Freer Markets, More Rules

A volume in the series

Cornell Studies in Political Economy

EDITED BY PETER J. KATZENSTEIN

A full list of titles in the series appears at the end of the book.

Freer Markets, More Rules

REGULATORY REFORM IN ADVANCED INDUSTRIAL COUNTRIES

STEVEN K. VOGEL

CORNELL UNIVERSITY PRESS

Ithaca and London

First published 1996 by Cornell University Press.
First printing, Cornell Paperbacks, 1998.

Printed in the United States of America

Library of Congress Cataloging-in-Publication Data

Vogel, Steven Kent.
　Freer markets, more rules : regulatory reform in advanced industrial countries
　　　p.　　cm. — (Cornell studies in political economy)
　Includes bibliographical references and index.
　ISBN 0-8014-3215-4 (cloth: alk. paper)
　ISBN 0-8014-8534-7 (pbk.: alk. paper)
　　1. Deregulation—Great Britain—Case studies　2. Trade regulation—Great Britain—Case studies.　3. Deregulation—Japan—Case studies.　4. Trade regulation—Japan—Case studies.　I. Title.　II. Series
　HD3616.G73V64　1996
　338.941—dc20　　　　　　　　　　　　　　　　　96-5054

Cornell University Press strives to utilize environmentally responsible suppliers and materials to the fullest extent possible in the publishing of its books. Such materials include vegetable-based, low-VOC inks and acid-free papers that are also either recycled, totally chlorine-free, or partly composed of nonwood fibers.

Cloth printing　　　10　9　8　7　6　5　4　3　2

Paperback printing　　10　9　8　7　6　5　4　3　2　1

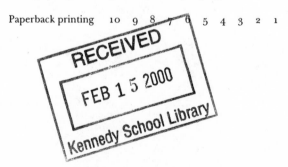

To my father

Contents

CONTENTS

PART IV: THE POLITICS OF REGULATORY REFORM

Tables

Figures

Acknowledgments

My greatest debt is to the many bureaucrats, politicians, business people, and scholars who generously agreed to be interviewed for this book. Many of them went far beyond what any researcher could reasonably expect, in setting aside their time and discussing matters in extraordinary detail. Some asked to remain anonymous, and in any case they are far too many to list here, but I am grateful to them all. At Berkeley, John Zysman, Barry Eichengreen, Gregory Noble, and Harold Wilensky helped me to focus the project and taught me much of what I know about political economy. I am indebted to the faculty and staff of the Berkeley Roundtable on the International Economy (BRIE) and the Department of Politics and Society at the University of California, Irvine, for support and advice. Dayanand Arora, Michael Borrus, Jennifer Holt Dwyer, Ian Ellison, Sir Nicholas Goodison, Stephen Glaister, Bernard Grofman, Masahiro Horie, Jun Iio, Philippe Jorion, Robert Kagan, Peter Katzenstein, Jonah Levy, Ulrike Schaede, Alec Stone, Koichi Tanaka, Osamu Toba, Ezra Vogel, and Charles Weathers all read portions of the manuscript and offered valuable comments. Two anonymous reviewers read the entire manuscript and considerably sharpened my thinking on numerous points. Many others helped to arrange interviews and otherwise facilitated my research. Among these, Andrew Davies, Masahiro Horie, Kunio Kinjo, Robin Mansell, Yoshio Nakamura, Takahiro Ozawa, Harumasa Sato, Masaaki Sakamaki, Hidesada Toriyama, Shuichi Uemura, and Douglas Webber deserve special mention. Yusuke Bannai, Patty Chookhae, Alexis Martinez, and John Remy provided superb research assistance. I enjoyed research affiliations with the European Institute of Business Administration (INSEAD) in France, City University in Britain, and the Institute of Fiscal and

Monetary Policy at the Ministry of Finance and the Foundation of Advanced Information and Research (FAIR) in Japan. Henri-Claude de Bettignies, Jill Hills, and Seizaburo Sato kindly arranged these affiliations. The Council for European Studies at Columbia University, the Japan Foundation, and the Social Science Research Council provided critical financial support. Andrew Lewis edited the manuscript, and Carol Betsch and Roger Haydon of Cornell University Press helped to guide it through editing and production. Finally, I thank my mother for passing on her insights into the world, many of which apply even to the arcane realm of regulatory reform. And most of all, I thank my wife, Susan, and my son, Justin, for their love and support, and for keeping me properly focused on life beyond this book.

S. K. V.

Freer Markets, More Rules

The Deregulation Revolution That Wasn't

Students of the former Soviet bloc can hardly exaggerate the transformation of Eastern Europe, but students of the advanced industrialized countries are hard pressed to find any comparable drama in the West. And yet over the past twenty years there has been a similar—though less spectacular—transformation of the relationship between governments and markets in the United States, Western Europe, and Japan. The transition in the West has been characterized not by violent demonstrations and drastic reform packages but by the accumulation of small and often seemingly insignificant measures, such as the removal of ceilings on interest rates for time deposits or the revision of rules regarding the licensing of taxis.

Some commentators have managed to find drama in the arcane world of fiscal reform, tax reform, and even regulatory reform. They describe developments in the advanced economies in terms of megatrends: globalization, privatization, deregulation. For these commentators, each of the trends implies stronger markets and weaker governments. As Richard McKenzie and Dwight Lee put it: "Growth in the enormous power of government is being checked by fundamental economic forces that transcend national boundaries. Governments have become weaker, at least relatively, and will surely become weaker yet."[1]

Globalization suggests that national economies are giving way to a single global market. Kenichi Ohmae describes this market as follows: "An isle is emerging that is bigger than a continent—the Interlinked Economy (ILE) of the Triad (the United States, Europe, and Japan), joined by aggressive

---

[1] McKenzie and Lee (1991), p. 17.

economies such as Taiwan, Hong Kong, and Singapore. It is becoming so powerful that it has swallowed most consumers and corporations, made traditional national borders almost disappear, and pushed bureaucrats, politicians, and the military toward the status of declining industries."[2] *Privatization* means that governments are selling off state assets, thereby redrawing the lines between the public and private sectors. John Naisbitt and Patricia Aburdene view this as a withdrawal of the state: "Globally the key to transforming socialism and the welfare state is the same approach that succeeded in Great Britain: privatization of state enterprises and private stock ownership. Some 100 other countries—from Chile to Turkey and from Brazil to Bangladesh—have also begun the process of rolling back the frontiers of the state."[3] And *deregulation* implies that governments are relinquishing their regulatory powers, getting out of the business of trying to control business. McKenzie and Lee contend that this has left governments virtually incapacitated:

> The recent revolution in computer and information technology has enabled firms to move assets around the world at the touch of a button. It has also caused an explosion of competition not only among businesses, but among national governments seeking to attract new business and to keep existing business within their borders. This competition has forced governments to reduce tax rates, spending and regulation and to lower trade barriers. The resulting loss of fiscal and regulatory power has put a severe crimp in the very ability of these governments to govern.[4]

These prophets of globalization, privatization and deregulation produce powerful images of markets overpowering governments, and firms outrunning them.[5] They are right that over the past two decades something has changed profoundly in how the governments of the advanced industrial countries regulate private sector behavior. But this transformation cannot be captured by a slogan, or even by a string of slogans. The rhetoric of globalization, privatization, and deregulation serves only to obscure what is really going on.

In this book, I use case studies to examine what has changed, and what has not changed, in how governments regulate industry. Unlike the authors quoted above, I find stronger markets but not weaker governments. Even in the paradigmatic case of government withdrawal—the deregulation movement—I find little net loss of government control. And even in the most dynamic and the most global of industries—telecommunications

---

[2] Ohmae (1990), pp. x–xi.
[3] Naisbitt and Aburdene (1990), p. 163. Toffler (1990, pp. 252–53) describes the privatization revolution in similar terms.
[4] McKenzie and Lee (1991), p. 1.
[5] Other works within this genre include Wriston (1992) and Boaz and Crane, eds. (1993).

and financial services—I find that governments are hardly overwhelmed by international market pressures. The universal logic of market forces has not compelled governments to respond in a particular, deregulatory way. In fact, these governments have responded to similar pressures in remarkably different ways.

I develop three propositions that challenge much of the conventional wisdom about "deregulation." First, I suggest that what we have witnessed has been reregulation, not deregulation. That is, the governments of the advanced industrial countries have reorganized their control of private sector behavior, but not substantially reduced the level of regulation. In part, the widespread misunderstanding of the deregulation movement reflects semantic confusion. People tend to use the term "deregulation" indiscriminately to refer both to the introduction of more competition within a market (what I shall call *liberalization*) and the reduction or elimination of government regulations (what I shall call *deregulation*)—as if these two were naturally associated. In the case of airline deregulation in the United States, they were in fact associated: we got freer markets and fewer rules. But in most cases of "deregulation," governments have combined liberalization with *reregulation*, the reformulation of old rules and the creation of new ones. Hence we have wound up with freer markets and *more* rules. In fact, there is often a logical link: liberalization requires reregulation.[6]

- In the "Big Bang" of 1986, for example, the British Stock Exchange boldly eliminated fixed commissions on stock transactions and opened Exchange members to outside ownership. Yet in the very same year, Parliament passed the Financial Services Act, producing a system of financial regulation infinitely more complex and burdensome than what it replaced.
- In 1985, the Japanese Diet approved three telecommunications laws, privatizing Nippon Telegraph and Telephone (NTT) and introducing competition in local, long-distance, and mobile telephone service. But the Ministry of Posts and Telecommunications (MPT) greatly augmented, rather than reduced, its regulatory powers.

The semantic confusion about deregulation, in turn, reflects a deeper logical confusion. Analysts tend to view governments and markets as having a zero-sum relationship, as if more of one necessarily implied less of the other.[7] But the Japanese cases demonstrate powerfully that there is no logical contradiction between more competition and greater government control. We shall examine in some detail how governments have rede-

[6] Polanyi (1944, p. 140) has made this same basic point about the historical evolution of free markets: "The introduction of free markets, far from doing away with the need for control, regulation, and intervention, enormously increased their range."

[7] Wolf (1988), for example.

fined the regulation of industry and assess whether this redefinition entails more or less government control.

Second, the governments of the advanced industrial countries have not converged in a common trend toward deregulation, but have combined liberalization and reregulation in markedly different ways. These governments have achieved different degrees of liberalization, adopted particular types of reregulation, and developed distinctive new styles of regulation. For example:

- When the British Stock Exchange enacted the "Big Bang," the government allowed large foreign investment banks to gobble up British brokers at will. The authorities saw no reason to protect inefficient firms. In contrast, the Japanese Ministry of Finance (MoF) structured financial reform precisely to insure that domestic financial institutions could survive.
- Over the course of the 1980s, the British government created a host of new independent regulatory agencies, from the Office of Water Supply (Ofwat) to the Securities and Investments Board (SIB). The government made these agencies semi-autonomous to ensure that they would make judgments on the basis of neutral criteria. In contrast, Japanese ministries have resisted any delegation of regulatory powers to outside agencies. In fact, even after the financial scandals in 1991 the MoF successfully fought off a movement to create an independent securities regulator.

In the cases, we look more specifically at how patterns of reregulation differ across countries. I have chosen to focus on the United Kingdom and Japan because they provide a good comparative fit: they began their reforms at the same time under similar circumstances and extended their programs to a similar range of sectors—with strikingly different results.

Third, the states themselves, even more than private interest groups, have driven the reform process. This proposition contrasts with the predominant school of thought on the politics of regulation, which suggests that interest group pressures are behind both regulation and deregulation. In fact, powerful private sector groups were often hopelessly divided over, adamantly opposed to, or simply not interested in regulatory reform. It was state actors who were committed to it. For example:

- In the United Kingdom, neither British Telecom (BT), nor telecommunications equipment manufacturers, nor corporate users ever demanded that the government privatize British Telecom or introduce competition in basic telephone service. Rather, the Thatcher administration and the Department of Trade and Industry (DTI) conceived, formulated, and implemented this policy.
- In Japan, neither the trucking companies nor their customers pushed the government to reform trucking regulations. But two government commis-

sions proposed reform anyway. The Ministry of Transportation (MoT) designed and implemented the new law—against the fervent opposition of many truckers.

Although not in a position to ignore the demands of private groups, state actors took the initiative in proposing reforms and in molding politically acceptable bargains. Thus the deregulation story is one rich in paradox. A movement aimed at reducing regulation has only increased it; a movement propelled by global forces has reinforced national differences; and a movement purported to push back the state has been led by the state itself. The conventional wisdom on deregulation cannot untangle these paradoxes, so we need a new framework with which to understand regulatory reform. In this book I seek to provide just that.

PART I

THE FORCES
FOR CHANGE

CHAPTER ONE

Understanding Regulatory Reform

Market-oriented regulatory reforms have been so prevalent throughout the industrialized world over the past two decades that they are commonly associated with a global deregulation movement. Thus in this book I focus on reforms of economic regulation, such as price or entry controls, and not reforms of social regulation, such as health or safety codes. Empirically, I offer an account of what really happened. As the single most important element in the current transformation of government-industry relations in the advanced industrial countries, regulatory reform is a critical development in its own right. And given that it is so widely misunderstood, it warrants a careful review. Theoretically, I use case studies to explore some of the core questions in comparative and international political economy.[1]

The study of regulation illuminates the larger relationship between government and industry, for regulation represents an essential mechanism of public control over private sector behavior. By studying regulatory reform, we learn more about how political-economic institutions shape policy choices and also about how these choices in turn reshape the institutions. The subject is well suited for comparative study because so many countries have enacted regulatory reforms in so many sectors during a relatively short period of time. Furthermore, by studying how different governments have responded to similar international economic and political pressures, we can explore the interaction between international pressures and domestic politics. When are international pressures so pow-

[1] See Eckstein (1975), Lijphart (1975), and George (1979) on the comparative case method.

9

erful that they override domestic political concerns, and when are they merely one element within a primarily domestic calculus? And by comparing sectors as well as countries, we can determine how national politics interacts with sectoral economics. When do sectoral markets fit national patterns of government-industry relations, and when are sectoral markets so distinctive that they override these patterns?

First, we need an analytical framework to guide us through the cases. In proper academic tradition, this chapter offers not one but three perspectives on regulatory reform, each of which implies a distinct interpretation of what regulatory reform has entailed, why it has occurred, and how it has evolved. Put simply, the first perspective suggests that markets have forced governments to deregulate, whereas the second contends that interest groups have driven reform. And the third claims that governments have reformulated regulations in response to a common set of pressures (outlined in Chapter 2), but have done so in distinctive ways reflecting their particular ideological and institutional legacies.

DEREGULATION AS THE TRIUMPH OF MARKETS OVER GOVERNMENTS

The most common perspective on regulatory reform views markets as the driving force behind change. In this view, market developments have directly produced deregulation by undermining regulation in practice and have indirectly spurred deregulation by increasing the costs of regulation relative to its benefits. In other words, in a world of dynamic markets, some regulations have ceased to work and others have ceased to pay. The overriding logic of market forces has forced all governments in the same deregulatory direction. This perspective appears in various forms, but most versions incorporate several if not all of the following four interrelated lines of argument.

First, marketplace changes have made regulation more costly and less beneficial. Many economists argue that much economic regulation is counterproductive, and that recent developments have only made it more so. The "public interest" school of regulation popular in the United States in the 1950s and 1960s stressed that regulation serves the public interest in the case of market failures such as natural monopoly, inadequate information, or externalities. More recently, however, economists studying regulation stress that government failure can be even worse than market failure. They suggest that regulation is only justifiable when one can demonstrate that a market failure exists, that regulation is the best method of correcting this market failure, *and* that the benefits of the regulation outweigh its costs. By such standards, they judge that most regulation is inefficient.[2] Furthermore, recent market developments have only made matters worse. In telecommunications, for example, technological advances have increased the "deadweight costs" of regulation—the distortion of resource allocation to the benefit of no one. Advanced technology has reduced capital investment costs and thereby increased the elasticity of supply and demand in many sectors. In other words, the quantities of goods and services that producers supply and that consumers demand are now much more sensitive to price. This means that even minor regulatory distortions can substantially dampen demand and stunt the overall growth of these sectors.[3]

Second, technological advances have undermined regulation in practice. In the financial sector, for example, advanced information technology has dramatically lowered transaction costs, enabling financial institutions to provide sophisticated new instruments at very low margins. These institutions have devised a wide range of "hybrid" financial instruments that defy the distinction between banking and brokerage and thus circumvent regulations founded on this distinction.[4] Likewise, new microwave and satellite transmission technologies have undermined regulations that presuppose a land-based network confined within national boundaries. These technological advances have produced *de facto* deregulation even in the absence of official regulatory changes by providing industry with new ways to evade regulation and otherwise rendering existing regulations obsolete.

Third, the globalization of markets has made it more difficult for national governments to control industry behavior. Technological advances have increased the mobility of capital, goods, services, and even firms, creating global markets in the place of national ones. In finance, for example, domestic authorities have less control over exchange rates or interest rates because these rates are too dependent on decisions taking place in markets outside their jurisdiction.[5] Likewise, governments cannot effectively regulate the activity of "domestic" firms, because these firms can circumvent national regulations through their operations abroad.

Fourth, and most critical of all, globalization has produced a competitive dynamic between national regulators that fosters deregulation. In global markets, firms can engage in *regulatory arbitrage*, moving their business or capital to the country with the most favorable regulations. So national authorities must compete to retain business and capital within their borders, and deregulation serves as a powerful tool in this new competi-

---

[2] See, for example, Niskanen (1993). Noll (1989, pp. 1255–58) summarizes this literature.

[3] Duch (1991, pp. 101–4) makes this argument explicitly, building on Becker (August 1983). Also see Peltzman (1989), pp. 18–21.

[4] Ely (1993), pp. 117–18.

[5] Wriston (1992).

tion. By relaxing financial regulations, for example, authorities allow financial institutions to offer more instruments at lower prices, and this environment attracts more capital and financial activity. Or by relaxing telecommunications regulations, they stimulate competition and encourage carriers to offer more services at lower prices, and this attracts multinational corporations to locate in their country.[6]

In one sense, the market-centered perspective embodied in these four lines of argument is beyond dispute: marketplace developments have clearly provided a powerful stimulus for regulatory change; however, proponents of this perspective often overstate their case, implying that markets not only stimulate regulatory change but determine its timing and nature. I contend that governments can respond to market pressures in a wide variety of ways. These pressures may cause some countries to deregulate, but they prompt others to reregulate. That some governments have tended more toward liberalization whereas others have tended more toward reregulation—in the face of the same market pressures—suggests that these pressures alone cannot explain policy outcomes. Indeed, market constraints themselves may be the product of past policies. As we shall see in Chapter 8, for example, Japanese officials confronted increased pressure to liberalize capital markets with the expansion of the market in Euroyen bonds, but these same officials opened the Euroyen bond market precisely so that it would have this effect.

In the primary case studies, we focus on two of the sectors where markets have been the most dynamic: telecommunications and financial services. These sectors lie at the heart of the technological revolution that has made possible the free flow of information and capital across borders, which many believe has undermined existing systems of regulation and changed the role of government forever.[7] Thus telecommunications and financial services are "crucial cases" for the market-centered perspective: for if the market forces the hand of governments anywhere, then it does so in these sectors.[8] We find, however, that the United Kingdom and Japan have responded to similar market pressures in strikingly different ways. Thus we must look beyond markets for a fuller understanding of regulatory change.

---

[6] McKenzie and Lee (1991) offer a popular rendition of this argument. Kane (1987) provides a more sophisticated version applied to finance in which he suggests that regulatory competition can lead to reregulation as well as deregulation. He argues that regulatory competition need not degenerate into a "competition in laxity," for companies will be attracted to countries that provide effective regulation where it is needed. Dyson (October 1986, pp. 28–30) summarizes the argument regarding competitive deregulation, and Cerny (1991, pp. 185–87) briefly outlines market-centered explanations of deregulation more generally.

[7] McKenzie and Lee (1991); Wriston (1992).

[8] A crucial case is one that presents near ideal conditions for confirmation of a given hypothesis. It can be used effectively to disconfirm a hypothesis, for if a hypothesis cannot hold true even in such a case, then it can be reasonably rejected. See Eckstein (1975).

DEREGULATION AS THE TRIUMPH OF INTERESTS OVER GOVERNMENTS

The second perspective suggests that interest groups drive deregulation. In many cases, the very industries that benefited from regulation in the past lobby for change because regulation no longer serves their interests. This argument builds on the most prevalent school of thought on the politics of regulation, a school that evolved directly from economic studies of regulation. As noted above, critics of the "public interest" school used empirical studies to demonstrate that regulation often decreases rather than increases economic welfare. But this finding suggested a puzzle: if regulation does not serve the public interest, then whose interest does it serve? George Stigler answered this question in a seminal article in 1971. Stigler assumes that regulators are rational actors trying to maximize the political benefits from enacting a particular policy. He contends that a small group with high stakes in a given policy, such as producers, will press their views more effectively than a much larger group with a smaller stake per capita, such as consumers. As a result, regulators are "captured" by producer interests.[9] Others have extended and refined the theory. Whereas Stigler envisions a unified group of producers supporting regulation, Sam Peltzman includes a wider variety of interests competing for influence over policy. Under Peltzman's formulation, producers do not always prevail, but they have an organizational advantage over consumers that helps them win out in many cases.[10]

The deregulation movement poses a major challenge to the theory of regulation. The theory suggests that producer groups prevail over consumers and thus perpetuate inefficient regulation, yet the U.S. government deregulated in a wide range of sectors despite strong opposition by well-organized producer groups. Moreover, as Martha Derthick and Paul Quirk note, economic studies pointing to the costs of regulation played a major role in promoting the cause of deregulation.[11] Ironically, by successfully propagating their critique of regulation, these economists undermined their own theory of the politics of regulation. Stigler and his colleagues had in effect sought to explain why policymakers were not listening to them—only to find that these leaders had started listening.

[9] Stigler (Spring 1971).
[10] Peltzman (1976). Noll (1989) offers an excellent survey of variations on the theory of regulation.
[11] Derthick and Quirk (1985). Wilson (1979, pp. 386–87) argues that American officials exposed as students in the 1960s to the critique of regulation went on to carry out the regulatory reforms of the 1970s: "Intellectual descriptions (and criticisms) of institutional arrangements come to have practical consequences. Any generalization about how government works is vulnerable to the behavior of persons who have learned that generalization and wish to repeal it."

More recently, theorists within this school of thought have argued that deregulation is consistent with the theory. They suggest that producer groups themselves have pushed for deregulation because the regulatory system has ceased to serve their interests, and that other groups in favor of deregulation have become more powerful. Theodore Keeler, for example, argues that rational regulators attend both to public interest and to special interest concerns, and after weighing the political costs, choose to deregulate when this will help them to maximize their support.[12] Peltzman suggests that regulators are likely to deregulate in response to a decrease in the economic benefits ("rents") that interest groups obtain from regulation. They deregulate when regulation becomes less effective so that continued regulation is pointless, or when regulation generates so few rents that continued regulation does not pay off politically.[13] Although these theorists manage to reconcile the theory with deregulation, they lose the power of Stigler's model. For if policy outcomes reflect competition between a wide range of interest groups, then how can we tell which group will win?

Although they accept the basic premises of these earlier works, other theorists have moved beyond the Stigler-Peltzman formulations to more sophisticated and open-ended versions of the argument. They still assume that regulators are rational actors trying to maximize their political benefits, but they define the interests of consumers and producers narrowly in accordance with economic theory and contend that small groups with concentrated interests tend to have more influence than large groups with diffuse interests. Barry Weingast's analysis of deregulation, for example, focuses on the principal-agent relationship between members of Congress and regulators. He suggests that regulators serve their political masters (members of Congress), who in turn serve their constituents, including producer groups. Although regulators may occasionally stray from the course set by these masters, Weingast emphasizes that legislators exercise considerable control over regulators even when they do not intervene directly in regulatory debates. Regulators are constrained in their actions simply because legislators *may* intervene.[14] He proposes an "equilibrium" model of regulation: the system is in equilibrium when the common interest in regulation among legislators, regulatory agencies, and producer groups remains stable over time. Deregulation occurs when court decisions, changing technology, or political entrepreneurs challenge this equilibrium. Although consumers are not likely to take up their own cause in the battle for deregulation, political entrepreneurs can mobilize this po-

[12] Keeler (1984).

[13] Peltzman (1989).

[14] This argument resembles Rosenbluth's (1989) argument about the Japanese Diet's oversight of the Ministry of Finance. I treat this point more fully in Chapter 8.

tentially powerful collective interest.[15] Similarly, Roger Noll and Bruce Owen characterize the U.S. regulatory debate as one of conflict among numerous interest groups, with producer interests having an organizational advantage but no absolute guarantee to prevail. They suggest that the U.S. government deregulated in response to external factors, such as market shifts, that realigned the balance of interests in favor of reform. In particular, producer groups decided that the costs of regulation outweighed the benefits and successfully lobbied for change.[16]

The theory of regulation and its successors miss the essence of the regulatory reform story because they build upon a distorted view of public and private interests. Proponents of the theory equate the public interest with the consumer interest, which they derive from economic theory. In the political arena, of course, consumers as citizens often act against this narrowly defined interest, demanding more regulation, not less. This notion of interest is useful as a neutral standard by which to judge policies, but these theorists get in trouble when they assume that because government officials do not serve the public interest *as the theorists define it,* then these officials must be serving some private interest. In other words, they allow their policy prescription to cloud their view of the political process: they look for private interests when policy does not accord with their vision of the public interest. In reality, however, there is no single public interest: disputes over the definition of the public interest lie at the heart of political debate. Government officials may legitimately disagree over how to define this interest in ways that cannot be explained in terms of their "capture" by private interests. Thus we cannot understand variations in regulatory policy until we understand how government officials in different countries define the public interest.

More broadly, the various renditions of the theory of regulation suffer from the weaknesses of any theory that focuses too exclusively on interest group pressures. Too often, their analysis degenerates into a search for winners and losers. But we must be careful not to equate winners and losers with proponents and opponents without carefully reviewing the evidence. Very often the interest groups that eventually benefit from a policy play little or no role in advocating and may even oppose the policy. They may misunderstand their true interest, they may lack enough information to assess their interest, or they may simply fail to act politically. As to regulatory reform, some of the greatest beneficiaries were new market entrants, whom did not even exist or had not yet decided to enter the market when the policies were formulated. Interest group models are also vulnerable to circular reasoning. They are prone to arguing that the most pow-

---

[15] Weingast (Winter 1981). Also see Weingast and Moran (1983).
[16] Noll and Owen, eds. (1983).

erful group got its way in a specific case, only to characterize this group as the most powerful because it got its way.[17]

Furthermore, interest groups models tend to overestimate how much interest group pressures determine policy outcomes. Even if we establish a relationship between group interests and policy outcomes, this does not imply direct causation. In practice, government officials choose among multiple policy options that will satisfy relevant interest groups. In other words, the distribution of societal interests may influence policy but still leave room for multiple outcomes, and not a single equilibrium.[18] Moreover, government officials themselves may shape interest group preferences, manipulate interest group pressures, or play one group off against another. Interest group models ignore the role of government officials and agencies as autonomous actors in the policy process. State actors have preferences that cannot be reduced to those of the most powerful groups in society, and they frequently act on these preferences.[19]

In some ways regulatory reform represents a crucial case for the theory of regulation and other models that focus on interest group pressures. After all, the theory of regulation was designed to explain regulatory policy. Regulation affects big business more directly than any other kind of policy. And what more powerful interest group is there than big business?[20] If interest groups are ever to dominate an issue, then regulatory reform should be that issue. Without a doubt, interest groups *do* play a large role in the policy process, and sophisticated interest group models that incorporate institutional factors can provide important insights. In the case studies, however, we find that interest group alignments were roughly similar across countries, and yet policy outcomes were strikingly different. For an explanation of these differences, we must look not to private interests but to public institutions.

REREGULATION AS THE REORGANIZATION OF GOVERNMENT CONTROL

As I noted in the Introduction, my own understanding of regulatory reforms since 1975 begins with the recognition that these reforms represent not deregulation but a combination of liberalization and reregulation. Many analysts have recognized an element of reregulation in these reforms, but maintain that the dominant trend is one of deregulation.[21] A

---

[17] Gourevitch (1986), p. 58.

[18] Steinmo and Thelen, eds. (1992), p. 9; Goldstein and Keohane, eds. (1993), p. 17.

[19] Nordlinger (1981).

[20] Lindblom (1977), pp. 170–88.

[21] Swann (1988, pp. 1–2), for example, notes that reforms have involved reregulation as well as deregulation, yet his title, *The Retreat of the State*, reveals which trend he considers dominant.

far smaller group has recognized reregulation as central rather than incidental to the reforms.[22] I build upon this basic insight, taking it two steps further by distinguishing different types of reregulation and explaining different patterns of reregulation across countries. In Table 1, I set out four broad categories of reregulation in order to analyze the relationship between liberalization and reregulation and to help us distinguish between different patterns of reregulation in the case studies. Government authorities introduce *pro-competitive reregulation* in order to create competition, by offering regulatory advantages to competitors or imposing disadvantages on incumbents, in markets such as basic telephone service where competition is not likely to arise naturally. They also may adopt auxiliary regulations to improve the conditions for competition. For example, they might strengthen corporate disclosure requirements when liberalizing bond markets because investors need access to corporate information to make informed choices. Authorities employ *juridical reregulation* by adding more detail to existing regulations, by putting tacit rules into written form, or by putting administrative rules into legal form. They may do so in order to cope with the growing complexity of markets or to adjust to more rigorous international regulatory standards. They typically make regulations more codified and legalistic as the number and variety of market

Table 1. A typology of regulatory reforms with selected examples

	EMPHASIS ON LIBERALIZATION	EMPHASIS ON REREGULATION
	Pro-competitive reregulation	Juridical reregulation
Undermines government control over industry	a. designing regulation to handicap incumbents or to help competitors b. adding regulations to facilitate the effective operation of markets c. strengthening antitrust regulations and/or their enforcement	a. putting informal rules into legal form (juridification) b. putting tacit rules into written form (codification) c. formalizing consultation / improving procedures to ensure accountability
	Strategic reregulation	Expansionary reregulation
Enhances government control over industry	a. giving regulatory advantages to domestic firms b. using regulation to take away the advantages of foreign firms c. promoting/protecting domestic firms so they can cope with liberalization	a. creating new regulations to enhance bureaucratic authority b. replacing old regulations with new ones in order to retain regulatory control c. extending regulations to new areas

[22] Among these, I am particularly indebted to the work of Borrus et al. (May 1985), Hills (1986), and Moran (1991).

players increases. Authorities engage in *expansionary reregulation* when they create new regulations in order to prevent the loss of bureaucratic authority that can accompany the liberalization process, or when they simply take advantage of the process to expand their powers. They implement *strategic reregulation* when they favor particular firms, often national champions, within a newly opened market.[23] They may design regulations to discourage the entry of foreign competitors or to give regulatory advantages ("regulatory subsidies") to domestic firms. They typically try to soften the impact of liberalization in order to protect domestic producers from the potential onslaught of foreign competition.

All four types of reregulation are related to liberalization, but the two on the left in Table 1 (pro-competitive and strategic) are specifically aimed at liberalization, whereas the two on the right (juridical and expansionary) merely complement the liberalization process. More critical for our purposes, the two on the top (pro-competitive and juridical) undermine governmental control over industry, whereas the two on the bottom (strategic and expansionary) enhance this control. Pro-competitive and juridical reregulation undermine government control because they reduce administrative leverage and limit discretion, whereas strategic and expansionary reregulation enhance government control because they increase administrative leverage and bolster discretion. Thus just as liberalization may imply more or less regulation, reregulation may imply more or less government control over industry. In addition to these four types of reregulation, governments may also engage in actual *deregulation,* which like pro-competitive and juridical reregulation tends to reduce government control.

In contrast to the market and interest group perspectives on regulatory reform, my understanding of regulatory reform entails a focus on state institutions to account for distinctive national patterns of reregulation. I do not reject the market and interest group perspectives outright, but rather incorporate them into my own model. I incorporate market forces into the model, as we shall see in the next chapter, not as determinants of reform outcomes but as stimuli to which states respond in a wide variety of ways. Likewise I recognize that interest groups powerfully constrain state actors, but suggest that national patterns of regulatory reform derive primarily not from differences in the definition or organization of interests but from differences in how these interests are mediated by state institutions.

While recognizing the power of market forces and interest group pressures, I prefer a framework that focuses on state institutions because it explains national variations in regulatory reform better than any other.[24] I

---

[23] Borrus et al. (May 1985) first introduced this term.

[24] Thus my approach builds upon a voluminous literature on the state and national variations in the institutions of economic policy, including Shonfield (1965), Katzenstein, ed. (1978), Zysman (1983), and Evans, Reuschemeyer and Skocpol, eds. (1985), among many others.

favor this approach for two simple reasons: it enjoys certain advantages as an analytical framework, and it is especially well suited to this particular story. An analysis that focuses on state actors is likely to be more parsimonious than one that emphasizes private groups, for there are typically fewer important state actors than private groups. And as noted above, in a policy arena in which a large number of interest groups compete, an interest group model loses much of its explanatory power because it becomes very difficult to demonstrate which groups influenced the outcome. Moreover, state actors are typically closer to the final decision process, and thus their imprint on policy outcomes may stand out more clearly. In particular, when decisions are made sequentially in some unforeseen way, state actors play the critical role in guiding the decision path. As one City of London lobbyist put it: "The regulators are all at the table where the legislation is made—and we are not."[25]

Furthermore, in the specific case of regulatory reform, state actors' preferences are simply too important to ignore. This may seem ironic, given popular images of markets and interests pushing back the frontiers of the state, but regulatory reform is about more than liberating markets. It also addresses two things that typically concern state actors far more than private-sector actors: finding new ways to raise government revenue and designing new mechanisms of policy implementation. These two goals constitute the core agenda of regulatory reform, one that is easily obscured by the rhetoric of "liberalization" and "deregulation." These goals play prominently in the case studies that follow. In telecommunications, for example, regulatory reform has been coupled with privatization, and state actors' concerns about generating revenue through privatization have powerfully shaped regulatory change. And in financial services, state actors' preoccupation with servicing the national debt has similarly colored reforms. Moreover, regulatory reform by definition involves reformulating the mechanisms of policy implementation, so it affects the very ability of state actors to perform their functions, which is why they insist on giving their own needs and preferences high priority as they pursue regulatory reform. Thus a model that focuses on state institutions best explains the essential variation in national approaches to regulatory reform, provided it is supplemented by other variables as needed.

---

[25] Interview with J. P. K. Tillett, deputy secretary, British Bankers Association (July 27, 1990). March and Olsen (1989, pp. 11–14) describe a "garbage can" model of decision making in which policy outcomes depend as much on timing as on logic or intent: "Problems, solutions, decision makers, and choice opportunities come together as a result of being simultaneously available." I would add that the availability of decision makers depends on their location, and state actors are likely to be strategically positioned at the moment of decision.

To understand the role of state institutions, we must first recognize that states are both "actors" and "structures."[26] As actors, state agencies and the officials in these agencies formulate goals independently of the input of specific societal groups, and these goals inform their participation in policy formulation and thereby affect policy output. State actors can insulate themselves from outside pressures or actively change interest group preferences.[27] When I suggest that the state can be autonomous, I do not mean that state actors can ignore societal interests but merely that their preferences cannot be reduced to those of societal interests. Likewise, I do not mean to imply that the state is monolithic. In fact, in the case studies I shall not refer to "the state" but rather to the specific institutions that constitute it: the chief executive, the cabinet, the bureaucracy, the legislature, political parties, and the courts.[28] I shall use the term "government" to refer to these institutions as a collective whole. In order to make the analytical distinction between state and society it is critical to evaluate the degree to which these institutions are autonomous from societal pressure. In general, the chief executive, the cabinet, the bureaucracy, and the courts tend to be more autonomous from this pressure than the legislature or political parties, so an assessment of state autonomy often hinges on an analysis of the relationship between these institutions.

Given that the state is both an actor and a structure, it follows that we should examine both the *ideas* that inform it as an actor and the *institutions* that define it as a structure. We can apply this perspective to our analysis of the cases by thinking in terms of national approaches to the regulation and promotion of industry, which I shall call *regulatory regimes*, comprised of specific constellations of ideas and institutions. For our purposes, we can make this analysis quite concrete, for we are only interested in the ideas and institutions of government policy toward industry.[29] As to ideas (or regime *orientation*), we are concerned with state actors' beliefs about the proper scope, goals, and methods of government intervention in the economy, and about how this intervention affects economic performance. These beliefs will reflect these actors' adherence to broad doctrines, such as economic liberalism; their predisposition toward certain functional tasks, such as revenue generation; and their commitment to

---

[26] Skocpol (1985).

[27] Nordlinger (1981) distinguishes three types of state autonomy—Type III, in which state and societal preferences converge; Type II, when the state alters societal preferences; and Type I, when the state acts against societal preferences—and he describes in some detail the strategies that state actors can use to enhance their autonomy.

[28] Krasner (1984, p. 224) argues that the state should be viewed as a totality. I suggest that one can view the state as a single coherent structure without insisting that it is a unitary actor.

[29] Wilensky and Turner (1987) suggest how national approaches toward industrial policy are in turn linked to labor-market and social policies.

specific policy mechanisms, such as licensing authority. As to institutions (or regime *organization*), we shall focus on the organization of those state actors concerned with industry and the relationship of these actors to the private sector.[30] The ideas and institutions of a given regime are interrelated, but the analytical distinction remains important nonetheless because they have independent effects on policy outcomes. Moreover, only by distinguishing between these two components of a regime can we discern how ideas and institutions interact. And as we shall see below, this interaction is integral to the process of regulatory reform.[31]

The *orientation* of a regulatory regime constrains policy choices by defining what is acceptable or conceivable, thus shaping state actors' reactions to external forces and their receptiveness to new ideas. Given that signals from the marketplace and the private sector are often unclear or conflicting, ideas affect how state actors respond to these signals.[32] In regulatory reform, for example, ideas influence how officials interpret market trends, apply lessons from abroad, and determine how new regulations should be put into practice. Ideas are important analytically because they structure state actor's preferences and thereby eliminate one of the greatest potential weaknesses of a state-centered model: that it tells you that state actors lead without telling you where they are likely to go. Without this element, a state-centered model can leave the state as a black box, powerful yet devoid of content.[33] Commentators have generally rejected ideological explanations of regulatory reform, but they typically equate ideology with party ideology, and I have specifically defined regime orientation in a way that transcends particular party platforms.[34] I suggest that regime orientation tends to survive transfers of power because it is partly rooted in the bureaucracy, and because major parties within a country often share certain core beliefs about the proper scope, goals, and methods for the regulation and promotion of industry. These

[30] Lehmbruch (1992, p. 31) adopts a similar framework, employing somewhat different language. He suggests that the institutional framework of economic policy has two dimensions: the ideological interpretation of the relationship between state and economy (ideas), and the organization of the state and of its linkages with the organized economy (institutions).

[31] Eisner (1993, p. 1) and Francis (1993, p. 43) offer alternative definitions of a regulatory regime. Francis defines a regulatory regime in terms of the degree of centralization of regulatory authority and the extent of delegation of regulatory responsibility to the private sector. Thus he limits his definition to two elements of what I call the organization of a regime. Eisner's definition is closer to my own in that he includes both ideas and institutions. He describes a regime as "a historically specific configuration of policies and institutions which structures the relationship between social interests, the state, and economic actors in multiple sectors of the economy."

[32] Hall, ed. (1989); Goldstein (1993); Goldstein and Keohane, eds. (1993).

[33] Hall (1986), p. 15.

[34] See, for example, Hills (1989) and Gary Becker, "When the Going Gets Tough, Ideology Gets Flexible," *Business Week* (January 22, 1990).

commentators also note that the beginning of the U.S. deregulation movement preceded the change in government ideology associated with Ronald Reagan's ascent to power. But I do not suggest that orientation explains *why* reforms occurred, only *how* reforms have evolved in different countries once begun. We shall address why they occurred in the following chapter.

The *organization* of a regulatory regime constrains choices by structuring the incorporation of interest groups, defining state capabilities, and shaping state and societal interests. In fact, we learn more about how interest group pressures influence policy by focusing on institutions than we do with a simple interest group model, for we understand how institutions mediate these pressures. Institutions shape state capabilities by defining the relationship between the state and industry and dictating how policies are formulated and implemented. And institutions can even shape state and industry preferences.[35] In the case of regulatory reform, for example, state actors judge new proposals in part by assessing their impact on existing institutions. (We shall look much more closely at what the concepts of regime orientation and organization mean in practice when we introduce the British and Japanese cases in Chapter 3.)

In this book I take this approach one step further by combining the study of national patterns with sectoral analysis. I do this by applying this same conception of regulatory regimes at the sectoral level. That is, we can say that the British government as a whole is characterized by a particular regulatory regime, defined by certain characteristic ideas and institutions, but this overall national regime does not preclude considerable variation across sectors.[36] *Sectoral orientation* will generally reflect national orientation, but may have some distinctive features. Typically it will reflect the bias of the dominant agency or agencies in the sector, and this may reflect the agencies' particular history, mission, or jurisdictional responsibilities. Thus the Bank of England tends to view financial regulation with a particular concern for its impact on the market in gilt-edged shares, because the Bank's jurisdiction includes managing the sale of these shares. And the officials of Japan's Ministry of Finance (MoF) are particularly obsessed with preventing bank failures, because they feel that their record of preventing failures in the postwar era promotes confidence in the financial system. *Sectoral organization* naturally parallels national organization,

---

[35] In this sense, my analysis fits within the historical school of the "new institutionalism," along with Steinmo, Thelen, and Longstreth, eds. (1992), and many others. On the variety of "new institutionalisms," see Hall and Taylor (September 1994).

[36] This perspective is thus consistent with much of the literature on sectoral policy networks or sectoral governance. See, for example, Wilks and Wright, eds. (1991); Campbell, Hollingsworth, and Lindberg, eds. (1991); and Hollingsworth, Schmitter, and Streeck, eds. (1994). Atkinson and Coleman (April 1992) provide a review. Few have linked sectoral analysis back to national-level variations; Shafer (1994) is a notable exception.

because it includes national institutions such as the chief executive, the cabinet, the national legislature, and the supreme court; however, it may exhibit certain particularities, such as more or less centralization than the national norm. In practical terms, sectoral organization refers to the organization of the most important state actors in the sector and their relationship to the relevant industry. Thus in finance, the United Kingdom's sectoral regime prior to reform was characterized by a division of labor between the Bank of England, the Treasury, and the Department of Trade and Industry (DTI), whereas Japan's was characterized by a centralization of power within the MoF. And it was also characterized by loose ties between government agencies, banks, and industry, whereas Japan's was characterized by much tighter links.

So where does a nation or a sector get its particular regulatory regime? My primary purpose in this book is to define the various national regulatory regimes prior to reform and then to explain how these have shaped distinct reform outcomes. Thus I do not offer a full-fledged theory of regime change, leaving this more daunting task for future work; however, I can accomplish several more modest tasks. First, I offer a simple model of regime change and indicate how national regimes evolved prior to the reforms of the 1980s. Then (in Chapter 3), I return to this question as it pertains specifically to the United Kingdom and Japan. Finally, in the case study chapters, I specify how several particular sectoral regimes evolved from 1980 to 1995.

At the broadest level, a nation's regulatory regime reflects its history of industrialization. As Alexander Gerschenkron has demonstrated, the timing of industrialization affects both the philosophy of the industrializing elite and the institutional mechanisms of the industrialization process.[37] Once in place, these basic sets of ideas and institutions have evolved only relatively slowly. They generally change in response to developments that produce a gap between state goals and state capabilities. And all else being equal, a larger gap will produce a greater change. Thus regimes have changed the most at times of crisis, such as the Great Depression or World War II, which dramatically redefine capabilities or transform existing institutions.[38] They have evolved more incrementally in response to particular historical experiences such as recessions or strikes that made leaders question the wisdom of the prevalent regime or that rendered the institutional mechanisms of the regime less effective. Still, the ideological and institutional elements of a regime evolve according to distinct rhythms. That is, ideas tend to change more gradually, as new ideas filter in or as the relative weights of different ideas shift. Institutions tend to evolve in a pat-

---

[37] Gerschenkron (1962).
[38] Gourevitch (1986).

tern of "punctuated equilibrium," in which long periods of stasis are interrupted by brief periods of rapid change.[39]

Furthermore, we can use an analysis of ideas and institutions to show how gaps between goals and capabilities lead to regime change. As noted above, policy goals reflect regime orientation (ideas) and capabilities reflect regime organization (institutions). And ideas and institutions are closely linked. To put this simply, a state's capabilities are likely to reflect its goals over time, and its goals are likely to reflect its capabilities: goals and capabilities tend toward equilibrium in the long run. Of course, a mismatch (disequilibrium) is possible, but the linkage between goals and capabilities has important implications in the case of such a mismatch. A government without the institutional tools it requires is likely to try to develop them, and a government with institutions inappropriate to its goals is likely to eliminate them, redefine them, or allow them to atrophy. For example, a government determined to achieve high growth through an active industrial policy is likely to develop the capability to implement such a policy.[40] If the government is unable to develop these capabilities, then this failure is likely to discredit the goals themselves, creating a new equilibrium between goals and capabilities.[41] To examine this interaction in more depth we must first review the forces that propelled so many governments to initiate regulatory reforms in the first place.

[39] See Krasner (January 1984), pp. 240–43, on the notion of punctuated equilibrium.

[40] The capability to implement an industrial policy will not necessarily make that policy successful in the sense of promoting growth, but will allow that policy to be effective in the more limited sense that it will be implemented and have some (positive or negative) impact.

[41] Raymond Duch (1991, pp. 115–16) addresses this issue of the linkage between ideas and institutions and arrives at the opposite conclusion: institutional structures are independent of national predispositions toward a particular kind of policy change. As evidence, he notes that liberal Britain experimented with corporatist institutions in the 1960s although these failed to take root, and statist France experimented unsuccessfully with liberal institutional innovations in the 1980s. I would argue that his examples prove my point rather nicely: institutional changes are not likely to take hold in the absence of a complementary policy orientation.

Chapter Two

Why Change the Rules?

Governments have been changing regulations ever since they began making them, but the wave of regulatory reforms that began in the mid-1970s and continues today is unprecedented. More countries are reforming regulations in more sectors than ever before. Why has regulatory reform become so pervasive? I propose three answers, each of which offers a partial explanation. First, market change, driven largely by technological developments, has undermined existing systems of regulation. Second, the theory and ideology of deregulation, backed by the economic and political power of the United States, have diffused internationally. In some cases, the U.S. precedent itself has been a major impetus for reform; in other cases, the U.S. government and U.S. multinationals have actively pressed for reforms abroad. Third, the macroeconomic shifts since the first oil shock in 1973 have made "deregulation" an attractive political program. Ruling parties in the United States, the United Kingdom, and Japan have used the deregulation movement to promise economic benefits without increasing government spending. Each of these three trends produced a gap between governmental goals and capabilities, and as we saw in the previous chapter, such gaps form a primary impetus for changes in regulatory regime.

I do not seek to validate or to reject any one of these explanations definitively, but rather to specify how each has affected the events of the past twenty years. No one factor caused the regulatory reform movement, so the best we can do is to define the influence each factor has had. I do this by examining each in turn and then analyzing what each can and cannot explain. We should also keep in mind that these are not purely exogenous variables, for each factor interacts with the domestic political processes examined in more depth in the chapters to follow. These trends have influenced domestic regulatory debates, but they have also been manipulated and partially driven by actors within those debates.

TECHNOLOGICAL DEVELOPMENTS AND MARKET FORCES

As we saw in the previous chapter, rapid market change has limited the effectiveness of some regulations and has rendered others obsolete. But the degree of change, and thus the urgency of regulatory reform, varies considerably from sector to sector. An extension of the analysis to the two sectors highlighted in the case studies, telecommunications and financial services, should clarify *how* market changes challenge existing regulatory regimes and provide important background for the case studies to follow. In both of these sectors, three major types of market change have directly affected regulation. First, technological developments and innovation have created new markets outside the scope of existing regulations, such as satellite communications or offshore financial markets. This has threatened regulators with the possibility that firms will bypass the framework of regulation. Second, innovation has blurred the distinctions between lines of business, undermining regulatory systems that presuppose these distinctions. In telecommunications, technology has bridged the divide between computers and communication; and in finance, innovation has challenged the traditional demarcation between banking and brokerage. Third, markets have become more international, making it more difficult for national authorities to control private sector behavior within their borders. For example, financial authorities have more difficulty controlling interest rates now that borrowers and lenders can seek higher returns in foreign markets.

The Telecommunications Revolution

In all of the countries examined here, the telecommunications sector has historically been dominated by a monopoly service provider. The telecommunications operator was a private monopoly in the United States, a public corporation in the United Kingdom and Japan, and a government administration in France and Germany.[1] The operator had a monopoly on local and long-distance service and on the provision of telephones and often other equipment as well. In all these countries, the telecommunications regime incorporated several fundamental principles.

---

[1] The Japanese telecommunications operator became a public corporation in 1952; the British telecommunications operator, in 1969.

First, the operator should be a monopoly because telecommunications was a "natural monopoly," meaning that economies of scale were so great that a single operator could provide service more efficiently than two or more competing operators. Competition would result in the costly duplication of investment in infrastructure. Second, the government, whether as the regulator or as the operator itself, should ensure that the telecommunications sector serves the public interest broadly defined. In practical terms, this meant that the telecommunications operator should provide universal service at a uniform price irrespective of geographical variations in the cost of providing the service. Third, the telecommunications system should be managed as a single integrated network in order to maintain uniform technical standards and to maximize interconnection—that is, to ensure that any telephone would be able to connect to any other.

The rapid advance of telecommunications technology in the postwar era challenged each of these basic principles of telecommunications policy. The first open challenge invariably came in the United States. Three technological challenges transformed the sector: the development of advanced terminal equipment, the advent of microwave and satellite transmission, and the creation of sophisticated "value-added" services combining data processing with communications. In most countries, the operator had a monopoly on at least the first telephone, ostensibly to ensure that the equipment would not damage the network. But as the possibilities for terminal equipment expanded, it became clear that a single operator could not provide the full range of equipment that users would ultimately demand. Electronics firms wanted to be able to provide terminal equipment, and users wanted to be able to buy this equipment. In the United States, the first challenge to the equipment monopoly came in a 1956 court decision that allowed the Hush-a-Phone Company to market a device to attach to telephones to make it easier to communicate in noisy areas. In other countries as well, the monopoly over equipment provision was often the first to be challenged.

New transmission technologies challenged the regulatory system even more fundamentally because they offered a means of contesting the monopoly in basic telephone service. Corporations could bypass the monopoly carrier by creating their own private lines using these technologies. Microwave technology had an advantage over wired communications in that it required less investment in infrastructure, it was not dependent on securing a right-of-way on land, and it could be transmitted from mobile terminals. At the same time, it could only offer a cost advantage in selected niches of the market, and it relied on the limited resource of the radio spectrum. In the United States, Microwave Communications International (MCI) challenged American Telephone & Telegraph's (AT&T) monopoly in 1963 by proposing a microwave link between St. Louis and

27

Chicago. Satellite technology provided a further challenge, with the added complication that it could easily cross national borders and thus defy the ability of any single national regulator to control it. Satellite technology had the benefit of being able to transmit signals even to remote or mountainous areas, but it had the disadvantage of greater cost. In the 1972 "Open Skies" decision, the Federal Communications Commission (FCC) ruled that companies should be able to compete freely to provide satellite communications service.

The gradual erosion of the barrier between communications and computers posed a third challenge. The advance of microelectronics and the transition from analog to digital transmission technology made it easier to send large quantities of information rapidly and inexpensively, and to interface between computers and communications channels. This presented regulators with a fundamental problem because the communications sector was strictly regulated but the computer and data processing sectors were hardly regulated at all. Regulators were confronted with two basic questions. First, to what extent should they allow data processing companies to use the network to deliver their services? If they allowed these companies to interconnect with the network, they would have to find some way to distinguish data services from communications even though many advanced services actually combine the two. Otherwise, companies claiming to be data service providers could "resell" lines, in effect competing with the monopoly carrier as telecommunications operators using the carrier's own lines. And second, to what extent should they allow the dominant operator to enter the business of data communications services? The operator would presumably have an overwhelming advantage in marketing these services and might be tempted to leverage its monopoly power to extend into this new area. In the United States, the Department of Justice first addressed this problem in 1956, when it upheld the Bell System's monopoly in telephone service but prohibited Bell from providing data services itself. The regulation of data communications services has posed a dilemma for other countries as well, often setting the stage for broader reform.

All of the major industrial countries have faced the same basic regulatory challenges brought on by advances in terminal equipment, transmission technologies, and value-added services. Most have moved gradually to introduce competition in telecommunications, at least in some market segments (Table 2). Their primary motivation to do so has come from the threat of international competition. They have judged that liberalization could help them gain or retain competitive advantage in a variety of ways. First, and most important, liberalization would lower telecommunications costs and facilitate the development of new products and services, thus enhancing productivity throughout the economy. Second, liberalization

Table 2. Milestones of telecommunications reform in five countries

Type of regulatory change	United States	United Kingdom	Japan	France	Germany
System reorganization	AT&T divestiture 1984	BT privatized 1984	NTT privatized 1985	FT separated from ministry 1990, privatization planned	DBP Telekom separated from ministry 1990; privatized 1995
Network liberalization	MCI starts 1971	Mercury starts 1982	Competitors licensed 1985	No	No
VAN liberalization	Computer I 1971 Computer II 1980	Liberalized 1981	Liberalized 1971, 1982, 1985	Liberalized 1987, 1990	Liberalized 1989
Equipment liberalization	Carterphone 1968, AT&T divestiture 1984	Liberalized 1981	Liberalized 1985	Liberalized 1990	Liberalized 1989
Mobile liberalization	Independent cellular service 1983	Two networks licensed 1986	Two consortia licensed 1987	Competitor licensed 1988	Competitor licensed 1990
Satellite liberalization	Open Skies 1972	Satellite services liberalized 1988	Two carriers licensed 1985	Liberalized 1986	Competitors licensed 1990

would stimulate the growth of the telecommunications industry itself, including equipment manufacturers as well as advanced service providers. Third, a liberal telecommunications regime would attract multinational corporations. The United Kingdom, for example, has tried to use telecommunications reform to persuade multinational corporations that rely heavily on telecommunications networks, such as financial institutions, to locate there rather than on the Continent. And fourth, liberalization would make domestic operators more price-competitive than their foreign rivals so that they could beat out these rivals in the international telephone service market.[2]

The liberalization of telecommunications markets has inevitably been accompanied by reregulation. Because of the dominant position of the incumbent carriers, all countries that have introduced competition in basic telephone service have employed pro-competitive reregulation to enhance the new carriers' ability to compete. They have constrained the dominant carrier's ability to "rebalance" rates—to raise local call rates so that they can lower long-distance rates more rapidly—in order to undersell their competitors in long-distance service. The British government took the most extreme measures to jump-start competition, protecting the new carrier, Mercury, from any other market entrants for a period of seven years. The Japanese government adopted the most interventionist approach to managing competition, carefully controlling the dominant carrier's pricing policy and its introduction of new services.

The countries in this study have also reorganized the dominant telecommunications operator. The United States broke up its private monopoly carrier into a long-distance carrier and regional operating companies, and France and Germany have separated the regulatory and operational functions of their post, telegraph and telephone (PTT) organizations. The United Kingdom, Japan, and Germany privatized the public operator, and France plans to follow suit. Authorities in these countries have argued that there cannot be effective competition without privatization. On the one hand, a public corporation would be unfairly burdened with a public service obligation and hampered with political intervention, which would impede its ability to compete. On the other hand, a public corporation would have an unfair advantage because it would not have to pay attention to its bottom line, knowing that it could always count on financial relief from the government.

Although the technological developments outlined above create the backdrop for telecommunications reform, they have not simply driven change but have interacted with corporate and government strategies.

[2] Other accounts of the technological forces behind telecommunications reform include Hills (1986), Bar and Borrus (October 1989), and Bickers (1991).

Companies develop the technologies they do within the context of the existing system of regulation, and in some cases they are actually motivated to innovate by their desire to overcome regulatory constraints and thus to break into new markets. Government policy establishes the environment in which innovation takes place and shapes the direction in which it evolves.[3] Thus there is a "dialectical" relationship between innovation and government policy, a dynamic we shall explore further in the case of financial services.[4]

The Financial Revolution

The financial revolution is linked to the telecommunications revolution, for the advance in telecommunications technology has directly affected financial markets. New computer and communications technologies have greatly reduced the transaction costs involved in providing financial services. This has transformed the cost structure of financial institutions by enabling them to make a profit at smaller spreads. It has also facilitated arbitrage activity—trading designed to take advantage of price differentials across markets—over long distances. Technological change has interacted with private sector adaptation and government policy to produce a global wave of regulatory reform.

Whereas market forces have applied roughly similar pressures in the major industrial countries in the telecommunications sector, the dynamics have varied more in finance because of differences in market structure, the degree of insulation from international markets, and fiscal and monetary policy priorities. Ironically, the rigid segmentation between banks and brokerage firms in the United States has created incentives for financial innovation not found in countries without such barriers, such as Germany. Countries with relatively insulated financial markets have been able to postpone reform longer than those more integrated into international markets. And national priorities for regulatory policy vary depending on whether countries are trying to attract or to keep out foreign capital, and whether the government itself is burdened with a large debt.

Regulatory arbitrage has motivated national authorities to reform regulations to attract financial institutions or capital or to prevent their flight. Some suggest that competition between regulators tends to degenerate into a "competition in laxity," but others contend that it makes regulators perform better just as marketplace competition makes firms more productive.[5] The governments of the advanced industrial countries differ in

---

[3] The literature on technological trajectories illustrates this point particularly well. See, for example, OECD-BRIE (October 1989) and Dosi, Tyson, and Zysman (1989).

[4] Kane (May 1981 and 1987).

[5] See Kane (1987).

their priorities within this regulatory competition. For those countries trying to attract foreign capital, such as France and Italy, the authorities created new investment instruments to induce foreigners to invest in their
country's assets. British authorities, in contrast, sought to use regulation to
attract foreign financial institutions to the City. They felt that the country
would benefit because these institutions bring valuable foreign exchange
into the economy. They were painfully aware that London was losing market share to New York and Tokyo and hoped to reverse this trend by gaining a new lead in regulatory innovation. Japanese authorities were less
driven to liberalize for the sake of Tokyo as a financial center because they
gave higher priority to system stability, and because they were confident
that the strength of the Japanese economy would benefit the Tokyo market over the long run.

The biggest threat to national regulators beginning in the 1960s was
the rise of the Euromarkets, markets based in a currency other than that
of the home country. By far the largest Euromarkets were based in dollars
and located in London. As "offshore" markets, they were not subject to domestic regulations such as reserve requirements and interest rate controls,
making them attractive both to borrowers and lenders. The Eurobond
market became particularly popular, with volume rising rapidly in the
1970s and 1980s. National regulators have had to adapt in order to limit
the movement of financial activity away from domestic markets into these
new markets.

Meanwhile, institutional investors in the major financial markets
pushed brokers to liberalize commissions and thus to pass along more of
the costs savings from technological advances. These investors were accounting for a larger and larger share of stock trading, so their influence
on the securities houses was substantial. They felt that the commission
price structure subsidized individual investors at the expense of institutional investors. Commissions depended primarily on the volume of the
trade, even though large trades do not require much more work than
smaller ones.[6] In the United States, institutional investors undermined the
system by bypassing the New York Stock Exchange (NYSE) and executing
trades in regional or over-the-counter markets. In the United Kingdom,
brokers increasingly offered "sweeteners," such as free research or other
gifts, to compensate for high commission rates. On May Day in 1975, the
Securities and Exchange Commission (SEC) liberalized commissions, and
this increased the pressure on other markets to liberalize to avoid losing
business to New York. In some cases, the governments' own needs for fi-

[6] Commissions were scaled such that they were lower (as a percentage of trade volume) for
larger trades, but institutional investors felt they were not scaled enough. This premise has
since been born out by the market, as liberalization has decreased costs for large trades and
increased costs for small trades. Schreiner and Smith (Summer 1980).

nancing contributed to the process. Bank of England officials supported the removal of fixed commissions under the Big Bang in 1986 in part because they felt that this would increase liquidity in the market for government securities, or "gilt-edged shares." In Japan, the government's issuance of a large quantity of bonds with ten-year maturities beginning in 1975 created a large secondary market in the mid-1980s, leading the government to loosen restrictions on short-term money markets as well (see Table 3 for examples of some of the major financial reform measures).

Macroeconomic shifts beginning in the early 1970s greatly amplified the pressure for reform. As the world switched from a fixed to a flexible exchange rate system, national authorities began to take more freedom with monetary and fiscal policy because they believed that they no longer needed to worry about the "external constraint"—that is, they would not have to intervene to balance the current account because this would presumably happen naturally.[7] Furthermore, the U.S. government responded to its economic difficulties by pursuing inflationary policies in the 1970s, then tightening monetary policy in the 1980s while continuing to expand fiscal policy. This combination of events provided a catalyst for financial reform in two ways. First, the resulting imbalances created huge international capital flows, increasing the "leakage" from domestic financial systems. Second, high inflation led to higher and more volatile interest rates, putting added pressure on authorities to allow interest rates to rise to market levels.[8] The authorities themselves accelerated the process by enacting measures to liberalize capital flows. The United Kingdom and Japan, for example, revised their foreign exchange laws in 1979 and 1980, respectively. This step had a catalytic effect, because it facilitated arbitrage with international markets, which in turn created more pressure to liberalize at home.

Increasing competition for higher returns has continued to fuel the trend toward disintermediation, whereby corporations gradually shift from "indirect" financing, or borrowing from banks, to "direct" financing, or the issuance of stocks or bonds. In countries like the United States and Japan where the banking business was strictly separated from the brokerage business, this trend worked to the detriment of the commercial banks. But it also gave these banks a powerful incentive to innovate—to develop market-based financial instruments more closely resembling those offered by securities firms—and to lobby their governments for regulatory reform. In the United States, both commercial and investment banks tried

---

[7] In fact, these authorities were mistaken because they failed to understand that international capital flows would undermine the adjustment mechanism that was supposed to bring current account imbalances quickly back to equilibrium. See Meerschwam (1991), pp. 43–46.

[8] Ibid., pp. 37–66.

Table 3. Milestones of financial reform in five countries

Type of regulatory change	United States	United Kingdom	Japan	France	Germany
Fixed commissions	Abolished 1975	Abolished 1986	Began liberalization 1994	Abolished 1988	Reduced 1980s
Exchange controls	Removed 1970s	Removed 1979	Removed 1980	Removed 1985	Removed for exports 1961, imports 1981
Deposit interest rates	Phased out 1980–86	Liberalized 1971	Liberalized 1980–95	Partially liberalized 1985	Liberalized 1967
System structure	Holding company cross-entry allowed 1987	Limited barriers, further eased 1980s	Entry by separate subsidiary allowed 1992	Limited barriers, further eased 1980s	Universal banking
Money market funds	Introduced 1974	Introduced 1971	MMCs 1985	Introduced 1983	Introduced 1994
CDs (negotiable)	Created 1961, liberalized 1971–73	Introduced 1968	Phased in 1979–85	Introduced 1985	Introduced 1986

to invade each other's turf by creating "hybrid" instruments such as government bond funds and mortgage-backed securities.

As in the telecommunications case, financial liberalization has been coupled with reregulation. Financial authorities have increasingly coordinated their movements precisely to avoid "competing for laxity" in prudential rules such as capital adequacy requirements. They have strengthened disclosure requirements to facilitate informed market decisions in a financial marketplace governed more by prices and less by relationships. And they have substantially stiffened regulations governing insider trading and other fraudulent practices.

In both the telecommunications and finance sectors, market changes take us quite far in explaining why so many countries have undertaken regulatory reform. But they cannot explain the extension of regulatory reform to other less dynamic sectors. They are not entirely irrelevant in these other sectors, for even less dynamic sectors are affected by developments in the wider economy. In trucking, for example, the integration of the Japanese economy with other markets increased pressure for regulatory reform because the U.S. government viewed excessive regulation as a structural barrier to trade. Or in the gas sector, British authorities responded in part to the prospect of competition from sources abroad. Nonetheless, market changes cannot explain why deregulation has taken on the character of a political movement. Why have some countries—the United States, the United Kingdom, and Japan—applied the logic of reform to one sector after another? Why has reform so often been couched in terms of the rhetoric of "deregulation"? And in the telecommunications and finance sectors, why did so many countries respond to market pressures only during the 1980s, when many of these pressures existed much earlier?

THE INTERNATIONAL DIFFUSION OF DEREGULATION

The deregulation movement began in the United States. In telecommunications the watershed came with the antitrust suit launched by the Justice Department against AT&T in 1974, and in finance it came with May Day in 1975.[9] And deregulation as a movement really began in 1975, when Senator Edward Kennedy initiated a series of hearings on airline regulation. The movement then quickly spread to trucking, the railroads, the environment, and occupational safety. Academic criticism of the inefficiencies of regulation combined with political entrepreneurship to pro-

[9] The U.S. role as the vanguard is less clear cut in finance, because other countries had experimented with deregulation earlier. Nonetheless, Moran (1991) argues persuasively that U.S. influence was critical.

duce a new policy fashion.[10] To this day, deregulation has proceeded furthest in the United States, although both the United Kingdom and Japan
have pursued reforms in enough sectors that they could be said to have
full-fledged movements as well. The progression of regulatory reform initiatives from the United States to the United Kingdom and Japan and beyond leads one to ask whether the United States played some role,
intended or not, in promoting reform abroad.[11]

The United States influenced regulatory debates elsewhere in three basic
ways. First, U.S. initiatives produced a *competitive dynamic*. As noted in the
analysis of market forces, U.S. regulators liberalized telecommunications
and financial services in order to make these two industries more efficient
and to provide the benefits of this greater efficiency to industry as a whole.
This in turn provided a competitive threat to other governments, which
then considered matching the U.S. liberalization. Some European officials
became concerned that domestic corporations might suffer from higher
telephone rates or fewer financing options than were available in the
United States, or that liberalization might encourage business activity and
capital to shift to the United States. For example, British authorities liberalized stock commissions in part because they feared that London would lose
more stock trading activity to New York since May Day commission liberalization had made it cheaper to trade in New York. The specific response to
U.S. initiatives, however, varies widely depending on how officials conceive
the interaction between regulation and international competition.

Second, U.S. followers engaged in *policy imitation*. In practice, the competitive dynamic and policy imitation are often intertwined, but the two
remain analytically distinct. In some cases, in fact, other countries have im-
itated U.S. initiatives without feeling any competitive threat from these initiatives. In the case of trucking or railroad deregulation, for example, the
competitive dynamic does not apply, but a demonstration effect does. Government officials in other countries often studied the U.S. experience
before embarking on their own reforms. Under the Thatcher administration, for example, Department of Industry (DoI) officials were assigned a
reading list, including files on the U.S. court cases involved in deregulation.[12] Japanese Ministry of Finance (MoF) officials sent teams to study the
U.S. experience in dismantling some of the regulatory barriers between
banking and the brokerage business. The chairman of the administrative
reform committee that recommended the liberalization of telephone ser-

---

[10] Derthick and Quirk (1985).

[11] Hills (1986) and Moran (1991) stress the U.S. influence on regulatory reforms elsewhere, applying this argument to telecommunications and financial services, respectively.
See Ikenberry (1990) for an analysis of policy diffusion applied to privatization.

[12] Interviews with DTI officials (July 1990). Bosanquet (July–September 1981) reproduces
the general reading list, although this does not include the telecommunications files.

vice and the privatization of Nippon Telegraph and Telephone (NTT) recalls that debates within the committee often centered on the question of whether the U.S. experience represented the beginning of a global trend. "We really were not sure whether this was an isolated case, or the start of a trend," he explains. "But if it were the latter, we certainly would not want to be left behind."[13] Interest groups with a stake in regulatory reform have also learned from the U.S. example, often only demanding changes in their own countries once they observed developments in the United States. British and Japanese telecommunications users did not even perceive the need for a major regulatory overhaul before the U.S. reform process built up momentum in the 1970s. Their perceptions of what would be technically and politically feasible, and economically beneficial, were transformed in light of the U.S. experience.

In addition, U.S. economists espousing the economic theory of regulation have strongly influenced opinion leaders abroad. This ideology had its greatest influence in the United Kingdom, where economists and policymakers heralded the teachings of the U.S. school. Bank of England officials combed the U.S. literature on financial regulation before writing their "Blue Skies" report that anticipated the Big Bang.[14] And Michael Beesley and other proponents of telecommunications liberalization built on the U.S. industrial organization literature. The U.S. proponents of deregulation have given regulatory reform a distinct vocabulary and rationale. Powerful figures in Western Europe and Japan have eagerly adopted their rhetoric, if not always their policy prescriptions.

Third, the U.S. government has applied *direct pressure*—generally not for sweeping reform programs abroad, but for more specific liberalization measures that would help U.S. exporters of goods or services. Nevertheless, these demands sometimes had the effect of promoting wider reform. For example, U.S. pressure for reciprocal access to the telecommunications equipment market gave the German government an incentive to open this market, and opening the equipment market led directly into the larger reform process. The U.S. government made its broadest appeal for liberalization in the case of Japanese financial markets because senior officials at the time believed that this would help U.S. exports overall by strengthening the yen (see Chapter 8). In some cases, U.S. pressure has provided a critical stimulus breaking deadlock within the domestic reform debate.[15] U.S. multinationals have also

[13] Interview with Hiroshi Katō, dean, faculty of policy management, Keiō University (May 14, 1991).
[14] Interviews with Andrew Threadgold, chief executive, Postel (October 25, 1991), and Sir David Walker, chairman, Securities and Investment Board (October 23, 1991).
[15] Webber (April 1990) argues that foreign pressure was critical in both telecommunications and finance in Germany, and Tadokoro (1988) makes a similar argument concerning finance in Japan.

played a part in policy debates abroad, particularly in the United Kingdom. The British subsidiaries of American-owned firms were among the first to call for telecommunications liberalization. These firms knew the American experience best, and they were eager to benefit from the same freedoms that they enjoyed at home.[16] American financial firms also influenced Japanese financial reform by supplying "wish lists" to the U.S. government, although they were very careful not to offend the MoF.

Although the United States has been highly influential, we should not overlook other actors that have played an important part in diffusing deregulation policies. The United Kingdom has strongly influenced the debate in the rest of Europe and Japan. On privatization, it has taken the global lead, for it has had more to privatize than the United States and has gone further with privatization than any other country. And beginning in the late 1980s, the European Community (EC) emerged as a major force in defining regulatory policies in Europe. French and German initiatives were often tied to EC directives.

Once again, we have to be careful not to presume an overly simplistic one-way causality. U.S. experience provided a stimulus, but was often used by domestic actors for their own purposes. In fact, domestic interest groups often interpreted the U.S. experience in a way to buttress their own cases. For example, British proponents of the breakup of British Telecom heralded the divestiture of AT&T as an unqualified success, whereas the unions portrayed it as an unmitigated disaster. Japanese securities houses claimed that the U.S. government wisely erected formidable "firewalls" between banks and their securities subsidiaries, but the banks contended that these firewalls were not really as high as they seemed. Furthermore, Japanese authorities have been prone to exaggerate the level of U.S. pressure when it suits their purpose to do so. In a few cases, they have even resorted to requesting pressure from American authorities.[17]

Like the market change explanation, the international diffusion explanation captures an important part of the truth. It helps to explain the common rhetoric and theory behind deregulation efforts, and the extension of deregulation to less dynamic sectors in the United Kingdom and Japan. But it does not really explain why the deregulation movement took hold. Why did it catch on in the United States in the first place? After all, new ideas have to meet the real or perceived needs of the time in order to have any impact. Government leaders must see some political benefit in order to take up a new cause.

---

[16] Interviews with British telecommunications user group representatives (July 1990).
[17] Prestowitz (1989), p. 477.

THE POLITICS OF ECONOMIC SLOWDOWN

U.S. political leaders launched the deregulation movement in the mid-1970s; British and Japanese leaders followed in the late 1970s. During this particular period these leaders found special merit in making a cause of the seemingly mundane business of rewriting and dismantling rules. The economic literature that suggested a need for deregulation had been accumulating for decades, but there was something about the post–Oil Crisis world that made deregulation programs particularly attractive. For most advanced industrialized countries, the Oil Crisis of 1973 marked the transition from rapid postwar economic growth to slower growth (see Table 4). Many of these countries faced severe economic difficulties in the

Table 4. GDP growth in five countries at constant prices, 1965–1994

	United States	United Kingdom	Japan	France	Germany
1965	5.6	2.5	5.8	4.8	5.3
1966	6.0	1.9	10.4	5.2	2.9
1967	2.6	2.3	11.0	4.7	–0.2
1968	4.1	4.1	12.2	4.3	5.6
1969	2.7	2.1	12.1	7.0	7.6
1970	—	2.3	10.2	5.7	5.0
1971	3.1	2.0	4.3	4.8	3.0
1972	4.8	3.5	8.4	4.4	4.3
1973	5.2	7.4	7.6	5.4	4.8
1974	–0.6	–1.7	–0.8	3.1	0.1
1975	–0.8	–0.7	2.9	–0.3	–1.3
1976	4.9	2.8	4.2	4.2	5.5
1977	4.5	2.4	4.8	3.2	2.6
1978	4.8	3.5	5.0	3.3	3.4
1979	2.5	2.8	5.6	3.2	4.0
1980	–0.5	–2.2	3.5	1.6	1.0
1981	1.8	–1.3	3.4	1.2	0.1
1982	–2.2	1.7	3.4	2.5	–1.1
1983	3.9	3.7	2.8	0.7	1.9
1984	6.2	2.3	4.3	1.3	3.1
1985	3.2	3.8	5.2	1.9	1.8
1986	2.9	4.3	2.6	2.5	2.2
1987	3.1	4.8	4.3	2.3	1.5
1988	3.9	5.0	6.2	4.5	3.7
1989	2.5	2.2	4.8	4.3	4.0
1990	0.8	0.4	4.8	2.5	4.9
1991	–1.2	–2.0	4.3	0.8	3.6
1992	3.3	–0.5	1.4	1.3	1.2
1993	3.1	2.3	0.1	–1.5	–2.3
1994	4.1	3.8	0.6	2.7	1.6

SOURCE: IMF International Financial Statistics

1970s as they tried to adjust to rising oil prices and resulting inflation. Governments faced a particular dilemma: the growth in demand for government services began to outpace the growth in governments' resources for meeting this demand. People had become accustomed to rising standards of welfare, and hard times were only increasing the need for welfare services. But with slower growth in income, governments faced tough choices: they could limit spending, increase taxation, or finance the gap between revenues and expenditures through debt. Politically, most governments were wary of raising taxes. Unable to cut spending significantly, the United States, the United Kingdom and Japan all experienced substantial budget deficits in the late 1970s.

Some commentators have described this situation as no less than a crisis of the welfare state. Interest groups were making more and more demands upon the state, and the state was simply unable to meet them.[18] James O'Connor (1973) argued that capitalist states were bound to face a fiscal crisis because they were offering more services than they could afford to provide. In one sense, the deregulation movement turns these arguments on their head. Governments in the late 1970s and early 1980s embarked on a project to do precisely what they were not supposed to be able to do: to cut expenditures and to reduce their role in the economy.

They were only able to do so, however, because the growth of state activity itself came to be questioned. Economic slowdown prompted opinion leaders to question established modes of government intervention, from Keynesian demand management to industrial policy.[19] The mass media and influential groups began to attack the overextension of the public sector, including excessive government regulation of business. Conservative parties exploited this opportunity, blaming economic difficulties on too much taxing and spending and too much government intervention. They also seized the moment to attack labor unions, suggesting that labor demands and labor-backed policies had produced the economic crisis in the first place.

In this context, the appeal of deregulation as a political strategy begins to make sense. First, in an era of growing public debt, it offers the possibility of cutting government expenses or at least controlling their growth by reducing administrative costs. Second, it offers a way to turn a political liability into an asset, by employing a rhetoric of cutting waste and eliminating inefficiency to turn a necessity, the reduction of government services, into a popular cause. Finally, to the extent that regulation hampers business productivity, deregulation promises to improve economic performance without any increase in government expenditure. That is, in a time

[18] See, for example, Crozier, Huntington, and Watanuki (1975) and Dahrendorf (October–December 1980).
[19] Hall (1986 and April 1993).

of economic austerity, deregulation has the ultimate virtue in that it is virtually costless in terms of tax dollars. And even better, it is linked to privatization, a policy that actually *produces* revenue with no visible cost to the taxpayer.

Each of these forces for change—market shifts, the export of U.S. regulation, and macroeconomic changes—provides a partial explanation for the widespread movement toward regulatory reform in the advanced industrial countries. The three explanations are complementary, but they are not of equal force or scope. The first explanation is the most powerful, yet the narrowest. It is powerful because market changes compelled governments to respond, but it is narrow because it applies only to dynamic sectors like telecommunications and financial services. It also suggests that reform will be more widespread across countries in dynamic sectors than in more stable sectors. The second explanation is less powerful, and less narrow. It helps to explain why governments have adopted a similar rhetoric of deregulation and why they have moved toward the more legalistic approach to regulation common in the United States. It is less powerful because the U.S. experience provided an important stimulus, but did not really force a response. The third explanation is the least powerful, but the broadest. It suggests how economic conditions provided a political opportunity, making deregulation and neoconservative ideology particularly attractive. This provided the preconditions for a deregulation movement, but conservative parties only seized the opportunity in certain countries. Continental European countries were less susceptible to such a movement because of their stronger social-democratic traditions and greater public support for government programs.

What all three explanations suggest, however, is that the countries in this study have responded to a common set of challenges. These explanations account for the elements of convergence among the advanced industrial countries. They explain why all countries have responded similarly in those cases where market incentives have been strongest, for example, in liberalizing interest rates. They explain the common rhetoric of deregulation adopted in many different national contexts; however, they cannot address the even more remarkable variance in how these countries have responded to these challenges. These countries may have adopted a common language of "deregulation," yet they have given it a very different substance. The countries we examine vary considerably in how they liberalized, how they reregulated, and how they transformed government-industry relations. I summarize the essence of the argument in Figure 1. These countries have faced similar challenges, yet have responded differently. In the remainder of this book, I seek to describe and to explain this variation in responses.

Figure 1. The basic argument in diagram form

Common Forces for Change		
Marketplace changes	U.S. "deregulation" exported	Macroeconomic trends
• Exerts strong pressure to respond	• Exerts medium pressure to respond	• Exerts weak pressure to respond
• Applies only to dynamic sectors	• Applies to all sectors	• Applies to all sectors
• Applies to all countries	• Applies to all countries (some more than others)	• Applies to all countries (but not all respond)

Specific National Responses

Regime orientation affects
    • how government officials interpret these forces.
      E.g., do these forces compel a liberal response?
    • what kinds of measures are considered appropriate.
      E.g., should governments manage the liberalization process?
 	
Regime organization affects
    • who controls the reform process.
      E.g., can bureaucrats resist party initiatives?
    • how government officials try to shape reform.
      E.g., do officials seek to preserve certain capabilities?

CHAPTER THREE

The United Kingdom and Japan: Two Paths to Regulatory Reform

The United Kingdom and Japan began their regulatory reform programs at the same time and under similar circumstances, and extended their programs to a similar range of sectors. They were similarly influenced by the U.S. deregulation movement and faced common international market pressures. Thus they provide a good comparative fit: any differences in reform outcomes are likely to reflect differences in domestic politics.[1] The British and Japanese governments adopted a similar rhetoric of "liberalization" and "deregulation," yet produced strikingly different reforms. This divergence cannot be explained by a market or interest group model, but only through an examination of the ideas and institutions that shaped the two countries' reform strategies.

THE POLITICAL CONTEXT OF BRITISH REFORM

The Old Regime: Arm's-Length Interference

As noted in Chapter 1, at the broadest level a government's regulatory regime reflects the historical legacy of industrialization. Beyond this, the ideas and institutions that comprise the regime evolve in response to particular historical experiences, such as the Great Depression and World War II. The British regime has been characterized by an intellectual tradition of liberalism and a political tradition of limited government. As Alexander Gerschenkron has demonstrated, early developers did not require powerful institutions to initiate the industrialization process. The

[1] Lijphart (1971), pp. 687–91.

United Kingdom industrialized in an era of simple textile processing when little capital was required to begin production. Thus private entrepreneurs could initiate industrial breakthrough without relying on heavy government intervention.[2] E. J. Hobsbawm offers a more political argument, although one not inconsistent with Gerschenkron's. He suggests that the British landed elite was distinct from Continental elites in that it was involved in trade and industry. This meant that the landed elite allied with the emerging industrial class and did not oppose industrial development. Thus manufacturing entrepreneurs were able to launch the industrial revolution without requiring state intervention to overcome elite resistance. As the United Kingdom faced greater competition in the twentieth century, the country's industrialists remained disinclined to look to the state for support because they adhered to a laissez-faire philosophy and could rely on the British empire as a secure market.[3]

After the Second World War, the Labour government built the foundations for a more active role in industrial affairs by nationalizing key industries and introducing a system of planning. But these institutions, which gave the government the potential to shape industrial development in theory, did not serve this purpose in British practice. Unlike their French counterparts, British nationalized industries were never incorporated into the apparatus of the state. Similarly, the government was unable to reach a consensus over how to use the planning system, so it quickly degenerated into a mechanism for distributing the resources designated for reconstruction. Meanwhile, the government failed to undertake more sweeping institutional reforms, such as reforms of the civil service or the financial system, that might have enabled it to play a more active role in promoting economic growth. Despite some noteworthy initiatives, the Labour Party ultimately failed to break away from an arms-length orientation toward industry.[4]

Although the British government's policy toward industry has varied somewhat between administrations and sometimes within the same administration, it is still possible to identify basic features of a British regulatory regime that hold true for the postwar era prior to 1979. The Labour Party and the Conservative Party differed sharply in rhetoric, yet far less in practice when in power. This relative continuity rested on a broader consensus on government policy. Dennis Kavanagh suggests that both parties

[2] Gerschenkron (1962).

[3] Hobsbawm (1969). Also see Leys (1983), pp. 229–33.

[4] Zysman (1983, pp. 180–87) argues that British leaders failed to make necessary institutional reforms because they were unable to reach a political settlement regarding the distribution of benefits from growth. Hall (1986) also attributes the United Kingdom's relatively poor economic performance to institutional weaknesses. He suggests, for example, that the British state lacks a strong central agency concerned with industry, and that the British private sector is divided between financial and industrial capital.

shared basic assumptions about the overall orientation of policy throughout the postwar period, and neither was willing to deviate much from this common ground.[5] Indeed, despite reform, some of the features of this regime remain in place even today.

We shall refer to the postwar regime's orientation prior to reform as *regulatory*.[6] This denotes a particular perspective on the proper scope, goals and methods of government regulation and promotion of industry (see Table 5). Concerning the scope of intervention, government officials believed that the range and depth of intervention should be restricted. They felt that they should be able to achieve prosperity through effective macroeconomic management without interfering in the management of private enterprises.[7] For British industrialists frustrated by constant government interference in their business affairs, this characterization may appear a bit naive. Yet British government officials and industrialists alike spoke in terms of government "intervention," which belies a fundamental difference in attitude between British officials and their counterparts in Japan or France. British officials did not assume that government intervention was inherently legitimate, but felt that it required a specific rationale. In the case of the nationalized industries, they may have interfered with management, but viewed their role as one of monitoring public managers rather than working directly with them for a common purpose.

Concerning the goals of intervention, government officials sought to enhance the efficiency of the existing market structure more than to alter this structure. Their primary role was to enforce fair rules of competition between market players and then leave these players to compete freely.

Table 5. Comparing British and Japanese regulatory regimes prior to reform

	United Kingdom	Japan
Orientation (ideas)	Regulatory	Managerial
1. Proper degree of intervention	Low	High
2. Goal of intervention	Efficiency	Growth
3. Regulatory philosophy	Procedural	Strategic
Organization (institutions)	Segmented	Fused
1. Organization of the bureaucracy	Fragmented	Centralized
2. Government's ties with industry	Detached	Engaged
3. Bureaucratic autonomy	Medium	High

[5] Kavanagh (1990), especially pp. 26–62.

[6] This distinction builds upon Johnson's (1982) notion of a "regulatory state" and Zysman's (1983) concept of the government as a "regulator" and "administrator" but not a "player."

[7] Shonfield (1965), pp. 88–120.

Unlike the French, German, or Japanese, the British government did not ordinarily try to develop long-term plans for industry or to restructure industry to create a new basis for growth. In practice, this meant that when they did intervene, they were more likely to do so in an *ad hoc* manner for purely political considerations than in a systematic manner for developmental purposes. They did not spontaneously promote growth industries so much as reactively protect declining ones. Beyond this, the British government promoted competition through an active antitrust policy, establishing the Monopoly and Mergers Commission (MMC) in 1948 and the Office of Fair Trading (OFT) in 1951, and strengthening the OFT's powers in 1970.[8] This contrasts to the pattern in Japan, as we shall see, where ministry officials tried to undermine antitrust policy because it threatened their developmental goals.

As to the methods of intervention, the government did not use the financial system to allocate funds to growth sectors, but rather relied on direct subsidies from the budget. In practice, this severely constrained the government's ability to implement industrial policy because of the Treasury's tight control over expenditures. The government did use incentives such as tax breaks to encourage investment, but generally avoided measures designed to favor a particular company or group of companies—with the obvious exception of national champions in serious trouble. As to regulation, the government used it to enforce fair competition within markets and to protect consumers from fraud rather than to support domestic industry. The government's style of regulation was "procedural" in the sense that regulators were more concerned with following proper procedures than with promoting industry. They strove to regulate as neutral judges rather than as sponsors of British industry or of specific companies.[9] They were not immune to the temptation to rig technical standards to benefit domestic suppliers, but unlike the Japanese or French governments they did not integrate regulation into a larger industrial policy.

Although the political mainstream supported a compromise position favoring selective intervention, members of Parliament (MPs) from the right wing of the Conservative Party kept a more radically liberal tradition alive. They argued for a bold move away from government intervention in the economy, including the abandonment of industrial policy and the reduction of welfare expenditures. In industrial policy the party balanced elements of liberalism and activism, although even the activist side never advocated a fundamental restructuring of industry. Think tanks associated with the party, such as the Centre for Policy Studies and the Institute for Economic Affairs, helped to popularize the neoliberal critique of govern-

[8] See Grant (1989), pp. 96–101.
[9] On the British preference for maintaining a judicious neutrality between firms, see Shonfield (1965), especially pp. 154–55.

ment intervention.[10] Although this was not the dominant strain of thought within the government prior to 1979, it was influential enough to deter greater moves toward intervention and to foster the impulse for a bold move away from intervention in the 1980s.

The regime's organization was *segmented* in the sense that the bureaucracy was decentralized, the government was detached from industry, and the bureaucracy was relatively vulnerable to influence from the political leadership and private groups. The government bureaucracy was decentralized in two senses: authority over a given domain was divided by multiple agencies, and the activities of these departments or agencies were not tightly coordinated. The Treasury was the lead agency in economic policy, but it focused on controlling expenditures and overseeing macroeconomic policy rather than promoting industry. In the making of industrial policy, no single agency dominated. The Department of Industry (DoI) was periodically merged with other departments and then reorganized again throughout the postwar era, and never gained the power to coordinate a national industrial policy.[11] The DoI was remarkably constrained compared to Japan's Ministry of International Trade and Industry (MITI), for it shared jurisdiction over industry with the Treasury and had to contend with more powerful political leaders, more independant regulatory agencies, and more assertive courts. The British central bureaucracy differed markedly from the Japanese bureaucracy in that civil servants were not nearly so strongly attached to the status and authority of their department: they were more accustomed to bureaucratic reorganization and less protective of their department's jurisdiction.

Moreover, government agencies did not have the strong links to manufacturing corporations or banks that would enable them to manipulate private sector actors in the pursuit of industrial policy goals. In other words, the sectoral networks between bureaucrats and business people were looser than they were elsewhere, and this inhibited the cooperative pursuit of national goals.[12] British officials had fewer sanctions and rewards to offer the private sector, and they were reluctant to use the leverage they did have for strategic purposes. The government maintained ownership of some major industries, but lacked the close working relationship with these industries that French authorities used as a powerful instrument of industrial policy. Likewise it lacked the strong ties with

[10] See Seldon (1989) on the role of the Institute of Economic Affairs, and Haas and Knox, eds. (1991), for a compilation of Center for Policy Studies papers.

[11] The Departments of Trade and Industry merged in 1973, subsequently separated, and then merged again in 1983.

[12] Numerous studies (e.g., Hansard Society, 1979) have addressed this issue throughout the postwar era.

banks characteristic of France, Germany, or Japan, and this effectively precluded using the financial system to preferentially allocate funds.[13]

The British bureaucracy was relatively vulnerable to pressures emanat-
ing from the political leadership or from society at large. It was more insulated from these pressures than the U.S. bureaucracy, but less insulated
than the Japanese or French bureaucracy. The structure of the British government allowed the ruling party to infiltrate the bureaucracy more easily
than was possible in Japan or France. This does not mean that British bureaucrats were mere servants of their political masters, but that it was easier for British politicians to enact new initiatives than it was for Japanese or
French politicians. The fact that prior to 1979 British politicians rarely attempted to push through major reforms that were not supported by the
bureaucracy is more a reflection of the underlying policy consensus than
of institutional constraints. Furthermore, the fragmentation of power to
multiple agencies gave interest groups more points of entry into the policy
process. And the government did not systematically incorporate certain
peak associations representing capital and labor like the more corporatist
governments of Continental Europe. This structure facilitated reform because new pressure groups were more likely to gain a hearing, and more
entrenched groups such as major producers and labor unions were less
likely to have a veto over reform.[14] In addition, British civil servants were
much more open to new ideas from outside experts than Japanese officials, who insisted on cultivating in-house expertise.

The Political Origins of "Deregulation": The Thatcher Revolution

To understand how these ideas and institutions shaped British reforms
in the 1980s, we should first review how they interacted to produce a
broad liberal reform program in the first place. As noted in the previous
chapter, institutions inconsistent with the dominant policy orientation are
likely to atrophy or to evolve into institutions more consistent with prevalent goals. When the British government nationalized major industries after World War II, it gave itself the potential to intervene strategically in
these sectors. Yet lacking the strong interventionist impulse of postwar
France, the relationship between the government and the nationalized industries evolved into one that precluded rather than facilitated such intervention. Likewise, policies that are inconsistent with the government's
institutional structure are bound to falter. Thus the Labour governments'
attempts at industrial policy in the 1960s and 1970s were stillborn in the
absence of institutional reforms because the government lacked the ca-

[13] Zysman (1983).
[14] Duch (1991, especially pp. 107–10) makes this argument concerning British telecommunications reform.

pacity to coordinate and implement such a policy effectively. And most critical for our own story, the failure of these initiatives in turn discredited industrial policy altogether by the late 1970s, opening the way in the 1980s for bolder moves away from intervention. For a government without the will or the means to implement an effective strategy of intervention, an anti-intervention strategy of privatization and deregulation became the "industrial policy" of choice.

In addition, the strong tradition of liberalism within British politics provided a would-be liberal reformer such as Margaret Thatcher with an ideological foundation she would have lacked in France or Japan. Thatcher did not develop her ideology within a vacuum, but borrowed from ideas already prominent in society and within a faction of her party. Her enthusiasm for neoliberal policies was further fueled by influence from the United States and from global trends evident in the 1970s that favored these policies (see Chapter 2). Thatcher herself must also be given some credit, for she turned a dilemma into an opportunity. She and her colleagues transformed a policy of cutting back the government's role into an industrial strategy in its own right. In a time when government budgets were bound to be tight, this had particular appeal. For the economy as a whole, it offered the chance to improve productivity without increasing spending. And for industry more specifically, it provided a means of enhancing productivity without increasing government intervention.[15]

The administration that came to power in 1979 represented a sharp break not only with the outgoing Labour government, but also with all previous Conservative governments. Although earlier Tory governments had employed a rhetoric of rolling back the state and unleashing market forces, none had ever been so ideologically driven or so determined to carry out liberal reforms. The radicalism of Thatcher and her colleagues grew in part out of their disgust with Labour's attempts to solve the country's economic problems from 1974 through 1979. Even more, however, their frustration was directed at the previous Conservative government under Edward Heath, which had traitorously abandoned its pledge to move away from intervention in the economy.[16] The Conservatives lost two elections in 1974, in part because of a crippling strike by mining workers. The party subsequently elected Margaret Thatcher over Heath in protest, and the leadership shifted ideologically to the right.

---

[15] Gamble (1988) suggests that Thatcher actually cut back government in order to make it more effective: to reestablish its "hegemony."

[16] Young (1989), pp. 84–85. Heath had won power in 1970 on a platform promising a withdrawal from industrial sponsorship, but reversed course in 1972 as his administration bailed out several major industrial corporations, including Upper Clyde Shipbuilders and Rolls-Royce.

In opposition, Conservative MP Keith Joseph founded the Centre for Policy Studies, where he and Thatcher and other colleagues began to sketch out "market solutions" to economic problems to put into practice when they returned to power. Their basic philosophy was quite simple: the government should intervene in the economy less, leaving companies and consumers freer to make their own decisions. They believed that excessive government intervention threatened both economic efficiency and individual liberty. The government should restrict itself to those tasks which require central leadership, such as providing national defense and overseeing monetary policy. In terms of macroeconomic policy, Thatcher and her colleagues moved from Keynesian demand management to monetarism.[17] They believed in cutting taxes and spending and controlling inflation by tightly constraining the growth of the money supply. In microeconomic policy, they replaced a halfhearted industrial policy with an approach that demanded less government, not more. They sought to narrow the scope of intervention through liberalization and privatization.[18]

The Thatcher agenda, as developed at the Centre for Policy Studies and articulated in the Party Manifesto of 1979, put a top priority on attacking the power of unions. This was more than revenge for the political cost of the miners' strike. The Thatcher group believed that union power was partially responsible for the country's economic woes. Unions had exacerbated inflation and undermined the competitiveness of industry by pushing for higher wages. To make matters worse, union influence over management was making companies less productive. The Thatcherites also struck at unions for political reasons, to weaken the Labour Party's support base.[19] The Thatcherites' interest in privatization was directly related to the assault on union power. Privatization would allow them to transform public sector unions into private-sector unions, which were typically less unified and less active. And it would give privatized enterprises the opportunity to shed excess workers. In addition, Thatcher and her colleagues hoped that widening share ownership could promote entrepreneurial values, to the political benefit of the party and the economic benefit of the country. They envisioned a range of other possible economic benefits from privatization: the companies would become more productive and would be able to raise funds in capital markets; the government would funnel less money into them; and most important of all, perhaps, the government would gain a windfall from the sale.[20]

[17] Hall (April 1993).

[18] On the philosophy of the United Kingdom's New Right, see Bosanquet (July–September 1981), Gamble (1988), and Kavanagh (1990).

[19] Their disdain for the unions was exposed in its baldest form when a secret paper by Nicholas Ridley was leaked to the *Economist* (May 27, 1978).

[20] In addition, both popular and elite opinion were highly critical of the nationalized industries. For the government perspective, see National Economic Development Office (1976) and H. M. Treasury (1978).

THE POLITICAL CONTEXT OF JAPANESE REFORM

The Old Regime: Ministerial Guidance

As a late developer, Japan required huge amounts of capital to industrialize. Under Gerschenkron's formulation, this required a mechanism for transferring capital to the corporate sector, and Japanese leaders used the institutions of a powerful state to accomplish this task.[21] Japan lacked the Anglo-American tradition of liberalism, and government officials and industrialists alike considered government involvement in industrial affairs to be both natural and appropriate. Since the Meiji Restoration in 1868, the government led the effort to modernize. It gradually developed the specific tools of industrial policy in the prewar years and strengthened these institutions during the militarist era. After the war, government leaders were all the more determined to achieve rapid economic recovery, and after the Occupation they substantially strengthened the institutions of industrial promotion.[22]

Postwar Japan's basic orientation prior to reform can be described as *managerial* (see Table 5). As in the British case, this characterization denotes a particular perspective regarding the appropriate scope, goals, and methods of government intervention in industrial affairs. Japanese officials viewed government intervention in industrial affairs as a natural component of economic policy. They believed that the government should actively shape and restructure markets as well as regulate industry.[23] Although the government owned very little of Japanese industry, it used a wide range of policy tools to control the allocation of capital to industry, to manage the terms of competition within specific industries, and to facilitate cooperation between firms.[24] Japanese ministries practiced "market-conforming intervention."[25] This meant that they supported industry without obliterating market signals, and they managed the economic adjustment process without halting it altogether.

Japanese officials put top priority on rapid economic growth. They tried to restructure markets and guide industry to make it more competitive internationally and to move the economy toward more capital and skill-intensive sectors. They discouraged "excess competition" among firms within a given industry because they believed that Japanese corporations were inclined to compete for market share to the point of eliminating

---

[21] Gerschenkron (1962).

[22] Johnson (1982).

[23] Johnson (1982); Sakakibara (1990); Hiwatari (1991); Tsuru (1993).

[24] See Samuels (1987), especially pp. 1–22, on the relative lack of state-owned industry in Japan. Representative works in the considerable literature on Japanese industrial policy include Magaziner and Hout (1980); Johnson (1982); Eads and Yamamura (1987); and Johnson, Tyson, and Zysman, eds. (1989). See Noble (1989) for a review.

[25] Johnson (1982), p. 29.

profits and threatening the survival of some of the players within the market. They were more concerned with market stability than efficiency narrowly defined. They feared corporate failure not only because they wanted to protect established firms but also because they felt that failure in some industries, like telecommunications or banking, imposes unjustifiable costs on the general public as both taxpayers and consumers.[26]

Japanese ministries employed a wide range of tools in a comprehensive industrial policy. Among other things, they selectively allocated credit to favored sectors, promoted research collaboration across industry, and disseminated information to industry. To implement these policies, they combined a substantial array of licenses and permits with a flexible and informal system of "administrative guidance." They did not generally tie their "guidance" of industry to a specific incentive or threat, but the potential for reward or punishment was implied. The ministries had such a wide arsenal of rewards or punishments that most firms complied with all but the most unreasonable directives.[27] Rather than trying to increase competition among firms, ministry officials restricted it through an elaborate system of licenses, permits, and other regulations.[28] Officials proudly referred to this system as "supply and demand adjustment" (*jukyū chōsei*), arguing that competition beyond a certain point becomes unnecessarily disruptive. Ministries also used licenses to control firm behavior indirectly. A license signified the ministry's approval of a market entrant as a responsible player that would meet government quality and safety standards, would not compete excessively, and would abide by ministry guidance. The Japanese approach to regulation was "strategic" in the sense that the regulation of industry was not considered an activity distinct from the promotion of industry. Rather than separate the functions of sponsorship and regulation by creating independent regulatory agencies, Japanese ministries integrated regulation into a policy of industrial sponsorship. The same ministry typically undertook both tasks and often used the leverage inherent in this duality of function to pursue its goals. For example, ministries could use the licensing system to protect incumbents; they could use

[26] See Hiwatari (1991), especially pp. 42–62, on how the Japanese government "organized" markets.

[27] See Johnson (1982), pp. 266–77, for two well-known examples of the threats behind "guidance." Recent studies focusing on manufacturing sectors (Haley 1986; Noble 1989) have questioned the extent of ministerial authority, citing examples of companies that have defied MITI guidance. The point is not that ministry guidance is always obeyed, however, but that the practice of issuing guidance that is routinely followed under normal circumstances profoundly affects the pattern of competition and cooperation in Japanese markets. This guidance is even more effective in service sectors because it is backed by more extensive formal regulatory powers.

[28] Hiwatari (1991).

price regulation to increase profitability; or they could use quality standards to discriminate against foreign producers.[29]

The regime's organization was "fused" in the sense that bureaucratic power was centralized, the government was closely engaged with industry, and the bureaucracy was relatively autonomous. Unlike the British, Japanese policy networks were tightly integrated with a single "lead ministry" at the center. Ministries deferred less to political leaders, regulatory agencies, or the courts and enjoyed clearly defined jurisdictions in terms of the industries they oversaw. Even so, they were still constantly seeking to protect or to augment their already considerable powers. Ministerial officials tried to maximize the power of their own ministry because this would enhance their own prestige and allow them to pursue policy goals with less resistance from other ministries or industry groups.[30]

Compared to British government departments, Japanese ministries had much stronger links with industry. They operated through denser networks of communication with the private sector, typically interacting with the firms under their jurisdiction through officially sanctioned industry associations.[31] The industry associations both articulated industry demands to the ministry and disseminated ministry directives to member companies. In addition, government and industry were tied by the practice of officials "descending from heaven" (*amakudari*) into private sector jobs after retirement at about the age of 55. This meant that the ministries had to be sensitive to industry demands, but it also meant that they had a much greater capacity to guide industry and to implement a state-led industrial strategy.

The Japanese bureaucracy was relatively insulated from interest group demands and ruling party interference. Government officials certainly could not ignore societal actors, but they enjoyed relative autonomy in the sense that they had a greater ability than their counterparts in the United States or the United Kingdom to tailor their responses to these demands in a way that promoted their own interests and the public interest as they defined it. They were in a better position to act on their own preferences because they were less likely to have their initiatives undermined, contradicted, or overturned by independent regulatory agencies, the Diet, or the courts. They were able to leverage permits and notifications into the power to "guide"

[29] On the latter, see D. Vogel (Winter 1992).

[30] A *Nihon Keizai Shimbun* poll found that 95 percent of upper-level bureaucrats put the interests of their own ministry first, even though 72 percent conceded that this should not be the case. *JEI Report* 2A (January 17, 1992), p. 8. Aoki (1988, pp. 272–73) stresses that Japanese bureaucrats seek to maximize their ministry's influence because their personal opportunities depend on this influence.

[31] Works in what Noble (1989) calls the "New Japan, Incorporated School" stress the close interaction between the bureaucracy and industry, but do not share Johnson's (1982) view that the bureaucracy is the leading partner. See, for example, Samuels (1987) and Okimoto (1989).

companies in other matters because they were not subject to codified regulatory procedures and their decisions could not be effectively challenged through judicial review. Although many scholars of Japan's political economy note the unusual powers of the bureaucracy, others stress the bureaucracy's ultimate accountability to the ruling Liberal Democratic Party (LDP).[32] The precise dynamics vary considerably across issue areas, but I contend that the bureaucracy remained relatively autonomous in many areas of economic policy despite the potential for LDP intervention. We shall explore this point in more detail, however, in the case studies to follow.

The Political Origins of "Deregulation": Administrative Reform

We can understand the evolution of Japan's postwar political economy in terms of the interaction between ideas and institutions. After the war, the U.S. Occupation authorities introduced social and political reforms that have had an enduring impact on Japanese society, yet those reforms aimed at reorienting government regulation and restructuring industry failed to take hold in the absence of a complementary economic ideology. For example, the Occupation authorities created five independent regulatory commissions on the model of U.S. agencies, but the central ministries took away their independence after the U.S. authorities departed. The Ministry of Posts and Telecommunications (MPT) absorbed the radio regulatory agency, and the Ministry of Finance (MoF) took over the Japanese Securities and Exchange Commission. The Fair Trade Commission (FTC) remains the sole survivor, but it has been emasculated by MITI and other ministries that have sponsored legislation providing exemptions from antitrust regulations. By the 1970s and 1980s, however, the ideological mainstream began to shift slightly, as some Japanese leaders proposed decentralization and deregulation and the U.S. government pressured Japan to liberalize its economy. Nevertheless, in the face of daunting institutional barriers, Japan's "neoliberal" reforms have ended up bold in rhetoric but not particularly liberal in substance.

In Japan, the "deregulation" movement came under the rubric of the Second Provisional Commission on Administrative Reform (*rinji gyōsei chōsakai*, or "Rinchō" for short), which was officially established in March 1981. The administrative reform movement has a variety of sources, but three factors were particularly important.[33] First, some Japanese leaders

---

[32] Johnson (1982) and Zysman (1983), for example, stress bureaucratic autonomy, but Satō and Matsuzaki (1986), Inoguchi and Iwai (1987), Muramatsu and Krauss (1987), Curtis (1988), Rosenbluth (1989), and Ramseyer and Rosenbluth (1993) emphasize accountability to the LDP.

[33] More detailed interpretations of the Rinchō include Kumon (Spring 1984), Kambara (1986), and D. Itō (1988). Kawakami and Masuda, eds. (1989), Hiwatari (1991), and Ōtake (1994) analyze Japanese neo-conservatism more generally.

came to question the highly centralized system of government that seemed to have served them so well. For example, Prime Minister Kakuei Tanaka's plan for the revitalization of the Japanese Archipelago was in part designed to decentralize "Japan, Inc."[34] Of course, Tanaka had more strictly political motivations as well, namely, to establish his status as a national leader by articulating his own "vision" and to create a rationale for increased spending on politically fruitful public works projects in remote areas. Nonetheless, there was a more rationally motivated element to the plan: the devolution of governmental authority. Similarly, the Rinchō's advocates saw the commission as a mechanism to move Japan away from an overly rigid governmental structure. Administrative reform—in the eyes of the politicians and the public but certainly not in the eyes of the bureaucrats—was an attempt to decentralize political authority away from the lead government agencies.

Second, more specifically, in the late 1970s the government had begun to run huge budget deficits. Prime Minister Tanaka had boosted public spending in the early 1970s, and this led to fiscal problems as economic growth rates slowed after the first Oil Shock. Prime Minister Takeo Fukuda was forced to try to stimulate growth through government spending. The LDP pushed the MoF to abandon its commitment to balanced or nearly balanced budgets. Many scholars date the ascent of the LDP's power, at the expense of the central ministries, from this period.[35] The big corporations, represented above all by the Federation of Economic Organizations (*keizai dantai rengōkai,* or "Keidanren" for short), resented the increase in corporate taxes as government spending swelled, and they were afraid that they would have to pay an increasing share of the burden of financing the debt. They were particularly bitter because they felt that the government was growing less fiscally responsible just when they were struggling to cut costs in the face of the two oil crises. They realized that the only alternative to higher taxes would be reduced government spending, and only a large-scale reform like the administrative reform program could possibly achieve meaningful spending cuts. The MoF had a common interest with the business community in cutting the deficit and hoped to use the administrative reform program to set new spending limits.

Third, the ruling LDP used administrative reform as part of a strategy to realign its political support base. The LDP was losing some of its dominance in rural areas, and in any case the population was migrating to urban areas. The LDP could not stall the political effects of this trend forever by postponing redistricting so that rural districts would remain overrepresented. LDP leaders felt they had to liberalize the economy

---

[34] Tanaka (1972).
[35] Satō and Matsuzaki (1986); Inoguchi and Iwai (1987).

somewhat to maintain strong economic growth and to appease the urban middle class, which so often paid the price for the party's pork-bar-
rel support for farmers and owners of small businesses.[36] This was a
dangerous political strategy because the LDP could not afford to alien-
ate these constituents either. Nevertheless, the LDP was able to limit the
damage by creating artificial outside pressure for administrative reform
in the form of an independent council, the Rinchō. Rank-and-file LDP
members could therefore portray themselves as defenders of their constituents' interests against the Rinchō. Seizaburō Satō argues that this
gave the LDP the best of all worlds: they could get the same political
credit for holding the line on subsidy spending that they would normally
get from pushing through spending increases.[37] Although many factors
contributed to the party's continued strength in the 1980s, the fact that
the party maintained strong support despite declining subsidy payments
suggests that this political strategy paid off.[38] When the LDP finally did
lose power in 1993, its demise was due more to political scandals combined with party infighting than to cutbacks in subsidies and other popular programs.

The biggest single target of the Rinchō's drive for reform was the Japan
National Railways (JNR), which had become a symbol of government
waste. The JNR had been running enormous deficits for years, at taxpayers' expense. Some LDP leaders also saw JNR reform as a way to break
public sector unions. The Japanese labor movement had been divided between the more militant public sector unions and the more pragmatic private sector unions, most of which were organized as company rather than
sector-wide unions. In 1975, the JNR union, Kokurō, brought much economic activity in urban areas to a halt with a week-long strike for the right
to strike, infuriating conservative politicians and business people alike.[39]

More immediately, the specific timing and nature of the second
Rinchō had to do with two elections and the person of Yasuhiro Nakasone. LDP leaders were bitterly disappointed after they failed to make any
significant gains in the elections of October 1979, and they attributed
this failure to their proposal for a consumption tax. This experience convinced the business community and the MoF that the only way to balance
the budget would be to cut expenditures. Zenkō Suzuki became prime
minister upon the sudden death of the popular Prime Minister Masahiro
Ōhira, and the LDP won a massive victory in the double general election

[36] Funabashi (1988, p. 92) attributes this strategy to Prime Minister Yasuhiro Nakasone.
[37] Personal communication.
[38] See Curtis (1988) and Inoguchi (1990) for an analysis of the LDP's continued strength
in the 1980s.
[39] On the JNR reforms, see Kusano (1989), Iio (1993), and Mochizuki (1993). Iio suggests
that the administrative program was not primarily targeted at the unions.

(Lower and Upper House) of June 1980, partly due to a sympathy vote in the wake of Ōhira's death. Suzuki placed his two most dangerous political rivals, Nakasone and Toshio Kōmoto, in relatively low-status cabinet positions: director-general of the Administrative Management Agency (AMA) and director-general of the Economic Planning Agency (EPA), respectively. Nakasone and Kōmoto led the two smallest LDP factions, but they were also the most viable candidates for prime minister. Tanaka, the infamous boss of the largest faction, was not yet ready to relinquish that role, as he would have to if one of his protégés were to become prime minister. In any case, Nakasone set out to make the most of his new job. If he could not get an important post, then he would make his post important. The outgoing director-general, Sōsuke Uno, understood Nakasone's dilemma quite well, since he was from the same faction. Uno instructed the AMA's staff to come up with "something big" to keep Nakasone occupied—and for the AMA this could only mean administrative reform. Nakasone took to his assignment with remarkable zeal, and what was originally a plan for some modest regulatory overhauls soon became a comprehensive reform movement. Various groups tried to manipulate the Rinchō to espouse their own priorities, including cutting government spending, breaking the unions, removing regulations, and privatizing the public corporations. Suzuki appointed Keidanren leader Toshio Dokō as chairman of the Rinchō in 1981, thus ensuring Keidanren's wholehearted support. Not to be outdone by Nakasone, Suzuki himself became a strong supporter of reform, staking his political career on its success. Nakasone then became the reform's most powerful proponent when he took over as prime minister in 1982.

The Rinchō preached a new philosophy of government. Dokō and other key members believed that a government which governs least, governs best. Ultimately, however, they had to relinquish control over the implementation of the reforms to the bureaucracy. They felt that they would not be able to push through effective reform without the support of the central bureaucracy, particularly the MoF. They judged that the first Rinchō in the 1960s had failed precisely because it did not have the MoF's support. For their part, the more powerful ministries realized that they could not stop administrative reform outright, so they chose rather to turn the reform into something they could support. Retired and active bureaucrats represented in Rinchō councils made an effort to neutralize initiatives that could diminish the authority of their ministries. The bureaucrats redefined deregulation in terms of limiting the growth of bureaus and reorganizing functions rather than in reducing the degree of governmental authority over the private sector.[40] Indeed, the MoF only

[40] D. Itō (1988).

gave the Rinchō its full support in exchange for a pledge not to threaten the MoF's sacred turf, financial regulation. In the end, the administrative reform program's greatest achievements came in those areas supported by MoF officials concerned with fiscal balance. "Administrative reform" largely became an exercise in limiting government spending and privatizing public corporations.

THE ARGUMENT IN BRIEF

Thus the particular interaction between ideas and institutions in the postwar period helps us to understand how the United Kingdom and Japan came to undertake major regulatory reforms in the 1980s and offers us the first clues to why they adopted such different reform programs. Still, the primary impetus for these reforms remains the developments common to all advanced industrialized countries outlined in Chapter 2. And the primary explanation for the divergent British and Japanese responses to these developments lies in the distinct ideological and institutional legacies described in this chapter. This argument operates at several distinct levels. First, the regulatory regimes prior to reform bias nations toward one of two fundamental approaches to regulatory reform, either "pro-competitive disengagement" or "strategic reinforcement." Second, we can replicate the analysis of regulatory regimes at the sectoral level to understand smaller variations across sectors within a given country. And third, we can supplement this analysis by incorporating variables outside the basic explanatory framework. I recognize that my central variables (regime orientation and organization) cannot explain reform outcomes in their full range and complexity. I merely suggest that this framework explains the essence of the regulatory reform story better than any alternative framework. Thus I have consciously designed the case studies to present events in their full complexity. Then in the conclusion I reassess what the framework can and cannot explain in light of the evidence.

The central framework consciously excludes core variables—such as interest group alignments, labor organization, industry organization, and political parties—that one might reasonably expect to see highlighted more than they are here. I give them secondary attention not on principle, but on pragmatic grounds. They are all important to the story, yet not essential to the core argument. I have already discussed the analytical difficulties with the interest group approach in Chapter 1. In addition, the case studies demonstrate that interest group alignments were remarkably similar across countries, so it makes sense to focus on the *intermediation* of these interests in order to explain differences in outcome.[41] Labor unions have resisted neoliberal reforms in all of the countries examined here, but their greatest achievement has been in slowing down reforms rather than in redirecting them. Thus the differences in the strength and organization of unions across these countries have not substantially altered the basic patterns of reform. Industry organization is more critical to the analysis, as we shall see, but it is only meaningful at the sectoral level because sectors—telecommunications and trucking, for example—vary so widely in their structure. Thus industry organization helps us to explain the difference between Japanese and German financial reform, for example, but it cannot account for the striking *similarity* between Japanese financial reform and Japanese airline reform. The political parties in power help us understand why some countries have taken up reform more zealously than others but cannot explain differences in reform outcomes. In fact, where we have seen transfers of party control over the legislature and/or the chief executive's office (Japan in 1993 and 1994; the United States in 1992 and 1994; France in 1986, 1988, and 1995), we have not seen any fundamental break in regulatory reform programs.

To summarize the argument briefly, the British postwar regime's combination of a regulatory orientation and a segmented structure led the government to respond to new challenges by moving boldly away from intervention in the market. It engaged in *pro-competitive disengagement*: it actively intervened to promote competition, devolved regulatory power to independent agencies, codified and legalized regulation, and enacted regulatory change in an uneven and adversarial manner. The net effect has been to undermine the government's ability to guide or promote industry. In contrast, the Japanese regime's combination of a managerial orientation and a fused organization led the government toward *strategic reinforcement*: it managed the liberalization process, resisted any devolution of regulatory power, protected ministerial discretion, and enacted change in a smooth and coordinated fashion. The government reinforced critical mechanisms of control in order to maintain its ability to guide or promote industry. Although both the United Kingdom and Japan have combined liberalization with reregulation, the British government has been inclined toward those types of reregulation (pro-competitive and juridical) which undermine its capacity to

[41] In telecommunications, for example, we will find that in all the countries telecommunications operators were willing to accept liberalization, but wanted to maximize their own freedom and minimize that of their competitors. Favored equipment suppliers opposed reform because it threatened their relationship with the dominant operator, although they recognized that it might expand the overall market. And corporate telecommunications users favored reform because they believed it would lower long-distance telephone rates and allow them greater flexibility to create private networks and develop complex value-added networks.

guide industry whereas the Japanese government has been biased to-ward those types of reregulation (strategic and expansionary) which re-inforce this capacity (see Table 1). Thus the United Kingdom and Japan both wind up with freer markets and more rules, but in one case the new rules attenuate governmental control whereas in the other they do not.

	United Kingdom	*Japan*
Market competition	Increases	Increases
Government regulation	Increases	Increases
Government control	Decreases	Remains the same

These contrasting outcomes are rooted in both ideological and insti-tutional differences. For example, as noted earlier in this chapter, British officials were more skeptical about the utility of industrial policy and more oriented toward improving the efficiency of the economy by facilitating competition than by creating a new basis of growth through industrial restructuring. So when confronted with new challenges, they were more likely to feel that these changes required a liberal response (disengagement). Japanese officials were more wedded to a tradition of protection and promotion and were more oriented toward creating the basis of growth through industrial restructuring. So when confronted with new challenges, they responded with pragmatic measures tailored to maintain as well as possible their ability to protect, promote, and re-structure domestic industry (reinforcement). Also, British officials viewed regulation as an activity distinct from industrial sponsorship, so when creating new regulatory systems they chose to devolve powers to new independent regulatory agencies. Japanese officials, however, sub-sumed regulation under industrial policy, so they refused to devolve regulatory powers away from the central ministries. Furthermore, the organization of the British state made the bureaucracy both less capa-ble of resisting pressures to disengage and less inclined to want to resist. British officials were less capable of resisting because their authority was more fragmented and because societal interests and political leaders were more powerful than in Japan. They were less inclined to resist be-cause they did not rely on the centralization of power and close links with the private sector to make their policy work. In contrast, the orga-nization of the Japanese state made the bureaucracy better able and more inclined to resist disengagement. Japanese officials were more ca-pable of resisting because they enjoyed more centralized authority and greater autonomy from political pressures. And they were more in-clined to resist because they did not want reform to undermine the close ties with industry and the leverage over industry that they valued so highly.[42]

[42] As Hall (September 1994, p. 25) has noted, private sector actors may also resist reforms that undermine institutions *they* value. This then reinforces the basic propensities I observe. I have not introduced these private sector preferences as a distinct variable at this stage for two practical reasons: the two central variables explain this effect sufficiently for our purposes, and these preferences vary considerably across sectors depending on the industry's structure. Furthermore, we shall find that to the extent that state actors' preferences about the utility of institutions diverge from those of private sector actors, the patterns of "reinforcement" in Japan reflect state actors' preferences more than private sector actors' preferences. For example, reforms have been structured to maintain ministerial leverage over industry more than they have been structured to protect linkages among members of industrial groups (*keiretsu*). I am indebted to an anonymous reviewer for clarifying my thinking on this point.

Part II

REGULATORY REFORM IN THE UNITED KINGDOM

CHAPTER FOUR

Telecommunications:
The Creation of Competition

In less than five years, from 1980 through 1984, the British government under Margaret Thatcher enacted the most radical pro-competitive reform of telecommunications anywhere in the world. The government not only went beyond the measures proposed by those interest groups which favored liberalization, but it went further than most proponents of reform within the government could have imagined in 1979. In this brief period, the government separated the postal and telecommunications sides of the Post Office; privatized the telecommunications side; and introduced competition in telecommunications equipment, value-added services, mobile communications, and long-distance and local telephone service. Furthermore, it combined liberalization with institutional reform, creating a new independent regulatory authority, the Office of Telecommunications (Oftel), with a mandate to use regulation to promote competition.

And yet more than a decade later, many of the proponents of liberalization and deregulation—whose wildest dreams were in so many ways surpassed—remain dissatisfied.[1] The Thatcherite vision of the withdrawal of government intervention and the promotion of free competition between market players, so straightforwardly articulated in the Conservative Manifesto of 1979, became riddled with contradictions as it encountered the complexities of the telecommunications sector. As we noted in the Introduction, liberalization and deregulation contradict each other more than they complement each other. The goal of liberalization—competition— requires more regulation, not less. In the view of the primary architect of

[1] Beesley and Laidlaw (1989) and Ellison (1990), all of whom were directly involved in the reform process, offer representative critiques.

Britain's new price regulation scheme, Stephen Littlechild, the extra regulation required to create effective competition should be temporary: it should be phased out as competition takes hold.[2] Nonetheless, competition shows no signs of gaining this level of strength, and Oftel officials openly doubt whether it ever will. Moreover, some argue that the government lost its initial enthusiasm for liberalization in the face of the practical necessities of privatization. The government declined to break up British Telecom (BT) along the lines of American Telegraph & Telephone (AT&T), not because of any persuasive economic rationale, but because this would complicate and delay privatization. And by deciding to privatize, the government took on a substantial financial stake in the valuation of BT shares, making it reluctant to subject BT to too much competition.[3]

Both the boldness of reform and the contradictions embodied in it find their roots in the perceived failures of the 1970s and in the Conservative Party's proposed solutions for the 1980s. In the telecommunications sector even more than other sectors, the government was able to move aggressively because of the widespread perception that previous policies had failed. As with regulatory reform more generally, Britain's response to new challenges in the sector was powerfully conditioned by the ideas and institutions of the regulatory regime prior to reform. Britain's unique approach was shaped by the goals of the Thatcher administration and the specific government agencies involved, and by the particular constraints and possibilities offered by the British political system.

THE OLD REGIME

The British telecommunications reforms have been radical by any standard, but they are all the more remarkable given how traditional a regime they replaced. Prior to 1981, Britain had a fairly typical post, telegraph, and telephone authority (PTT), with a public corporation (a government agency prior to 1969) serving as the monopoly provider of all services. By the early part of the twentieth century, government officials had become convinced that the sector was a "natural monopoly": high economies of scale implied that any duplication of investment by competitors would decrease, rather than increase, efficiency. In addition, the system's proponents felt that a government PTT would be able to pursue larger public goals, such as the provision of universal service and investment in public infrastructure, without extracting unfair profits from consumers. For crit-

---

[2] Littlechild (February 1983).

[3] Vickers and Yarrow (1988), Bishop and Kay (1988), and Beesley and Laidlaw (1989), among others, criticize the government for putting privatization before liberalization, arguing that liberalization reaps greater benefits in terms of enhancing efficiency.

ics of the system, however, government control opened the door to political interference that undermined efficiency, often for reasons that had little to do with the larger public interest.

The government's role in telecommunications has been a matter of contention from the outset. Bell Telephone Company began service in Great Britain in 1878, Edison Telephone Company in 1879. They subsequently merged to form the United Telephone Company. The British Post Office, however, won a court battle in 1880, claiming that its monopoly over telegraph services should extend to other electrical means of communication, including the telephone. The Post Office licensed the United Telephone Company to provide service, but it also began to build up its own network. The Post Office purchased the telephone company's trunk lines in 1895, primarily to protect its telegraph revenues. In 1898, a Select Committee of the House of Commons debated the merits of monopoly and competition and recommended that the Post Office and local authorities compete with the telephone company, which had been reorganized as the National Telephone Company (NTC). With the passage of the 1899 Telegraph Act, six new local companies began service, but all except one were subsequently bought out by the Post Office or the NTC.[4] In 1912, after a prolonged debate over the costs and benefits of government ownership, the Post Office bought out the NTC in order to guard its own revenues, to gain control over telephone service, and to unify the network.[5]

In the postwar era, government policy incorporated numerous and conflicting goals. The Post Office retained a strong orientation toward public service, stressing equitable service, high technical standards, and a unified network. At the same time, however, the Post Office put a priority on satisfying defense requirements. In practice this meant favoring investment in long-distance lines at the expense of local service. Likewise, the Post Office favored export businesses in accord with a general government policy of promoting exports. But this policy hurt British exporters of telecommunications equipment because it stunted the growth of their domestic market.[6] The Post Office ended up compromising its stated goals of universal service and network expansion by suppressing household demand, the area with the greatest potential for growth.

Government officials sought to support the telecommunications equipment industry, but were ambivalent about how to achieve this goal. Similar to PTTs elsewhere in Europe and in Japan, the Post Office cultivated a small group of "court suppliers" and allotted shares of procurement to these suppliers according to a system of bulk-purchase agreements. In the 1960s, the Labour government decided that there were too many switch-

---

[4] Hull, the one local authority not bought out, still provides its own service.
[5] Pitt (1980), pp. 23–41; Hills (1986), pp. 79–89.
[6] Pitt (1980), p. 106.

ing manufacturers and arranged a merger of three of them: General Electric Company (GEC), Associated Electrical Industries (AEI), and English Electric. Government officials subsequently began to question the cartel arrangement itself, arguing that cooperation among suppliers and between the Post Office and suppliers had made the suppliers less productive. As a corrective measure, they introduced competitive bidding for contracts.[7] But competitive sourcing only prevented the suppliers from achieving economies of scale, making them less fit for international competition.

The shortcomings of British telecommunications policy were rooted in the organization of the regime. The Post Office's status remained ambiguous, neither independent enough to function as an enterprise nor integrated enough to work as a government agency. Even more critical, it was plagued with financial uncertainty because of its reliance on the Treasury for funds. As soon as the government took control of the telecommunications system in 1912, critics began to point to weaknesses in its organization. In particular, they charged that the Post Office bureaucracy was too rigid to respond to technological changes and that heavy government supervision prevented Post Office officials from managing the organization in an efficient manner. The British Post Office certainly lacked the independence of the U.S. Bell system, but it actually enjoyed more autonomy than the French or German PTTs. Still, the British government's involvement in the sector was more likely to be counterproductive because there was no consensus on policy goals and no effective coordination between the various agencies involved in telecommunications policy. Post Office officials consistently sought to achieve greater autonomy, but the Treasury and Parliament were reluctant to give up their power to intervene. The Treasury had substantial powers of oversight because it controlled the budget and was the lead agency in economic affairs, yet it tended to subject the sector to its own macroeconomic priorities rather than to value the development of the telecommunications system itself. Meanwhile, members of Parliament (MPs) periodically lobbied for specific measures to improve or expand telecommunications services on behalf of their constituents.

The government launched a series of inquiries into the Post Office organization beginning in the 1920s and continuing until the telecommunications side was separated in 1981. Douglas Pitt notes with some irony that the government demonstrated an extraordinary will to reform the telecommunications function yet little capacity to do so.[8] In 1932, the Bridgeman Commission recommended limiting Treasury oversight and

[7] Hills (1986), p. 86.
[8] Pitt (1980).

reorganizing the Post Office to permit it to operate the telecommunications system with less interference from other government agencies.[9] In the postwar era, a major investigation into public services led the Labour government to transform the Post Office from a government department into a public corporation in 1969. The government separated the operation of the telecommunications and postal services, but yielded to demands from the Union of Postal Workers (UPW) to maintain the two functions within a single organization.[10]

Unlike France or Japan, the United Kingdom never tried to incorporate the Post Office into a larger national strategy for economic growth. In many ways the Post Office actually enjoyed relative freedom from routine regulation or oversight—a freedom it would lose, ironically, with liberalization and privatization. The Post Office developed its own plans and even performed some regulatory functions, setting standards for telecommunications equipment and issuing licenses to outside providers of telecommunications services. Nevertheless, the Post Office was plagued by periodic political interference and above all by Treasury control over its budget. The Treasury tightly restricted investment when the Post Office was a government department and continued to constrain borrowing after the Post Office became a public corporation in 1969. The Treasury would not allow public corporations to borrow in private markets, fearing that they would invest irresponsibly while counting on the government to bail them out if anything went wrong.[11] At the same time, the Treasury restricted public sector borrowing, because an increase in the "Public Sector Borrowing Requirement" (PSBR) could fuel inflation. The Treasury also occasionally held down telephone rates as a means of controlling inflation. The Post Office thus fell victim to the Treasury's preoccupation with macroeconomic management and the stop-and-go economic policy that characterized much of the postwar era. In some ways, this regime gave the Post Office the worst of all worlds: political interference and Treasury control without a coherent government strategy. This legacy helps to explain why British authorities, unlike their Japanese counterparts, were ultimately willing to cede so much of their authority over the sector.

The regime was actually more centralized than that of many other sectors in Britain, for it was built around a single government monopoly. In fact, the disjuncture between the regime and that more typical in other sectors suggests why British telecommunications reforms were so radical. The reforms of the 1980s finally gave the telecommunications regime the fragmented structure characteristic of most other sectors in Britain. Under the old regime, the government failed to supply the leadership or the

---

[9] Ibid., pp. 70–96.
[10] Duch (1991).
[11] Swann (1988), p. 233.

funding to support state-led network development on the French model, or to allow the Post Office the freedom to grow independently on the U.S. model. Britain was left with a telecommunications policy driven neither by the state nor by the market. On the one hand, the government sought to expand service but failed to cultivate household demand or to invest adequately. On the other hand, it sought to make the Post Office more efficient, but failed to give it the freedom to operate like a commercial business. Given these problems, the British telecommunications sector was destined to fall behind its rivals, making major reform increasingly imperative. With governments of both parties lacking the will or the institutional capabilities to pursue a state-led strategy, British telecommunications reform was eventually bound to head more firmly in the other direction.

New Challenges

By the 1970s, the Post Office was coming under increasingly widespread attack. It was unable to raise prices in the early 1970s because of the Treasury's anti-inflationary policies, and this only exacerbated its financial troubles. When it finally raised prices in 1975, this incited outrage from both corporate and household users. It was falling behind its Continental neighbors in labor productivity, and it was lagging in the all-important race toward digitalization. It had created a British digital switching technology, System X, in cooperation with the equipment manufacturers. It began to introduce the system, but found itself far behind because of constraints on capital spending.[12] Furthermore, it was increasingly unable to meet the demands of its users, particularly sophisticated multinational corporations. These corporations had become accustomed to the wider range of telecommunications equipment and advanced services available in the U.S. market, where liberalization was well under way. Britain lagged particularly in advanced terminal equipment because the Post Office had a stronger hold on the equipment market than most Continental PTTs.

In 1975, the government created a special committee, the Carter Committee, to investigate problems at the Post Office. The committee had three negative findings: the Post Office was less efficient than PTTs in other major countries, not responsive to customers' needs, and still ori-

---

[12] The Post Office consistently invested less than the common carriers in all four of the other countries treated in this study. Per capita investment figures for common carriers (three-year moving average in U.S. dollars at 1980 prices and exchange rates) are as follows: for 1975–77—United Kingdom $53, Japan $58, Germany $58, United States $71, and France $85; and for 1977–79—United Kingdom $44, Japan $59, Germany $65, United States $81, France $105. OECD (1988), p. 104.

ented toward standardized telephone service rather than to the growing range of new services that had become technologically possible.[13] The committee report recommended partial liberalization of the telecommunications equipment and value-added services markets, and proposed a separation of the telecommunications side from the postal service.[14] The Labour administration at the time proposed some minor reforms in response, but overruled any substantial market liberalization or reorganization of the Post Office.[15]

When Margaret Thatcher's team came to power in 1979, it did not have to convince anyone of the need for telecommunications reform. The Carter Report had already outlined several measures that were not likely to encounter substantial political resistance, and the Post Office was in no position to protest. In the case of value-added services, business users favored liberalization, and the Thatcher government was more than willing to accommodate them. And in the case of the separation of the postal and telecommunications functions, the main union for telecommunications workers, the Post Office Engineering Union (POEU), strongly supported the move. For years, telecommunications workers had played a subordinate role to postal workers within post offices, and they were eager to gain the higher status and wages of a more demanding and sophisticated sector. The UPW opposed the move, but the split between the unions made it easier for the government to proceed.[16]

We already have two clues to why telecommunications reform was so much more radical in Britain than elsewhere. First, the old regime's performance was particularly bad, and therefore the need for reform was obvious to all. Second, the government that came to power in 1979 had an unparalleled commitment to neoliberal reform. The Conservative Party shifted ideologically to the right after 1974; it consolidated a program based on this ideology during its period of opposition; and this program brought it to power in 1979 in part because of a widespread perception that government intervention in industrial affairs had failed. The realignment within the Conservative Party and the election victory were both in part attributable to the economic problems of the 1970s and the Labour Party's inability to address them effectively. Yet these clues still do not tell us how the Conservatives managed to uproot the old regime. This required them to convert—or to subvert, some might say—the civil service.

[13] Morgan and Davies (October 1989), p. 7.
[14] Department of Industry (July 1977).
[15] The government outlined its response and its rationale for not taking bolder action in Department of Industry (July 1978).
[16] Grande (April 1987) argues that the German situation differs from the British case precisely because German postal and telecommunications workers were unified in a single union.

LIBERALIZATION

The Thatcher administration destroyed the old telecommunications regime in the United Kingdom more thoroughly than the Nakasone administration did in Japan, primarily because of its superior ability to infiltrate the civil service. The British Broadcasting Corporation (BBC) television series "Yes Minister" caricatures how civil servants can manipulate their ministers to undermine efforts at reform.[17] In reality, however, British ministers have a far better chance than their Japanese counterparts of imposing their agenda on civil servants. British civil servants are taught that their role is to serve their ministers, and generally they take this mission seriously. They accept that ministers make policy and they implement it. Still, the Thatcher administration went beyond accepted norms in terms of pursuing its own goals irrespective of the concerns of civil servants.

The sponsoring department for telecommunications was the Department of Industry (DoI), a target particularly ripe for conversion to Thatcherism. The department had never had the chance to develop a clear departmental mission, for it had been disassembled and reassembled throughout the postwar era. Department officials were not particularly devoted to an activist industrial policy. In the 1970s, they had been more involved in the thankless duty of propping up industrial losers than in the heroic task of supporting future winners. In telecommunications, the department had already begun to shift its priority from equipment manufacturers to users before the Thatcher government came to power. The department focused increasingly on the promising area of "information technology" (IT), hoping that growth in this sector would help to compensate for the decline of manufacturing industries. This shift then colored the department's approach to reform, pushing it toward bold liberalization irrespective of the potential impact on equipment suppliers.

The new secretary of state was none other than Sir Keith Joseph, Mrs. Thatcher's most trusted adviser and ideological soulmate. Joseph was by any standards an unusual minister. In the words of one of his deputies: "He was an extraordinary intellectual, a fine man—and thoroughly unsuited for the role of minister. He was so intellectually honest that he had great difficulty in running a department."[18] Joseph came to the DoI with a mind to abolishing many of its functions. So if bureaucrats, as William Niskanen has argued, are determined to maintain or augment their power, how could Joseph possibly succeed?[19] Niskanen's argument is much more pertinent to Japan, for British civil servants are less interested in power for power's sake than their counterparts in Japan. Moreover,

[17] The series also comes in a book version: Lynn and Jay (1989).
[18] Interview with former DTI official (October 1991).
[19] Niskanen (1971).

these were unusual times, and those civil servants who believed in a more active industrial policy were in no position to argue. Joseph and his successors, some of the most radically liberal members of the Conservative Party, systematically dismantled those sections of the department which handled industrial policy. "Our policy," remarks one civil servant, "was to wind up the Department of Industry."[20] Joseph issued a reading list to his civil servants in order to convert them to his cause, including specific readings on telecommunications.[21] He chose a young civil servant, Ian Ellison, to be his private secretary. Ellison had joined the department in 1974 and had spent three years at the Office of Fair Trading (OFT), the agency in charge of antitrust regulation. Ellison was a "conviction civil servant": he believed in the government's program. The private secretary controls the minister's door, his appointment book, and his correspondence. He serves as a double agent: he presents the minister's case to the ministry, and the ministry's case to the minister. Ellison was particularly effective in articulating Joseph's message to his colleagues and thus diffusing potential resistance to the government's initiatives.

Joseph's disdain for industrial policy was particularly pronounced in telecommunications. He had no qualms about deserting the equipment industry and focusing on the needs of the wider community of telecommunications users. By liberalizing equipment and services, he felt that the government could help business users to become more efficient and thus strengthen the entire economy.[22] In connection with its shift in priorities, the DoI began to solicit more advice from business users. The Telecommunications Managers' Association (TMA), the primary organization representing large users, first became involved in policy issues at the time of the Carter Committee hearings. TMA officers found Conservative MPs, in opposition at the time, particularly receptive to their plea for greater freedom in using public lines for advanced value-added services. When the new government came to power, the TMA found that the doors in Whitehall "suddenly swung wide open."[23] The DoI encouraged business users to participate in policy debates because these users formed a constituency in favor of liberalization and because they provided a source of technical expertise outside BT. Although these users were involved throughout the reform process, their influence over the outcome should not be exaggerated.[24] As one user representative put it: "Our views were acceptable to the civil servants and the politicians at the time—'choice'

---

[20] Interview with former DTI official (October 1991).

[21] Bosanquet (July–September 1981).

[22] Interviews with former DTI officials (October 1991).

[23] Interview with Stephen Finch, independent consultant and former director of the TMA (July 23, 1990).

[24] Morgan and Davies (October 1989), among others, attribute a greater role to these users.

and 'competition' were music to Mrs. Thatcher's ears. But if she had said that telecommunications come last, then we wouldn't have been able to do a thing."[25]

In 1980, the government created the position of Minister of Information Technology within the DoI, and Kenneth Baker became the first to hold the position. His duty was both to oversee the liberalization of telecommunications and to develop a strategy for Information Technology. Baker believed that cable technology held the key to development in the IT sector, and that cables would eventually carry everything from television to interactive data services. In 1982, the Information Technology Advisory Panel (ITAP), a group within the Cabinet Office, completed a report outlining a long-term vision for IT. The ITAP report recommended that the government develop a coherent policy for the information industry so that Britain could emerge as a leader in the business of selling information and advice.[26] The IT division within DoI was inclined to actively promote the IT sector, but this stance often ended up conflicting with the telecommunications division's drive to liberalize.

In a July 1980 statement, Joseph outlined the government's plans for liberalization of the telecommunications sector. First, the government intended to separate the telecommunications operator, to be known as British Telecom, from the Post Office. Second, the government planned to privatize Cable & Wireless, a company whose primary business lay in telecommunications services overseas, especially in Commonwealth territories such as Hong Kong. Finally, the DoI would assume the power to issue licenses for market entry into any segment of the telecommunications market, in consultation with BT.[27] In particular, the government planned to open the markets for telecommunications equipment and for value-added services.

Although the Carter Report had recommended the liberalization of equipment and value-added services, few had even considered allowing competition in basic telephone service.[28] Certainly no major group had ever lobbied for such an option. Most DoI officials accepted that telephone service was a natural monopoly and assumed that any proposal for

[25] Finch interview (July 23, 1990).

[26] Dyson (October 1986), p. 42.

[27] See Solomon (September 1986) for a brief insider's account of the reform process. Solomon was assistant secretary for the telecommunications industry in the early 1980s. Other accounts of the liberalization and privatization process of varying scope and detail include Hills (1986), Morgan and Davies (October 1989), Cawson et al. (1990), and Duch (1991).

[28] One user group representative recalls: "We were just hoping for some competition in customer service. We never even dreamed of competition in the network. Some of the Conservatives were interested in privatization, but this had not occurred to us." Interview with George McKendrick, executive director, International Telecommunications Users' Group (July 31, 1990).

liberalization would meet virulent opposition, most of all from the Post Office itself. Yet in a meeting with department officials one day, Joseph proposed the unimaginable: Why not allow network competition? The civil servants, straining themselves just to refrain from laughter, pulled out the expected arguments: telecommunications is a natural monopoly; network integration would be undermined; safety and quality standards would suffer. Unconvinced, Joseph asked them to think about it.[29] The civil servants eventually went along, but the reluctance of some was reflected later in the cautious terms they set out in licenses for BT and its new competitor. Their first task was to find a potential competitor, so they promptly passed their plans along to City financial institutions. Before the end of the year, Barclays Bank, British Petroleum, and Cable & Wireless formed a joint venture, Mercury Communications Ltd., and they announced a business proposal in the summer of 1981. Mercury would focus on long-distance and international service. At the time, government officials had not decided whether Mercury would only provide private lines or whether it would be able to interconnect with BT's network.

The department considered several proposals for opening the mobile telephone services market. The Post Office argued that multiple providers would only take up more valuable space on the radio spectrum. Others argued that this sector badly needed some form of competition as well. The government came up with an innovative solution, with multiple layers of competition. Two network operators, Cellnet (60 percent owned by BT) and Racal Communications (now Vodafone), would compete, but could not sell directly to customers. Thirty-odd service providers would then market the services, and hundreds of dealers would rent or sell the handsets. This approach has been remarkably successful: the market has boomed, with 25 to 30 percent annual growth through the 1980s, and Vodafone has gained a substantial share of the market.[30]

For value-added services, the department commissioned an economist from the London Business School, Michael Beesley, to write a report on the feasibility of competition and to recommend how much competition to allow. The government chose Beesley knowing his liberal inclinations, but they left him to develop his own approach. His recommendations were more radical than even the Thatcher government could accept. He argued that resale should be liberalized completely.[31] This meant that potential competitors could lease lines from the Post Office and then resell them with or without adding value. In effect, they could compete with the Post Office using the Post Office's own network. For Beesley, it really did not matter whether telecommunications was a natural monopoly or not.

[29] Interviews with former DTI officials (1990–91).
[30] *Economist* (October 5, 1991), Survey of Telecommunications, p. 8.
[31] Beesley (1981).

He believed that creating competition would have such a positive impact on the incumbent's productivity that this would outweigh any possible cost in terms of lost economies of scale.[32] The government balked at his suggestion, deciding to allow resale only if value was being added. Competitive telephone service would have to be provided on a separate network.

Shortly before the legislation passed, DoI deputy secretary Jonathan Solomon founded a consultative committee on telecommunications policy, soliciting views from users, manufacturers, the unions, and the Post Office itself. Solomon was known to be unusually open to input from the outside. Nevertheless, the DoI did not design these meetings to solicit outside opinions so much as to build support for its own initiatives and to facilitate implementation. These sessions allowed the department to "sound out" the potential response to its proposals and to work out some of the technical details of the legislation.[33] Solomon continued to hold these meetings through much of the debate over privatization, until Secretary of State Norman Tebbitt abruptly abolished the committee in 1983 because of some embarrassing press leaks. Meanwhile, the POEU tried to mount an opposition to the reforms. The union made an extraordinary effort to refute Beesley's paper, producing a line-by-line critique.[34] At the stage of parliamentary debate, the union's position was considerably weakened by the fact that it favored one of the major elements of the legislation—the separation of telecommunications from the Post Office, but opposed the other—the termination of the Post Office's monopoly.

The British Telecommunications Act passed easily in July 1981. It shifted more responsibility to the DoI by giving it the right to issue licenses and leaving it considerable discretion in writing the licenses. Some critics had suggested transferring these duties to an independent regulatory body, but the government decided to leave them with the department. The Act gave regulatory powers to both the department and to BT itself, but offered little guidance to how these powers should be divided.[35] In practice, the department controlled the licensing of competitors and BT set technical standards. DoI officials quickly realized that the 1981 Act had not produced a satisfactory regulatory framework and began working on new legislation almost as soon as it passed.

At this point the government's plans for network competition faced a final challenge from the union. POEU leaders, infuriated because they not only had to accept competition but had to support it through interconnection,

---

[32] Interview with Michael Beesley, professor, London Business School (July 19, 1990).

[33] Interviews with Finch (July 23, 1990), Darlington (October 22, 1991), and DTI officials (1990–91).

[34] Interview with Roger Darlington, National Communications Union (October 22, 1991), and Beesley interview (July 19, 1990).

[35] For example, Section 15 of the act gives the authority to issue licenses to both BT and the department. *British Telecommunications Act 1981* (1981).

took action. They refused to interconnect the exchange at Mercury head-quarters or to perform maintenance services for members of the Mercury consortium. Mercury then took the union to court and won in the Court of Appeal in November 1983. DoI officials also had to resolve the sticky issue of setting the terms for Mercury's license. Mercury representatives were worried that they would not be able to compete with BT while also investing in a new network. They demanded preferential terms to help them penetrate the market, asking for the exclusive right to compete with BT for a given period of time. Otherwise, they argued, Mercury and the other competitors would simply eat each other up "like so many minnows." The government gave in, and in November 1983 Secretary of State Kenneth Baker announced what came to be known as the "duopoly policy." Mercury would retain its exclusive right until 1990, at which time the policy would be reviewed.

PRIVATIZATION

In retrospect, it is easy to view the privatization of BT as somehow inevitable given the Thatcher administration's ideological determination and BT's dismal reputation. But no group outside the government advocated such a move. And as it came to power, the Conservative Party only declared its intention to privatize three companies: British Aerospace, British Shipbuilding, and the National Freight Corporation.[36] The policy was one of privatization primarily for manufacturing companies, not utilities. Geoffrey Howe, Thatcher's first Chancellor of the Exchequer, believed that the government should only privatize companies in sectors where the company already faced competition. He feared a private monopoly far more than a public one.[37] As Conservative leaders gained experience in power, however, they accumulated more detailed evidence of the nationalized companies' poor performance, they encountered difficulties in improving this performance, and they became frustrated with their inability to cut back government spending. And most important, Thatcher herself became more committed to a privatization program.[38] Even so, when Secretary of State Peter Jenkin announced that BT would be privatized in July 1982, the news took almost everyone by surprise.[39] Many

[36] Conservative Party (1979). As Margaret Thatcher (1993, p. 677) herself puts it: "Now that almost universal lip service is paid to the case for privatization it is difficult to recall just how revolutionary—how all but unthinkable—it seemed at the end of the 1970s."

[37] Swann (1988), pp. 259–60.

[38] Ibid., pp. 226–28, 236–38.

[39] For example, Beesley (interview, July 19, 1990), an outside consultant to the department, and Bruce Laidlaw (interview, October 24, 1991), then a DoI economist specializing in telecommunications regulation, both report that they knew nothing of the plans prior to the announcement.

within the government felt that privatization of a public utility simply would not be possible. As Solomon recalls: "It was conventional wisdom that privatization could not be popular; that the sale of BT was too big for the U.K. equity market to absorb; that a private monopoly would crush all competition."[40] In short, there was every reason to believe BT would not be privatized.

The most compelling argument in favor of privatization was that it would allow BT more freedom to invest. As noted above, BT was not allowed to raise money in private markets, and its borrowing was limited by the infamous PSBR. Investment in telecommunications was bound to be profitable over the long term because it would bring down transmission costs, but there was a limit to how much of the cost could be extracted from users through higher prices. Treasury officials had considered the privatization of BT along with several other nationalized industries in the late 1970s, but they were never able to reach a consensus on the costs and benefits of such a move.[41] In 1981, Treasury and DoI officials, along with BT executives, made an extensive effort to find a better way of financing investment in the telecommunications infrastructure. They carefully reviewed several proposals for the issuance of bonds. The most promising candidate came to be known as the "Busby" bond, named after the bird in BT commercials. The Busby bond would carry a relatively low fixed return initially, shifting to a variable rate at a specified time. After heroic efforts at a compromise, talks finally broke down because City advisers insisted that they would not be able to place the bonds unless the government would guarantee them—and the Treasury simply refused. The DoI then negotiated to raise BT's borrowing ceiling for 1981–82 by £200 million, overcoming substantial resistance from the Treasury. BT had already caused an uproar by raising telephone rates substantially in October 1981, arguing that it had to do so in order to finance investment. When it became clear in March 1982 that BT had failed to spend the additional funds allotted for investment, DoI leaders were outraged. "For civil servants," as one such civil servant put it, "there is no more heinous offense than not spending money that has been allocated."[42] Following this episode, DoI officials were no longer in any mood to go to bat for BT, and they were just a bit more likely to consider privatization.

Broader forces certainly influenced the final decision to privatize, but the immediate source of the decision came not from the Treasury, the prime minister, or any private sector group—but from two civil servants in the DoI who were working on telecommunications liberalization. In March 1982, they sent a memo to the secretary of state suggesting that pri-

[40] Solomon (September 1986), p. 188.
[41] Interview with former Treasury official (July 1990).
[42] Interview with former DTI official (October 1991).

vatization would be necessary in order to assure effective competition. Otherwise, BT would always be able to rely on state finances in a pinch, and a private competitor would never have a fair chance. Competition could only have its intended effect—stimulating BT to improve productivity—if BT itself had to rely on private markets for finance.[43] Jenkin responded to the memo by calling a meeting of a small group of civil servants involved in telecommunications policy. The meeting did not result in any decision, but he assigned the team the task of investigating the possibility of privatization. They were to look into the practical aspects of both the flotation itself and the mechanisms of regulating competition. The original memo to the secretary of state was accompanied by a Cabinet paper, a note to other Cabinet members suggesting that the issue be discussed at a Cabinet Committee meeting. The Cabinet Committee simply decided to create a ministerial committee and a parallel official committee to look into the matter.[44] Within the official committee, the Treasury representatives were surprisingly hesitant. They were still unsure whether the proceeds of the sale would compensate for the loss of income from BT revenues, and they were concerned about the practical problems involved in such a large sale. In addition, they feared that such a huge issuance of stock could disrupt something dear to their hearts: the market for "gilt-edged" shares (government bonds).[45]

The government decided in favor of privatization in May 1982 and publicly announced the decision in July. The unions, predictably, were outraged. Led by the POEU, the telecommunications unions launched a massive campaign against privatization. They operated on several fronts. First, they prepared precise arguments against every aspect of liberalization and privatization. They maintained that BT should operate for public service not profit, and that privatization would undermine BT's welfare function of providing universal service at a reasonable cost. Second, they mobilized their members for massive rallies and petition campaigns. And third, they went on strike. About 2500 operators at BT International went on strike for ten weeks from October through December 1983.[46] But BT managers "locked out" the striking workers, taking over the exchanges at night and somehow keeping them running. The action ended in com-

---

[43] Interviews (1990–91).

[44] Ministerial committees bring a small group of ministers and junior ministers together to discuss a particular issue. They are typically matched with larger interdepartmental official committees of civil servants working on the same issue.

[45] Interviews (1990–91). One civil servant recalls that most members of the official committee were caught completely off guard by the proposal. "The overriding tone," he says, "was 'Good God! What have these ministers done?!' " Interview, October 1991.

[46] Moon, Richardson, and Smart (1986, p. 345) stress the extent to which the unions pursued an "outsider" as opposed to an "insider" strategy because they were effectively excluded from the relevant policy community.

plete failure, with the cost to the unions running to £3 million. Looking back on the war over reform, union official Roger Darlington concedes that the unions lost almost every battle.[47] Despite repeated defeat on the larger issues, however, the unions continued to work on the specific terms of reform, pushing for stricter technical standards and fewer restrictions on BT's activities.[48]

BT, for its part, was divided. The managers were initially incensed that they had not been consulted. In general, however, top managers went along, for they knew that they would enjoy large pay increases after privatization. They also hoped that privatization would allow them greater freedom to move into new areas of business. But they played down their enthusiasm for privatization in public so that they would not antagonize the unions. Middle managers, particularly engineers, were more hesitant, because they still believed in a single unified network. The Society of Telecom Executives, a group of BT managers, produced a strong critique stressing that privatization would lower quality standards and threaten research and development.[49] Rank-and-file workers, most of whom were union members, feared for their jobs. As a firm, BT did not lobby for or against privatization, but BT managers fought vigorously to make sure that the terms of reform favored BT as much as possible. In particular they pressed for greater business freedom and a "light rein" of regulation.

The equipment manufacturers were more reluctant. Some felt that privatization could lead to greater demand and higher prices for telecommunications equipment, but most simply feared losing their preferential relationship with BT. Lord Weinstock, chairman of GEC, used his position in the House of Lords to campaign publicly against privatization, and incorporated this campaign within a larger attack on the government's economic policy.[50] But his best efforts were not enough to alter the outcome. Department of Trade and Industry (DTI) officials had subtle ways of buffering themselves from complaints from BT's "court suppliers," organized as the Telecommunications Equipment Manufacturers Association (TEMA), as from other pressure groups. For example, they would publicly complain that BT was obstructing progress through TEMA as its agent, and then embarrassed BT executives would quickly put TEMA back into line.[51] In the end, the government was perfectly willing to sacrifice the equipment manufacturers for the cause of reform, as they ultimately did.

[47] Darlington interview (October 22, 1991).
[48] See Thomas (1986) for a review of union efforts to oppose the privatization of BT and other public corporations.
[49] The Society of Telecom Executives (July 1983).
[50] Young (1989), p. 362.
[51] Interview with former DTI official (July 1990).

Corporate users had never asked for network competition, let alone privatization.[52] Yet given the government's initiative, they were more than happy to go along. In fact, some of them actively lobbied in favor of BT's breakup. Mostly, they hoped to use the reform legislation as an opportunity to press for further liberalization of the use of lines. Household user groups were hardly enthusiastic about privatization. They were comfortable with the access they enjoyed through the consumer councils attached to BT, as well as to other nationalized enterprises, and they were concerned that privatization would diminish their influence.

The opponents of reform do claim one victory, the prevention of the breakup of BT. The unions would like to take credit for this, and there is some evidence that they did play a role. Insiders contend that union leaders worked out a deal with government representatives whereby they would moderate their protest in exchange for a pledge not to break up BT.[53] Nonetheless, BT itself, the Treasury, and City financial advisers probably deserve more credit than the union. The government did not decide not to break up BT, but simply never decided in favor. In addition to the union, the management of BT lobbied intensively against breakup. Officials from DoI's IT division were sympathetic with the opponents of breakup, for they hoped that a stronger BT would become the flagship company for an internationally competitive British information industry. Likewise, the Treasury opposed breakup because it would make it more difficult to sell BT. More practically, BT managers were able to persuade the government that they simply could not straighten out their books for several years.[54] One City firm estimated that it would take three to four years to separate BT's accounts into long-distance and local, or regional divisions. TMA representatives, who favored breakup, independently estimated that it could be done in twelve months, but they were not in a position to override BT and BT's advisers in the City. In any case, the government was eager to move forward in order to pass the privatization bill before the next election.

The combination of liberalization and privatization required the government to overhaul its system of regulation—to introduce pro-competitive reregulation. The regulatory system would have to prevent BT from engaging in restrictive practices and it would have to set out fair terms for competition. This involved first deciding who would do the regulating. Unlike Japan, where two ministries waged an epic turf battle for the job, the obvious candidates in the British case wanted nothing to do with it. DoI officials considered keeping the regulatory powers for themselves, but quickly eliminated this option. Unlike their Japanese counterparts, they

[52] Finch interview (July 23, 1990) and Cawson et al. (1990), p. 93.
[53] Interviews (1990–91).
[54] Thatcher herself (1993, p. 680) offers this explanation for privatizing BT as a whole.

did not view their regulatory authority over industry as a critical tool of telecommunications policy. Moreover, they agreed with the Conservative Party that an independent regulator would be less susceptible to manipulation by a future Labour government. They wanted to protect the progress they had made from the whims of future governments.[55] Moreover, advisers from the City were emphatic on this point: people would not subscribe to a share issue unless regulation could be insulated from the hazards of political alternance. The government then offered the job of telecommunications regulation to the OFT, but the OFT politely declined. It did not want to be distracted from its obligation to monitor other sectors, and it did not want to take on an issue that was bound to be complicated by politics.[56] Conservative Party leaders were somewhat reluctant to create a new regulatory agency, for they had attacked Labour for its propensity to create more and more quasi-autonomous nongovernmental organizations, popularly known as quangos. They did not want to be in the uncomfortable position of creating more new agencies themselves. Nevertheless, they realized that this was the only viable option, and formed the Office of Telecommunications (Oftel) on the model of the OFT. Oftel has since become the standard for other utility sectors, and Britain now boasts four more such regulators: the Office of Gas Supply (Ofgas), the Office of Water Services (Ofwat), the Office of Electricity Regulation (Offer), and the Office of the Rail Regulator (ORR).

Meanwhile DoI officials began to review the possible approaches to regulation. A study group under Malcolm Bradbury proposed a modified rate of return system with differential rates for the various market segments. Sir Alan Walters, Prime Minister Thatcher's economic adviser, produced a scathing critique of the plan. He claimed that it would distort incentives, by inducing firms to overinvest, for example. He proposed a far more elaborate scheme, "output related profits levied," which would tax companies in inverse proportion to profits: the more you make the less you pay. This gives the companies an incentive to raise output, but creates perverse effects when changes in external circumstances, such as an oil crisis, force output down. In any case, City advisers were horrified with the plan because it could endanger the selling of BT. The government then assigned an economist, Stephen Littlechild, to evaluate the two proposals, and to offer his own solution. In February 1983 Littlechild came up with a price-capping scheme, known as RPI-X, whereby telecommunications rates could not rise by more than the retail price index minus a certain percentage. Littlechild designed this system to rely primarily on neutral criteria and therefore limit the regulator's discretion and make implementation

[55] Interviews with former DTI officials (1990–91).

[56] As we shall see in the following chapter, the OFT was heavily involved in a restrictive practices case against the Stock Exchange at the time.

more straightforward. The price-cap approach ensured that at least some efficiency gains from technological progress would be passed on to the consumer. Price capping creates its own distortions, however, because it gives the operator an incentive to cut costs but not to improve the quality of service. Some recent economic analyses have recommended some combination of rate of return and price capping.[57] Littlechild's view prevailed, and the "X" in RPI-X was set at 3 percent. There was some debate over which BT prices would be included in the price-cap formula, but the government finally decided to include residential and business rentals as well as all domestic telephone calls, but to exclude private lines, public telephones, and international calls.[58] Littlechild explicitly argued that regulation of the telecommunications sector was designed to facilitate entry for a short period of time and should be phased out as competition took hold.[59] Littlechild's basic formula has subsequently been applied to other sectors. At the last moment, Bruce Laidlaw, who was beginning to question the government's commitment to competition, given the practical requirements of selling BT, managed to persuade Littlechild to incorporate a commitment to further pro-competitive measures in his report. Specifically, Littlechild's report concluded by recommending seven steps to encourage competition, such as allowing unlimited domestic and international resale and the shared use of private lines among closed user groups. BT officials, who had received a draft without the seven points, protested that the civil servants "had got to Littlechild." And indeed they had.[60]

Under the original plans, the DoI expected to pass the second telecommunications reform bill in the fall of 1983 and then begin selling shares after the election. But Prime Minister Thatcher chose to call elections early, in June 1983, given her enormous popularity after victory in the Falklands War. After the election, the DoI merged with the Department of Trade, becoming the DTI. The election gave the civil servants more time to work out the details of the legislation, and the bill finally passed in April 1984. Parliament had been on the sidelines throughout most of the debate. When the Act came before Parliament, however, the MPs naturally became more involved. Particularly in the House of Lords, some of the more independent Lords subjected the legislation to careful scrutiny. The unions briefed the Labour MPs line by line, so that they could question the government as convincingly as possible. For their part, the user groups worked with the Conservative MPs, hoping to filter in revisions that would give them greater freedom in leasing and using lines. The most substantial revisions to the bill came to Clause 3, which outlines the responsibilities of

[57] Stelzer (Summer 1988); Veljanovski, ed. (1991).
[58] Hills (1986), p. 128.
[59] Littlechild (February 1983), pp. 38–39.
[60] Interviews (1990–91).

the DTI and Oftel. The clause was greatly expanded to include language that committed the government to consider the interests of consumers in general and to certain special groups, such as the disabled or the elderly, more specifically. By focusing on Clause 3, however, the MPs only fell into the civil servants' trap. DTI officials had deliberately placed this "propaganda clause" at the beginning of the bill, knowing well that parliamentary committees work through the clauses in order. "The idea was to get everyone to worry about this," confessed one official, "so they would not have time to scrutinize later sections."[61] After more than a month of debate on Clause 3, the government "guillotined" the bill, meaning that it set a timetable to plow through the remaining sections. In the end, parliamentary revisions were relatively minor, and the bill passed with little difficulty.[62]

The new legislation gave both the DTI and Oftel important roles in crafting Britain's new regulatory regime: the DTI would issue licenses to the new competitors, and Oftel would interpret, enforce, and sometimes revise license conditions. The DTI's new license for BT, which went into effect in August 1984, required BT to connect licensed competitors to its network. Furthermore, it prohibited BT from a wide range of potentially anticompetitive practices. For example, BT could not use monopoly profits in one line of business to subsidize another. Likewise, BT could not engage in "undue preference and undue discrimination," that is, favoring its own businesses at the expense of its competitors. DTI officials thus attempted to compensate for the fact that BT was not broken up by using license conditions to prevent BT from capitalizing on its potentially unfair advantage: its integration of a wide range of businesses.[63]

The DTI chose Bryan Carsberg, a professor of accounting at the London School of Economics and a consultant to the department, as director general of Oftel. In his judgments after taking office, Carsberg leaned strongly in favor of competition, ruling more often against BT than for it. In his most critical ruling, in October 1985 Carsberg set out new terms of interconnection that strongly favored Mercury. The previous year, BT and Mercury had signed an initial agreement on interconnection, known as the "Heads of Agreement," but Mercury refused to honor the terms and appealed to Oftel. Carsberg ruled that BT must allow full interconnection so that any subscriber from either network could reach any other. Moreover, he set out interconnection charges such that Mercury would pay BT

---

[61] Interview with former DTI official (May 1993).

[62] In their study of the legislative process, Moon, Richardson, and Smart (1986, p. 350) come to a conclusion entirely consistent with my own: "The outcome of the Telecommunications Act reflects more the priorities and methods adopted by the departments and ministers directly involved than those characteristic of the 'traditional' policy community."

[63] Vickers and Yarrow (1988), pp. 211–12.

for its portion of the tariff at a substantially discounted rate. Finally, he established a timetable for BT to achieve interconnection, requiring BT to create thirty-six exchange linkages by March 1986.[64] Carsberg took his mandate to promote competition quite seriously and believed in carrying it out in a rather "proactive" manner. He felt that the regulator sometimes must assist the entrant, thereby forcing the dominant player to become more productive. "This might not be necessary if we had a conscientious and productive monopoly," notes Carsberg, "but we feel that we have a rather lazy and inefficient one."[65]

THE DUOPOLY REVIEW

The duopoly policy was reviewed in 1990. The DTI officially directed the process, but Oftel was a full partner. In principle, the DTI was concerned with the broader policy issues, and Oftel with the more technical details. In practice, of course, the policy could not be formulated without reference to these details. The primary mission of the review was to determine whether network service should be open to competition beyond the two carriers, BT and Mercury. As it turned out, the review provided an opportunity to reevaluate the mechanics of regulation, but not to deliberate broader issues of telecommunications policy. The DTI did not have the inclination to delve into these broader issues, and Oftel did not have the authority. Despite Oftel's legal obligation to consider matters of social and industrial policy, in practice it did not have the power to move beyond regulatory issues. The duopoly review was thus bound to disappoint many observers, for it would not address their concerns.

The DTI and Oftel chose to make the duopoly review a public debate. They issued a consultative document in November 1990 and solicited comments from the general public.[66] They received more than two hundred submissions, most coming from businesses: large users or firms interested in getting into the telecommunications business. Consumer groups, unions, and local authorities also offered their views. Nevertheless, the central battle pitted BT against Mercury. Mercury, to no one's surprise, argued for the continuation of the duopoly policy. The company's representatives devised what they called a "Second Force" argument: open competition would only result in fratricide among the competitors, so new entrants should only be allowed if they work with Mercury rather than against it. Mercury should be able to make alliances with cable television

[64] Ibid., pp. 217–20.
[65] Interview with Sir Bryan Carsberg, director general of Oftel (October 22, 1991).
[66] Department of Trade and Industry (November 1990).

companies, but BT should not.[67] In contrast, BT managers argued that the duopoly policy should be removed, and BT should be given greater freedom to move into new lines of business.

On the surface, the DTI and Oftel worked together fairly harmoniously. Secretary of State Peter Lilley and Director General Bryan Carsberg appeared jointly at the press conference announcing the final decision in March 1991. Yet there were signs of a subtle discrepancy in views between the two, further complicated by the Treasury's interest in the matter. The DTI was the most anxious to open competition; the Treasury the most concerned with strengthening BT. Oftel stood somewhere in between, believing more strongly than the DTI that competition would still require quite a bit of regulation. The whole debate was colored by Treasury's having scheduled a major sale of BT shares for late in 1991.

The DTI and Oftel agreed from the beginning that they would end the duopoly policy, opening the network service market to more competition. They had more difficulty determining the terms of competition. In the final report in March 1991, they announced that they would no longer limit the number of possible entrants. Unlike the Japanese authorities, who continue to micromanage the competition after liberalization, they would issue licenses to any qualified applicants and then simply let the market decide from there.[68] "We do not believe in beauty contests," explained one DTI official.[69] They would also phase out the tariff structure that had helped Mercury to enter the long-distance market by rebalancing tariffs—lowering long-distance call rates relative to local rates. Since the review, more than 130 new competitors have poured into the market, with the greatest new threat to BT coming in the form of cable companies that use discounts on telephone service to lure cable TV subscribers. With the United Kingdom being the only country in which cable companies can offer telephone service, U.S. firms have invested billions in British cable firms in order to get a piece of the action. BT executives and sympathetic MPs now fear that U.S. firms are gaining altogether too strong a toehold in the British market.[70]

As it turned out, the most controversial decision was made outside the review itself. As part of the process, Oftel had to renegotiate the terms of BT's license, including the terms for the competitors' interconnection with BT. Although a final decision was contingent upon the outcome of the review, Carsberg began discussions with BT in late 1990. BT argued strenuously that its competitors should have to compensate BT for its obligation to provide unprofitable local service, or what BT executives

---

[67] Interview with Stephen Young, director of public policy, Mercury Communications (October 21, 1991).

[68] Department of Trade and Industry (March 1991).

[69] Interview with DTI official (October 1991).

[70] *Economist* (July 16, 1994).

called the "access line deficit." They argued that this should be paid in the form of an access charge beyond the discounted toll charges Mercury already paid to BT. Carsberg accepted the point and made an initial agreement with BT concerning the determination of these charges.

Mercury and other potential competitors were outraged. They found Oftel's action particularly surprising because the earlier consultative document seemed to have dismissed the notion of access charges. In some sense, the dispute arose naturally from the structure of the decision process. Carsberg was supposed to negotiate solely with BT first, then come up with a proposal, call for outside comments on the proposal, revise the agreement if necessary, and then go back to BT. And of course he had to rely on BT for much of his data. Mercury representatives suspect that the Treasury had gotten to Carsberg, requesting a judgment favorable to BT in order to facilitate the impending public offering of BT shares—but Carsberg denies this.[71] The truth is probably more subtle. Even if the Treasury did not pressure him directly, Carsberg could not help but be influenced by the upcoming share offer. And he was well aware that the duopoly review as a whole would require the approval of the Treasury and the prime minister. In the end, Mercury and the potential new competitors managed to convince Carsberg that the arrangement he had worked out with BT would deter new firms from entering the market and would severely damage Mercury's profitability. Carsberg then revised his decision. In his own words he did some "fine tuning," but in the words of others he performed a complete "U turn."[72] He maintained that BT had a right to receive access charges, but he prohibited BT from levying them until Mercury had gained 10 percent of the market or combined competitors had gained 15 percent. BT then had its turn to protest. BT could have refused to agree to the new terms, in which case the issue would have been referred to the Monopolies and Mergers Commission (MMC). This would probably not advance BT's interest in the long run, for there was certainly no guarantee that the MMC would rule in BT's favor. Nevertheless, the threat was a potent one, for the MMC review process would probably take a full year, making it impossible to issue shares before the elections scheduled for 1992. The government had only sold 51 percent of BT at the time, meaning that a future Labour government could regain a majority stake by repurchasing two percent.[73] BT conceded at the eleventh hour, and the DTI soon began considering new licenses.

[71] Carsberg interview (October 22, 1991).

[72] Carsberg interview (October 22, 1991); other interviews (October 1991).

[73] In fact, the Labour Party, which had openly threatened to buy a majority stake in BT if elected only a year early, had lost interest in doing so by 1991. A policy aide to one Labour Party leader reported that the party was more interested in changing regulation than in regaining ownership (interview, October 1991). The government sold another 33 percent stake in December 1991. The Conservatives held onto power in the April 1992 elections, and the government then sold its remaining 22 percent share in July 1993.

As it turns out, U.S. telephone companies have quickly emerged as the most formidable new entrants in the market. Unable to get into the cable television business in the United States due to regulatory restrictions, they have used the British market as testing ground for the provision of integrated telecommunications and entertainment services. They now dominate the British cable market and have been offering telephone service in conjunction with cable service at rates 10 to 15 percent below those of BT. Meanwhile, BT is handicapped from fully striking back because it cannot offer broadcasting services directly until 2001.[74]

Although competition has clearly increased since the duopoly review, BT remains dominant. According to Oftel estimates, BT had 95.3 percent of call revenues in the local market in 1993–94, 86.0 percent in domestic long-distance, and 73.4 percent in international service. BT served 96.0 percent of business telephone lines in 1994 and 97.8 percent of residential lines.[75] Oftel has charged that BT engages in anticompetitive practices, whereas BT complains that excessive regulation impedes its competitiveness on world markets. In 1995 BT referred a dispute with Oftel to the MMC, contesting Oftel's proposals about how to allow customers to keep their telephone numbers when switching from BT to other telephone companies. Then in July 1995, Oftel published yet another review of the regulatory regime, recommending a substantial increase in its own powers to investigate and punish BT's anticompetitive practices.[76]

THE NEW REGIME

The story of British telecommunications reform closely mirrors the larger story of British reform outlined in Chapter 3. Throughout most of the postwar era, an ambivalent mix of market-oriented policy, political intervention, and Treasury constraints on spending produced poor results in the telecommunications sector. The British government was disinclined to follow the French model of state-led network expansion. And the dismal performance of the sector in the 1970s opened the door for a bold move in the other direction, toward greater competition and indirect regulation rather than direct control. The new Thatcher administration, and Keith Joseph in particular, succeeded in rallying DTI officials to their cause. The result was a radical reform that heralded a new ideology of regulation, created new institutions, and produced a new regulatory style. The British government invented a mode of regulation, designed not simply to allow competition but to create it: a sort of "affirmative action" pro-

[74] *Economist* (November 26, 1994).
[75] Cave (August 1995), p. 46.
[76] *Financial Times* (October 3, 1995).

gram for market entrants. Unlike their Japanese counterparts, British officials have actively promoted intermodal competition—competition across
market segments such as mobile and land-based communications. In the
other haven of pro-competitive reform, the United States, the government
has adopted policies to help entrants, but it has leaned more toward a laissez-faire version of liberalism. In the United Kingdom, two contradictory
strands of pro-competitive thought coexist uneasily: one argues for simply
releasing natural competitive forces; the other for going one step further
and creating these forces in markets like telecommunications where competition may not naturally occur.

Beyond the basic pro-competitive nature of reform, the subtleties of
British telecommunications policy today represent a careful balance between the views of the DTI, Oftel, and the Treasury. The contradictions
between laissez-faire liberalization and proactive liberalization are embodied in the subtle differences in philosophy between the main government
agencies involved: the DTI and Oftel. Whereas DTI officials believe that
pro-competitive regulation should be removed as quickly as possible, Oftel
officials are more committed to continuing regulation. As one DTI enthu-
siast put it, "Our approach is that regulation is a transitory affair. Regulation is only a surrogate for competition, an engine for change. If we
succeed, we will eventually deregulate ourselves out of a job."[77] Oftel officials see things quite differently: the government will always have to monitor competition. "In order for there to be effective competition without
regulation," Carsberg notes, "we would need to have perhaps three viable
competitors in each market segment—and I do not expect to see this happen in my lifetime. Our services will be required for a long, long time."[78]

Another contradiction within the government's program is reflected in
a discrepancy between the goals of the DTI and those of the Treasury, with
Oftel between the two. As we have seen, the new government's passion for
creating and nurturing competition bogged down somewhat in the face of
the practicalities of ensuring a successful sale of BT. The government has
been afraid to create too much competition for fear of undermining its
program of selling BT shares. The gap between the DTI and Treasury
views became more apparent with the duopoly review; the Treasury preferred terms favorable to BT, whereas the DTI was more interested in improving the conditions for BT's competitors. Even within the Treasury,
there was a perception gap between those in the shares division, who were
narrowly focused on the share price, and those in the policy division, who
had broader concerns. And within the DTI, there was a discrepancy between those in the telecommunications division, who believed in competi-

[77] Interview with DTI official (July 1990).
[78] Carsberg interview (October 22, 1991).

tion first and foremost, and those in the information technology division, who hoped that BT would be strong at home so that it could take on the competition abroad.

The British telecommunications reform is most distinctive in that the government has created an independent regulator, Oftel. By combining regulatory reform with institutional innovation, the United Kingdom has changed its regime more drastically than even the United States. The United States has a tradition of independent regulatory agencies dating back to the early part of the century, so "deregulation" represented a change in the structure of markets, not government institutions.[79] Most countries have liberalized without creating an independent regulator. France and Germany have separated the telecommunications regulator from the operator, but have not separated the regulator from the sponsoring ministry. The Japanese government has also maintained the regulatory function within the sponsoring ministry.

	Before reform	*After reform*
Operator:	Post Office	BT, Mercury, others
Regulator:	Post Office	Oftel
Sponsor:	DTI	DTI
Owner:	Government	Shareholders

By creating an independent regulator, the British government has further fragmented authority within the telecommunications regime. Under the old regime, the government controlled the provision of telecommunications services through a public corporation. It had no need to regulate because it could control the operator directly: the operator itself was part of the equipment of the state. As such the operator was free from regulation, but not from political interference. The government's designs for the operator often conflicted with the operator's primary mission, providing reliable service at a reasonable cost, and this conflict prompted calls for reform. By establishing Oftel, the government rendered its means of control less direct, separated regulatory responsibilities from the sponsorship function, and created an agency with an institutional interest in procompetitive regulation. Even within the realm of regulation proper, powers are divided between the DTI, which issues licenses; Oftel, which enforces and revises licenses; and the MMC, which amends licenses when the carrier in question and Oftel cannot agree.[80]

---

[79] Of course, U.S. reforms have included some institutional changes, but nothing like the complete restructuring of regulatory institutions in the United Kingdom. In the case of airline deregulation, the United States did take the unusual step of actually eliminating a regulatory agency, the Civil Aeronautics Board (CAB).

[80] Foster (1992), p. 272.

The system of direct control was not replaced by the sort of informal regulation described as typically British by David Vogel, but by a much more formal and legalistic (juridical) variety of regulation influenced heavily by the United States.[81] In this sense, Oftel represents a break in regulatory style as well as an institutional innovation. Oftel has less authority than the Federal Communications Commission (FCC), but it operates under a system of formal procedures and regulations that leave little room for flexible interpretation. In fact, users have complained about the rigidity of the licensing system. The regulatory process itself has transformed from an administrative to an adversarial process. Instead of government officials gradually phasing in regulatory changes as necessary, the process now involves a more disjointed sequence of complaints from certain parties, defenses from others, and finally judgments by the regulator.

Finally, the British telecommunications case offers us some more clues to the relationship between the ideas and institutions of regulatory policy. The organization of the regime influences the content of policy by creating certain possibilities and excluding others. On the one hand, regulation could never be truly "fair" without the creation of an independent regulator. By segmenting decisions, this system creates the possibility for *judicial* regulation. Like a judge in court, Oftel has the ability to limit the scope of its judgment to the particular merits of the case. Otherwise, Oftel would be internalizing fundamental conflicts of interest, such as the interest in protecting consumers versus that of promoting BT. The British telecommunications regime has moved strongly toward a more juridical style, whereby each agency has only a limited role. On the other hand, telecommunications policy can never be truly coherent if regulation is left to an independent regulator. By fusing, rather than segmenting regulatory and policy decisions, other countries retain the capacity for *strategic* regulation. What a British or U.S. official might see as a conflict of interest, a Japanese or French official might see as interrelated issues that must be dealt with in a coherent fashion. The latter would contend that the role of government is to incorporate conflicting values into coherent solutions, not to parcel problems out to islands of limited authority. When French telecommunications minister Paul Quilès says that telecommunications is "too important to leave up to the market," he is not just saying that he distrusts the market. He is arguing that the government needs to retain the capability to pursue larger goals. Unlike the British government, the French government is oriented toward intervention and possesses an institutional structure that facilitates this intervention. Other countries have diverged from the

---

[81] D. Vogel (1986).

Anglo-American pattern of regulatory reform because they have wanted to keep regulatory and policy decisions in the same office. The challenge of regulatory reform in other countries—including Japan, France, and Germany—is precisely one of trying to unleash market forces without undercutting government capacity.

Chapter Five

Financial Services: The Big Bang and the Proliferation of Rules

The British financial revolution of the 1980s offers the most spectacular example of how deregulation and reregulation can coincide. In the space of two weeks in the autumn of 1986, London experienced the boldest of both: the abolition of restrictive practices by the Stock Exchange *and* the inauguration of a new, more extensive and intrusive system of regulation. On October 27, in what is referred to simply as the "Big Bang," the London Stock Exchange abandoned fixed commissions on stock transactions; eliminated the system of single capacity, whereby financial service firms could serve as market makers or brokers but not both; and opened membership to banks and foreign financial institutions. On November 7, Parliament passed the Financial Services Act (FSA), which resulted in a new private regulatory agency, five self-regulatory organizations (SROs), dozens of compliance departments, and thousands of memos trying to explain the new rules to frustrated practitioners.[1] The FSA may have revolutionized life in the City even more than the Big Bang, for in matters of regulation it replaced the informal with the formal, the flexible with the rigid, and the personal with the legalistic. If there is a logical contradiction between "deregulation" in the sense of unleashing competition and "reregulation" in the sense of adding more rules, then the City of London has brazenly defied this logic.

London's particular combination of liberalization and reregulation is unusual in the degree to which the two movements operated separately from each other. The Big Bang and the FSA represent two separate debates, two distinct decision processes, and two different compromises.

---

[1] The original five SROs have since consolidated into three.

And yet the two are linked. They share a cast of characters: the Bank of England, the Treasury, the Department of Trade and Industry (DTI), the City financial institutions, the prime minister, and the Parliament. The Stock Exchange and the Office of Fair Trading (OFT) lead in the Big Bang but play smaller parts in the FSA. More important, the two episodes reflect a common set of trends, trends pushing toward both more open competition and more regulation.

THE OLD REGIME

The City of London has long held a special place in the British economy, and in British politics as well. The City of London occupies a square mile of prime real estate in the eastern end of the borough of London and boasts its own mayor and city council. It has a resident population of only about 6000, but a workday population of over 500,000. It houses the Bank of England and the headquarters of most of the United Kingdom's major banks and brokers as well as branch offices of many of the world's largest financial institutions. The core institutions of the City—the Bank of England, the Stock Exchange, and Lloyd's, the insurance market—date to the late seventeenth century. City financial institutions developed as the British empire grew, financing the two great missions of that empire: commerce and war. The City's merchant banks played only a limited role in the Industrial Revolution, for manufacturing entrepreneurs had relatively modest demands for capital, and regional banks handled most of the lending that was required. By the early nineteenth century, London had taken its place as the world's premier financial center, with sterling serving as the dominant currency. With the end of the Napoleonic Wars, the bank shifted more funds abroad to support trade activities. Even a century ago, City institutions were criticized for "funding every railway in the world apart from their own."[2]

The City's historical development distinguishes it from other financial centers in several interrelated ways. First, the City has a strong bias toward international over domestic markets, and wholesale over retail markets. City institutions include domestic retail banks and small brokerages, but the City's real strength lies in the more sophisticated and professional markets. Second, the City has more developed equity markets and concentrates less on bank lending than financial centers in other countries.[3] Third, the City has looser ties to domestic industry. The strength of the City institutions in international finance makes them less concerned with

---

[2] Kerr (1986), p. 26.
[3] Zysman (1983).

domestic industry, and the emphasis on equity markets implies a more distant relationship between the financial institutions and industry. This gap between financial and industrial capital makes it more difficult for the government to coordinate an industrial policy, and it means that financial interests are less likely to coincide with industrial interests in the political arena.[4] In fact, numerous critics have blamed Britain's relative economic decline on the City.[5]

In the postwar era, the government has had an industrial policy for the financial sector, but no financial policy for the industrial sector. That is, it has strongly supported the City's role as a financial center, but it has not tried to use the financial system as a tool of industrial policy in the way that has been common in Japan or France. Occasionally, the government has intervened in industrial finance. The Bank of England, for example, has quietly encouraged financial institutions to support industry through hard times.[6] Yet the government has not had any more comprehensive strategy for guiding the allocation of credit to industry. Meanwhile, the government has supported the development of the City as a global financial center by limiting the tax and regulatory burden on financial institutions. The government's emphasis on preserving the leading role of the City, even at the possible expense of British industry or British financial institutions, was reinforced by its experience with the Euromarkets. Bank of England officials actively cultivated the Euromarkets—markets denominated in offshore currencies, mostly dollars, which are not subject to national regulations. They felt that the City as a whole would benefit from being the dominant center for Euromarket trading. British financial institutions may have lost out to the Americans and Japanese as the biggest underwriters of Eurobond issues, but the British economy has profited from the foreign exchange and high-grade employment generated by financial activity based in London. Since the advent of the Euromarkets, Bank officials have become strong advocates of liberalization. They have not been particularly protective of domestic institutions because they are primarily responsible for wholesale markets, where British firms are highly competitive. Furthermore, they have felt that a liberal regulatory environment would attract business to London.[7] As we shall see, this orientation

---

[4] Zysman (1983), for example, argues that the City-industry gap helps to explain the British government's inability to find a solution to relative economic decline in the postwar era. Likewise, Hall (1986) suggests that the "organization of capital," and specifically the relationship between finance and industrial capital, helps to explain the divergence in postwar economic policy between Britain and France.

[5] See, for example, Hutton (September 1991). This concern was also paramount in a broad review of the financial system in the late 1970s. Committee to Review the Functioning of Financial Institutions (1978 and 1980).

[6] The Bank launched such an "industrial lifeboat" operation in the early 1980s in order to limit the damage from the recession. See Reid (1988), pp. 218–20.

[7] Interview with Bank of England official (October 1991).

strongly colored their approach to reforms in the 1980s. In comparison to Japanese financial authorities, they have been less concerned with the fortunes of domestic manufacturers or bankers and brokers and more concerned with the health of their financial center.

As to style of regulation, the British authorities distinguished between the more cosmopolitan merchant banks and stockbrokers in the City, which they exempted from routine interference, and the domestically oriented building societies and smaller brokers outside London, which they regulated more tightly.[8] They left most regulation in the wholesale sector up to self-regulatory bodies, whereas they regulated the retail sector more directly. They were extremely sensitive to accusations of being soft on financial institutions that engage in fraudulent practices with the assets of the proverbial "Aunt Agatha." In investment services, the Stock Exchange generally regulated the wholesale sector whereas the Department of Trade supervised the retail sector. In banking, the Bank of England licensed first-tier banks whereas the Treasury licensed second-tier banks. Beyond this, the Department of Trade oversaw the Stock Exchange and other self-regulatory organizations, and the Treasury oversaw the Bank in its capacity as a regulator.

The Bank of England, the primary regulator in the banking sector, practiced a flexible and informal approach to regulation. Bank officials prided themselves on their ability to understand the markets and the players. They referred to their approach to regulation as "market-determined," meaning that they relied more on market signals about the health of a particular bank than on detailed scrutiny of bank records.[9] They met informally with practitioners on a regular basis. Without any legal authority prior to 1979, they relied primarily on moral suasion—yet Bank "requests" were faithfully observed. Of course, the Bank did have some leverage to back up its requests: for example, banks relied on the Bank to provide liquidity. In practice, the Bank occasionally ran into trouble because of the ambiguity in its division of labor with the Treasury. In the case of the banking crisis of the 1970s, Bank officials did not feel responsible for the secondary, or "fringe," banks because they did not license them.[10] But Treasury officials defined their regulatory role narrowly, simply certifying that the secondary banks had certain features of banks that would allow them to be exempted from the Moneylending Laws. Thus neither the Bank nor the Treasury claimed full responsibility for regulating these banks, with catastrophic results.[11] In the 1980s, the Bank

[8] Moran (1991), p. 61.
[9] Moran (1986), p. 18.
[10] On the now-obsolete distinction between "primary" and "secondary" banks, see ibid., p. 11.
[11] Ibid., pp. 84–96.

and the Treasury clashed because the Treasury sought greater authority over bank regulation, particularly in the wake of the failure of Johnson Matthey Bankers in 1984.[12]

Within the City, the ideology of self-regulation reigned. The system thrived precisely because of the cultural homogeneity of the practitioners and the geographical proximity of their offices. Self-regulation was based on frequent informal contact between regulators and practitioners. The City's bankers and brokers greatly preferred this approach because the regulators knew the institutions better and could regulate their activities more flexibly. Practitioners assumed that self-regulation implied light regulation reflecting an insider's knowledge of the markets. Most important, of course, the practitioners simply preferred to be free from political interference. The business of finance was highly specialized, and the intrusion of politics into the City could only create problems. As we shall see in Chapter 8, Japan's old regime was characterized by a similar closeness between regulator and practitioner. Britain broke away from this pattern rather dramatically with the FSA; Japan has not made a similar break.

The most important self-regulatory organizations, the Stock Exchange and Lloyd's, were at the same time regulators, markets, and industry cartels. They provided the market infrastructure and controlled the competition. The Stock Exchange, for example, limited entry into the marketplace by controlling its own membership and by fixing prices for brokerage commissions. It established rules for its members both to protect members from excessive competition and to protect clients from fraud. The most important protection for the client was the single capacity rule, whereby a firm could either be a "jobber" or a "broker" but not both. Jobbers were the wholesalers of shares: they made a "book" of shares in certain stocks, arranging trades with buyers and sellers and sometimes buying or selling on their own account in anticipation of future trades. Brokers were agents, who bought and sold shares from jobbers on behalf of their clients, and earned commissions on these trades from the clients. The jobber-broker split eliminated the potential conflict of interest between principals, who trade on their own account, and agents, who trade on behalf of clients.

Within the regime, the Bank of England played a critical role as the intermediary between City financial institutions and the central government departments, particularly the Treasury. Beginning after the First World War, the Bank increasingly took up the role of protecting the City from political pressures. The interwar period brought an increase in government intervention in markets and more democratic political institutions, and the Bank under its legendary governor Montague Norman stepped in

---

[12] Reid (1988), pp. 211–41.

to shield the City from both of these outside pressures.[13] This created a distance between the government departments and City institutions that contributed to the government's inability to incorporate financial institutions into an industrial strategy. At the same time, it impeded the capacity of City institutions capacity to communicate their views directly to the government. The Bank served as spokesman both for the City within the government and for the government within the City. After the Second World War, however, the Bank gradually became more independent from City interests. The Bank was nationalized in 1946 and subsequently became more integrated into the government's macroeconomic policy process. The Bank promoted the welfare of the City as a whole, but generally would not represent specific institutions or groups of institutions in Whitehall. Bank officials were guided by their strong attachment to the health of the City as a financial center, by their belief in flexible regulation and due respect for markets, and by the requisites of their central functions as a central bank and banking regulator.[14]

The Bank's role as intermediary inhibited City institutions from lobbying the government directly, but did not diminish their political influence more broadly. The City was extremely powerful, but the peculiar organization of the sectoral regime strongly affected the nature of this power. The City's power came first and foremost from its importance within the economy. This meant that governments were forced to consider the greater welfare of the City irrespective of whether City actors actively demand such consideration. Thus the government was unwilling to devalue the pound in the 1960s and 1970s, despite the damage an overvalued pound was doing to British exporters, because they felt that devaluation would shake confidence in London as a financial center. The City was far less effective when it came to lobbying on specific policy issues. Where City institutions succeeded in influencing more specific decisions, they typically did so through informal contacts with individual members of the government. The City institutions only really developed lobby groups in the 1970s because they felt that the Bank of England was not adequately representing their interests in debates leading up to the Banking Act of 1979.[15]

NEW CHALLENGES

In the 1970s, the British banking sector experienced a cycle of deregulation and reregulation that bears close parallels to the capital market reforms of the 1980s. The banking reforms, however, responded primarily

[13] Moran (1991), pp. 62–63.
[14] Moran (1986), pp. 46–53.
[15] See Moran (October 1981).

to domestic economic and political pressures, whereas the City revolution of the 1980s responded more to international pressures. In 1971, the government deregulated deposit interest rates under the Competition and Credit Control Act. The Bank of England felt that it had no choice but to make this move because clearing banks were quickly losing market share to building societies that enjoyed special tax benefits. The clearing banks were losing out precisely because they were the favored members of the banking family and thus were expected to follow stricter guidelines concerning capital reserves and the use of their assets. The 1971 Act freed them to compete more effectively. The subsequent secondary bank crisis then prompted a movement toward reregulation with the Banking Act of 1979. This finally gave the Bank of England the legal authority to do what it had been doing all along, to regulate banks. It also greatly strengthened, extended, and formalized regulatory procedures.[16]

The reforms of the 1980s thus focused on capital markets. As the gap between London's highly competitive and sophisticated international markets and its protected and traditional domestic stock market became more pronounced, more people began to call for reform. In 1979, the newly elected Thatcher administration provided an important catalyst for reform by eliminating exchange controls. This move followed naturally from the administration's avowed antagonism toward restrictions on competition. This then made it much more difficult for the Stock Exchange to insulate itself from the international market. The ability to "swap" assets into other currencies offered new possibilities for circumventing restrictions on particular types of transactions.[17]

The growing presence of foreign financial institutions in London, particularly U.S. and Japanese firms, also increased pressure for change. The big U.S. and Japanese brokers had large capital reserves, which only made the weaknesses of the British houses more apparent. The U.S. firms promoted financial instruments not provided for under the 1958 Prevention of Fraud Act. Furthermore, the traditional informal style of regulation was less appropriate in a market populated by financial institutions of diverse national origins. Foreign firms were less receptive to moral suasion. That is, they were less likely to be persuaded to pass up opportunities to make a profit in the name of the City's greater welfare. More immediately, the failure of Norton Warburg and several other major financial scandals precipitated calls for a new regulatory framework for investment services.

The clearest sign of trouble was that British shares were increasingly being traded abroad. In particular, the New York market, which had deregulated commissions in 1975, took a large portion of business in British

---

[16] See Moran (1986), especially pp. 113–39.
[17] Goodhart (Summer 1987), p. 14.

stocks through American Depository Receipts (ADRs), receipts for non-U.S. shares that are held in U.S. banks. The Stock Exchange actually considered liberalizing commissions for international shares, but council members turned down this proposal because they were afraid that the effects would "leak" to domestic shares. Moreover, domestic brokers had a competitive disadvantage vis-à-vis foreign "dual capacity" traders who could both collect and execute orders.[18] And British securities houses were severely undercapitalized relative to U.S. and Japanese firms. This meant that the market was less liquid and thus less attractive both for issuers and investors. Jobbers were often unable to match large trades because they did not have the capital to support a given market position. Although insufficient capital had less dire circumstances for brokers, they still required some reserves as a cushion in order to weather extended bear markets.[19]

Like New York and Tokyo, London gradually felt the increasing weight of institutional investors. The institutional investors not only took an increasing share of transactions, but they became a larger presence in City politics. They felt that commissions should be much lower for large trades. Commissions per share decreased as volume increased, yet institutional investors were still effectively cross-subsidizing individuals because larger trades entail virtually no additional costs for the brokers. Brokers responded to these concerns by adding various "sweeteners" for institutional clients. They provided research for free or even sent gifts. In addition, brokers began to undermine the spirit of the single capacity system by getting into the "put through" business: they would arrange trades on their own and then execute the trade through a jobber to establish the right price. Despite this erosion in the old system of fixed commissions and single capacity, however, most Stock Exchange members were not inclined to abandon it altogether without a good fight.

The Big Bang

The long road toward the Big Bang began with a legal challenge to the Stock Exchange based on restrictive practices law. In 1973, the Conservative government passed the Fair Trading Act, strengthening measures to prevent and to punish restrictive practices and bolstering the OFT's ability to enforce these measures.[20] Both major political parties supported competition policy, although the Conservatives emphasized market liberalization and antitrust enforcement whereas Labour stressed consumer protection. In 1976, the Labour government extended the OFT's juris-

[18] Reid (1988), pp. 33–34.
[19] Ibid., pp. 37–38.
[20] Moran (1991), p. 69.

diction to services, including financial services. The Stock Exchange was subsequently required to submit its rule book to the OFT. The OFT was to judge whether the rule book contained restrictive practices and could refer the rule book to the Restrictive Practices Court if it found infractions. The Stock Exchange Council lobbied the government for an exception to the 1976 order, arguing that the Stock Exchange was a "market" and not a "service," and therefore should not be subject to restrictive practices law.[21] Stock Exchange chairman Nicholas Goodison appealed to the secretary of state for Prices and Consumer Protection, Roy Hattersley, arguing that the Stock Exchange's inclusion was no more than an unfortunate but potentially costly accident. Despite this effort, the government ultimately declared in February 1979 that the Stock Exchange would not be exempted, and the director general of the OFT, Gordon Borrie, promptly referred the rule book to the Restrictive Practices Court.[22]

Goodison had taken over as chairman of the Stock Exchange in 1976. The senior partner in a medium-sized brokerage firm, he was the Exchange's youngest chairman ever at age 41.[23] He was convinced that the Stock Exchange needed reform so that it would not be bypassed by increasingly sophisticated institutional investors. In particular, he believed that membership should be opened in order to bring more capital into the market and to strengthen the Exchange's international position. Most Stock Exchange members, however, resisted such changes. They felt that reform would compromise their interests by intensifying competition, cutting profits, and inevitably forcing many firms to sell out in order to avoid failure. Even so, brokers were not as bound to fixed commissions as press reports implied, for the system was already starting to break down as brokers offered large clients more and more "sweeteners." Beyond their material interest in protecting their economic rents, the members simply believed in the merits of single capacity trading. They felt that the structural regulation embodied in the single capacity rule effectively protected investors and relieved the Stock Exchange of the need for more burdensome conduct regulations. The Stock Exchange Council repeatedly debated the possibility of reform, including the abolition of single capacity, throughout the 1970s. "Each time," Goodison notes, "we leaned toward endorsing change—and yet we never went over the brink."[24]

Meanwhile, a few voices in the City began to question the fixed commission system. Institutional investors argued that commissions should be negotiable, particularly for the frequently traded gilt-edged securities. In

---

[21] Several institutions were exempted.
[22] Moran (1991), pp. 69–70.
[23] Reid (1988), p. 34.
[24] Interview with Sir Nicholas Goodison, chairman, TSB Group, and former chairman, Stock Exchange (October 29, 1991).

general, however, investors were reluctant to complain too loudly. Despite their frustrations with the Stock Exchange, they hesitated to risk upsetting the peace in the City. In fact, Borrie and his staff had a rather difficult time recruiting witnesses to testify against the Exchange in court.[25] Likewise, the clearing banks and foreign financial institutions did not actively demand membership on the Exchange. Curiously enough, no law prevented banks from becoming members—only Stock Exchange practice, tacitly supported by the Bank of England, stood in their way. The greatest pressure to open membership came from within the Exchange, from member firms that hoped to link up with banks.

Given their failure to have the rule book exempted, Stock Exchange leaders began to prepare a defense. They could not really rationalize some of the more egregious practices on their own merits, but they believed wholeheartedly in the virtues of the single capacity system. David LeRoy Lewis, a council member and chairman of the large jobber Ackroyd & Smithers, developed what became known as the "link" argument: you could not maintain the single capacity system without fixed commissions, and thus both must be preserved. He maintained that with liberalized commissions, competitive pressures would push jobbers and brokers to bypass the system. Brokers would match deals between their own clients, and jobbers would arrange deals and then execute them through friendly brokers at a discount, thereby undermining single capacity.[26] Meanwhile, the lawyers continued to argue that a market is fundamentally different from a service, and therefore the Stock Exchange should never have been subject to restrictive practices legislation in the first place.

From the Stock Exchange officials' point of view, the case prevented them from taking any further action to promote reform on their own. Their lawyers cautioned them not to publicly discuss any proposals for reform because this could jeopardize the case. The Exchange was pushed into a defensive position—forced to defend the indefensible. Goodison recalls the horror of the situation with some anguish many years later.

> The full enormity and complexity of the whole thing had not come in on us at first. . . . The formality of the case prevented us from discussing solutions. The court case was by nature an antagonistic process. You could not postulate: "If we do this, then would the government drop the case?" This would be seen as an expression of weakness. It really was a ridiculous position to be in![27]

Goodison continued to look for ways to release the Exchange from the OFT action. In particular, he stressed that any decision would cause enor-

[25] Reid (1988), pp. 40–42.
[26] Ibid., pp. 28–30.
[27] Goodison interview (October 29, 1991).

mous disruption to the market, and "the market" of course included the government's own gilt-edged market. He approached Director-General Borrie himself, offering to discuss whatever measures might be necessary to persuade the government to drop the case. Borrie refused, reminding Goodison that the OFT had to review the rule book in its entirety and could not negotiate on individual practices. So the case would have to take its course.

When the Thatcher government came into office, Goodison approached the new secretary of state for trade, John Nott, hoping once again to find a way to avoid the court battle. Nott refused, but the government did put a provision into the Competition Act of 1980 that would allow the Exchange a "stay of execution" so that it could reorganize in the event of an unfavorable decision. The government at that point did not want to be seen as too close a friend of the City and did not want to undermine the authority of the OFT. Goodison repeated his plea with Nott's successor, John Biffen, but the reply was the same. Goodison found support for his cause from former prime minister Harold Wilson, who had chaired a committee reviewing the operation of the entire financial system from 1977 through 1979. The committee report, which came out in 1980, argued that an independent commission should undertake the task of reviewing Stock Exchange practices.[28] In October 1980, Wilson wrote to Prime Minister Margaret Thatcher, suggesting this route. Thatcher responded in November, saying that she had considered this possibility but had decided against it.[29]

The Bank of England had not been heavily involved in the debate to this point, but the Bank's intervention proved to be the turning point in the evolution of the Big Bang. Although the Bank had little formal authority over capital markets, it had a keen interest in the Stock Exchange because the Exchange organized the trading of gilt-edged securities. And of course it had a major stake in the Big Bang because the proposed reforms would bring down commissions—including the substantial commissions the government paid to city firms when issuing gilt-edged securities. And beyond its direct interest in the market, the Bank felt a responsibility for the overall health of the City. In 1982, David Walker, a former Treasury official, was appointed as one of four executive directors at the Bank, in charge of Industrial Finance. This section was concerned with finance for industry and for the "non-bank" City, meaning primarily the securities and insurance markets. Walker and his deputies were deeply concerned about the fate of the Stock Exchange. Although the City was a world leader in many areas of finance, it clearly lagged in domestic securities. Without changes, Walker

---

[28] Committee to Review the Functioning of Financial Institutions (1980).
[29] Reid (1988), p. 36.

felt that the situation could only get worse, indeed, that it could have a negative impact on other markets. Walker was troubled by the shift of trading in British shares to New York and the lack of liquidity in the market. He also felt that the Exchange's trading system was inefficient, just as New York's Big Board had been before May Day in 1975.[30] His concerns partly reflected what he was hearing from City practitioners, but like most Bank officials he was far more concerned with the overall health of the City as a market than with the strength of particular British institutions. London's role as a financial center served the best interests of "U.K. Inc." by attracting foreign capital and generating high-grade employment. Furthermore, Walker was seriously troubled by the OFT case:

> We started to realize the awkwardness of the court process. The OFT had a long list of antitrust counts, many of which were warranted. But we were worried about the process. . . . We thought: Let's assume the OFT succeeds. Then we might be into 1986 and the court would say A to Z practices are in breech of antitrust law. It would not say that any new plan was acceptable. So if we came up with a new system, it was still possible that we would have the same process all over again.[31]

To make matters worse, a ruling against the Stock Exchange would permanently subject the rule book to OFT regulation.

Walker assigned a young Bank official, Andrew Threadgold, to draw up a "Blue Skies" plan: forget about the court case and all political constraints and try to imagine how the Stock Exchange would operate in an ideal world. Threadgold studied the American literature on stock markets, and he and other Bank officials visited the New York Stock Exchange (NYSE) and studied the Nasdaq (the National Association of Securities Dealers Automated Quotation) system. He produced a report in November 1982, which envisioned an Exchange with membership open to banks and negotiable commissions. It proposed a competing market maker system like Nasdaq that could make the most of available computer technology.[32] The report was never publicly released but was circulated within the Bank, where officials welcomed the conclusions in principle but doubted the plan's practicality.

Lord Richardson, the Bank's governor, gave Walker his blessing to try to negotiate an out-of-court settlement in January 1983. Officials within the Bank's Gilts Division initially remained uncommitted, however, for they were generally satisfied with the performance of the jobbers in the gilts

---

[30] Interview with Sir David Walker, chairman of the SIB and outside director of the Bank of England (October 23, 1991).

[31] Walker interview (October 23, 1991).

[32] Interview with Andrew Threadgold, chief executive, PosTel Investment Management Ltd. (October 25, 1991).

market. The Gilts Division was a major power center within the Bank, and it was the division with the greatest direct stake in the market. Trading in gilt-edged securities consistently exceeded the value of all other securities in the market. By the end of the year, Division Director Eddie George and his staff were persuaded that reform would improve the operation of the market and signaled their approval. With this, the full weight of the Bank shifted behind reform, and George himself anchored the effort to reform the gilts market.[33]

Walker embarked on a series of informal lunch meetings with senior executives from jobber and broker firms to explore avenues for reform and to convince them that change was necessary. Walker notes: "These were 'let your hair down' sessions, as you might say. I rather deliberately gave the practitioners the full force of my vision. There was certainly some shock and horror that a director of the Bank would even suggest abandoning fixed commissions and single capacity. Initially they found the very idea offensive. But by the end of March 1983, I noticed some willingness to entertain the notion of change."[34] Walker then took his case to the two interested departments: the Treasury and the Department of Trade. At the Treasury, Chancellor Geoffrey Howe, a former solicitor general himself, was reluctant to endorse the plan, for he felt it was inappropriate to interfere with the OFT proceedings. Within the Department of Trade, the head of the financial affairs division, Philip Brown, shared Walker's concern with the untidy aspects of the court process. The department was paralyzed, however, because the head of the competition policy division steadfastly supported the OFT process. The two Department of Trade division chiefs both diplomatically stated their cases to the ministers, but the result was simply deadlock. Although Goodison had lobbied the department for the abandonment of the case, the OFT's Borrie had made a similar effort to ensure that the case proceeded.[35]

The secretary of state at the time, Lord Cockfield, played a critical role in formulating the all-important agreement that would take his successor's name.[36] Cockfield was initially hesitant to interfere, but he sympathized with the Bank's concern that reform should proceed more quickly. He was a firm believer in the Thatcher ideology of free markets and a rabid opponent of restrictive practices. He figured that if the Stock Exchange would agree to abandon some of the worst offenses, then he could arrange a deal to have the case dismissed. Walker's hopes that he could arrange a

---

[33] Walker and Threadgold interviews (October 1991).

[34] Walker interview (October 23, 1991).

[35] Interview with former Department of Trade official (October 1991).

[36] Cockfield went on to serve as European Community (EC) commissioner and to contribute to the formation of a single European market.

deal with Cockfield were dashed when elections were called for June 9. Walker and Goodison were distraught, for the case was expected to go to court in January of 1984.[37]

The Conservative election victory brought in a new Cabinet. The new Chancellor of the Exchequer, Nigel Lawson, was an adamant free trader and felt that anything that would hasten the abolition of the restrictive practices—even if it meant bypassing the OFT—should be welcomed. The new secretary of state for the reunited DTI, Cecil Parkinson, was briefed on the case and met with Borrie on June 27 and then Goodison on July 1. Goodison had sent Parkinson a handwritten letter, warning that he could not guarantee the "integrity" of the market in the event of an unfavorable judgment. When the two met, Parkinson offered the deal: eliminate fixed commissions and make some constitutional changes to the Exchange, and the OFT case would not go to court. Goodison accepted immediately. "I had been working on this for three years," comments Goodison, "but I still think he was surprised that I agreed so quickly—for he was new to the process."[38] The *Guardian* revealed that the government was considering an out-of-court settlement on July 19. The prime minister confirmed the story in the House of Commons that afternoon, and the "Goodison-Parkinson" agreement was official.[39] Parkinson did his best to explain the merits of the agreement in a House of Commons statement, but opposition MPs and media critics still denounced the agreement as a constitutional outrage and a blatant sellout to City interests. The most cynical saw it as repayment for City contributions to the election campaign. But brimming with the confidence of a resounding victory, the ruling party simply did not care. Borrie, who had only heard of the plan in his own meeting with Parkinson several days before Goodison's turn, was understandably furious. He and his staff had worked for years on the case, and their findings would never be put to use. Borrie argued that the case could only be dismissed through an act of Parliament and not by a simple government order. The government accepted this view, and Parliament passed the measure on March 13, 1984.

The agreement did not touch on the question of single capacity, and in fact the government was in no hurry to abandon the practice, because it eased the fears of private investors. Parkinson publicly declared that single capacity should be retained, if possible. DTI officials were surprised when Exchange leaders explained that their "link" argument was likely to hold, and thus single capacity would not survive. This made the department's efforts to develop a new regulatory framework all the more imperative.

Goodison was left with the unpleasant task of persuading the forty-seven members of the Stock Exchange Council to approve the changes. To

[37] Walker interview (October 23, 1991).
[38] Goodison interview (October 29, 1991).
[39] Reid (1988), p. 48.

make matters worse, small and medium-sized firms were disproportionately represented on the council. "In retrospect," Goodison admits, "I
took a great risk in agreeing without prior approval, even if I did feel that
I knew my council member's views."[40] Even so, Goodison's case was
strengthened by two factors. First, although the weaker Exchange members would effectively be voting their firms out of business, they would be
paid very handsomely to do so. They could expect clearing banks or foreign firms to pay dearly to buy them out, and they were not disappointed.
Second, the OFT case remained a horrible enough alternative to push
them toward action. Although some still believed they could win the case,
most were soberly realistic about their chances. On July 22, the Council
approved Goodison's original package of concessions.[41] Some Exchange
members continued to resist after this first vote, and Goodison had to
lobby valiantly in order to pass related measures in 1983 and 1984.[42]
Goodison had agreed to enact the changes by 1986 without really knowing how long it would take to prepare. Walker had originally envisioned a
gradual transition toward negotiated commissions, but Exchange officials
felt that market forces would overwhelm any effort to manage the transition. Meanwhile, Nigel Lawson, the long-standing Chancellor of the Exchequer and a thoroughbred Thatcherite, pressed for full liberalization
without delay. It was shortly after this that a Bank official first coined the
phrase now used universally to describe what was to take place on October
27, 1986: the "Big Bang."[43]

Released from the torture of the restrictive practices action, the Exchange finally began to look more carefully at how to modernize the trading system. The exchange took study groups to visit U.S. exchanges: the
NYSE with its floor-based continuous auction system, and Nasdaq with its
automated competing market-maker system. Exchange officials were
much more impressed with the latter, and they developed London's new
Stock Exchange Automated Quotation (SEAQ) trading system on the Nasdaq model. Their conclusions closely paralleled those of Threadgold's
"Blue Skies" report, probably not so much because they borrowed his
blueprint but because they based their conclusions on the same model.[44]

With the Big Bang impending, City institutions began the inevitable restructuring. The Bank of England, and Walker in particular, mediated in
some of the alliances and buyouts that developed. Walker and his team believed that the market would be characterized by many niche players but only
six to eight truly integrated financial services firms: perhaps two British firms,

---

[40] Goodison interview (October 29, 1991).
[41] Reid (1988), p. 70.
[42] Ibid., pp. 53–55.
[43] Walker interview (October 23, 1991).
[44] Reid (1988), p. 54.

two U.S., one or two Continental, and one or two Japanese. In stark contrast to their Japanese counterparts, the British authorities did little to protect domestic financial institutions from the onslaught of new competition. As expected, the vast majority of the smaller British jobbers and brokers were quickly gobbled up by larger players. Meanwhile, S. G. Warburg and Barclays emerged as Britain's national champion full-service firms.[45] Likewise, in the gilt-edged market the Bank licensed all twenty-nine qualified applicants for market-maker positions and let them fight it out in the savage competition of the free market. Bank officials were eager to improve the liquidity of the market, and they felt that the market itself, not they, should pick the "winners." They suspected that only twelve to fifteen of the licensees would survive, however, and their estimates turns out to have been right on target.[46]

Despite all the fanfare, the actual day of the Big Bang was relatively uneventful. The surviving firms had expanded in anticipation of the Big Bang, leading to substantial overcapacity and an inevitable fallout. The new competitive environment did not hit brokers right away, however, because the bull market of the mid-1980s smoothed the transition. The competition hit home after the 1987 crash, with many firms cutting personnel in order to survive. In a broader sense, the Big Bang symbolized a cultural shift that had begun long before that day in 1986 and would continue long after. The gentlemen's luncheon was replaced by the power breakfast, civilized rivalry was replaced by cutthroat competition, and discrete self-regulation was replaced by a nightmare from America: the proliferation of regulatory bodies, the endless creation of rules, and an invasion of lawyers.

THE FINANCIAL SERVICES ACT

The origins of the FSA, like those of the Big Bang, date back to the mid-1970s. Officials at the Department of Trade, the department responsible for overseeing the securities industry, recognized that in a world of increasingly diverse and sophisticated investment services the 1958 Prevention of Fraud Act was dangerously outmoded. They were only pushed to act in 1981, however, when a series of scandals highlighted the weaknesses of the regulatory system.[47] City practitioners had long argued that the DTI

---

[45] Reid (1988, pp. 51–70) examines City reorganization in more detail. Kerr (1986) and *Midland Bank Review* (Spring 1986) offer charts of the new alliances. Warburg later encountered serious troubles, and was bought out by the Swiss Bank Corporation. *Economist* (February 18, 1995), p. 72, and (July 1, 1995), pp. 66–67.

[46] Interview with Bank of England official (October 1991); Reid (1988), pp. 63–65; *Bank of England Quarterly Bulletin* (February 1989), pp. 49–57. With the increase in new government debt in the early 1990s, the number of dealers recovered to nineteen by 1994.

[47] The most prominent of these scandals involved the collapse of Norton Warburg. This scandal was highly politicized because many small investors lost their savings.

was not equipped to regulate the stock market, but even DTI officials came to question the system's adequacy. The situation grew even worse as the Thatcher administration began to cut department personnel. Senior civil servants eventually warned the secretary of state that they could no longer effectively administer the act. One civil servant recalls: "The situation became increasingly embarrassing. We were taking appalling risks. But when asked to devise an alternative we only had a rag-bag of thoughts, not a legislation, nothing concrete. We had no ability to think up a new act."[48] Department officials considered setting up a Royal Commission, but these commissions were in disrepute for the length of time they often took to propose very little. So instead, in July 1981 the department decided to assign the momentous task of devising a new regulatory framework to a one-man commission by the name of L.C.B. Gower, the country's leading authority on company law.

Gower chose first to produce a consultative document, a "green book," with an outline of the problem and suggested solutions, and then to solicit comments. In the document, which appeared in 1982, Gower tried to compromise between statutory regulation by the central government and self-regulation. The system would center on self-regulatory organizations, but would be tied to a legal framework through oversight by a central government department or regulatory agency. He tried to reassure potential City critics by stressing that he understood "(1) that it would be self-defeating to impose restrictions so severe that they cannot be complied with except at disproportionate trouble and expense, and (2) that it would be detrimental to the national interest if controls were disproportionately strict in comparison with those of other financial centers to which the business could move."[49] Gower spent more than a year lunching with City executives, tapping their views on how the new system should work. Nonetheless, the City's response to the document was rather chilly. In Gower's own words: "A few of the responses to the Discussion Document accused me of having an excessive passion for logic and tidiness, of wishing to regulate for the sake of regulating, and of thinking it was both possible and desirable to protect fools from their own folly."[50] Above all, City firms feared that the new system would allow lawyers and the courts to take over the business of financial regulation.

City attitudes changed somewhat before the second report appeared in 1984 because the Goodison-Parkinson agreement intervened, making the need for a new regulatory framework more pressing. The demise of single capacity would require creating some new, and inevitably more complex, means of protecting investors from fraud. Integrated financial service

[48] Interview (October 1991).
[49] Gower (January 1982).
[50] Gower (January 1984), p. 5.

firms would bring in a whole new range of possible conflicts of interest, and the invasion of more foreign firms would make self-regulation less practical.

Gower's second report, released in January 1984, provided an outline much closer to the system that eventually emerged. Gower recommended establishing a central regulatory authority, either the DTI or an independent agency, which would delegate statutory powers to private self-regulatory organizations. The central authority would establish a core set of regulations, and the self-regulatory organizations would have to develop their own more detailed rules in harmony with these core rules. Gower was concerned that the system should incorporate enough of a self-regulatory element to insulate it from Parliament, for he feared that parliamentary intervention would hold up the regulatory process.[51]

In 1984, the Bank of England set up its own study group on regulatory reform, chaired by Sir Martin Jacomb. The committee's report was never released, but it differed from Gower's report primarily in that the central authority would itself be a private organization. It would have the free hand of a private organization, but would receive its powers from the government.[52] The Board would be appointed jointly by the Bank and the DTI. The Committee members were most interested in wresting regulation away from DTI officials, whom they viewed as obsessed with political appearances and indifferent to the concerns of honest businessmen.[53] They need not have worried, for as in the telecommunications case it turned out that no one wanted the job. In stark contrast to their Japanese counterparts, DTI officials had no interest in taking on such a cumbersome and thankless task. A small minority within the Bank of England thought that the Bank should take over, thus becoming more of a one-stop regulator.[54] Senior Bank officials were convinced, however, that this could only mean trouble. They had already experienced the headaches of regulating "fringe" institutions with the secondary bank crisis. In any case, they figured that they could exert some influence over securities markets via their authority over banks, which would become major players in the investment business. (By contrast, Japan's Finance Ministry officials have adamantly insisted on maintaining unified regulatory control over the banking and securities industries.)

[51] Interview with former DTI official (October 1991).
[52] Kenneth Berrill (Summer 1986, p. 16), the first chairman of the regulatory organization, the Securities and Investment Board (SIB), argued that a private organization would be preferable because it could afford the salaries required to attract a first-rate professional staff.
[53] Interview with Sir Martin Jacomb, chairman, PosTel Investment Management (May 4, 1993).
[54] Threadgold interview (October 25, 1991).

The DTI issued a white paper with its final plans for reform in 1985. The government basically accepted the Gower plan with the modification that the central regulator, which was subsequently designated the Securities and Investment Board, would be a private organization as envisioned in the Bank of England's study group report.[55] Parliament then passed the legislation in November 1986. Despite Gower's efforts to incorporate practitioners' feedback, City interests never fully mobilized to express their views. For its part, the Bank of England was preoccupied with the Johnson Matthey affair. "Without the scandal," suggests one bank official, "the Bank's role in the process would have been different, and the final legislation would have been less problematic. The FSA went adrift because it got in the hands of DTI lawyers."[56] The largest financial lobby group, the British Bankers' Association (BBA), was never able to speak out for the City as a whole, since it found itself in frequent conflict with the merchant banks' industry association. And many City practitioners were simply too preoccupied with the coming Big Bang to take part in the regulatory debate. As noted above, City institutions are not particularly effective for lobbying on specific issues, and in the case of the FSA this weakness came to haunt them.

City institutions only really became active late in the process, when the DTI had already developed its framework, so they were only able to make revisions at the margins. They tried to exempt wholesale markets from those regulations obviously aimed at protecting individual investors. Section 43 of the Act reflects their effort, incorporating special exemptions for certain transactions between professionals. The Association of Corporate Treasurers also pushed through a revision at the eleventh hour. These corporate financial officers were mortified to find that their investment activities would come under the Act and managed to have these excluded. City firms also revolted—unsuccessfully—against the Act's notorious Section 62, which provides channels for investors to sue brokers for damages.

City practitioners still did not comprehend the full ramifications of the FSA until it came into effect. Early in 1987, they received an enormous rule book from the Securities and Investment Board (SIB), only to be followed by even more detailed regulations from up to five self-regulating organizations, depending on their range of activities. This incited a more forceful rebellion from City practitioners, who argued that the FSA could undermine the gains from the Big Bang. They were particularly disgruntled with how the new SIB chairman, Kenneth Berrill, had interpreted elements of the law. For example, they objected to his rigid definition of "equivalency," the principle whereby SRO rules must be at least as protec-

[55] DTI (January 1985).
[56] Interview (October 1991).

tive of the consumer as the core rules established by the SIB. In addition, some practitioners protested the SIB's insistence on "polarization," whereby branch offices could not act as both principals, selling their own investment products, and agents, providing investment advice. Polarization penalized banks, which could operate more efficiently if their branches could engage in both activities, to the benefit of insurance companies, which were accustomed to this separation. The OFT challenged the polarization principle, contending that it was anticompetitive, but the SIB prevailed. City concerns were echoed by members of the DTI's deregulation task force, who attacked their own departmental colleagues in the financial services division for regulatory excesses. As one member of the task force puts it, "The FSA is the DTI's Achilles' heel."[57]

Economists attacked the FSA for increasing the costs of regulation. Touche Ross estimated the first-year costs of the Act at a whopping £1 billion.[58] David Lomax, an adviser to the National Westminster Bank, estimated the annual maintenance costs for the SIB and the SROs at £20 million, and the total costs to City firms, including the internal costs of compliance, at over £100 million.[59] Charles Goodhart, a former adviser to the Bank, made a personal campaign of the issue, stressing that Gower and the DTI failed to perform any cost/benefit assessment.[60] Moreover, these costs may actually fall hardest on those whom the act was supposed to benefit: private investors. Given the high cost of compliance with regulations applying to transactions with private investors, some brokers have simply stopped selling to these investors. Likewise, the legalization of regulation may also backfire on private investors. The infamous Section 62 of the Act, which gives investors the right to sue for a violation of regulations, has prompted the SIB and the SROs to adopt more detailed rules to defend practitioners against lawsuits. And the investment firms, in turn, have developed practices to protect themselves rather than the investors, including special contracts designed to limit their liability to their clients.[61]

City practitioners focused their frustration on the person of Berrill, who argued that he was only following the law.[62] "The City practitioners demanded Sir Kenneth's head on a plate," notes one former civil servant

[57] Interview with former DTI official (July 1990).
[58] *Institutional Investor* (May 1988), p. 58.
[59] Cited in Goodhart (1988), p. 18.
[60] Goodhart (1987) and Seldon, ed. (1988). A London Business School study (Franks and Schaefer, March 1993) compared the costs of Britain's regulatory system to that in other major countries and found that the British system is not significantly more expensive. The study recommended that the system be further decentralized, with the SIB giving the SROs greater autonomy.
[61] See Claire Makin, "First, Big Bang, now Big Brother," *Institutional Investor* (May 1988), pp. 58–61.
[62] Berrill retorted in a magazine interview: "Remember, it's the government's act entirely. . . . Every dot and comma is the government's." *Institutional Investor* (May 1988), p. 60.

rather bluntly, "and in an extraordinary act of treachery—they gave it to him."[63] In February 1988, DTI Secretary of State Lord Young and Bank Governor Robin Leigh-Pemberton jointly announced that Berrill would be replaced by none other than the Bank of England's own David Walker.[64] Walker tried to bring back some of the flexibility of the old system, while leaving in the statutory bite. His approach combined three levels of regulation. At the highest level, the SIB would have a set of ten core principles. Then it would have forty more specific core rules, based on the ten core principles, that apply to all investment businesses. The self-regulatory organizations would then develop detailed regulations based on the SIB's core rules. Because the SROs are "voluntary" organizations, they have the ability to punish members on the basis of an infraction against a core rule—that is, an infraction against the spirit but not the letter of the rule book.[65] Walker proved far more popular than Berrill, even though the regulatory burden did not ease that much. Walker also played a critical role as a liaison between the Bank and the SIB, a role the Bank valued greatly. Some of those actually dealing with compliance matters were less appreciative, for Walker's reforms effectively meant that they had to rewrite their internal rule books one more time.[66]

In recent years, criticisms of the FSA regulatory regime have only grown louder. With the occurrence of more financial scandals, notably the Maxwell and Bank of Credit & Commerce International (BCCI) affairs, critics suggested that the new regime was not only costly but ineffective as well. The fragmentation of the regulatory system has been central to the problem, because firms turned down by one self-regulatory organization could try their luck with another and because the regulatory authorities have failed to coordinate their efforts effectively.[67] In 1992, the Treasury took over the DTI's supervisory responsibilities over the FSA regime, giving the system greater coherence at the ministerial level although not at the regulatory level. In 1994, the SIB concluded a comprehensive review of the system. It proposed clarifying the definition of trading violations, promoting more cooperation with criminal prosecutors, and improving the surveillance of trading practices. In addition, it recommended greater transparency in equity trading, meaning that quotes and prices should be more accessible to public view. The SIB also encouraged the consolidation of the SROs, with a new Personal Investment Authority (PIA) taking over for two other SROs and most of one other—the Life Insurance and Unit

---

[63] Interview with former DTI official (October 1991).

[64] Walker had articulated his preference for a light rein of regulation several years prior to this. *Bank of England Quarterly Bulletin* (December 1983), pp. 499–501.

[65] Firms not joining SROs are regulated directly by the SIB.

[66] Interview with a senior compliance officer at a major merchant bank (October 1991).

[67] *Economist* (November 9, 1991), p. 96.

Trust Regulatory Organization (LAUTRO) and the Financial Intermediaries, Managers, and Brokers Regulatory Association (FIMBRA), and the Investment Management Regulatory Organization (IMRO).[68] Within a year, the SIB was reviewing its report once again, suspecting that market-makers were abusing their special privileges to their own advantage.[69] Meanwhile, British regulation has become increasingly intertwined with European Union (EU) initiatives. Concerning investment services, EU leaders agreed in December 1992 to a regime that would allow investment firms to operate with a European "passport" throughout the EU on the basis of home-country authorization, effective January 1996. For British regulatory authorities, this has meant harmonizing their own regulations more fully with EU standards and preparing to allow firms authorized by other national authorities to operate in Britain.

THE NEW REGIME

Although finance is a very different business from telecommunications, and British finance is unusual in itself, Britain's financial reform shares some basic themes with its telecommunications reform: bold liberalization, the decentralization of authority, and the formalization of regulation on the U.S. model. As we noted earlier in the chapter, the regulatory reforms of the 1980s were preceded by an earlier cycle of liberalization and reregulation in the 1970s. And beyond the Big Bang and the Financial Services Act, other financial reforms in the 1980s featured these same basic themes.[70] In the banking sector, the government gave banks new freedoms in lending activities by removing the system of "corset controls" in 1980. But under the 1987 Banking Act, after the Johnson Matthey failure, the government substantially strengthened the Bank of England's authority over banks. The Bank, for example, gained new powers to regulate large loan exposures and to screen bank takeovers.[71] In the case of the building societies, Britain's savings and loan institutions, the government passed legislation in 1986 to expand the range of activities in which building societies could engage. While building societies would still be required to maintain 90 percent of their commercial assets in mortgage loans, they

---

[68] *Economist* (February 26, 1994), pp. 79–80.

[69] *Economist* (February 15, 1995), pp. 71–72. The SIB issued a report on this problem in June 1994, curtailing some of the market makers' privileges but leaving many others intact. *Economist* (June 24, 1995), pp. 67–68.

[70] Reid (1989, p. 56) argues that the combination of bold liberalization and extensive reregulation is characteristic of the Thatcher administration: "The Thatcher government . . . detects no inconsistency between giving greater play to what are seen as benign market forces and at the same time seeking to clamp down sharply on malpractice."

[71] Reid (1988), pp. 257–58.

were allowed to commit up to 5 percent of their assets to unsecured loans. This enabled them to diversify into related financial services such as credit cards and money transmission accounts. At the same time, however, the government further decentralized authority by creating yet another regulatory body, the Building Societies Commission; it also formalized and strengthened regulation. The Building Societies Act defines the limitations on Building Societies activities and sets out detailed criteria for prudent management. If a society violates its regulatory constraints, the Commission has the authority to impose new conditions for continued authorization as a building society or to revoke authorization altogether.[72] The Act accelerated a consolidation of the industry that shrank the number of societies by more than half to eighty-four from 1980 through 1994.[73] The government completed a major review of the Act in January 1995, giving the building societies more powers to compete directly with banks.[74]

Of course, as noted at the outset of this chapter, the combination of bold liberalization with massive reregulation was embodied most vividly in the virtual coincidence of the Big Bang and the FSA. Together, these two episodes demonstrate a characteristically British pattern of regulatory reform, one which we shall define in more detail in the following chapter. Yet the two episodes themselves almost appear to move in different directions: one removes restrictions on market competition, and the other adds regulations on market behavior. We can unravel this paradox in several ways. First, there is the logical link stressed throughout this book: greater competition often mandates more regulation, not less. Second, there is a difference in substance. The Big Bang deals foremost with the regulation of prices and entry, and the Thatcher government opposed such restrictions on competition. But the FSA concerns the regulation of fraudulent practices, and the government firmly supported such supervision where necessary. And third, and perhaps most important, there is a difference in jurisdiction. The Bank of England played the critical role in the Big Bang, whereas the DTI took the lead with the FSA. As argued in Chapter 1, different agencies within a government may embrace distinct policy orientations depending on their specific history, jurisdiction responsibilities, and functional requirements—and these different orientations shape how these agencies steer the reform process. Thus which agency takes the lead on a specific issue becomes critical.

In the case of the Big Bang, Bank of England officials stressed the overall health of the City over the fate of specific British financial institutions and therefore embraced radical liberalization. They firmly believed that

---

[72] Boleat (August 1987).
[73] *Economist* (May 7, 1994).
[74] *Economist* (April 1, 1995), p. 62.

less regulation and greater competition would ultimately benefit the City as an international financial center. And they had the institutional capacity to mediate a bargain between the Stock Exchange and the government. Beyond this, members of the Thatcher government—and Secretaries of State Cockfield and Parkinson in particular—were so completely devoted to the virtues of competition that they were willing to entertain a deal that would eliminate the Stock Exchange's restrictive practices more quickly and more certainly than the court process. In addition, the OFT case provided a credible threat that helped to push the Stock Exchange into action. The Stock Exchange probably would have acted on its own eventually, but it might not have come up with such a bold solution in the absence of this threat.

Meanwhile, the DTI view of the world pushed the FSA in a strikingly different direction. The DTI was primarily concerned with preventing scandals that would undermine the credibility of DTI bureaucrats and embarrass their political masters. Thus it leaned toward more regulation rather than less, and it sought counsel from lawyers more than from brokers. British economist Charles Goodhart has devised a model that explains this rather nicely and turns the theory of regulation on its head. He contends that government agencies tend to respond to public perceptions derived from celebrated cases of fraud and therefore lean toward overregulation. Officials discount cost concerns (efficiency) because they are more afraid of the public's outrage over a major scandal than they are of industry groups' displeasure with being overregulated.[75] This model explains the trend toward more comprehensive regulation of financial services, such as insider trading, far better than the theory of regulation. Nevertheless, the FSA regime stresses the protection of investors, not firms. "Our philosophy is not to keep weak firms afloat," reports one senior regulator. "We want to wind them down quickly, with minimum pain to their customers."[76]

The FSA has greatly extended the scope and added to the density of regulation. Moran suggests that it embodies three long-term trends: codification, juridification, and institutionalization. In other words, unspoken rules are now written down; informal codes of conduct have become rigid laws; and new practices have become embodied in a new set of institutions.[77] David Llewellyn describes the new "regulatory mix" slightly differently. He suggests that the Act extends regulation to a much wider range of financial services; it is more "interventionist" in the sense that it imposes more precise requirements with regard to specific business practices; and it replaces the regulation of "institutions" with the regulation of

[75] Goodhart (1987).
[76] Interview with SIB official (April 1993).
[77] Moran (1991).

"functions." That is, because the distinction between different types of financial institutions is blurring, the self-regulatory organizations divide their regulatory duties by what the institutions do (provide insurance or sell stocks) rather than by what they are (insurance companies or brokers). Thus institutions that perform multiple functions are subject to regulation by multiple SROs.[78] In theory, the erosion of barriers between market segments could lead to the recentralization of regulatory authority just as well as to the diffusion of authority. In fact, a 1973 report on the financial system recommended that regulatory authority over financial services be centralized in the DTI.[79] Yet precisely the opposite occurred: the compromise between statutory regulation and self-regulation added a middle layer of regulation between the government and the SROs. And the creation of multiple SROs for different functions further diffused authority and led to the duplication of regulatory responsibilities.

[78] Llewellyn (August 1987).

[79] Inter-Bank Research Organization (1973). More recently, a think tank known as the Centre for the Study of Financial Innovation has proposed creating an umbrella regulator to be known as the Financial Services Supervisory Commission. *Economist* (May 7, 1994).

Chapter Six

Regulatory Reform British Style: The Separation of Regulatory Powers

The British government chose to regulate the telecommunications and financial services industries for very different reasons, so naturally it reformed regulation in these two industries for different reasons, at different times, and in different ways. Yet behind the obvious differences, reforms in these two sectors follow a common pattern. But to generalize about the British approach to regulatory reform, we must first survey regulatory reforms in other sectors. After all, telecommunications and financial services share certain characteristics, such as rapid technological progress and the internationalization of markets. We can identify a wider pattern only by extending our analysis to other sectors.

REGULATORY REFORM IN OTHER SECTORS

Broadcasting

The British government's regulatory reform program has taken perhaps its most bizarre turn in the field of broadcasting. As the Thatcher decade began, the broadcasting regime was both simple and popular. The television sector was characterized by a duopoly of the public British Broadcasting Corporation (Channels BBC-1 and BBC-2), which was financed by license fees, and Independent Television (Channel 3), which was financed by advertising revenues. The BBC dominated radio as well, with a monopoly on national radio and some competition from private stations in local markets. The Independent Broadcasting Authority (IBA) had the dual function of running the Independent Television (ITV) network and regulating independent television and independent radio. The

Home Office had responsibility for overall broadcasting policy as well as for supervision of the IBA.

The Thatcher administration began with two important yet relatively uncontroversial reforms. First, it opened the cable television market. In 1981, the Home Office licensed thirteen new independent cable operators. Prior to this, cable companies only had been able to relay transmissions from established broadcast stations. Then in 1982, the Information Technology Advisory Panel (ITAP) report recognized cable as a critical element in government plans for the rapid growth of the information technology sector.[1] The 1984 Cable and Broadcasting Act built on the report's recommendations, introducing cable television on a permanent basis and creating the Cable Authority to regulate competition. Second, in 1982, the government created Channel 4, a national station with a mandate to provide programming for minority audiences. The new channel found supporters on both the Left and the Right who felt that the new station would give more expression to their views.[2] Thatcherites liked it because it would bring in entrepreneurial producers to challenge the existing duopoly.[3]

In 1985, the government appointed the Peacock Committee to investigate the possibility of commercializing the BBC, a proposal favored by Mrs. Thatcher herself. The Committee recommended a major overhaul of broadcasting regulation, featuring the familiar mix of more competition and more regulation with a novel twist: it proposed to auction off ITV licenses. It suggested that the auction would provide much-needed revenue, which could be used to pay for the BBC. It also recommended additional regulation as a surrogate for free market competition, which could never be fully attained in the broadcasting sector: "Collective provision and regulation of programs does provide a better simulation of a market designed to reflect consumer preferences than a policy of laissez-faire."[4] Under the subsequent 1990 Broadcasting Act, the government opened independent television and radio stations to competition, establishing a new regime to auction licenses and regulate competition. The Act also required the BBC and ITV to obtain at least 25 percent of their programming from independent producers. It divided the IBA's regulatory responsibilities between two new regulators: the Independent Television Commission (ITC) and the Radio Authority. The new authorities were specifically designed to serve as independent regulators, as opposed to the IBA, which was both regulator and broadcaster. In addition to these two new regulators, the government had already created the Broadcast Standards Council in 1989 to promote higher standards of de-

[1] Information Technology Advisory Panel, Cabinet Office (1982).
[2] Curran (1992), pp. 91–92.
[3] Thatcher (1993), p. 635.
[4] As quoted in Curran (1992), p. 93.

cency in program content. The net result has been greater institutional confusion within the sector, since the Home Office, the Office of Fair Trading (OFT), the Office of Telecommunications (Oftel), the Broadcasting Complaints Commission, and the Broadcasting Standards Council are all involved in broadcast regulation in addition to the three primary regulators.[5] Then after John Major took over, the sponsoring authority shifted from the Home Office to the Department of National Heritage.

As in the telecommunications and finance cases, the new regulatory regime reflects a shift from informal supervision to legalistic regulation. The regime's philosophy is to specify regulatory requirements clearly in licenses, codes, and guidelines, and then leave the licensees freedom within this framework—rather than to advise or intervene on specific programming decisions. The ITC does not preview programs or screen program schedules, but rather evaluates program content after the fact. It has more regulatory bite than its predecessor, since it can levy fines in the case of infractions, as well as issue warnings, require public apologies, or shorten or withdraw licenses. The regulatory system is now more severe, more extensive, and more complex. "We are supposed to have a lighter regulatory touch than the 'Nanny' IBA," notes the ITC's Peter Monteith, "but this is not the case at all. We regulate now more than ever."[6]

The new competition reached a frenzied pitch in 1991 as incumbent stations and new challengers jousted for the sixteen independent television franchises to be auctioned in October (Table 6). The auction had some unusual quirks. Bidders were to be evaluated on both the quality of their proposed programming and the monetary value of their bid. But to add to the suspense, a bidder could bid too high as well as too low. That is, the ITC could deny a franchise if it judged that a candidate had bid more than it could afford. A total of forty-one groups ended up bidding for franchises. Confident incumbents won franchises for as little as £1000, whereas Carlton bid a whopping £43 million—to be paid annually, plus an adjustment for inflation—for the London weekday franchise. Some of those who won paid so dearly that they have barely survived their own victory, and ITC officials worry publicly whether these franchises will maintain quality standards. Recognizing that many of the franchises are too small to compete either domestically or internationally, the government invited a series of mergers by relaxing restrictions on takeovers in November 1993.[7] Fourteen companies failed to pass the quality threshold, and three lost because they were judged to have bid too much. One of those that overbid, TSW Broadcasting, appealed the decision through judicial

---

[5] Glencross (1991).

[6] Interview with Peter Monteith, public relations officer, ITC (May 5, 1993).

[7] *Economist* (November 27, 1993), p. 60.

Table 6. The Channel Three franchise auction, October 1991

License area	Winner (bid in 1993 £1000s)	Other applicants (bids in 1993 £1000s)
Borders & Isle of Man	Border Television (£52)	
Central Scotland	Scottish Television (£2)	
Channel Islands	Channel Television (£1)	* C13 Group (£102)
E., W. & S. Midlands	Central Independent TV (£2)	
East of England	Anglia Television (£17,804)	* CPV-TV (£10,125)
		* Three East Television (£14,078)
London Weekly	Carlton Television (£43,170)	* CPV-TV (£45,319)
		Thames Television (£32,794)
London Weekend	LWT (£7,585)	* Consortium for Independent Broadcasting (£35,406)
North of Scotland	Grampian Television (£7,200)	* C3 Caledonia (£1,125)
		* North of Scotland TV (£2,709)
North-East England	Tyne Tees Television (£15,057)	North-East Television (£5,010)
North-West England	Granada Television (£9,000)	* North-West Television (£35,303)
Northern Ireland	Ulster Television (£1,027)	• TVNi (£3,100)
		* Lagan Television (£2,712)
South & S.E. England	Meridian Broadcasting (£36,523)	Carlton Television (£18,080)
		* CPV-TV (£22,105)
		• TVS Television (£59,758)
South-West England	Westcountry Television (£7,815)	* Telewest (£7,266)
		• TSW Broadcasting (£16,117)
Wales & W. of England	HTV Group (£20,530)	C3W (£17,760)
		* Channel 3 Wales & W. (£18,289)
		* Merlin Television (£19,367)
Yorkshire	Yorkshire Television (£37,700)	* Viking Television (£30,116)
		White Rose Television (£17, 403)
National Breakfast-time	Sunrise Television (£34,610)	Daybreak Television (£33,261)
		TV-am (£14,125)

SOURCE: ITC

* Failed to pass quality threshold

• Overbid

review, but lost the appeal. Four incumbents lost their franchises because they were outbid, including the popular Thames Television in London. The newly dethroned Mrs. Thatcher wrote a personal letter of apology to the station's president, recognizing that this unfortunate outcome was the unintended consequence of her zealous pursuit of competition as prime minister.[8] In 1995, the ITC ran a second auction, for the new Channel 5, with its own strange twists. Media magnate Rupert Murdoch's New Century Television bid a surprisingly paltry £2 million, and two other candidates suspiciously submitted identical bids of £22.002 million.[9]

[8] Davidson (1992) captures the spirit of the franchise auction in its full frenzy.
[9] *Economist* (May 6, 1995), pp. 55–56.

Transportation

The government has moved somewhat more cautiously in the transport industries because of even greater political sensitivity and the Department of Transport's relatively conservative approach. It began with the long-distance coach industry, which had several qualities that made it a prime candidate for liberalization: the technical and financial barriers to entry were low; the industry already had an element of competition with other means of transport; and most critical, the government anticipated little political resistance to reform.[10] The deregulation of trucking in 1968 was widely regarded as a success, and even the Labour Party had considered a partial deregulation of busing in the late 1970s. In its 1979 Manifesto, the Conservative Party only mentioned one specific sector as a target for deregulation: buses. Conservative MP Norman Fowler had written a paper recommending deregulation in the busing industry, and he encouraged the party leadership to include his proposal in the Manifesto.[11] Fowler himself became Thatcher's first secretary of state for transport, so he naturally pressed ahead to fulfill the Manifesto commitment. As in the case of telecommunications reform, zealous ministers successfully converted civil servants who were comfortable with the status quo. The new government moved quickly, passing the Transport Act in October 1980. The Act effectively eliminated price and entry controls for long-distance coaches, shifted the burden of proof in license disputes from the applicant companies to the regulatory authorities, and established trial areas for deregulation in local bus service as well. The Act simultaneously strengthened the Traffic Commissioners' regulation over bus drivers' licenses and vehicle maintenance standards, because it would become more difficult to monitor standards directly as more private companies entered the business. The project succeeded in the short run; a large number of companies entered the market and prices dropped dramatically. Six smaller companies joined to form a national consortium, British Coachways. But the National Bus Company (NBC) quickly responded by matching its competitors' prices and improving its services and pushed British Coachways out of business in January 1983.[12]

The government then decided to move further.[13] Under the 1985 Transport Act, it privatized NBC as fifty-two separate regional companies and deregulated local bus service, except in London. Its primary motiva-

[10] Interview with Patrick Brown, permanent secretary, Department of Transport (October 29, 1991).

[11] Fowler (1977).

[12] Most economists who have studied the reform agree that there have been benefits from competition in terms of higher quality if not lower prices. See, for example, Jaffer and Thompson (November 1986), Hibbs (1989), and Glaister (1991).

[13] The Department announced its intentions in Department of Transport (July 1984).

tion was not to promote competition, but to reduce spending on subsidies.[14] It eliminated general subsidies so that local authorities wishing to subsidize unprofitable lines would have to solicit competitive tenders. The local authorities proved to be the strongest opponents of the reforms, for the Act threatened their sovereignty over local transport systems. The government skillfully neutralized union opposition, presenting the reform as an expansion of consumer choice and disguising their goal of facilitating cost reductions through layoffs. New companies have entered the market, but there have been widespread complaints of predatory behavior on the part of incumbents. The OFT had reportedly received 570 such complaints by 1995. Meanwhile, the quality of service had degenerated and the buses themselves had deteriorated so greatly by 1995 that the government began making plans to reregulate the industry.[15]

After much debate over the regulation of London's taxis, Steven Norris, a junior minister in the Department of Transport, managed to put modest reform on the agenda in 1994. The sector is divided into two groups: "black" cabs, which are subject to strict regulation in exchange for the right to ply for hire for customers off the street, and mini-cabs, which must rely on calls but which are virtually free of regulation. The irony in this case is that the mini-cabs have called for more regulation to make them more legitimate and therefore more competitive with the black cabs. Norris and his colleagues therefore proposed that the government strengthen regulations for the mini-cabs and drop some of the most arcane regulations still governing the black cabs.[16]

In the airline sector, the United Kingdom has led Europe in liberalization. In 1984, the Civil Aviation Authority (CAA) conducted a comprehensive review of airline regulation, recommending liberalization combined with pro-competitive regulation to control the dominant player, British Airways.[17] On the basis of the CAA review, the government opened domestic routes to free entry and reduced price regulations to a notification requirement. But the government rejected CAA proposals for measures to actively promote competition, such as transferring some of British Airways' routes to other carriers.[18] Vickers and Yarrow argue that the government was reluctant to foster too much competition because it was simultaneously planning the privatization of British Airways.[19] Shortly after privatization, British Airways solidified its dominant position by buying out British Caledonian. Under the 1986 Airports Act, the government pri-

---

[14] Glaister (1991).

[15] *The Times* (October 24, 1995).

[16] *Economist* (April 2, 1994), pp. 56–57.

[17] Civil Aviation Authority (1984).

[18] Department of Transport (1984).

[19] Vickers and Yarrow (1988), pp. 342–66. Also see Swann (1988), pp. 241–43, 275–79.

vatized the British Airports Authority and introduced a new regime to regulate airports. The British government has also pushed for further liberalization within the European Union (EU). The EU liberalized price and market entry regulations substantially under its Third Aviation Package of 1993, and the European Council has since committed to further liberalization by 1997.

Britain arrived at railway reform relatively late, but has gone farther with innovative modes of pro-competitive reregulation than any other country. The government had considered privatization throughout the 1980s, but stalled in the face of three problems. The privatization would be especially difficult because British Rail was unprofitable; the regulatory changes would be unusually complex because of the particularities of railway economics; and the policy as a whole would be politically sensitive, since the public had a strong emotional attachment to the railways. Even as the government decided to move forward in 1990, the relevant departments and ministers debated at length how they should proceed. The more radical liberalizers, including Thatcher herself, argued that the railways should move toward the road transport model, with the government providing an infrastructure on which service providers could freely compete. The more moderate group proposed that British Rail be divided into private monopolies, including an intercity (long-distance) rail service, a freight company, and several regional railways.[20] The government announced its decision in 1992: a single public track authority, Railtrack, would provide the infrastructure, and the government would auction franchises to service providers. The potential franchisees could offer either a positive or negative bid: that is, they could bid to pay for a lucrative franchise, or they could demand a subsidy to provide unprofitable service. In principle, the government would award the franchise to the candidate offering the highest bid, or demanding the lowest subsidy. Parliament passed the Railways Act in November 1993, producing a regulatory system of daunting complexity. Railtrack determines train routes and provides the network, and charges the franchisees for its services. The franchising director defines the services to be franchised and then offers these to independent train operators under competitive tender. And a new independent regulator, the Office of the Rail Regulator (ORR), licenses the operators, sets the rules of fair play for competition between operators, and regulates the prices that Railtrack charges the operators and that operators charge passengers. As in telecommunications, privatization and regulatory reform have had the paradoxical effect of reducing the operator's freedom and strengthening government regulation. The overlapping of regulatory jurisdiction combined with the

[20] Thatcher (1993), pp. 686–87.

inherent ambiguities of the legislation has increased the possibility that regulatory matters will have to be resolved through litigation. The government has recognized that the new regime opens up the possibility of franchisee failure, and the legislation makes provisions for the government to intervene to provide service in the case of such failure. If the government chooses to close a particular route, it is required to hold public hearings before doing so.[21] The new regime went into effect in April 1994, and the rail system was plagued by a series of strikes by rail workers that continued through September. In May 1995, the government announced more detailed plans for the regulatory regime, pledging to restrict the franchisees' ability to raise fares.[22] The government scheduled the first auction for December 1995 and the privatization of Railtrack for April 1996, ensuring that the process would be well under way before any Labour administration could attempt to unravel it.[23] In the meantime, the independent companies created in anticipation of privatization have wreaked havoc on railway service: raising prices, canceling services, and refusing to invest in new railway cars.[24]

The Public Utilities

The greatest regulatory change, excluding telecommunications and finance, has come in the public utilities: gas, electricity, and water. In each of these cases, the government has combined privatization with liberalization and reregulation. The government has encountered the most trouble with British Gas (BG), which it privatized as a whole in 1986. Critics have argued that the government could have created competition much more effectively by breaking up BG, but that it refrained from doing so in the interest of a successful privatization.[25] The Gas Act of 1986 established a new independent regulator on the model of Oftel: the Office of Gas Supply (Ofgas). The Act divided the market into two sectors: a "tariff" sector serving primarily household customers and a "contract" sector serving large corporations. Ofgas regulates prices in the tariff sector, but BG can negotiate prices freely in the contract sector. The authorities liberalized the contract sector because they felt that BG would face effective competition from other sources of energy. Ofgas uses an RPI-X price-cap formula like Oftel, but has added an extra variable to the formula to account for fluctuations in the cost of gas supplied to BG.

---

[21] Glaister and Travers (April 1993).

[22] *Economist* (May 20, 1995), pp. 54–55.

[23] The *Economist* (January 21, 1995, p. 20) reported that 64 percent of British voters opposed the privatization and only 16 percent approved.

[24] *Sunday Times* (October 15, 1995).

[25] For example: Vickers and Yarrow (1988), pp. 245–81; Veljanovski (1991).

Since the regulatory system began operation, BG has clashed frequently with Ofgas and the OFT. As Sir James McKinnon, director-general of Ofgas until 1993, put it: "BG's position was that gas is *their* business. So you could not expect them to like the competition policy. In fact, they have done everything they could to prevent competition. We have had a bad relationship with them, unfortunately but perhaps inevitably, and the acrimony has only increased over the years."[26] From BG's perspective, Ofgas has gone far beyond its remit to allow competition and has actively promoted BG's competitors. BG executives were outraged that they would be required to assist their own competitors by allowing access to BG pipelines and by providing backup for these competitors in the case of a sudden shortage. In 1987 the OFT referred BG to the Monopoly and Mergers Commission (MMC) for monopolistic pricing in the contract sector. The MMC ruled against BG in October 1988, subjecting BG to new restrictions.[27] In response to the MMC judgment, the OFT and Ofgas conducted a joint study of the contract sector, finding that competitors had gained only one to two percent of the market. As a result they proposed that BG give up more than 50 percent of the contract market to competitors and allow some liberalization in the retail sector as well. They threatened a referral to the MMC if BG would not agree, and BG conceded in December 1991. Ofgas infuriated BG executives further by publicly stating that BG should be broken up in order to allow true competition in the gas market. By August 1992, BG was so frustrated with Ofgas that it took the risky step of initiating its own appeal to the MMC for an extensive review of gas regulation.[28] BG contended that Ofgas unreasonably restricted its rate of return in certain business segments and constantly changed regulations, making it impossible for the company to set long-term plans. In 1993, the MMC offered its judgment: BG must be broken up.

For water, the government privatized the regional monopoly suppliers in 1989. The water companies have been allowed to diversify, but they still face no competition in their core business. The new regulator, the Office of Water Supply (Ofwat), has also adopted a variant of the RPI-X formula for price regulation. In addition, Ofwat has introduced a regulatory innovation that has been recommended by economists for some time: yardstick competition. Ofwat compares the rates charged in different regions—factoring in cost differentials—to assess the relative cost performance of each group. If one regional company charges rates considerably higher than Ofwat judges to be reasonable, Ofwat can force it to lower

---

[26] Interview with Sir James McKinnon, director general, Office of Gas Supply (May 4, 1993).

[27] Borrie (1991), p. 88.

[28] Technically, the DTI made the appeal on BG's behalf, after BG executives approached DTI Secretary of State Michael Heseltine. Ofgas also made its own appeal at the same time.

them. Even so, water prices—unlike telecommunications, gas, and electricity prices—have risen considerably faster than inflation.[29] The government also replaced its direct control over water resource development prior to privatization with yet another independent regulator, the National River Authority, in 1989. Nicholas Ridley, environment secretary at the time, had argued persuasively that water authorities should not be permitted to combine supply and regulatory functions.[30]

The government has gone the furthest toward creating competition in the case of electricity, breaking up the electricity company prior to privatization in 1990. It separated the national grid, considered to be the natural monopoly component of the business, from nineteen other companies. Stephen Littlechild, the author of RPI-X himself, took over as director general of the new regulatory body, the Office of Electricity Regulation (Offer). Littlechild has argued that Offer has benefited from the experiences of the other new regulators and enjoys more "teeth" than its predecessors. Specifically, Offer can resolve disputes between electric companies and their customers, and it has greater powers to demand information from the companies.[31] Yet ironically, Littlechild has come under heavy criticism for being too lenient on the regional electricity companies. Electricity company profits and executive salaries soared under the RPI-X formula that he inherited from the government, and he failed to fully rectify the situation when he revised the formula in August 1994 (effective April 1995). He then publicly announced plans to cut prices further in March 1995, violating the spirit of the price-cap regime, which calls for revisions only once every five years. To make matters worse, his timing was more than a little bit suspicious, coming two days after the government had sold shares in two electricity generating companies.[32] He then ordered a second round of price cuts in July. Even so, potential profits in the sector have continued to generate takeover activity, including the September 1995 buyout of one regional electric company by Southern Electric of the United States.

The Deregulation Unit

Beyond these sectoral initiatives, the Department of Trade and Industry (DTI) has taken the lead in a deregulation program that spans all lines of business. The effort began as a departmental initiative under Keith Joseph to eradicate many of the department's industrial policy functions—to dismantle the old Department of Industry. But the DTI only transformed

[29] *Economist* (August 13, 1994), p. 64.
[30] Thatcher (1993), p. 682.
[31] Littlechild (1991), pp. 114–15.
[32] *Economist* (March 11, 1995), p. 74.

deregulation into a heroic task under Lord Young in 1987. The DTI had begun a modest economy-wide deregulation program in 1985, focusing on the elimination of bureaucratic procedures that pose an unnecessary burden on businesses, especially smaller businesses. Meanwhile, Young had organized an informal task force on deregulation in the Cabinet Committee in 1985, and he took it with him as he moved to the Department of Employment in 1986 and to the DTI in 1987, where it became the Enterprise and Deregulation Unit. Prime Minister Thatcher enthusiastically supported the idea. "While other ministers bring me problems," she was quoted as saying, "Lord Young brings me solutions."[33]

The purpose of the Unit was to attack excessive regulation by all government departments. It worked through a policy of "embedding," whereby a representative in each department would be assigned to promote deregulation within the department. But these representatives inevitably turned into double agents more loyal to their departments than to the Deregulation Unit, and instead of promoting the Unit's mission, ended up defending their departments against the Unit. The Unit developed a system of "efficiency scrutinies," whereby departments had to assess the costs of compliance for any new regulations, and then justify that cost. Officials within the Unit were only too aware that they were creating a bureaucracy to eliminate excessive bureaucracy. Thus the Unit remained "temporary" in status, subject to review every year or two. Lord Young also hoped to use the Unit to promote an enterprise culture. In a 1988 white paper, DTI officials attacked the interdependent relationships between government, business, and the unions, which they characterized as British "corporatism." They claimed that the private sector should be left alone as much as possible, left to regain its entrepreneurial spirit.[34] They coupled the publication of the white paper with a publicity campaign under the theme of "Releasing Enterprise." By fostering an enterprise culture, the new administration found a way to put a positive light on a policy for industry that centered on paring down the government's role and allowing market forces to operate more freely.[35]

Prime Minister John Major subsequently revived and redirected the deregulation initiative. In 1991, Major introduced the "Citizen's Charter," a program to improve public services through liberalization and regulatory and administrative reform. After the 1992 elections, the government merged the Civil Service Department and part of the Treasury into the Office of Public Services and Science, which administers the Citizen's Charter. Under the Charter's "Next Steps" program, the government ini-

[33] Interview with DTI official (July 1990).
[34] DTI (1988).
[35] On the DTI under Lord Young, see Grant (1989), especially pp. 90–93 and 102–3, and Wilks (Autumn 1989).

tiated a bold civil service reform to separate the functions of policy and implementation and gradually devolve routine implementation, such as the issuing of drivers' licenses, to quasi-autonomous executive agencies. Beyond this, the government introduced the "market-testing" of some civil service functions: putting them up for private-sector tender. In a July 1994 white paper, the government announced a further devolution of bureaucratic power, making departments much freer from central control. The report also proposed liberalizing the civil service labor market, giving civil servants greater opportunities for advancement but considerably reduced job security.[36] Major also focused on deregulation through a new program initiated in 1993 operating out of an invigorated Deregulation Unit at the DTI. The Unit shifted its emphasis from new regulations to existing regulations. Each department submitted a complete list of its regulations, and these were then scrutinized by task forces made up of civil servants and business people. The task forces recommended ways to eliminate unnecessary regulations and ease the burden of necessary ones. The government used a high-profile publicity campaign and a short, one-year time-frame for action to maximize the initiative's impact.[37] The only weakness in the exercise was that zealous civil servants often found the private sector representatives less than enthusiastic about deregulation. In any case, in January 1994, Board of Trade president Michael Heseltine announced with great fanfare a deregulation bill that would eliminate or revise 350 pieces of regulation.[38]

THE BRITISH PATTERN OF REGULATORY REFORM

Having reviewed evidence from five sectors, we can now characterize the British pattern of regulatory reform, a pattern that holds true across remarkably diverse sectors. I call this pattern "pro-competitive disengagement" because it involves both the active promotion of competition and a further detachment of government from industry. This pattern of regulatory reform has four main characteristics (see Table 7).

1. *The government aggressively promotes competition without managing market entry or exit.* The government has intervened heavily to promote competition, but generally has not tried to manipulate the outcome of its liberalization policies in terms of winners and losers in the marketplace. The government has aggressively employed pro-competitive reregulation to liberalize markets, formulating new rules to favor competitors over incumbents. Oftel, for example, has consciously used its regulatory powers

---

[36] *Economist* (July 16, 1994), pp. 47–48.
[37] Interview with Vivian Brown, head of the Deregulation Unit, DTI (May 6, 1993).
[38] *Economist* (January 22, 1994), pp. 60–61.

Table 7. The British pattern of regulatory reform

Regime orientation:	Regulatory
Regime organization:	Segmented
Overall pattern of reform:	Pro-competitive disengagement

1. The government aggressively promotes competition without managing entry or exit. (bias toward *pro-competitive* reregulation)
2. The government fragments regulatory authority.
3. The government codifies and juridifies regulation. (bias toward *juridical* reregulation)
4. The government implements reform in an uneven and adversarial manner.

to help BT's competitors. Likewise, Ofgas has tightly constrained BG in the hope of fostering competition. Beyond setting these new rules, however, governmental departments and the new regulators have not tried to manage the transition toward greater competition. For example, when it came to admitting new dealers to the trade in gilt-edged shares, the Bank of England deliberately chose not to control entry. Bank officials were certain that the market could not support more than fifteen dealers, but they were perfectly happy to let twenty-nine enter a crowded market and then fight it out. In the case of the telecommunications duopoly, of course, the government initially limited entry to a single firm, but this was considered a practical necessity in order to create competition. DTI officials were persuaded that only a unified firm would survive competition with British Telecom (BT), for multiple competitors would only kill each other off—to the benefit of BT. When it came to the duopoly review, however, the DTI insisted that there would be no more "beauty contests." The government would not try to analyze market potential and then choose between license applicants, but would let in as many firms as applied and then leave them to the mercy of the marketplace.

Likewise, the Thatcher government did not try to limit market exit. It pursued pro-competitive reform to the point where it welcomed the failure of specific firms, even British firms. Thatcher and her colleagues believed that competition would make some firms stronger, but they accepted that it would eliminate others. In fact, they felt that many of these firms *should* fail. In telecommunications, the British government was astonishingly indifferent to the welfare of the equipment manufacturing industry. The government declared that it was happy to buy its telephones from abroad—and it meant it. The result has been the merger of General Electric Company (GEC) and Plessey, a precipitous drop in world market share, and the loss of thousands of jobs. In the finance case, the government was similarly indifferent to the fate of British stockbrokers. In broadcasting, the government introduced a franchise auction system that eliminated several established and respected broadcast companies.

Those in the Thatcher camp envisioned the United Kingdom as a service economy and a business center for the world. The government allowed uncompetitive British manufacturers to fail, but also encouraged foreign multinationals to locate in Britain—even in competition with domestic firms. This explains why government officials have been particularly attuned to the competitive dynamic between national regulators examined in Chapter 1. They have promoted "deregulation" because they believe that it makes the United Kingdom more attractive as a location for manufacturing, commerce, or finance. In contrast, Japanese government officials have been far less concerned about retaining a competitive advantage in regulation, for they are more interested in strengthening their own manufacturers and banks than in attracting those of other countries. The British government's willingness to allow free market entry and exit also reflects a broader acceptance of the market disruptions inherent in the liberalization process. It has not made any special effort to smooth the transition to greater competition, but has welcomed the disruptions involved. In contrast, the Japanese government has tried to orchestrate the liberalization process to minimize exactly this kind of market disruption.

2. *The government fragments regulatory authority.* More than any other country, the United Kingdom has coupled regulatory reform with institutional reform, shifting power from central government departments to new independent regulatory agencies. The government has created twelve major new independent regulatory agencies since 1979, including those for telecommunications, financial services, gas, water, electricity, and broadcasting (see Table 8). In telecommunications, the DTI now shares power with Oftel. And in financial services, the Treasury and the Bank of England now share power with the Securities and Investments Board (SIB) and the self-regulatory organizations. Remarkably, in neither case did the central agencies try to retain regulatory authority. This sort of institutional reform would be extremely difficult in the United States because of constitutional limits on reorganizing the state. It would be equally unlikely in Japan where central ministries zealously guard their authority. The British government began this pattern of institutional reform with Oftel, in part because City advisers insisted on a neutral regulator. Beyond their ideological preference for the separation of regulation from policy, Thatcher administration officials favored independent regulators because of the dynamics of alternance in British politics. The party in power wants to be able to infiltrate the bureaucracy, but by the same token wants to guard it from future infiltration by the other party. Thus Conservative Party leaders were keen to establish independent regulators that could not easily be "captured" by the Labour Party. The creation of these new regulators im-

Table 8. Major British regulatory agencies

Agency	Year formed	Industry regulated
Economic regulators		
Civil Aviation Authority	1971	Airports
Office of Telecommunications	1984	Telecommunications
Office of Gas Supply	1986	Gas
Office of Water Services	1989	Water
Office of Electricity Regulation	1990	Electricity
Office of the Rail Regulator	1993	Rail transport
Financial regulators		
Building Societies Commission	1986	Building societies
Securities and Investments Board	1986	Investment business
Quality regulators		
HM Inspectorate of Pollution	1987	All
National Rivers Authority	1989	Water
Broadcasting Standards Council	1990	Broadcasting
Independent Television Commission	1991	Television
Radio Authority	1991	Radio
Competition regulators		
Monopolies and Mergers Commission	1948	All
Office of Fair Trading	1951	All

Source: Adapted from Veljanovski, ed. (1991), p. 11.

plies a real loss in the government's capacity to intervene in markets. The government has created a more complicated bureaucracy to enforce regulation, so we still cannot refer to British reform as "deregulation" in the literal sense. But by separating the functions of regulation and sponsorship, the government has made it more difficult to integrate regulation into a broader industrial policy.

3. *The government codifies and juridifies regulation.* David Vogel and others have characterized the British regulatory style as particularly informal and consensual, but regulatory reform in the 1980s has moved it distinctly toward a more "U.S.-style" approach based on neutral criteria, fixed procedures, formal debate, and openness to appeal.[39] This decreases the bureaucracy's power by defining its authority and minimizing its discretion. Not surprisingly, these characteristics are most pronounced in the new regulatory agencies, such as Oftel and the SIB, and the least so in older agencies, such as the Health and Safety Commission. In part this trend follows naturally from the government's pro-competitive policy, which requires stronger and more sophisticated regulation to enforce competition. In addition, however, the belief in proper procedure and fair competition have made the United Kingdom particularly susceptible to

[39] D. Vogel (1986).

the American disease: more lawyers and ever more complex and detailed rules. And the British government's strong reliance on academic advisers—economists and lawyers such as Littlechild and Gower—has also pushed British regulation closer to the U.S. model. The government developed the RPI-X scheme precisely to ensure that regulation would be neutral, and the regulators have been developing more complex and sophisticated versions of RPI-X ever since. Likewise, the government has added new layers of complexity to the regulatory regimes in finance, broadcasting, and rail transport.

4. *The government implements regulatory reforms in an uneven and adversarial manner.* Without the corporatist links between government and industry, and without effective policy coordination within the government, no one agency has been able to orchestrate enduring resolutions to regulatory policy debates. Although the British system is still far from the adversarial U.S. model, regulatory reform has made it more prone to appeal and prolonged iterative decision making at the implementation stage. The new regimes in telecommunications, financial services, and the public utilities have all been characterized by repeated clashes between the new regulators and the regulated industries. And more often than not the process of negotiation and appeal has been extended, to the satisfaction of neither party. The most extreme case has come in the case of gas, where disputes have resulted in two debilitating appeals to the MMC, and public warfare between the BG and Ofgas by 1992.[40] In telecommunications, Mercury and BT have fought an extended regulatory battle over the terms of interconnection that has hampered the ability of either party to make long-term plans.[41] In financial services, some City practitioners were so outraged with the proliferation of rules embedded in the Financial Services Act (FSA) that they organized to oust the SIB's first chairman. The Bank of England's David Walker then took over and devised a somewhat less cumbersome regime, but continued dissatisfaction with the regulatory regime led to yet another major review of the system under Walker's successor, Andrew Large.

In terms of the typology of regulatory reforms (Table 1), the British approach reveals a strong bias toward pro-competitive and juridical reregu-

---

[40] Commentators have been especially critical of the United Kingdom's unwieldy competition policy regime. The *Economist* (April 1, 1995, p. 47) charges that it is "unpredictable, uncoordinated, unfair, and unduly expensive." Maggie Urry of the *Financial Times* (August 3, 1992) offers an entertaining commentary on the potential risks and substantial costs involved in an MMC appeal: "Volunteering to go before the UK Monopolies and Mergers Commission is like offering to stand before a firing squad playing Russian roulette. . . . Being summoned before the tribunal, whose members sit round a semi-circular table, gives 'a feeling of corporate nakedness that can best be compared to appearing before the House Unamerican Activities Committee. It is a very thorough process.' "

[41] Vickers and Yarrow (1988), p. 219.

lation. As noted in Chapter 1, both of these types of reregulation imply a loss of governmental control over industry. The legacy of these reforms is likely to endure, particularly because they have involved such extensive institutional innovations and because pro-competitive ideology has become embedded in a set of new regulatory institutions. The new regulators have an institutional interest in competition policy and economic regulation. And any future government will find it difficult to reverse course because this would require subverting these independent regulators, undermining their powers, or eliminating them outright. Even a new Labour government would not be likely to undo the Thatcher and Major reforms. In its long period in opposition, the Labour Party has changed considerably. In the early 1980s, the party insisted that it would renationalize the privatized industries, but by the early 1990s it had come to accept much of the privatization and deregulation program. In fact, it has tried to distinguish itself by a virulent defense of the consumer and by its insistence that the regulators be given yet more teeth.[42] In March 1995, the party revised Clause 4 of its constitution,[43] officially abandoning its commitment to national ownership of the means of production.

[42] Interview with a policy staff member for a leading Labour MP (October 1991).
[43] *Economist* (March 18, 1995), p. 59.

Part III

REGULATORY REFORM
IN JAPAN

CHAPTER SEVEN

Telecommunications:
Reregulation with a Vengeance

As we have seen, what has been called "deregulation" has sometimes had the paradoxical effect of increasing the regulator's power. Some British or U.S. regulators may have been relieved that deregulation did not render them obsolete, and a few even may have tried to design reform specifically to maintain their authority. But only Japan's Ministry of Posts and Telecommunications (MPT) deliberately pursued regulatory reform as a means to augment its power. Japan's telecommunications reform thus provides the extreme case of reregulation: reregulation not by coincidence but by intent.

On the surface, the Japanese telecommunications story follows the pattern of British reform to an astonishing degree. Both governments initiated telecommunications reform as part of a neoconservative deregulation movement. Both were responding in part to the U.S. deregulation begun in the 1970s. Both started working seriously on legislation to liberalize the use of telephone lines in 1980 and passed legislation to privatize the telecommunications carrier in 1984. The managers of the two monopolies were ambivalent toward reform: they believed in the virtues of a public monopoly, but they also realized that reform could bring them higher salaries and greater freedom from political intervention. The unions officially opposed reform, but softened their opposition in exchange for certain concessions, the most important of which was a commitment not to break up the company. Most equipment manufacturers resisted reform because they feared that it would jeopardize their privileged relations with the dominant service provider. The major opposition parties protested the changes, arguing that the ruling parties were sacrificing the public interest in the name of private profits. And in the end, both countries privatized the carriers and introduced competition—albeit managed competition—to all segments of the market.

Despite these similarities, the Japanese political leaders and ministry officials who led the telecommunications reform effort pursued different goals from their British counterparts, guided the reform through a different political process, and produced a strikingly different new regulatory regime. Japan's MPT seized new regulatory responsibilities; whereas the United Kingdom's Department of Trade and Industry (DTI) passed them on to the Office of Telecommunications (Oftel). The MPT enhanced its role as a protector and promoter of the telecommunications industry, whereas the DTI all but absolved itself of this function. The MPT developed a regulatory system that leaves it considerable discretion over the many small decisions regarding changing prices or introducing new services, whereas Oftel devised a more rigid price cap system, which it supplements with periodic judgments on specific disputes.

The MPT's opportunity for advancement came with the growth of the sector it was supposed to be regulating: telecommunications. Prior to reform, the ministry exercised only minimal supervisory authority over the mammoth telecommunications operator, the Nippon Telegraph and Telephone Public Corporation (NTT). To make matters worse, the MPT's neighbor, the Ministry of International Trade and Industry (MITI), was threatening to become the lead ministry for the expanding information technology sector that joins communications with computers. The telecommunications case is thus unusual in the sense that the lead ministry was not trying to protect its authority over its proper jurisdiction so much as to establish this authority in the first place. The story of reform thus provides us with a unique opportunity to understand the foundations of ministerial authority, by analyzing what levers the MPT sought and what mechanisms it has employed to gain more influence over the industry.

The MPT did not initiate the telecommunications reform, nor did it design the reform without making substantial concessions to other agencies and to relevant interest groups. The U.S. precedent of deregulation highlighted the need for reform, and the Administrative Reform Commission (Rinchō) provided the immediate impetus domestically. But the ministry shaped the final content of reform more than any other actor. In fact, the MPT sculpted a regulatory system that plays havoc with the Rinchō's deregulatory intent. The ministry enhanced its own power and prestige, gaining an element of vengeance over NTT and joining MITI among the ranks of Japan's elite policy ministries. The MPT invented a new activist role for itself, complete with financial incentives for research and development and the promotion of private sector collaboration. Ironically, at a time when MITI was publicly renouncing industrial policy, the MPT was just getting started.

THE OLD REGIME

In Japan, the central bureaucracy controlled the development of modern communications systems from the beginning. Although a number of private companies had shown interest in getting into the telephone business, the government decided in 1889 to extend the Communications Ministry's monopoly over telegraph service to telephone service as well. It justified this policy on the basis that a government monopoly could best expand service to rural areas and preserve security, and in any case most other countries had government telephone monopolies.[1] The government began the transition from manual to automatic exchanges after the great earthquake of 1923, which destroyed much of the old network. It used two competing systems of connection, one German and one British, but manufactured in Japan under license. The incompatibility of the two systems effectively prevented the creation of an integrated national network. The telephone system was once again decimated, even more thoroughly, during the Second World War. The U.S. Occupation forces found the dismal state of the network a major hindrance in trying to organize economic recovery programs and soon issued a memorandum ordering the reorganization of the telecommunications system.[2]

The Ministry of Communications was subsequently split into two, one ministry for posts and the other for telecommunications. At the end of the Occupation, Prime Minister Shigeru Yoshida and others pushed for the creation of a private telecommunications carrier. Eisaku Satō, the minister of telecommunications at the time, opposed the plan, insisting that the ministry should provide all telecommunications services. The two sides in this debate reached a compromise in 1952 whereby the Ministry of Telecommunications became NTT, a public corporation with a monopoly over domestic telecommunications. The Ministry of Posts became the Ministry of Posts and Telecommunications, with supervisory responsibilities for NTT. Kokusai Denshin Denwa (KDD), a government-regulated corporation, became the monopoly provider of international telecommunications services. NTT was guaranteed a monopoly over domestic telephone and telegraph service and the supply of telephones.[3] The Diet had to approve NTT's budget on an annual basis and reviewed the corporation's plans for investment. NTT executives considered themselves civil servants rather than businessmen, and senior managers were regularly called to testify before the Diet. In 1956, after a scandal concerning excessive overtime payments in order to circumvent constraints on wages,

[1] Y. Itō (1986), p. 206.

[2] Hills (1986), pp. 102–3.

[3] On the early history of NTT, see Nippon Telegraph and Telephone Public Corporation (1977), especially pp. 4–19.

the Diet prohibited NTT from adjusting the portion of its budget allocated to wages. NTT workers were considered civil servants and thus were denied the right to strike.

After the war, government leaders incorporated telecommunications into their larger scheme for state-led economic growth.[4] They put a high priority on rebuilding the telecommunications infrastructure because this would both support the telecommunications equipment industry and enhance the productivity of corporate users. Nevertheless, they left the specifics up to the new public corporation, which after all had only just transformed from a government ministry. NTT set two specific targets related to its mission of building up the telecommunications infrastructure: fully meeting the demand for telephone service and creating a national direct-dial network. The goal of providing universal service was itself a daunting task, for in 1952 Japan had only 1.5 million telephones for a population of 100 million.[5] NTT was more effective than British Telecom (BT) in investing in the network because it came up with a unique source of funds. Prohibited by law from raising call rates, NTT generated more than half of its investment funds by requiring new subscribers to buy telephone bonds for ¥100,000 each ($278 at ¥360=$).[6] Subscribers could resell these bonds, along with the right to access which they represented, but would incur a loss in the transaction.

Like most European post, telegraph, and telephone authorities (PTTs), NTT developed a strong cooperative relationship with a group of telecommunications equipment manufacturers. NTT's "family" of suppliers centered around NEC, Hitachi, Fujitsu, and Oki Electric. NTT provided a stable market and performed basic research, but relied on the suppliers' participation in major research and development projects. NTT's Electrical Communications Laboratory, designed after the U.S. Bell Labs, worked together with the manufacturers in designing, manufacturing, and testing telecommunications equipment. NTT encouraged cooperation in research, but competition in manufacture. In most cases, at least two companies would produce test models of a given piece of equipment and compete for the procurement contract. NTT's research and development system was not only critical in developing Japan's telecommunications technology, but also in nurturing the computer and semiconductor industries.[7]

---

[4] Johnson (1982) and Tyson and Zysman (1989) are among the many who stress the role of the state in Japan's economic growth. See Noble (1989) and McKean (1993) for overviews of the considerable literature both supporting and criticizing this perspective.

[5] Hills (1986), p. 103.

[6] Anchordoguy (1989), p. 41.

[7] Ibid., especially pp. 39–42.

The basic principles of the postwar telecommunications system—monopoly service provision, uniform technical standards, high investment in infrastructure, and cooperative research and development—became more entrenched over time, particularly since they seemed to be remarkably successful. NTT attained its dual goals of universal service and nationwide direct dialing in 1977 and 1978. The Japanese regime, unlike the British, was characterized by a broad consensus on goals and a dependable means of providing capital for investment in infrastructure. In addition, the centralization of authority within NTT facilitated the network's rapid development. And yet the regime's peculiar structure also held the seeds of its own demise.

The regime's organization influenced the course of reform in two different ways. First, tensions in the relationships between the three major actors in telecommunications policy shaped their approach to telecommunications reform. MPT officials' lack of effective authority over NTT motivated them to try to manipulate the reform process to gain control over telecommunications policy. NTT, meanwhile, hoped to escape from political intervention without subjecting itself to equally debilitating ministerial control. Furthermore, the ambiguity in the division of labor between the MPT and MITI over the promising area of information technology created an epic turf battle between the two ministries. Second, the MPT officials' leading role in drafting and implementing the reform legislation gave them the capability to formulate the reform in order to enhance the ministry's prestige and maximize their own discretion.

Prior to reform, NTT was the dominant force within the telecommunications regime. NTT set the technical and safety standards for its equipment. NTT officials handled most of the "politics" of telecommunications policy—meaning relations with the Diet. And NTT controlled the research and development system. The regime was centralized, but in NTT and not the MPT.

By law, however, the MPT was designated as the lead ministry within the telecommunications sector. A lead ministry's jurisdiction is typically defined by the industries it oversees. The sectoral policy network is organized around the lead ministry through ministry-sanctioned industry associations.[8] Within this system, the MPT prior to reform was a ministry with some decisive weaknesses. It had very few "client" companies: only NTT, KDD, and the broadcasting companies. To make matters worse, as we have seen, NTT pretty much ran its own show. When NTT separated from the ministry in 1952, Japanese leaders gave the Diet control over NTT's budget but offered the MPT only minimal supervisory responsibilities. Legend has it that the "best and the brightest"

---

[8] See Wilks and Wright, eds. (1991), on policy networks in Japan.

from the ministry went to NTT. Those officials remaining at the ministry initially accepted NTT's *de facto* control over telecommunications policy because they were content to run the postal service and the postal savings and insurance system. The MPT maintained a small Telecommunications Supervision Bureau, with a staff of thirty to forty, but the position of one of the two lead inspectors in this bureau was reserved for an NTT official on a two-year rotation. Cynically viewed, one could say that NTT ran its routine business affairs and supervised itself through its office within the MPT.[9] The few MPT bureaucrats in the Telecommunications Supervision Office gradually became more frustrated with their lack of authority, and this frustration ultimately motivated their drive for regulatory reform.[10]

Liberal Democratic Party (LDP) Diet members intervened in telecommunications policy selectively, when they saw political advantage in getting involved. Generally they were more interested in using their influence to bring services to their districts than in debating telecommunications policy.[11] Beginning in the 1970s, LDP policy specialists increasingly formed "tribes" (*zoku*) centered around the various divisions of the party's Policy Research Council.[12] LDP members were particularly interested in becoming postal/telecommunications *zoku* because the postal system includes more than 30,000 branch post offices, which can be mobilized highly effectively at election time. Otherwise, these *zoku* benefited from ties to the construction and telecommunications equipment industries, both of which were important donors to the party. In 1983, more than two hundred LDP members formed the New Media Parliamentary Federation (*nyū media giin renmei*) to promote "Teletopias" and other telecommunications infrastructure projects in local areas.[13] Given the LDP's prolonged rule (1955–93), the opposition parties had relatively little influence on telecommunications policy. The Social Democratic Party of Japan (SDPJ) was involved by virtue of its ties with the NTT union, the Japan Telecommunication Workers Union (*zenkoku denki tsūshin rōdō kumiai*, or "Zendentsū" for short). Zendentsū was both unusually powerful and uniquely moderate: it never staged a strike, leaving it with an enormous strike fund, which could be used for political purposes. Its greatest source of power, however, was its influence over NTT itself.

[9] Johnson (1989), p. 190.
[10] Interview with Tetsurō Tomita, managing director, Fuji Television (December 21, 1990), interviews with MPT officials (1990–91).
[11] One LDP staff member lamented: "Unfortunately, our politicians do not understand questions dealing with bits-per-second and such." Interview, January 1991.
[12] The pathbreaking studies on the LDP's policy specialists are Nihon Keizai Shimbun (1983) and Inoguchi and Iwai (1987).
[13] Inoguchi and Iwai (1987), pp. 223–24.

New Challenges

The greatest strength of the telecommunications regime born in 1952 was that it facilitated concentrated investment in a unified network. Its greatest weakness was that it lacked the flexibility to satisfy the diverse needs of its users. Over time, this weakness became more pronounced as the regime failed to keep up with changes in the marketplace. The authorities did make some minor adjustments over the years. In 1957, for example, they allowed customers to provide their own extension (second) telephones. In 1970, they allowed customers to provide other attachments. But these makeshift adjustments were insufficient to respond to the rapid advances in telecommunications technology, and so the need for reform only grew.

In 1970, about a hundred young MPT bureaucrats organized a set of eight study groups to consider reforms in telecommunications policy. The group averaged thirty to thirty-five years old, with the rank of deputy section chief (*kachō hosa*) or the equivalent. In June 1971, they completed a report recommending the liberalization of value-added service markets and even questioning whether NTT should retain a monopoly at all. They proposed a "reorganization" of NTT, although they did not directly mention privatization. Even at this early date, these MPT officials saw reform as a way to position the MPT in its proper role as the lead agency in telecommunications field:

> Regarding the Ministry of Posts and Telecommunications, which oversees telecommunications policy at the present time, it seems as if the communications policy section were just incidentally attached to the core operational sections of the ministry. This arrangement leaves the ministry without a foundation upon which to build up a policy-making capability. In order to develop a new communications policy for this new era, we feel that it is all the more imperative to carry out a bold reform.[14]

In effect, the study group members proposed that the MPT be elevated from the status of an "operational agency" to a true "policy agency," like MITI or the Ministry of Finance (MoF). They divulged the contents of the report to the press, which applauded their recommendations, but the document itself was never officially released. In fact, MPT elders all but ignored the report because they were not prepared to undertake a reform of such proportions at that time. Nevertheless, the core group of reform-minded bureaucrats held on to their desire for change. When they gather these days, reports one member of the group, they congratulate them-

---

[14] MPT, Telecommunications Policy Issues Study Group (June 1971), p. 7.

selves on the fact that almost all of their recommendations were put into effect—albeit fifteen years after the fact.[15]

For their part, NTT managers saw problems as well. They believed in liberalization, but a particularly self-serving form of liberalization. They hoped to expand NTT's liberty to move into new areas, like value-added services, without threatening its monopoly in telephone service. They wanted greater freedom in setting prices, starting new services, and making personnel and investment decisions. They were particularly frustrated with the Diet's control over their budget, and the propensity of certain members of the Diet to interfere with routine business decisions. On at least five occasions after NTT's establishment, government advisory councils considered reforms to give NTT greater autonomy and flexibility in management. Among these, the Committee on the Basic Structure of the Three Public Corporations (*sankōsha kihon keieitai ni kansuru shōiinkai*), which reported in 1975, explicitly mentioned the possibility of privatizing or breaking up NTT into regional companies.[16]

Corporate users had their own concerns. They feared that without reform they would not be able to take full advantage of the new advanced terminal equipment and sophisticated telecommunications services that technological progress was making possible.[17] Nevertheless, users did not make any substantial efforts to appeal to the government for reforms until the late 1970s. And even then, they did not politicize their demands, but only quietly expressed their interest in gaining more freedom to develop value-added networks. As in the United Kingdom, they had not even imagined the possibility of network competition or privatization.

Major reform did not become a credible option until the 1980s, when the U.S. example combined with Japan's administrative reform campaign transformed the debate. As the United States began to liberalize its market and initiated the process leading to the breakup of American Telegraph & Telephone (AT&T), the MPT, NTT, Keidanren, and numerous research institutes sent a constant stream of teams to study the U.S. experience.[18]

[15] Interview with former MPT official (March 1991).

[16] NTT Corporation (1986) pp. 620–21. The MPT's Tomita (interview, June 22, 1993) contends that MPT officials persuaded the committee to include this in their recommendations. Hiroshi (Kan) Katō, a Keiō University professor who was on the committee (interview, May 14, 1991), recalls that the committee members deliberately stated that union members should not be given the right to strike "*so long as they remain in the public sector*"—precisely to instill the idea of privatization in the minds of the unions.

[17] The first surveys reporting these concerns appeared in 1969. Representative examples appear in Nippon Telegraph and Telephone Public Corporation, Management Survey Bureau (May 1971).

[18] As Tomita (1984) notes, Japanese authorities were concerned that they were falling behind the United States. The United States had allowed foreign attachments to the basic telephone set in 1968 but Japan only gradually liberalized its restrictions in 1972, 1982, and 1985. The United States had adopted its "Open Skies" policy in 1972, but Japan did not even launch a communications satellite until 1983. And the United States had allowed VAN services in 1973, but Japan only followed in 1982.

Meanwhile, the U.S. government began pressuring Japan to purchase more U.S. telecommunications equipment in 1978, but stressed the pragmatic issue of U.S. sales to Japan rather than broader questions of competition in basic services or the privatization of NTT.[19] When asked whether the U.S. government had a political strategy in trying to open the Japanese telecommunications market—in terms of allying with Japanese proponents of deregulation or pushing for broader reform—one U.S. negotiator replied that "the U.S. government did not have the resources, the interest, or the expertise to analyze the politics of telecommunications in Japan. We were doing our best just to address whatever happened to be on the trade agenda."[20]

Two important reports actually preempted the Rinchō's 1982 report proposing network competition and privatization. In 1980, a neoliberal think tank known as the Forum for Policy Innovation (*seisaku kōsō fōramu*) came out with a report recommending the liberalization of value-added network (VAN) services and suggesting that competition might be extended to basic telephone services as well. As to the regulatory structure, it anticipated that the rivalry between the MPT and MITI over the growing value-added services sector would only grow worse and thus proposed that a new agency be established to oversee the sector.[21] Also in 1980, the MPT organized an advisory council, the Telecommunications Policy Discussion Group (*denki tsūshin seisaku kondankai*), primarily to explore ways to liberalize the value-added services sector. The group reported in August 1981, recommending the full liberalization of value-added services, subject to MPT regulation of course. In addition, however, the report also suggested that the government should consider "a reform of NTT's management structure, including privatization."[22] In 1982, the Rinchō came out with its proposal: allow competition in all sectors of telecommunications services and privatize and "reorganize"—meaning break up—NTT. This proposal fundamentally reshaped the Japanese debate about telecommunications policy, and about deregulation in general. In the remainder of this chapter, we shall look in more detail at the two critical episodes in Japan's telecommunications reform: the liberalization of VANs and the privatization of NTT.

[19] In fact, U.S. officials originally were suspicious of proposals for NTT's privatization, seeing these plans as a possible excuse for not abiding by the 1980 procurement agreement. The MPT later actually tried to argue that the privatized company should not be held responsible for commitments made when it was a public corporation, but backed down in the face of U.S. protests.
[20] Interview with Glen Fukushima, former director for Japanese Affairs, Office of the U.S. Trade Representative (December 13, 1990).
[21] Seisaku Kōsō Fōramu (December 1980); interview with Hajime Hirota, executive director, Forum for Policy Innovation (July 23, 1991).
[22] NTT Corporation (1986), pp. 635–36.

THE LIBERALIZATION OF VALUE-ADDED NETWORK (VAN) SERVICES

By the late 1970s, the rivalry between MITI and the MPT over their common jurisdiction, the sector of information technology joining computers and communications, had evolved into a full-fledged feud focusing on the regulation of value-added networks.[23] For the MPT, the growth of the information technology sector presented it with the opportunity to increase its authority and to bring a whole new group of companies, the new VAN service providers, within its jurisdiction. For MITI, it offered a chance to stave off the threat of a real decline in power and status. MITI officials recognized that there was no longer any need for an industrial policy in many of the sectors it controlled. And to make matters worse, the leading-edge technologies of the 1980s and 1990s were outside MITI's exclusive domain. Not only did MITI have to spar with the MPT over information technology, but it had to contend with the Ministry of Education in software and the Ministry of Health and Welfare in biotechnology.

The two ministries adopted battle strategies designed to make the most of their respective strengths. On the one hand, MITI was not in a position to claim that it should regulate the sector, because the MPT had legal authority over telecommunications, and VAN services certainly involved telecommunications. On the other hand, MITI was in a position to exert *de facto* control over the sector by virtue of its ties with computer and software companies, which were likely to dominate the VAN business—so long as the MPT was not explicitly granted jurisdiction. Thus MITI pushed for the complete liberalization of VANs, but the MPT insisted that new entrants should be subject to MPT regulation. Both sides developed seemingly rational arguments to match their interests. MITI argued that any system of regulation that hampered the entry of U.S. VAN service providers would invite U.S. retaliation. For its part, the MPT declared that it needed to regulate entry in order to ensure that VAN providers would not hinder the sound management of the national telephone network by violating quality or safety standards. The MPT also insisted that it had to regulate foreign ownership for national security reasons.[24] The two ministries even tried to define the VAN service business in such a way that it would seem logically to fall within their own jurisdiction. The MPT called it "data communications," with the accent on the communications, whereas MITI called it "on-line information processing," with the accent on the information processing.

In terms of wooing the potential VAN service companies into its fold, MITI clearly began with the upper hand. In the late 1970s, as data pro-

---

[23] The MPT had begun liberalizing the VAN sector with modest reforms in 1971 and 1977. Kawakita (1985) and Johnson (1989) provide two of the best accounts of the VAN Wars. See Campbell (1984) on bureaucratic turf battles more generally.

[24] Prestowitz (1989), p. 472.

cessing firms began to realize the potential of the VAN business, they started to lobby MITI for reforms. They worked primarily through the Japan Information Industry Promotion Association (*nihon jōhō sangyō shinkō kyōkai*) and the Japan Software Industry Center (*nihon sofutoueā sangyō sentā*)—which later merged into the Information Service Industry Association (*jōhō sābisu sangyō kyōkai*)—both of which were associated with MITI. Some, however, tried to open channels with the MPT as well, recognizing that the MPT was really the lead agency in the telecommunications sector. They felt that being too closely associated with MITI could result in eventual retaliation by the MPT. In 1979, five of these firms officially revolted, choosing to work with the MPT rather than MITI. Kōya Aoi, who worked for Intec, one of the rebel firms, explains that his firm became suspicious because MITI officials seemed too blatantly political. Furthermore, the rebel companies felt that the MPT's proposal was more likely to get through: somehow they just could not imagine complete liberalization.[25] The VAN service providers thus split into two groups, mirroring the divide between their ministerial sponsors.

Meanwhile, the two ministries set up rival advisory councils. Not surprisingly, the policy council recommendations closely followed the positions of their respective ministries. In 1981, the MPT's council proposed a system whereby the MPT would regulate all VAN operators—just what MITI feared most. Of course, MITI's parallel advisory group recommended complete liberalization—just what the MPT feared most. Policy councils (*shingikai*), which are very common for Japanese ministries, range from the truly meaningful to the utterly powerless. In general, they are designed more to create a consensus around the ministry's plans than to bring in new ideas from the outside. The ministry officials choose the members carefully, so that recommendations will not be too unpredictable, and they discuss the issues at length with the members before hearings so that nothing too unexpected comes out at a given session.[26]

The MPT hoped to submit a law to the Diet based on its council's recommendations, but MITI objected vigorously. MITI felt that no liberalization at all was better than liberalization under MPT auspices. MITI outmaneuvered the MPT politically, enlisting the support of Keidanren and numerous influential Diet members. The LDP entered the discussion as arbitrator and decided to drop the bill. But the party did decide to liberalize VANs for small and medium-sized industries, under the MPT's framework. The LDP's solution reflected a shrewd political logic: it gave MITI the edge by rejecting the MPT proposal, but also tailored the bill to

---

[25] Interview with Kōya Aoi, adviser, information strategies, Industrial Bank of Japan (March 8, 1991). Prestowitz (1989, p. 471) suggests that the MPT coopted some MITI supporters by offering to limit foreign participation in VAN services.

[26] See Schwartz (1993).

a key party constituency, small businesses.[27] Representatives of small businesses had successfully argued that they were at a disadvantage under the existing rules, which allowed private networks within a single company but not connecting a company to outside parties.

In any case, by this time the Rinchō had presented its first report, and it became clear that the MPT would need to prepare major reform legislation, of which VAN liberalization would be but a small part. MITI proposed that telecommunications services should be divided as in the United States into "basic" and enhanced "services." Basic services would be subject to the MPT regulation, but enhanced services would be completely free. The MPT devised a different categorization based on ownership. Type I service providers, which own their own facilities, would need licenses from the MPT. Special Type II service providers, which do not own facilities but provide services to a large number of users over an extended area, would need permits. Basic Type II service providers, which operate in a more limited area, would only need to register with the MPT. MITI officials understood all too well that even registration would let the MPT meddle in the affairs of the companies, for they themselves were quite accomplished at using the slightest bit of formal authority to exercise administrative guidance. MITI officials eventually accepted the MPT's Type I/Type II classification, but insisted that permits and registration requirements be eliminated (see Table 9). When asked whether he and his colleagues designed their proposals to keep MITI out of their turf, one senior MPT official was surprisingly blunt: "Absolutely," he replied, "and we did everything we could to make sure that we got our way."[28]

Both sides enlisted the support of their respective LDP divisions (internal party policy committees). MITI worked with the Commerce Division (shōkō bukai) and the MPT with the Communications Division (tsūshin bukai). The divisions within the LDP's Policy Research Council are critical to the party's input into the legislative process.[29] MPT officials were determined to tap all their political resources because they felt they had lost the first round of the battle.[30] Realizing that its rival had learned a tactical lesson, MITI pulled out its final card: the United States. Within two days of a MPT-MITI meeting on the subject in February 1984, U.S. trade negotiators came flying to Tokyo to protest the MPT's effort to gain control over VANs. They feared that the MPT would use these regulations to keep out U.S. VAN companies, and they particularly objected to the MPT's pro-

[27] See Calder (1988), pp. 312–48, on the LDP and small businesses.
[28] Interview with MPT official (1991).
[29] Satō and Matsuzaki (1986).
[30] Inoguchi and Iwai (1987, pp. 222–26) cite this as an example of the growing influence of the LDP zoku in politics, although they note that the zoku's main role was to be cheerleaders for the two ministries. Muramatsu and Krauss (1987, pp. 545–46) mention this case as an example of "patterned pluralist" politics.

Table 9. MPT and MITI proposals for the regulation of telecommunications services

Type of service	MPT proposal	MITI proposal	Final outcome
Type I carriers			
Entry	Permit	Permit	Permit
Prices	Permit	Permit	Permit
Foreign equity	Less than 1/3	Less than 1/3	Less than 1/3
Special Type II carriers			
Entry	Permit	None	Registration
Prices	Notification	None	Notification
Foreign equity	Less than 1/2	None	None
General Type II carriers			
Entry	Notification	None	Notification
Prices	Notification	None	None
Foreign equity	None	None	None

SOURCE: Adapted from Inoguchi and Iwai (1987), p. 225.

posal to limit the foreign ownership of Special Type II VANs.[31] Tomita of the MPT insists that the Americans could only have been tipped off by MITI.[32] Even if he is mistaken, MITI clearly tried to make the most of the U.S. protest. U.S. negotiator Clyde Prestowitz recalls that MITI officials practically begged him to take action, since the U.S. government appeared willing to accept the MPT's registration requirements so long as there was no restriction on foreign ownership: "As MITI felt its ally weakening, I began receiving frantic calls from high MITI officials, urging me to make the Americans stand their ground. Didn't U.S. officials understand, they asked, that the real control was the bureaucratic procedures and not the equity restriction?"[33] MITI officials also made a special appeal to Prime Minister Nakasone because they sensed that the MPT had better ties with two of the LDP's "big three" leaders (*sanyaku*): Rokusuke Tanaka and Ryūtarō Hashimoto.[34]

For their part, MPT officials launched a massive public relations campaign to convince the business community of the need for liberalization *and* the need for some minimal level of regulation. One MPT official reports that for several months he had two train passes: one for the daily com-

[31] Prestowitz (1989), p. 469.

[32] Tomita interview (December 21, 1990). Prestowitz (1989, pp. 470–71) also mentions these meetings in his book on trade politics.

[33] Prestowitz (1989), p. 477.

[34] The "big three" refer to the top three party posts after the party president (who was also prime minister so long as the LDP ruled): the secretary general (*kanjichō*), the chairman of the General Council (*sōmukaichō*), and the chairman of the Policy Research Council (*seimu chōsakaichō*).

mute from home to the ministry, and another for the more-than-daily com-
mute from the ministry to Ōtemachi, Tokyo's business district and the
home of Keidanren. The ministry's strategy was to convince the business
community, which would enlist Keidanren, which would lobby the LDP. If
one overlooks step one in this strategy—the MPT convincing the business
community—then it looks like a classic case of pressure-group politics. But
then why would business leaders on their own be so convinced that they
needed some minimal level of regulation for VANs? In fact, the MPT was
manipulating the political process in order to pursue its own agenda.[35] In
the end, MITI lost out. The LDP forced the MPT to downgrade from permit to registration for Special Type II VAN companies, but left VAN services squarely within the MPT's jurisdiction.[36] To appease MITI somewhat,
however, the LDP required the MPT to notify MITI of all VAN permits and
registrations. One MPT official concludes dryly: "This just goes to show
that MITI never really believed in liberalization. Because once they had lost
the war, they started saying, 'Well then let's regulate VANs together.' "[37]

THE PRIVATIZATION OF NTT

The VAN Wars were merely one element within a larger debate over
telecommunications reform centering on the question of NTT's privatization. The Rinchō put privatization on the public agenda, but behind the
scenes the MoF was the real force driving the policy. Like their British
counterparts, a small group of officials within the MoF's Budget Bureau
began to consider privatizing public corporations in the late 1970s. They
declared 1978 the year of fiscal rehabilitation and revised the budget control system for NTT as part of this effort. They began to see some compelling reasons for privatization: it would eliminate the double regulation
of NTT by the Diet and the MPT; it would eliminate NTT's perverse incentive to maximize personnel and resist cost cutting; and most important, it would bring in substantial funds, which could be allocated to

[35] Interviews with Yoshio Utsumi, councillor, Ministry of Posts and Telecommunications
(January 28, 1991), and Hiroshi Tachibana, deputy director, Industry and Telecommunications Department, Keidanren (August 6, 1991). The language adopted in Keidanren position papers (compiled in Keidanren, January 1987) strongly supports this interpretation. In
these papers, Keidanren officials explicitly recognize the need for a new regulatory regime
and offer a sophisticated rationale for various types of regulation.

[36] Johnson (1989) looks at other issues of conflict between the MPT and MITI related to
telecommunications, including equipment standards, research and development, and satellite technology.

[37] Interview with MPT official (1991). In an interview in *Computopia* (January 1985, pp.
131–32), MITI Vice Minister Keiichi Konaga played down the MPT's victory by emphasizing
this concession: "The jurisdiction [over VANs] is shared by the two ministries. But because
the companies are supposed to register with MPT, MPT is the interface."

budget deficit reduction. The government divested 50 percent of Japan Air Lines (JAL) in 1979, and Budget Bureau officials then began considering the privatization of the "three public corporations" (*sankōsha*)—NTT, Japan National Railways (JNR), and Japan Tobacco and Salt. They were ambivalent about Japan Tobacco, because privatization could cut into the government's revenue stream. They were cautious about JNR, because they did not know how to handle its huge debt and because they were wary of dealing with the union, the National Railways Workers' Union (*kokutetsu rōdō kumiai*, or "Kokurō" for short). They were most enthusiastic about NTT, for it would bring the most money into the national coffers. One former MoF official recalls that he approached Hisashi Shintō shortly after he took over as president of NTT: "After a game of golf one day, I told Shintō about our thoughts on privatization. He just listened and did not respond. It seemed as though he had been considering the same idea, and had wanted to talk to me about it because he needed MoF to go along. But since I spoke first, he did not need to say anything at all."[38] MoF officials also exchanged views with the Rinchō, and the prospect of privatization helped to bring the ministry strongly behind the administrative reform program by 1981.

For its part, the Rinchō divided into four subcommittees in 1981, with the fourth subcommittee focusing on the reorganization of the three public corporations. The fourth committee was chaired by Hiroshi (Kan) Katō, a professor at Keiō University and a zealous proponent of the elimination of waste in government. Katō, who boasts a framed picture of American economist James Buchanan on his wall, considers himself part of a Japanese tradition of ardent believers in the strengths of private enterprise, dating back to Yasuzaemon Matsunaga who privatized and broke up the electric companies after the war. The sixteen-member committee included a diverse group of businessmen, academics, journalists, and union representatives, but the pro-reform forces had the clear majority. The committee, which began deliberations in 1981, focused initially on the JNR. They quickly realized how difficult it was going to be politically to push through the JNR's privatization and breakup. In particular, they faced the rabid opposition of the JNR's union, Kokurō, and the Socialist and Communist parties. Some members of the committee began to turn to NTT, which could provide a smoother test case before moving on to the more difficult case of the JNR.[39]

Meanwhile, the fourth committee began to find friends in a most unexpected place: NTT itself. In January 1981, Shintō succeeded Tokuji Akikusa as NTT's president. NTT had been suffering from a reputation for

[38] Interview with former MoF official (July 1992).

[39] Katō has authored or coauthored several volumes on his experiences with the Rinchō: Katō and Sandō (1983a), Katō and Sandō (1983b), and Katō (1984).

poor management, particularly after a scandal about illegal overtime al-lowances. NTT used this system of allowances to reward its employees be-cause it was not allowed to raise average salaries above those of civil servants in other public corporations like the JNR. Akikusa was in disfavor for having mismanaged the issue of opening NTT's procurement system to the outside, a problem that had been a source of great friction with the United States from 1978 to 1980, when an accord was reached. Akikusa had infuriated MITI as well as the Americans by declaring that NTT had nothing to buy from the United States except "buckets and mops."[40] Shintō already had a reputation as a rationalizer par excellence for his cost-cutting at Ishikawajima Harima Industries (IHI), a major shipbuilding firm. Toshio Dokō, Shintō's predecessor at IHI, was chairman of Keidanren and the newly created Rinchō. Dokō, who had considerable power throughout big business, personally "appointed" Shintō to take over at NTT.[41]

Shintō was selected with the explicit aim of cutting costs at NTT, al-though privatization itself was not on the agenda at the time of his ap-pointment. Dokō had privatization in mind, but Shintō claims that he did not realize this until about one month after he took office.[42] Shintō quickly recognized that NTT required a massive change in consciousness and set about trying to transform it.[43] In 1981, as one way of changing per-ceptions within the company, he set up a study group for young NTT offi-cials to look at issues concerning NTT's long-term future. The study group drew up three proposals: reform within the status quo, transformation into a "special corporation" such as the Bank of Japan, and privatization. Vice President Yasusada Kitahara and many within NTT's elite corps of en-gineers felt that privatization would threaten the company's commitment to basic research. Yet they felt that Shintō had the blessing of both Kei-danren and the Rinchō, and thus to oppose him would be futile.[44] Shintō did not publicly announce his own stance, preferring to say that he would leave the decision up to the Rinchō. Nonetheless, he privately agreed with the Rinchō to proceed with privatization on the condition that NTT not be broken up.[45] Having discussed the matter at length with the union, Shintō was convinced that the union would go along so long as there was no breakup.[46] Members of the fourth committee were encouraged by

[40] On the NTT procurement issue, see Curran (1982).

[41] Shintō recalls that he was contacted first by Dokō, but also by several other members of the Rinchō, including C. Itoh Chairman Ryūzō Sejima (Interview, May 14, 1991).

[42] Shintō interview (May 14, 1991).

[43] Shintō (1982 and 1985) articulates his philosophy in two books on his experiences at NTT.

[44] Interviews with NTT executives and a former NTT executive (1991).

[45] Shintō (May 14, 1991) and Katō (May 14, 1991) interviews.

[46] Union leader Komori (1988, p. 19) reports that in December 1981 Shintō pledged to the union that he would not agree to a breakup.

NTT's unexpectedly responsive attitude and took this as a green light to move ahead with privatization.

The union, Zendentsū, was officially opposed, yet actually quite ambivalent. Union leaders realized that they stood to profit from privatization: they could use the opportunity to push for the right to strike, greater flexibility in wages, and higher overall wages. The union's chief, Kazuo Oikawa, was particularly progressive and decided early on not to fight privatization but to make the most of it. Oikawa's successor, Akira Yamagishi, followed this line faithfully. The union remained officially opposed for two reasons: a blatantly supportive stance might have upset the rank-and-file and the SDPJ, and the union would be able to achieve more concessions from the LDP if it withheld its approval.[47] At the union convention in May 1984, the union officially decided to take this more realistic stance, and union leaders began an all-out campaign to make the most of the reform.

Two powerful groups related to NTT opposed privatization: retired NTT executives and the NTT "family" manufacturers. NTTs "old boys" were the most virulent, because they saw privatization as undoing their legacy. They believed that the concentration of money, brains, and technology in a single public monopoly was responsible for the sector's success, and one should not tamper with this formula. They felt that NTT's role as a regulator and an active participant in making policy was essential, and they refused to stand by idly as the MPT usurped NTT's power. Many of these "old boys" worked for the "family" manufacturers. NTT officials, like most government bureaucrats in Japan, have a custom of "descending from heaven" (*amakudari*) into lucrative positions in the private sector after retirement at around age 55. In the case of NTT, this system provided one more bond between NTT and its "family." The telecommunications equipment manufacturers association, the Communications Industry Association of Japan (CIAJ) did not officially oppose privatization. Some manufacturers, however, lobbied against privatization individually, especially those with close ties to NTT.[48] They appreciated NTT's role in funding research and development and providing a secure market for their goods. Nonetheless, they hesitated to lobby too openly, because the U.S. government might see opposition to reform as an effort to keep out imports, and this could threaten the increasingly lucrative business of exporting equipment to the United States.

Meanwhile, the MPT was still officially opposed to privatization. According to the conventional wisdom, the MPT opposed privatizing NTT

---

[47] Masao Komori (1988), who was secretary of Zendentsū at the time, provides a detailed account of Zendentsū's political efforts. Yamagishi's reflections are somewhat more abstract (1985 and 1989). Yamagishi went on to lead Japan's new umbrella union federation, the Japanese Private Sector Trade Union Federation (Rengō).

[48] Interview with Haruo Ozawa, president, CIAJ (March 5, 1991).

until it was inevitable, and then conveniently switched its stance to make the best of a bad thing.[49] In fact, however, the MPT was divided on the issue from the start. Those who had been involved in the 1971 study group on telecommunications policy strongly favored privatization, seeing this as an opportunity to enhance the ministry's status. And as we have seen, a ministry study group raised the possibility of privatization in a report in August 1981, before the Rinchō's first report. Then in 1982, another MPT-related group recommended restructuring NTT and mentioned privatization as a promising option.[50] Yūshin Morizumi, director of the Communications Policy Bureau, led the group that was more hesitant about privatization. He did not blindly oppose privatization, but argued that liberalization should come first. He feared that a private company might not be devoted to public service and might not invest sufficiently in infrastructure.[51] The Communications Policy Bureau officials eventually took a vote in July 1982, and the proponents of reform won. Morizumi was succeeded by Moriya Koyama, a strong supporter of reform. The bureau moved as one unit in favor of privatization from that time on, although officials were careful not to make it seem as though they had gone through too abrupt a change of mind. The public line was to be: the ministry had never opposed privatization, but had always had certain concerns.[52]

Between the appearance of the Rinchō's final report in 1982 and September 1983, the LDP leadership busily conducted the background political work toward coming up with a palatable proposal. The Tanaka faction, the largest and most powerful, played the pivotal role in formulating the LDP's approach to the reform. Kakuei Tanaka himself, like the other top LDP leaders, had committed his support to the Rinchō, although he reserved the right to differ on specific issues.[53] In July 1983, Tanaka faction elder Shin Kanemaru devised a shrewd way to coerce the more conservative LDP Communications *zoku*. He announced a proposal

[49] See, for example, Inoguchi and Iwai (1987), p. 222.
[50] Nippon Telegraph and Telephone Public Corporation Management Structure Study Group (November 1982).
[51] Interview with Yūshin Morizumi, member, House of Councilors (August 7, 1991).
[52] Interview with Mitsuo Igarashi, Deputy Minister for Policy Coordination, MPT (July 31, 1991).
[53] According to a member of the Rinchō staff, Tanaka invited Rinchō leaders Dokō and Sejima to a fancy Japanese *ryōtei* (garden restaurant) along with young Tanaka faction members to discuss administrative reform. Tanaka began with an apology for all the trouble that the faction had caused. By this he meant that the faction accepted partial responsibility for boosting spending and thus creating the fiscal crisis. Tanaka pledged his support for administrative reform, making sure that the faction members got the message that they were to go along. Interview with Kazuaki Tanaka, Deputy Director General, Administrative Management Bureau, MCA, July 25, 1991. Katō had his own meeting with Tanaka on the issue of NTT privatization. After a lengthy explanation, all Tanaka said was: "And how much do you expect to get for it?" Katō took this to mean that Tanaka was not about to object to a plan that would bring so much money into the national coffers. Katō interview, May 14, 1991.

that they could readily accept, a minor revision of NTT's status to that of a "public organization." Kanemaru designed the proposal to fail, as it did when the MoF and the LDP leadership overwhelmingly condemned it. This way, Kanemaru was able to tell the *zoku* that he had tried and convince them to accept a bolder proposal. Kanemaru was assisted by Rinchō officials and by Shintō himself, who discussed the issues at length with these *zoku* in order to gain their acquiescence. In addition, MoF officials pushed the *zoku* to go along because they were eager to get their hands on the revenues from privatization.[54] On September 6, 1983, Ryūtarō Hashimoto, chairman of the LDP's Committee on Administrative Reform, abruptly announced an eleven-point proposal. The proposal favored the privatization of NTT but not its breakup. It stated that the possibility of breakup would be reconsidered after ten years. NTT and Zendentsū had lobbied intensively against the Rinchō's proposal for breakup. They had promised acceptance of reform, in NTT's case, and only minimal resistance, in Zendentsū's case, in exchange for the withdrawal of the breakup clause.[55] Zendentsū not only used its own network in the SDPJ, but also directly lobbied the LDP. Hashimoto and company simply concluded that the reform would proceed much more smoothly if debate regarding NTT's breakup were postponed.

Once Hashimoto's proposal was out, the central battle became one over the terms of privatization, pitting NTT, with Zendentsū's support, against the MPT. In essence, NTT wanted more business freedom, whereas the MPT sought greater regulatory power. This battle had a couple of peculiar twists. First, because NTT was to become a private company, it was supposed to shed its role in making government policy. It was losing this function, however, at the very moment when it needed political influence the most, for it was fighting over the terms of its own transformation. The MPT increasingly insisted that NTT stay out of politics, that the MPT would handle all relations with the Diet. This would have been fine for NTT if its interests had matched those of the ministry, but it was quite awkward because they did not. NTT could not appeal directly to the Diet without incurring the wrath of the MPT, so it undertook a strategy of lobbying through its union, Zendentsū. At the early stages, MPT officials discussed the terms of the reform directly with top NTT officials, but once the Diet became involved, MPT officials tried to close NTT out of the process as much as possible.

Second, although the core element of the battle was a power struggle between the MPT and NTT, NTT was losing its attachment to political

[54] Muramatsu (Spring 1988), p. 127.

[55] In a panel discussion looking back at this period (Komori, 1988, p. 89), Hashimoto remarked: "I have heard of union-management harmony, but this was really too much. I mean the company's top executives and the union were saying the same thing!"

power *per se*. Unlike the MPT-MITI conflict, this was not a simple turf war between two government agencies seeking to extend their powers. For its part, the MPT clearly was seeking to maximize its authority. But NTT executives were already responding to the evolution in the corporation's identity, so they were more interested in fighting for business autonomy than political power. NTT old boys still saw things in terms of relative power, and that is why they fought privatization so adamantly. But Shintō and his staff were willing to give up their political role and certain regulatory powers. After all, it did not make sense for NTT to have regulatory responsibilities once it had competitors. They were more interested in fighting for the right to expand into new lines of business, and to choose investments and develop new services with a minimum of interference from the MPT. In September 1983, they set up a special office of twenty to thirty people, the System Reform Strategy Office (*seido mondai taisaku shitsu*), to develop the company's strategy for reform.

Concerning the Telecommunications Business Law, which would set out the terms of competition, NTT battled the MPT over the degree of market management. As we saw in Chapter 3, Japanese ministries are fond of second-guessing the market through "supply and demand adjustment." They most often intervene to prevent oversupply, either by restricting entry into the market or by directing firms to restrict production. NTT executives argued that the MPT should be barred from this practice because MPT officials could use it as a pretext to force NTT to cut back on research and development, on investment, or on its supply of services. The MPT argued that it would have to maintain the ability to make adjustments so that NTT would not overwhelm the competition. NTT also fought with the MPT over price and service regulation. NTT came up with some creative proposals in order to gain concessions: let the ministry regulate daytime rates but not night-time rates, or individual lines but not party lines. On most issues the MPT prevailed, leaving NTT reliant on the ministry's consent before changing prices or adding new services, but NTT managed to squeeze out a few minor victories. For example, NTT would be free to set the charges for moving or adding an outlet, although not for initial installation. Even where NTT prevailed, however, the MPT maintained the ability to intervene by asking NTT for information.[56] And MPT officials would not hesitate to offer "guidance" to NTT executives on the basis of the information they received. On the NTT Law, which would outline NTT's responsibilities after privatization, NTT managers disputed the definition of "principal" versus "secondary" businesses. Under the new law, NTT would be free in areas outside its principal business, but this left plenty of leeway for flexible

---

[56] Interview with Kōichi Tanaka, former NTT executive and managing director, Research Institute for Telecom-Policies and Economics (March 5, 1991).

Table 10. Major regulatory changes under the reform laws

Item	Primary authority before 1985	Primary authority after 1985
	The Telecommunications Business Law	
Entry	Diet Law designates NTT as the monopoly service provider.	MPT Requires MPT permit (for Type I), registration (Special Type II) notification (General Type II).
Prices	Diet Prices for basic services set by law; NTT free to set prices on certain items.	MPT Most price changes require MPT approval.
Service	Diet Basic guidelines set in law; items not covered subject to MPT approval.	MPT Major service changes require MPT permit.
Technical standards	NTT Set by NTT for network; set by the MPT for customer equipment.	MPT Set by the MPT's Telecommunications Deliberation Council.
	The NTT Law	
Budget	Diet Requires Diet approval.	NTT Business plan requires MPT approval; budget must be attached.
Personnel	Diet Subject to Diet approval through budget process; certain guidelines written into law.	NTT No special restrictions.

SOURCE: Compiled by the author, based in part on NTT (1986).

interpretation. NTT wanted the MPT to clarify this distinction so that MPT officials could not later expand the definition of "principle business" in order to constrain NTT's activities (see Table 10).

When it came to lobbying the Diet, Zendentsū took the lead, often working on NTT's behalf. In a massive political effort, Zendentsū focused on gaining the right to strike, guaranteeing flexible salaries, and maximizing NTT's business autonomy. Zendentsū used a number of political routes, including mass mobilization and lobbying SDPJ and LDP Diet members.[57] Zendentsū coached SDPJ Diet members who pushed MPT officials to clarify the scope of the ministry's proposed regulations over NTT in Diet hearings. Zendentsū and the SDPJ won some minor victories in revisions made in the Lower House Communications Committee. Specifi-

[57] On Zendentsū's role, see Komori (1988), Mochizuki (1993), and Ōtake (1994), pp. 117–42.

cally, the government agreed to reconsider granting the right to strike after three years; it determined that NTT would only have to file its spending plans with the MPT rather than apply for approval; and it clarified the definition of primary versus secondary business.[58]

CIAJ representatives pushed through some minor changes of their own, mostly by working directly with the MPT at the drafting stage. For example, they inserted a clause stating that all products must attain a standard that did not threaten the overall effectiveness of the network. They were only too aware that they enjoyed an advantage in their home market because they were more familiar with the quality standards and the standards were set high enough to keep out many cheaper imports—and they wanted to keep it that way.[59] They also appealed for a guarantee that NTT would continue its leadership in telecommunications research and development, thus indirectly subsidizing the entire equipment industry. Shintō, consistent in his private enterprise philosophy, argued that NTT should not have to conduct any research that would not pay off on the company's bottom line. Even so, the CIAJ convinced the MPT to include a clause in the law stating that NTT would conduct "public interest" research and development.[60]

The Diet passed three laws shortly after reopening on December 20, 1984: the Telecommunications Business Law, the NTT Law, and the Background Law for the Telecommunications Law, and these took effect on April 1, 1985. MPT officials hoped to use the proceeds from the sale for MPT-sponsored telecommunications research and development, but the MoF, MITI, and even NTT opposed.[61] The MoF struck a deal with the MPT and MITI whereby one third of the proceeds from privatization would be shared by the MPT and MITI for a new research and development facility, the Key Technology Center.[62] The remainder would be used for deficit reduction. The government issued the first block of 200,000 shares at 1,197,392 yen each (U.S. $11,974) in October 1986. It planned to sell one-half of the shares in four equal blocks annually beginning in 1986, but only sold part of the third block in 1988 because of a sharp drop in the share price, and then postponed further sales because of market conditions.

According to the NTT Law, the question of NTT's breakup was to be reviewed in five years. The MPT had reduced the ten years stipulated in the Hashimoto proposal to five in order to increase the chances of breakup, something MPT officials had increasingly come to favor. When time for

---

[58] *Computopia* (October 1984), pp. 50–54.

[59] U.S. negotiators eventually protested the MPT's technical standards and negotiated the removal of thirty-two of fifty-three technical specifications.

[60] Ozawa interview (March 5, 1991).

[61] MPT officials (interview, June 1993) argue that NTT executives only opposed because they did not want the MPT to become too powerful.

[62] See Johnson (1989) for an elaboration on this episode of the MPT-MITI feud.

the review arrived in 1990, the MPT came out most strongly in favor of breakup, with MITI opposed. MITI officials claimed that MPT officials were only in favor of breakup because they wanted another way to put NTT in its place, and MPT officials countered that MITI was only opposed because the MPT was in favor. Needless to say, NTT and Zendentsū were adamantly opposed. NTT's new competitors were in favor, but did not actively lobby on the issue. As expected, the advisory councils of the MPT and MITI came up with recommendations closely following the established positions of their respective ministries. Even the economists on the policy councils seemed to divide fairly neatly depending on which policy council they served—except for two who left the MPT panel because they felt their concerns were not taken seriously.[63] The MPT council stopped short of demanding breakup outright, but recommended a major reorganization possibly leading to breakup.[64] The MITI experts suggested that breaking up NTT would be extremely disruptive and should be postponed.[65] Keidanren concurred with MITI, after sending a study team in 1989 to study the U.S. experience with the breakup of AT&T.

The MoF proved to be the decisive force in this debate, pushing strongly against breakup because this could threaten the share price of NTT's stock, two-thirds of which it still owned. The MoF asserted its prerogative as majority owner of the corporation and refused to approve the breakup unless the MPT could demonstrate that the breakup would not violate the interests of taxpayers or shareholders.[66] In essence, the MPT had to prove that NTT would be worth as much or more in pieces as it was as a whole—something it was entirely incapable of doing. The LDP decided to deal with the issue in the relevant party committee. The committee chairman, Tsutomu Hata, persuaded the party's "big three" to delegate the decision to him. This is one way in which the LDP sometimes tries to insulate itself from political pressure, for an individual committee chairman is freer to do what he thinks best, whereas the big three would have to make political balance their first priority. The committee held a series of hearings, but Hata had no trouble in concluding that further consideration of a breakup should be postponed for another five years.[67]

Nevertheless, the LDP issued a policy statement along with its decision stipulating that (1) NTT must reorganize into long-distance and regional divisions, (2) NTT must rationalize (i.e. cut personnel), (3) the government must deregulate further, (4) the government must monitor NTT's returns

---

[63] Interview with Tsuruhiko Nambu, professor of economics, Gakushūin University, and member of MITI's council (February 22, 1991).

[64] MPT, Telecommunications Policy Council (March 1990).

[65] MITI, Industrial Structure Council, Information Industry Committee (January 1990).

[66] Interview with MoF official (June 1992).

[67] Interview with member of the policy staff, Policy Research Council, LDP (January 1991).

to its shareholders, (5) the government must review the situation once again in 1995.[68] The MPT attached a far more extensive list of conditions to its approval. Its statement ran for four pages and incorporated demands that NTT try harder in about every aspect of its business. In addition to the measures also appearing in the LDP statement, for example, the MPT declared that NTT must disclose more information about its cost structure, open its network to greater use by other carriers, improve interconnection with other carriers, create a special discount rate for other carriers accessing its network, establish a new telephone number system more equitable to the other carriers, increase the digitalization of the network, and facilitate the diffusion of its research and development results.[69] In essence, the MPT has used the threat of breakup for everything it is worth. Some have suggested that MPT officials do not even really want to break up NTT, but saying that they do makes it that much easier for these officials to keep NTT in line.

In 1993, Japanese politics underwent a major upheaval when a substantial group within the LDP defected and joined with opposition parties to form a coalition that ousted the LDP from power for the first time since 1955. Then the LDP returned to power in June 1994 in a coalition with the SDPJ and the Sakigake (Harbinger Party). In the short term, the political turmoil has given the bureaucrats even more leeway to proceed without fear of political intervention. In the longer term, reformist politicians like Ichirō Ozawa have vowed to impose more political control over the bureaucracy.[70] MPT officials remain confident, however, that the new MPT-run telecommunications regime will survive the political transition.

NTT's status was due for a second review in 1995, but political turmoil caused the government to postpone a decision until 1996. Once again, the MPT rallied the forces in favor of breakup, and NTT led the opposition. In October 1995, an MPT advisory council reviewed possible approaches to breakup, including vertical division into a long-distance company and one local carrier, and horizontal division into multiple local carriers. It appeared to lean toward the more radical horizontal breakup option. The MPT's case was strengthened by AT&T, which announced in September 1995 that it would divide itself into three companies in order to compete more effectively. MPT was further supported by a new Administrative Reform Committee (*gyōsei kaikaku iinkai*, or "Gyōkakui" for short) that proposed breaking up NTT and further deregulating the telecommunications market.[71] Even so, given strong opposition from NTT, the NTT "family"

---

[68] LDP statement dated March 30, 1990.

[69] MPT statement dated March 30, 1990.

[70] Ozawa (1993), pp. 55–64. In fact, the Hosokawa administration took a startling step in this direction in December 1993 when the MITI minister, a politician, asked one of his highest-ranking deputies to resign (see Johnson, 1995, pp. 224–31).

[71] *Asahi Shimbun* (November 18, 1995).

equipment manufacturers, and the union, the ruling coalition decided in March 1996 to postpone any decision on breakup for at least one more year.

THE NEW REGIME

The new telecommunications regime has three primary characteristics. First, the MPT has become the dominant force in the sector. Authority within the regime remains "fused" in the sense that it is centralized within a single agency. The unusual aspect of Japan's reform is that the dominance of NTT within the old regime has been replaced by the dominance of the MPT within the new regime. Regulatory authority has shifted in three fundamental ways. Control over the budget and personnel has shifted from the Diet to NTT with MPT supervision; responsibility for price and service regulation has shifted from the Diet to the MPT; and responsibility for technical regulation has shifted from NTT to the MPT (Table 10). In their own study of Japan's telecommunications reform, Noll and Rosenbluth make the extraordinary claim that "Japan's parliamentary and unitary (nonfederal) system of government gives the majority party in the Diet unfettered influence over the bureaucracy and over the regulatory process at every stage of implementation."[72] But if this were so, then why would the LDP willingly give up so much power? And why would it allow the MPT to undermine administrative reform by increasing its powers so dramatically? When SDPJ politician Sanji Mutō asked Hashimoto why the LDP let the MPT expand its regulatory powers so much, Hashimoto's response was less than impressive: "Well I have forgotten the details, but you [Mutō] certainly did bring a great number of matters to my attention, and at the time I would think 'well that really is terrible,' and then I would put in a call [to the MPT]. But they would give their own reasons for these regulations, and although we did have some of them corrected, clearly some have remained."[73] In other words, MPT bureaucrats turned an LDP "deregulation" initiative into the most extreme form of expansionary reregulation, and LDP leaders were simply helpless to stop them.[74]

---

[72] Noll and Rosenbluth (1995) p. 147.

[73] Komori (1988), p. 98.

[74] This case illustrates the peril in taking the Diet's formal authority over the bureaucracy at face value. Noll and Rosenbluth (1995) derive their interpretation of Japan's telecommunications reform from their presumption of LDP dominance while ignoring the evidence to the contrary. They simply assert, for example, that telecommunications users, manufacturers, and potential entrants provided the impetus for reform (p. 146), whereas in fact MPT officials had devised their outline for reform before users, manufacturers, or LDP Diet members became involved in the process—and before potential entrants had ever imagined that they could get into the telecommunications business.

	Before reform	*After reform*
Operator	NTT	NTT, others
Regulator	NTT	MPT
Sponsor	NTT	MPT
Owner	Government	Government, shareholders

Second, the MPT has taken up industrial policy—in sharp contrast to Britain's DTI which virtually abandoned industrial sponsorship under Thatcher. The MPT thus brazenly defies the Anglo-American notion of "deregulation." It has gradually tried to gain more control over telecommunications research and development, although its own budget remains dwarfed by that of NTT. The MPT's total research and development budget for 1994 came to 37 billion yen, compared to 291 billion for NTT.[75] The MPT has tried to compensate for its budgetary limitations by employing tax incentives to encourage private investment in telecommunications equipment, and by directing funds to telecommunications infrastructure projects through the Japan Development Bank (JDB). MPT-related JDB loans have grown from zero in 1985 to over 100 billion yen in 1994, about 5 percent of JDB's total.[76] The ministry is gradually increasing funding for its own telecommunications research laboratory, the Radio Research Laboratory. It uses projects at the Key Technology Center—which it oversees jointly with MITI—to encourage research and development collaboration between private companies. In particular, the MPT has directed a substantial portion of its Key Technology funds to the Advanced Telecommunications Research International (ATR), a public-private consortium of research labs it established in March 1986. Meanwhile, NTT claims that it cannot spend as much on basic research because its profits have decreased in the face of competition. This opens the possibility of an implicit bargain that could help out both the MPT and NTT: the MPT keeps up the competitive pressure on NTT through its price and service regulation, but the MPT and other government agencies help out NTT by shouldering more of the cost of telecommunications research. In June 1995, the MPT announced plans to revise two laws to bolster its ability to finance the telecommunications infrastructure. Among other measures, the ministry proposed using the proceeds from the NTT privatization to make low-interest loans to telecommunications and cable television operators.[77]

Third, the MPT has taken an unusually interventionist approach toward managing the competition in telecommunications services. It has not

[75] MPT and NTT data.

[76] MPT data. Yamada with Borrus (February 1992) analyzes the MPT's new industrial policy role at greater length.

[77] *MPT News* 6:7 (July 3, 1995). On Japan's plans for a National Information Infrastructure (NII), see West (February 1995).

adopted the DTI's laissez-faire philosophy, nor Oftel's juridical style of pro-competitive regulation. Rather it has opted for a highly discretionary style of administrative guidance more characteristic of the MoF or MITI— or the MPT's own broadcasting bureau. It has orchestrated the entry of competitors in each market segment. The MPT was involved in the establishment of all three new common carriers (NCCs) in the long-distance market. It originally hoped to limit entry to two carriers, but agreed to allow three because the Ministry of Transportation (MoT) insisted on sponsoring Japan Telecom, which uses lines along the railway network; the Ministry of Construction insisted on sponsoring Teleway Japan, which uses lines along the highway network; and the MPT wanted to have at least one truly private competitor. DDI Corporation, which primarily uses microwave technology, filled this role.

In the international market, the MPT was less anxious to encourage competition, but it eventually allowed two competitors: International Telecom Japan (ITJ) and International Digital Communications (IDC), the latter of which is partly owned by the United Kingdom's Cable & Wireless.[78] MPT officials look upon KDD as a favored child, in stark contrast to NTT, the overgrown renegade. KDD has readily accepted retired MPT officials as senior executives and has more eagerly cooperated with MPT guidance. An executive from one international carrier reports that the MPT initially refused to let it apply to compete with KDD, and only accepted its application after six months of detailed negotiations. Of course, as is the case with other Japanese ministries, the pre-application negotiations were more important than the application itself, and the application was quickly approved.[79]

In mobile services, the MPT itself arranged the consortia to compete with NTT. According to one U.S. negotiator, the MPT asked foreign firms trying to enter the paging and mobile telephone businesses to delay applications while the ministry assembled acceptable consortia of companies to enter these fields.[80] In mobile telephones, the MPT originally hoped to merge the potential competitors into one company using NTT technology. But after considerable pressure from the United States, the MPT allowed a second consortium led by DDI Corporation using Motorola technology. The MPT assigned the DDI consortium to the Kansai (Osaka) region and the other to the Kantō (Tokyo) region, but eventually required the Kantō carrier, Nippon Idou Tsūshin Corporation (IDO) to carry the

---

[78] The MPT allowed foreign participation despite considerable protest from KDD, among others. "What foreigners do not understand," explains one MPT official, "is that the private sector and not the MPT opposed foreign participation. They should thank us because we were the ones that made the private sector accept this." Interview, August 1992.

[79] Interview with telecommunications executive (July 1992).

[80] Prestowitz (1989), p. 484.

Motorola format as well. Nevertheless, IDO, which is closely affiliated with NTT, has strongly favored the NTT format in its infrastructure development, effectively preventing the Motorola format from significantly expanding its market share. The U.S. government vehemently protested this situation, and the MPT finally agreed in February 1994 to make IDO accelerate its investment in the Motorola-format infrastructure. In the satellite communications market, the MPT initially restricted the market to two competitors—Japan Communications Satellite Company and Space Communications Corporation—because it felt that three would be a crowd. But the United States pressured the MPT to allow another entrant, in the hope of promoting U.S. satellite exports, and the MPT licensed Satellite Japan. In August 1993, however, MPT officials discreetly orchestrated a re-merger of two of these carriers, leaving the market with two players once again.

The MPT has maintained a basic principle of market segmentation in telecommunications, much as it does in broadcasting or as the MoF does in finance. But ministry officials recognize that they will not be able to maintain this strategy forever, as technology advances and competition between carriers intensifies. Therefore, they have already begun quietly deliberating on how to reorganize the telecommunications market. They may borrow a practice from the MoF and arrange mergers between some of the carriers. The MPT would then use these mergers to bridge market segments, marrying international to long-distance carriers or joining long-distance carriers to local carriers. The MPT completed its first merger in 1992 when it arranged the bailout of Tokyo Marinet, a mobile service for the Tokyo Bay area.

Unlike Oftel, which uses a rigid price-cap formula, the MPT micromanages the competition between NTT and its major rivals by evaluating every price or service change in terms of its potential impact on the competitive balance. Typically, the MPT conducts extensive negotiations and demands enormous amounts of data before it permits such a change. If MPT officials are not inclined to permit a specific change, they may simply ask carriers not to apply because they would have to a provide written explanations if they were to formally deny a permit. Like other Japanese ministry officials, MPT officials have been known to leverage their formal authority in order to exercise "administrative guidance." For example, they demanded that the carriers explain in writing that customers can end up paying more with certain discount calling plans depending on their calling patterns, although they have no legal authority to enforce this demand. Similarly, they have advised Teleway Japan to expand its network more rapidly because it lags behind the other two new long-distance carriers. In the case of noncompliance, the threat of punishment is usually implied rather than explicit, and the punishment does not necessarily fit the crime. "If you make trouble in Edo (Tokyo)," remarks one executive from a major carrier, "then they get you back in Nagasaki."[81]

The formal procedure for price changes is quite straightforward: the carriers apply, and the MPT says yes or no. In practice, however, NTT executives claim that the MPT will not let them lower prices, and MPT officials contend that they have to force NTT to lower prices. Insiders suggest that the truth lies somewhere in between. The MPT was initially reluctant to let NTT lower prices too quickly for fear that this would hurt the competitors. More recently, however, NTT has become reluctant to lower prices because of declining profits. Unable to get NTT to lower prices in 1992, the MPT apparently persuaded Japan Telecom to move first.[82] From 1985 through 1993, NTT lowered the cost for a three-minute call from Tokyo to Osaka from 400 to 180 yen. The three new carriers initially held a 40 yen advantage over NTT for most calls until 1992, but the MPT then allowed NTT to cut the gap to 20 yen in 1992, and 10 yen in 1993.[83] In 1994 MPT introduced a completely new price structure, with higher starting prices but larger local calling areas. The MPT has evaluated the competitive situation quite differently in the case of international service, where it allowed KDD to close the price gap with its competitors very quickly. MPT officials argue that NTT has a greater advantage over its competitors than KDD does because it can offer the combination of local and long-distance service. Concerning the services it offers, the MPT has been reluctant to allow NTT to get too far ahead of its competitors. In numerous cases, the MPT has delayed taking action on an NTT application for a service change so that the new carriers have a chance to develop a comparable service. In particular, the MPT has been very slow to permit discount calling plans, because these would erode the new carriers' price advantage. Executives from the carriers complain that the MPT takes an average of four months to take action on permit applications, with some responses being delayed by more than a year.[84]

The MPT's heavy hand of regulation certainly violates the spirit of "deregulation," but has not prevented liberalization. The NCCs had 10.1 percent of the domestic telephone service market on a revenue basis, and 16.1 percent of the private line market in fiscal 1993. Competing carriers had 29.5 percent of the international telephone service market, and 37.8 percent of the mobile telephone market.[85] In addition, thirty-nine Special Type II and 1550 General Type II carriers (VAN service providers) had entered the market by 1994 (see Table 11). By fostering competition and

---

[81] Interview (June 1991).
[82] Interviews (1992).
[83] *JEI Report* 28A (July 28, 1995), p. 9.
[84] Interviews (1990–91) and internal company documents.
[85] *JEI Report* 28A (July 28, 1995), pp. 7–8.

Table 11. The growing number of competitors in telecommunications services

	1985	1986	1987	1988	1989	1990	1991	1992	1993	1994
Type I Total	2	7	13	37	45	62	68	70	80	86
NTT	1	1	1	1	1	1	1	1	1	1
KDD	1	1	1	1	1	1	1	1	1	1
Long-distance		3	3	3	3	3	3	3	3	3
Regional			3	4	4	7	7	7	8	10
Satellite		2	2	2	2	2	2	3	3	2
Mobile telephone				3	5	13	16	17	26	36
Paging			2	20	26	33	36	36	36	31
International				2	2	2	2	2	2	2
Other			1	1	1					
Type II total	85	209	356	530	693	841	943	1036	1179	1589
Special Type II		9	10	18	25	28	31	36	36	39
General Type II	85	200	346	512	668	813	912	1000	1143	1550
Total	87	216	369	567	738	903	1011	1106	1259	1675

SOURCE: MPT data.

yet tightly controlling the terms of competition, the MPT follows in a long tradition of market management cultivated by other Japanese ministries and nearly perfected by the MPT's across-the-street neighbor, the MoF.

CHAPTER EIGHT

Financial Services: The Ministry of Finance and the Perpetual Bargain

In the summer of 1991, Masaaki Tsuchida was roughly halfway through his term as director general of the Finance Ministry's Banking Bureau. When asked to reflect for a moment on the reform of the financial system, a top priority during his tenure, Tsuchida alluded to a deal made fifty years earlier. During the Second World War, the Ministry of Finance (MoF) and the Ministry of Commerce and Industry (now the Ministry of International Trade and Industry or MITI) swapped jurisdictions: the MoF passed alcohol over to MITI, and MITI gave up securities and insurance in return.[1] "Although probably no one realized what this would mean at the time," Tsuchida noted, "this has made it much easier for us to deal with financial reform today."[2]

Japan may never offer the universal bank—a single financial institution that can provide the full range of financial services from banking to broker-age to insurance—yet it has the closest thing in the advanced industrial world to one-stop financial regulation, all on the fourth floor of the MoF. The ministry's three financial regulatory bureaus—the Banking Bureau, the Securities Bureau, and the International Finance Bureau—control the regulation of all types of banks, securities firms, and insurance companies. MoF officials regard the breadth of their jurisdiction, which includes levying taxes and compiling the budget, as a critical source of their power and prestige.[3] More-

Portions of this chapter have appeared previously in Vogel (July 1994).
[1] Johnson (1982, pp. 142–43) notes that the MoF also gave up control over import and export licenses.
[2] Interview with Masaaki Tsuchida, director general, Banking Bureau, MoF (June 13, 1991).
[3] Rosenbluth (1989) argues that the MoF's ability to package bargains between industry groups depends on this broad scope of jurisdiction. The policy process then differs on those regulatory issues where the ministry shares jurisdiction with another agency, such as the MPT.

over the ministry is not simply a powerful bureaucracy: it is a singularly *political* institution. The MoF is not "autonomous" in the sense that it can formulate policy independently from the financial institutions, but it is not captive to these institutions either. The MoF is rather the master orchestrator of the political bargains that eventually emerge as financial policy. The ministry's structure strongly affects which interest groups have the most access to the policy process, and how policy is formulated and implemented. And when structuring these deals, MoF officials manage to filter in some of their own agenda: what they think is good for Japan, for the financial system, and, of course, for the ministry.

THE OLD REGIME

When Japanese authorities reconstructed the financial system after the Second World War, their highest priority was to devise a means of reliably allocating low-cost funds to industry and thereby promoting long-term economic growth. Economists still debate the efficiency of the postwar finance system, but agree that it certainly facilitated a massive transfer of funds from the personal to the corporate sector.[4] MoF regulatory policy in the postwar era was designed to promote industrial growth and to achieve several goals that MoF officials believed to be directly tied to the prospects for growth. Specifically, they sought to ensure the stability of the financial system, to maximize their own control over the system, and to facilitate the performance of other critical ministry functions such as managing fiscal policy. Toward these ends, Japanese officials structured and nurtured a financial system defined by five essential characteristics: the segmentation of different types of financial institutions, the dominance of indirect financing (bank lending), the maintenance of artificially low interest rates, relative isolation from international financial markets, and heavy regulation designed to prevent both entry to and exit from the market.

The Occupation authorities failed in many respects to transform the financial system, but they did leave Japan with Article 65 of the Securities and Exchange Law, modeled on the U.S. Glass-Steagall Act, which separated banks from securities houses. Japanese banks are further divided into commercial banks, including city banks, regional banks, and credit associations (*shinyō kinko*) and cooperatives (*shinyō kumiai*) ; seven trust banks, specializing in the management of trusts and pension funds; three long-term credit banks, focusing on long-term lending to industry; and one foreign exchange bank, the Bank of Tokyo. The government also cre-

---

[4] See, for example, Hamada and Horiuchi (1987), Imai (August 1989), and Tachibanaki (June 1991).

ated a number of government financial institutions, including the Japan Development Bank (JDB) and the Export-Import Bank, to support industrial investment and trade through subsidized financing. Meanwhile, the Ministry of Posts and Telecommunications (MPT) operated the huge postal savings system, a crucial organ for funneling personal savings to favored industrial sectors and government-sponsored development projects through the Fiscal Investment and Loan Program (FILP).[5]

The authorities promoted a "credit-based" financial system: that is, industry relied primarily on loans through banks, rather than on capital markets, for long-term financing.[6] The banks at the center of industrial groups (*keiretsu*) became the "main banks" for companies within the group, offering low rates and financial help when needed in exchange for the companies' business. The authorities deliberately handicapped bond markets with stringent issuing conditions and high minimum issue amounts. They gave securities houses a monopoly in bond underwriting, but compensated the banks by requiring issuers to provide collateral and designating the banks as trustees for the collateral. They tightly regulated trading activity and routinely intervened to control volatility in equity markets. They kept interest rates artificially low in order to control the cost of capital for industry and to facilitate the administrative allocation of capital for industrial policy purposes.[7] This implied a transfer of resources from the household sector, which received lower-than-market rates on its bank and postal deposits, to the industrial sector, which could borrow money at favorable rates. Below-market rates also created excess demand for capital, allowing the MoF, in conjunction with MITI and the Bank of Japan (BoJ), to allocate funds to preferred sectors.[8] The system of controlled interest rates also helped the banks, because it guaranteed them a healthy spread between the low rate they gave to depositors and the higher rate they charged industry for loans. This system only worked because the MoF also restricted capital inflow and outflow. Under the Foreign Exchange and Trade Control Law, the government limited cross-border financial transactions, insulating the Japanese economy from international finance and making it easier for authorities to control financial markets.

[5] On the linkage between postal savings and high savings rates, see Anderson (1990).
[6] This terminology comes from Zysman's (1983) differentiation between three basic types of financial systems: capital-market based (the United States and Britain), credit-based with administered prices (Japan and France), and credit-based and dominated by financial institutions (Germany).
[7] Meerschwam (December 1989) and Frankel (April 1990), among others, suggest that Japan's cost-of-capital advantage has been greatly exaggerated.
[8] See Johnson (1982) on the role of finance in MITI's industrial policy, Zysman (1983) on Japan as an example of a credit-based financial system, and Noguchi and Sakakibara (August 1977) on the MoF-BoJ mechanism for controlling the flow of funds. Calder (1993) argues that Johnson and Zysman overstate the role of the MoF and MITI and understate the role of the financial institutions themselves.

The MoF, and the Banking Bureau in particular, regulated financial markets with a heavy hand in order to maintain the stability of the financial system. Both the segmentation of the financial system and the regulation of interest rates served the purpose of limiting competition and thereby minimizing the risk of bank failure. MoF officials defined stability in terms of preventing failures altogether because they believed that failures would extract a high cost in terms of disruption to the economy and an even higher cost in terms of lost confidence in the ministry and the financial system as a whole. Ministry officials used their regional representatives to monitor the activities of local banks closely. If they suspected weakness, they would advise the bank in question and sometimes even send retiring MoF officials to take over the management of these banks.[9] They managed to prevent near-failures from becoming outright failures that could undermine public confidence by arranging mergers with other institutions.[10] "In terms of maintaining order," boasted Tsuchida of the Banking Bureau, "we feel we have an indisputable, remarkable record."[11] Ministry officials have been somewhat less protective of securities houses, but they have been notoriously conservative when it came to the stock market. They have relied on an elaborate set of "voluntary" trading rules backed by a smaller set of legal restrictions to limit volatility in the market.

The MoF's style of regulation depended on a close working relationship with the financial institutions themselves. MoF officials required a detailed knowledge of financial institutions' management and finances in order to intervene before problems got out of control. They relied on considerable administrative discretion, interpreting the law in a characteristically flexible manner.[12] They used administrative guidance to persuade banks to change their management practices, to direct securities houses to alter their trading practices, or to restrict insurance companies from investing in certain types of assets. Beyond prudential regulation, MoF officials also asked financial institutions to support their own policy goals: purchasing government bonds at favorable rates, or taking over struggling banks. They could normally count on compliance because they enjoyed the practitioners' trust and because they controlled an enormous array of permits and licenses that financial institutions needed to conduct their business.

---

[9] A *Yomiuri Shimbun* survey in 1979 reported that thirteen of eighteen banks with questionable financial standing had former MoF officials as executives, twelve in the position of president. Horne (1988), pp. 187–88.

[10] There were no outright failures prior to 1995—nor any new entrants, aside from foreign banks, since 1955 (Management and Coordination Agency data).

[11] Tsuchida interview (13 June 1991).

[12] Beller, Terai, and Levine (1992) offer a fascinating case study demonstrating how MoF officials inherited a securities law (the Securities and Exchange Law of 1948) closely patterned after U.S. law, and yet administered the law in a manner that broke completely with U.S. practice.

The MoF had a reputation for retaliating against rebel financial institutions, often imposing punishment not directly related to the offense. For example, the MoF has been particularly stingy in granting new branch offices to Daiwa Bank ever since the bank ignored MoF guidance and entered the trust business.[13]

Unlike the MPT, the MoF dominated the financial regime throughout the postwar period. Even among Japan's elite ministries, the MoF enjoys unusual power and prestige.[14] Within the financial sector, its only major rivals for authority are the Bank of Japan (BoJ) and the MPT. The MoF has supervisory powers over the BoJ, which usually defers to the MoF on policy issues. But when a problem directly affects the BoJ's central concern, monetary policy, the Bank is a bit more feisty. It has, for example, openly pushed for the establishment of a treasury bill market so that it can use open market operations more effectively as a tool in monetary policy. The MPT, which controls the immensely popular postal savings system, is more problematic for the MoF. MoF officials have been continually frustrated by the postal savings system because they cannot control the interest rates on postal account deposits.[15]

The ministry's decision-making procedures strongly favor some interests over others. The formal process centers on the policy councils (*shingikai*). As we found in the last chapter, ministry officials strongly influence the orientation of the councils: they screen potential members; they brief the members extensively; and they often draft the councils' final reports. MoF officials like to think of the policy council process as a sort of democracy among experts: they are pooling relevant and informed opinions before taking any action. But *shingikai* democracy is a very strange type of democracy indeed. The representation on these councils is heavily biased in favor of the industry that falls directly under the jurisdiction of the particular ministry, or bureau, sponsoring the council. Thus the Banking Bureau's policy council has more bankers than brokers, whereas the Securities Bureau's council has more brokers than bankers. Interested parties who do not fall directly under the relevant jurisdiction—including corporate borrowers as well as household consumers—are underrepresented. Even among financial institutions, the ministry incorporates some views more than others. The banks have the closest ties with the ministry, followed by the securities houses, insurance companies, and then non-banks. But along with representation within the MoF comes responsibilities to the MoF. The city banks are generally happy to accept MoF "guidance" as the price for unrivaled access to the ministry. They value this access as much for the in-

[13] As of 1990, Daiwa had 181 branches, compared to 220–520 for the other major city banks. MoF, Banking Bureau (1991), p. 397.

[14] This has generated a huge literature of popular books trying to analyze the MoF's power (Nihon Keizai Shimbun, 1992, and Toshikawa, 1995, for example).

[15] See Rosenbluth (1989), especially pp. 167–208.

formation as for the influence it provides: they like to know what the MoF is planning before it acts. For their part, the non-banks are equally satisfied with their nonrepresentation, as long as they can continue to enjoy the benefits of being relatively free from MoF control.

Representatives of the financial institutions also interact with MoF officials on a less formal basis. The major financial institutions all have at least one or two designated MoF-watchers (*mofu-tan*), who constantly shuffle between headquarters and the ministry, staying informed of the latest developments. Ministry officials welcome the contact with the private sector as much as the private sector welcomes the contact with ministry. They believe that their control over the financial system is a product of their close contact with the financial institutions. They use this contact to influence the financial institutions, just as the institutions use this contact to lobby them. They also feel that a cooperative relationship with financial institutions makes policy implementation more effective.[16]

LDP Diet members were normally happy to leave financial policy up to the ministry. Most Diet members did not understand the details of financial regulation and lacked the staff to support them in this area. Furthermore, they had relatively little interest in finance politically, for although banks and securities houses were important donors, they counted for very few votes. Banks in particular were very "clean" donors, meaning that they gave to the party as a whole more than to individual politicians. Thus they bought general goodwill, but not specific favors.[17] Far more LDP Diet members join the party Communications Division or Construction Division than the Finance Division, even though the Finance Division deals with the budget as well as with financial policy.[18] The party did intervene occasionally, particularly in response to public outrage over financial scandals. They did so not to usurp power from the MoF, but to prove to the public that they were working on the problem. The party would also intervene if a particular ministry or a group of financial institutions appealed for their help, although such appeals were relatively rare in the case of financial policy. The LDP could usually safely ignore the opposition parties. These parties might express their outrage whenever a financial scandal erupted, but they had little impact on the government's response.

---

[16] For example, Ulrike Schaede (1990) has found that although Japanese authorities took longer than other countries to make the decision to create a futures market, the market developed more quickly once it was permitted—precisely because the market players knew what to expect. Litt et al. (1990) provide further evidence.

[17] Rosenbluth (1989) argues that these donations bought substantial influence on specific policies. I contend, however, that the party's willingness to allow the MoF to pursue policies strongly opposed by some of Japan's most wealthy and powerful financial institutions (several of which are discussed later in this chapter) suggests otherwise.

[18] As of 1992, the Finance Division had 60 members, compared to 80 for Communications, 115 for Agriculture, and 151 for Construction. LDP (April 1992).

NEW CHALLENGES

The economic logic of financial liberalization in Japan differs from that of Britain because of the very different structure of Japan's financial system. The segmentation of the Japanese system, and the division between banks and brokers in particular, provides institutions with the incentive to circumvent this segmentation. Banks seek ways to act more like brokers, and brokers seek ways to act more like banks. Likewise, the limitations of the domestic bond market have pushed issuers to seek better conditions abroad. The very stringency of regulation creates incentives to innovate and to arbitrage between markets.

The most important impetus behind Japan's financial reforms has been the gradual trend toward disintermediation: the shift from bank lending to equity financing. By the 1970s the banks' best customers—those large industrial firms with the best credit ratings—were increasingly raising money in the Euromarkets rather than borrowing from the banks. Big business reliance on bank loans declined from 30.2 percent of funds in 1973–77 to 17.5 percent by 1978–82.[19] As companies moved more toward equity financing, the larger banks naturally became more interested in breaking into the securities business.[20] To make matters worse for the banks, they were simultaneously losing market share in savings deposits to the postal savings system.[21] The city banks' share of the overall financial services market declined from 35.4 percent in 1970, to 31.6 percent in 1975, to 25.8 percent in 1980.[22] The banks captured some of the Euromarket business, but the "Three Bureaus Agreement" of 1974 prohibited them from undermining the spirit of Article 65: they could not serve as lead underwriters of Euromarket bonds or otherwise threaten the securities firms' strength in this sector. MoF officials gradually allowed bankers and brokers to invade selected niches in each other's territory. In 1979, for example, the ministry permitted banks to issue high-denomination certificates of deposit, giving them an instrument bearing market interest rates. In 1980, in exchange, it granted securities houses the right to offer medium-term government bond funds (*"chūkoku"* funds), which combine market returns with liquidity approaching that of bank deposits.[23]

In the early 1980s, MoF officials slowly began to chart out longer-term plans for liberalization. In April 1983, the ministry's Financial System Re-

---

[19] Hamada and Horiuchi (1987), p. 249.

[20] On the economics of financial liberalization in Japan, see Rōyama (1989) and Tachibanaki (June 1991).

[21] The postal system's share of personal savings and deposits rose from 15.7 percent in 1965, to 19.0 percent in 1970, to 23.1 percent in 1975, to 29.8 percent in 1980. FAIR (1991), p. 465.

[22] Hamada and Horiuchi (1987), p. 227.

[23] Arora (1991), pp. 136–40.

search Council completed a report that recommended incremental liberalization of interest rates and desegmentation of the financial system.[24]
MoF officials wanted to make Japanese markets more efficient and to promote Tokyo as an international financial center, but more immediately
they recognized that they would have to create a fuller short-term market
in order to refinance the huge amount of government bonds that would
begin to reach maturity in 1985.

The Japanese themselves explain liberalization as the result of two *kokusaika*. "Kokusaika" can mean two very different things, depending on
which character is used for the "sai." The more common meaning, "internationalization," became one of Japan's most overworn catchwords of the
1980s. But "kokusai" also means government bond, and this second *kokusaika* ("government bond-ization," one might say) played a critical part in
the history of financial liberalization. The MoF issued the first national
bonds in 1966, but only began issuing large quantities in 1975. Given that
these latter bonds would begin to mature in 1985, and the government
could not possibly pay off the debt, the government was effectively creating a short-term market in government bonds. This, in turn, produced
pressure for further financial liberalization.

Although the momentum toward reform had begun to build, U.S. government pressure transformed the domestic debate. This was probably no
accident, for even those MoF officials and Japanese bankers and brokers who
favored reform felt that Japanese deregulation would have to begin exter-
nally and move internally. This runs counter to the standard economic logic,
which places internal liberalization first.[25] In Japan, however, political logic
won out over economic logic, for it was obvious to all parties that it would be
easier to push through external liberalization—improving foreign access to
the Tokyo market and promoting the internationalization of the yen, rather
than internal liberalization—deregulating interest rates and breaking down
the segmentation of the financial system. Furthermore, external liberalization would create added economic incentives for internal liberalization.[26]

The United States had its own peculiar reasons for bringing up financial
liberalization in 1983. The U.S. government's goal was not to help U.S. financial institutions so much as it was to help U.S. manufacturers, by
strengthening the yen relative to the dollar. Lee Morgan, chairman of

[24] Summarized in MoF, Banking Bureau (1983), pp. 20–22.
[25] See Caves, Frankel, and Jones (1990), pp. 538–39.
[26] Nomura Securities, Japan's largest broker, also promoted a foreign-led liberalization
strategy by proposing to enter the trust business in a joint venture with J. P. Morgan (see
Shiota, 1988). But MoF officials got the last laugh by requiring foreign firms entering the
trust business to tie up with Japanese trust banks, not securities houses. Some Japanese reporters (interviews, 1991) even claim that Nomura prodded the U.S. government to press
for financial liberalization by submitting a paper to the Treasury through its research arm,
the Nomura Research Institute.

Caterpillar Tractor and a leader of the Businessmen's Roundtable, led a movement calling for a correction of the yen-dollar rate imbalance, which he and others assumed was a primary cause of the enormous U.S. trade deficit. Morgan commissioned a report from Stanford economist Ezra Solomon and Washington, D.C., lawyer David Murchison, who concluded that the best way to realign the two currencies would be to open up Japanese capital markets and to internationalize the yen.[27] The U.S. government took up the issue at the November 1983 summit between President Ronald Reagan and Prime Minister Yasuhiro Nakasone, where the two sides issued a joint communiqué establishing a "Yen-Dollar Committee" to discuss financial liberalization in greater detail.

The MoF's first approach was to dust off their own preexisting plans for gradual deregulation, which had been outlined in the April 1983 policy council report, and to present these to the United States as their proposed response. But they quickly realized that the United States was looking for something much more far-reaching, and the Americans were not going to let the issue go. International Finance Bureau officials, who were convinced of the merits of major reforms, used the opportunity to convince their more conservative colleagues. They deliberately included senior Banking and Securities Bureau officials in many of the yen-dollar meetings to convince them to go along.[28] They leaked information about the talks in order to prepare domestic institutions for what was coming.[29] And most critically, from their point of view at least, they kept other ministries and politicians out of the process. The U.S. side had proposed wider discussions, but the MoF insisted that they be limited to the ministry and the Treasury.[30]

When the final Yen-Dollar Committee report came out in 1984, the Japanese press portrayed it as no less than a financial revolution. Some analysts warned that the reforms would incite chaos in Japanese financial markets. Yet none of the dire predictions came to pass. The MoF's own report in response to the yen-dollar talks revealed its strategy for reform: soften the impact of change and maintain ministerial authority. Among other things, the ministry emphasized that it would upgrade its supervisory capabilities, tighten disclosure requirements, and promote mergers between banks.[31] The ministry moved quickly on those issues with the least opposition: liber-

---

[27] Frankel (1984) summarizes the issues involved in the yen-dollar talks, persuasively arguing that the economic logic of the Solomon-Murchison report was flawed. Also see Funabashi (1988) on the yen-dollar talks.

[28] Interviews with Toyoo Gyohten, senior adviser, Bank of Tokyo, and former deputy minister, MoF (August 15, 1991), and Makoto Utsumi, senior adviser and former deputy minister, MoF (July 15, 1992).

[29] Ebato (1987), pp. 54–55.

[30] Utsumi interview (July 15, 1992). Tadokoro (1988) argues that the yen-dollar talks played a critical role in moving the domestic liberalization process out of a logjam.

[31] Ebato (1987), p. 67.

alizing the Euroyen bond market and allowing foreign institutions to set up trust subsidiaries. They then took on the more difficult and politically sensitive issues—interest rate liberalization and the desegmentation of the financial system—in their own particularly drawn-out fashion.

THE LIBERALIZATION OF DEPOSIT INTEREST RATES

Japan started liberalizing interest rates much later than the United States and went about the process much more deliberately—that is, slowly. The "deliberate" speed served two purposes: it made it easier for the ministry to get the losers (primarily the smaller banks) to accept their fate, and it gave the ministry and the smaller banks time to adjust. This delay defies the standard logic of economic theory because interest rate regulation impedes market efficiency and the exit of uncompetitive firms should enhance it. But given the MoF's priorities, the approach makes perfect sense. The MoF values stability and is willing to sacrifice short-term efficiency in order to ensure that the transition is smooth. During the interim period, the ministry actively worked with the smaller banks to make them more competitive. The "step-by-step" approach allowed it to monitor the impact of liberalization on the most vulnerable institutions. If things were going well, the MoF speeded up the schedule; if badly, it slowed it down. If one looks at the whole process as the MoF's attempt to realize two potentially conflicting goals—interest rate liberalization and the maintenance of their record of no bank failures—deregulation MoF-style starts to make sense. "We may have started a bit late," argues one MoF official, "but we have nothing to apologize about concerning the speed of liberalization. We are confident that we have gone about this the right way."[32]

MoF officials themselves recognized the potential benefits to be gained from liberalization early on, but did not rush into it because they felt that the system of regulated rates had some important advantages. First, as we saw earlier, the MoF used interest rate regulations to transfer resources from the household sector to the corporate sector, and to direct funds to preferred sectors. But the MoF no longer needed to do this once the corporate sector became a net creditor, and the government itself became the main debtor in the country. Second, the ministry itself had an interest in keeping interest rates low because this helped it control the cost of servicing the national debt. Third, the system facilitated control over the financial system. Regulated interest rates decreased the likelihood of bank failure, and made the financial institutions heavily dependent on the MoF. Fourth, MoF officials felt that the regulated system helped Japanese finan-

---

[32] Interview with MoF official (June 1991).

cial institutions compete abroad, because they had access to cheap funds from their depositors.

For its part, the BoJ supported liberalization largely by not interfering on behalf of the smaller banks. One Bank official recalls a meeting between Bank Governor Haruo Maekawa and the top leadership of the Federation of Credit Associations (Zenshinren), including the association's legendary boss, Tetsugorō Ohara. Ohara and his followers made an impassioned appeal for Maekawa to put a stop to liberalization, but Maekawa flatly refused. "Liberalization cannot be stopped," Maekawa told them, "so you better get ready."[33]

The different types of banks varied in the degree of their opposition to deposit interest rate liberalization. All would lose out in the short term, because they would have to offer higher interest rates, thus increasing their cost of funds. But the city banks were in a stronger position to weather this storm and felt that in the long term higher rates would help them to compete with securities firms. Even the city banks, however, did not push for early liberalization. According to a 1985 survey, five of seven city banks reported that "given the characteristics of our financial system, interest rate liberalization should be pursued much more moderately than in the United States," and six of seven stated that "interest rate liberalization should be advanced gradually, after observing trends."[34] The regional banks were more hesitant about liberalization, and the credit associations and the agricultural cooperatives (*nōkyō*) were outright opposed. LDP members traditionally supported the smaller banks and the agricultural cooperatives, but did not intervene to defend them from liberalization.

Consumers, who in theory should support deposit interest liberalization the most, were distinctly uninterested. A survey by the nation's largest consumer group, the Housewives' Federation (*shufu rengōkai*, or "Shufuren" for short), found that consumers felt more comfortable if all the banks had the same interest rate.[35] One MoF official recalls that he could not find a single consumer representative to testify before a policy council in favor of interest rate liberalization. When he finally found one consumer representative who felt that consumers would benefit from liberalization, the representative still refused to speak out. "Personally I would like to see liberalization," he responded, "but my organization has come out against it. They want more regulations, not less."[36]

For MoF officials, liberalizing deposit interest rates also meant coping with the sensitive issue of postal savings. The ministry and the commer-

---

[33] Interview with BoJ official (July 1992).

[34] Economic Planning Agency, Comprehensive Planning Bureau (1986), p. 233.

[35] Interview with Hatsuko Yoshioka, deputy director, Secretariat, Shufuren (August 6, 1991).

[36] Interview with MoF official (February 1991).

cial banks feared that the banks would be decimated if the postal system were allowed to compete for deposits on the basis of price. Commercial banks argued that the postal savings system would have an unfair advantage in price competition because post offices do not have to worry about the bottom line and enjoy a built-in network of more than twenty-thousand branches. In the past, MPT officials had opposed liberalization just as much as the commercial banks, but they shifted their stance in the early 1980s because they recognized that liberalization could benefit postal savings at the expense of the banks. In fact, one MPT official recalls staying up all night in early 1983 fighting with MoF officials about how to word the response to a question regarding interest rate liberalization that was to be asked at the next day's Diet session.[37] The precise wording of the response was critical, for it would be an official expression of the government's attitude toward liberalization. The MoF side wanted to reply that the government would "promote liberalization as appropriate," with the emphasis on the "as appropriate." The MPT wanted to state that the government would "actively address it," with the emphasis on "actively." In the end, the prime minister came up with his own wording: the government would "promote it steadily."[38] In April 1994, in anticipation of the liberalization of demand deposits in October, the two ministries reached an agreement whereby the postal system would preserve a substantial interest rate advantage (about one percent) over commercial banks but would link its rates to those offered by the banks.[39]

In 1985, the Banking Bureau began to deliberate the liberalization of interest rates in an informal advisory policy council to the director general of the bureau. The MoF began liberalization with the largest time deposits. Rosenbluth argues that this approach reflects a predictable political logic, for it helps large institutions, not household savers.[40] I suggest that this simply reflects an economic logic, for large depositors are precisely those who can bypass bank deposits and seek higher returns elsewhere. It also reflects a MoF logic: to do last that which hurts the vulnerable institutions most. Banking Bureau officials created a most elegantly drawn out schedule of liberalization, with incremental decreases in the minimum amount for market rates being announced at precise six-month intervals (see Table 12). They used the liberalization schedule as a warning to the smaller and weaker firms to strengthen their management or to link up with other banks.

---

[37] The opposition Diet members customarily—although not always—give the ministries one-day advance notice of what questions they will ask.
[38] Interview with MPT official (June 1991).
[39] *Tokyo Business Today* (September 1994), pp. 47–51.
[40] See Rosenbluth (1989).

Table 12. The deregulation of deposit interest rates
(minimum units in ¥ million with allowable term in parentheses)

	Negotiable CDs	Large time deposits	Small time deposits	MMCs	Super MMCs
May 1979	500 (3–6 mos.)				
Jan. 1984	300 (3–6 mos.)				
Apr. 1985	100 (1–6 mos.)			50 (1–6 mos.)	
Oct. 1985	100 (1–6 mos.)	1000 (3 mos.–2 yrs.)		50 (1–6 mos.)	
Apr. 1986	100 (1–12 mos.)	500 (3 mos.–2 yrs.)		50 (1–12 mos.)	
Sept. 1986	100 (1–12 mos.)	300 (3 mos.–2 yrs.)		30 (1–12 mos.)	
Apr. 1987	100 (1–12 mos.)	100 (3 mos.–2 yrs.)		20 (1 mo.–2 yrs.)	
Oct. 1987	100 (1–12 mos.)	100 (1 mo.–2 yrs.)		10 (1 mo.–2 yrs.)	
Apr. 1988	50 (2 wks.–2 yrs.)	50 (1 mo.–2 yrs.)			
Nov. 1988		30 (1 mo.–2 yrs.)			
Apr. 1989		20 (1 mo.–2 yrs.)			
June 1989		20 (1 mo.–2 yrs.)			3 (6 mos.–1 yr.)
Oct. 1989		10 (1 mo.–2 yrs.)			3 (3 mos.–3 yrs.)
Feb. 1990					1 (3 mos.–3 yrs.)
Apr. 1991					0.5 (3 mos.–3 yrs.)
Nov. 1991			3 (3 mos.–3 yrs.)		
June 1992					no minimum

SOURCE: FAIR (1991), p. 333, MoF and Bank of Japan data.

Frustrated with the slow progress, Deputy Assistant U.S. Treasury Secretary David Mulford demanded in 1990 that Japan completely liberalize interest rates within one year. The Treasury was convinced that artificially low rates were helping Japanese financial institutions to compete in the United States and Europe.[41] By 1990, MoF officials were much less receptive to Mulford's cries, for they had already developed their schedule and were not going to be bullied about at this late stage. "After my last yen-dollar meeting in Washington [in 1991], I told Mulford that we agree on the process but disagree on the speed," notes Makoto Utsumi, who was MoF deputy vice minister at the time. "The United States is ahead of us on deregulation, but look what our forerunner has done. It has created a river of deregulation and this river is running too fast. It has broken down the river's banks, and inundated many towns and villages. We prefer not to follow this example."[42]

In October 1994, the ministry finally completed the liberalization process, lifting restrictions on all demand deposit interest rates. Even so, few banks raised their rates significantly and 90 percent of Japanese banks kept their rates on ordinary accounts within a narrow band of 0.22 to 0.25 percent per year. In July 1994, Kansai University Finance Professor Shōzō Ueda had already filed a request with the Fair Trade Commission (FTC) to investigate bank collusion on small-lot time deposits, which had been liberalized in June 1993. FTC officials began an investigation, but they warned Ueda that they would need material evidence of collusion before they could take any action against the banks: uniform interest rates in themselves did not constitute sufficient evidence.[43]

FINANCIAL SYSTEM REFORM

Fairly early on in the process of liberalization, it became clear that the MoF would have to take on the ugliest of regulatory problems: the segmentation of the financial system itself. As noted above, the division between banks and securities companies began to erode in the late 1970s and early 1980s, when banks won the right to sell and deal in government bonds, and securities firms were allowed to market medium-term government bond funds. Meanwhile, the ministry also confronted the problem

---

[41] This potentially contradicts another common argument made on the U.S. side: that liberalization will ultimately strengthen Japanese financial institutions. One U.S. embassy official was so convinced with the logic of this latter argument that he suggested in the mid-1980s that the U.S. government stop pressuring Japan to liberalize altogether—effectively letting MoF and the Japanese finance industry hang themselves. Interview with former U.S. Embassy official, August 1990.

[42] Utsumi interview (July 15, 1992).

[43] *Tokyo Business Today* (March 1995), pp. 12–13.

of the divisions among the banks themselves, as city banks began to push for entry into investment management and long-term lending. The MoF would have to craft an elaborate, multilayered deal to reorganize the whole financial system.

The Banking Bureau's policy council, the Financial System Research Council, first began to deliberate system reform in 1985. Not surprisingly, the Banking Bureau was more anxious to deal with the matter than the Securities Bureau, because banks had more to gain by getting into the securities business than securities houses had to gain by getting into the banking business. Knowing well that it could not reform the system successfully without the Securities Bureau's participation, the Banking Bureau requested that the Securities Bureau's council, the Securities and Exchange Council, begin discussing the matter as well. The Securities and Exchange Council only began formal deliberations in 1988, approaching the issue primarily as one of redefining the limits of the securities business, and only then considering opening this business to new entrants such as banks. Each council was appropriately biased in favor of the industry it oversaw. Although the numbers varied slightly from time to time, the committee of the Financial System Research Council that produced its final report on reform in 1991 had ten representatives from the banking industry and four representatives from the securities industry. The counterpart committee of the Securities and Exchange Council had nine representatives of the securities industry and three representatives of the banking industry. The two councils periodically came out with interim reports, each biased slightly toward its own side, with the Financial System Research Council always advocating more extensive liberalization than the Securities and Exchange Council. In principle, each council examined five possible scenarios: (1) piecemeal reform within the present structure (essentially, maintenance of the status quo), (2) mutual entry through single-business subsidiaries (i.e., banking or trust or securities subsidiaries), (3) mutual entry through multifunctional subsidiaries (i.e., wholesale investment banking subsidiaries), (4) mutual entry through a system of holding companies, and (5) universal banking (see Figure 2). The securities firms preferred piecemeal reform—the status quo, in effect—whereas the city banks favored universal banking.

Each group of institutions waged a heroic lobbying effort. At least one representative from each group of institutions testified before both policy councils. The institutions developed sophisticated rationales to back their defense of their interests and presented these rationales in the form of research reports to the councils. The city banks, for example, argued that universal banks would provide financial services the most efficiently and offer users the most convenience.[44] Securities houses claimed that the city banks would

---

[44] For example, Fuji Bank Research Department (September 1987).

Figure 2. Five scenarios for financial system reform

1. Piecemeal reform
2. Separate subsidiaries

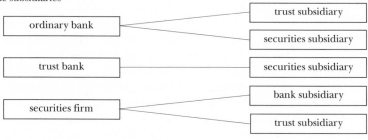

3. Multifunctional subsidiary

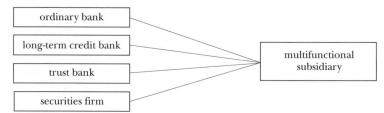

4. Holding company

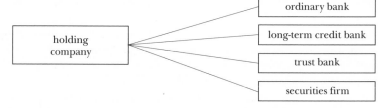

5. Universal bank

have undue influence on underwriting clients and would be susceptible to conflicts of interest. The city banks were not only lobbying for the right to enter new businesses, they were preparing for entry. Fuji Bank, for example, had its trust and securities divisions simultaneously contributing to the lobbying effort and preparing to do business as soon as they received a license.[45]

The Banking Bureau report that appeared in May 1989 narrowed the choices to the separate subsidiaries or multifunctional subsidiary options.[46] Ministry officials never seriously considered either universal bank-

---

[45] Interview with Fuji Bank executives (June 1991).
[46] MoF, Banking Bureau, Financial System Research Council (May 1989).

ing or the status quo option. They were committed to some desegmentation yet were concerned that universal banking would make regulation more difficult, produce conflicts of interest, make banks too powerful, and generally disrupt the financial system more than they could tolerate. And they rejected the holding company option because it would require revision of antitrust law. Many Banking Bureau officials initially preferred the multifunctional subsidiary option, because it would be more efficient than requiring institutions to set up a separate subsidiary for each new line of business. It also played right into the hands of one of Japan's most powerful corporations: the Industrial Bank of Japan (IBJ). It would allow city banks or securities companies to set up multifunctional investment banking subsidiaries, so long as these subsidiaries were separated from their retail operations. But if the law was designed in a manner favorable to IBJ and the other two long-term credit banks, then these institutions would be able to become full-service investment banks without even forming subsidiaries—because they had virtually no retail business at all. The securities houses opposed this option, insisting on either the status quo or—as as a second choice—the separate subsidiaries option. Of the choices available, the city banks logically should have preferred the more liberal multifunctional subsidiary option, but decided to short-circuit IBJ's ambitions by backing the separate subsidiaries option, since they could not have universal banking.[47] Before interim reports from both councils appeared in July 1990, the BoJ also came down clearly in favor of the separate subsidiary option. BoJ officials opposed universal banking because they believed that money-supplying institutions should not carry the risks of the securities business. Following this logic, they were equally opposed to multifunctional subsidiaries, for these subsidiaries would not only still be banks involved in the securities business, they would not even have the stable supply of funds that comes from a retail base.[48] Meanwhile, Banking Bureau officials were losing their enthusiasm for the multifunctional subsidiary option as well, for they realized that this would involve far more complex revisions of Japanese law than the separate subsidiary option.

The Banking Bureau's July 1990 report clearly leaned toward the separate subsidiary option.[49] Although the Securities Bureau report remained vague on this point, Securities Bureau officials were prepared to accept this option under certain conditions, and so the debate became more specific.[50] The Banking Bureau had the more difficult task, because it had to

---

[47] *Nikkei Kinyū Shimbun* (January 14, 1991).

[48] Interview with BoJ official (July 1991).

[49] MoF, Banking Bureau, Financial System Research Council (July 1990a/b). The report candidly reveals one important reason why MoF officials favored this option: it would make it easier for the ministry to monitor and regulate the market players.

[50] MoF, Securities Bureau, Securities and Exchange Council (June 1990).

consider the balance of interests among the various types of banks while at the same time negotiating with the Securities Bureau over the terms of a settlement on the barriers between banking and the securities business. In particular, they had to find a way to placate the trust banks and long-term credit banks, which would be losing their cozy cartels.

At this stage, the principal battle between the banks and the securities houses focused on the conditions of cross-entry: the scope of business in which subsidiaries could engage, and the designation of firewall barriers between parent firms and the subsidiaries. The banks naturally wanted to widen the scope of securities functions they could perform, whereas the securities houses wanted to narrow this scope. The banks wanted to minimize the firewall barriers between parent firms and subsidiaries, whereas the securities houses demanded the strictest firewalls possible.[51] The securities houses indicated that they would accept bank entry into the underwriting business but not brokerage and recommended strict restrictions on the flow of funds, personnel, and information between parent firms and subsidiaries. The banks protested vehemently, arguing that such restrictions would undermine the potential benefits of expanding into the securities business. The securities houses figured that if a few reasonable restrictions deterred the banks from entering the securities business altogether—then all the better.

By May 1991, when the two councils came up with their final report, their positions had become much closer.[52] The settlement worked out between the two bureaus operated on the principle of protecting the core business of each industry group in the short term, but allowing cross-entry at the margins. Thus banks would be allowed to underwrite bonds, but could not sell stocks. And banks and securities firms could engage in land or estate trusts but not in the most lucrative segments of the trust business: loan trusts, a form of savings instrument, and pension trusts, which manage corporate pension funds.[53] The press widely denounced the settlement as the product of too many political compromises. The ministry had made so many concessions to industry groups trying to protect their turf that cross-entry would be meaningless.[54]

And yet MoF officials interviewed in June 1991 were visibly pleased with themselves.[55] They offered slowness as a concession to those who would

---

[51] Fuji Research Institute (September 1990).

[52] Interviews (1991). The two reports are MoF, Banking Bureau, Financial System Research Council (May 1991), and MoF, Securities Bureau, Securities and Exchange Council (May 1991). For more detailed analysis of the reports and the positions of the various industry groups, see *Kinyū Zaisei Jijō* (June 17, 1991), *Kinyū Bijinesu* (July 1991), and *Ekonomisuto* (July 15, 1991).

[53] Sneider (1993).

[54] For example: *Yomiuri Shimbun* (June 7, 1991), *Nihon Keizai Shimbun* (June 8, 1991), and *Kinyū Bijinesu* (July 1991). Also see Miwa (1993).

[55] Tsuchida interview (June 13, 1991); other interviews (June 1991).

eventually lose out in the multilayered deal: the trust banks, the long-term credit banks, and the securities firms. They also vowed to offer the first licenses to those firms that deserved some compensation from the deal, most notably the long-term credit banks. Nonetheless, they were convinced that they could transform what initially appeared as a muddled compromise into meaningful reform over the long term.[56] They described their philosophy by way of aphorism: "Bear it small, but grow it big" (*chiisaku unde, ōkiku sodateru*). They would eventually allow cross-entry into the full range of banking and securities businesses, producing clear sets of winners and losers. Although all sides would gain something and lose something in the original settlement, the policy victory for some (the city banks) differs fundamentally in nature from the compensation offered to the others (trust banks, long-term credit banks, securities houses).[57] That is, the banks won the war over Article 65, for they would get into the securities business. Meanwhile, the securities houses only received compensation: a delay and some fairly stringent conditions attached to bank entry into the securities business. And the compensation offered to the securities houses would be temporary, whereas the victory won by the banks would be permanent. In the eyes of MoF bureaucrats, however, the losers in the political arena need not end up as losers in the marketplace, for the ministry would give them time, and perhaps some guidance, to adjust to their fate.

Critically, the ministry itself would retain the discretion to determine the timing and the extent of cross-entry. MoF officials could monitor the impact of a given move before proceeding to the next step. Best of all, from the perspective of the MoF officials, this discretion gave them new leverage over the industry, leverage they had been losing in an era of economic liberalization. They effectively created a new queue for the all-important licenses for new subsidiaries. They knew well that they could make or break financial institutions depending on how they determined the order and timing of entry, and how they defined the scope of business in which the new subsidiaries could engage. And until they had given out the last license and clarified the last detail of the reform, they would have a powerful new card to play.

The LDP kept remarkably quiet throughout the process of formulating the financial system reforms. By 1991 a few Diet members, notably the chairman of the party Research Commission on the Financial System (*kinyū seido chōsakai*), Tetsuo Kondoh, began to utter a cry for bolder reform. Far from taking up the defense of the weaker institutions, Kondoh

---

[56] Interview with Ryūichiro Tachi, professor emeritus, Tokyo University, and chairman, Financial System Research Council, MoF (July 15, 1991), and other interviews (1991).

[57] Calder (1988) describes the "compensation dynamic" as an integral element in Japanese politics at a broader level.

argued that the MoF should move more decisively in favor of reform. Kondoh personally advocated the holding company option, and in a June 1991 interview he vowed that he would push this option through regardless of what the MoF might say.[58] Yet when the legislation came up for debate in 1992, Kondoh was quietly on the sidelines, having been appointed labor minister in the interim. Also in 1991, another LDP finance expert, Shunjirō Karasawa, resurrected an old proposal for a Finance Agency, which would break off the three financial bureaus from the rest of the MoF. He argued that this would move finance officials beyond balancing political interests and permit them to start thinking about the broader national interest. Yet when this comment hit the papers, an embarrassed Karasawa did his best to play down the point after receiving some unfriendly telephone calls from the ministry.[59]

By the time that the financial system reform legislation reached the Diet in the spring of 1992, two unforeseen developments had transformed the debate: the stock market went into free fall, and a major financial scandal erupted. Both of these developments had profound implications for how the ministry managed the reform process and plotted the restructuring of the financial industry. The stock market plunge weakened both securities firms and banks, making it easier for the ministry to coerce institutions to accept ministry plans for mergers and other forms of reorganization.[60] But this also meant that few firms were strong enough to buy out others on their own, and the government might have to assist the mergers financially. In addition, institutions on both sides of the Article 65 wall would have that much less desire to move into new areas, so the ministry could permit cross-entry without worrying too much about any immediate market disruption.

The scandal broke in June 1991, when a *Yomiuri Shimbun* article revealed that Japanese securities firms had paid enormous sums to their top corporate clients as compensation for losses resulting from the stock market crash. Although compensating clients itself is not illegal under Japanese law, it is illegal to solicit business by guaranteeing minimum returns, and widespread compensation effectively proved that brokers had made such guarantees. Reporters suspected that officials at the National Tax Agency, perhaps even Director-General Masahiko Kadotani, a former director-general of the MoF's Securities Bureau, leaked the story because they were enraged that compensation payments were not being reported for tax purposes. The weekly journal *Tēmisu* published these allegations in its July

---

[58] Interview with Tetsuo Kondoh, member, House of Representatives (July 11, 1991). Kondoh boasted to the *Yomiuri Shimbun* that he and his colleagues would ensure a "radical reform, led by politicians" (June 8, 1991).
[59] Interview with Shunjirō Karasawa, member, House of Representatives (July 12, 1991).
[60] The Nikkei average fell from a high of ¥38,916 in December 1989 to a low of ¥14,309 in August 1992.

17 issue, but withdrew the entire issue from newsstands within hours of its appearance, apparently in response to strong political pressure.[61]

At first, the scandal appeared as a blessing in disguise for the ministry. For by utterly discrediting the securities industry, the scandal effectively muted the most powerful group opposing meaningful reform. Moreover, it provided a convenient rationale for the ministry to increase its regulatory control over the industry. As it turns out, however, the scandal soon turned against the ministry. News commentaries suggested that the MoF's close relationship with the securities firms prevented it from serving as an effective regulator. Prime Minister Toshiki Kaifu charged the third Provisional Council on the Promotion of Administrative Reform (*rinji gyōsei kaikaku suishin shingikai*, or "Gyōkakushin" for short), led by business leader Eiji Suzuki, with the task of recommending regulatory changes. Suzuki swiftly declared his own preference: Japan should set up an independent securities regulator on the model of the U.S. Securities Exchange Commission (SEC). The LDP began deliberating reforms as well, and a solid majority within the party supported the SEC option.[62]

For the ministry, this was a threat of the ultimate sanction: dismemberment. If Japan were to have an independent securities regulator, the MoF would no longer be able to orchestrate bargains between securities firms and other financial institutions, for it would no longer enjoy such broad jurisdiction. The ministry would lose some of its leverage over financial institutions because it would not command such a wide array of punishments and rewards. And the ministry would lose regulatory discretion, because it would have to negotiate many issues with a regulatory commission that was bound to have a more formal and legalistic approach to regulation. Not surprisingly, MoF officials launched an all-out effort to stave off this threat. They developed a sophisticated and arduous rationale for their position, and they bombarded both the new Gyōkakushin and the LDP with extensive briefings on the subject. They argued, for example, that creating a new agency would violate the spirit of administrative reform, that the ministry needed to regulate banking and securities together precisely because the two sectors would begin to merge under system reform, and that in any case SEC-type regulation was unnecessary within the MoF's regulatory regime.[63] "The ministry outmaneuvered us with their logic," conceded one LDP staff member.[64]

---

[61] *Nihon Keizai Shimbun* (July 10, 1991).

[62] Interview with policy staff member, Policy Research Council, LDP (July 1992).

[63] With respect to the new Gyōkakushin, the MoF got some help from Management and Coordination Agency (MCA) officials who serve as the Gyōkakushin staff. MCA officials helped to dissuade the commission from officially proposing an independent regulator, and they sculpted the commission's report in accordance with the MoF's wishes. See James Sterngold, "Japanese Learn a Lesson in Bureaucratic Rule," *New York Times* (November 4, 1991).

[64] Interview (June 1992).

The reform legislation that emerged from the LDP-MoF deliberations created a new securities regulation commission within the ministry, with a substantially enlarged staff. As a concession, the ministry agreed that the top three positions within the commission would go to non-MoF officials. Despite this minor intrusion of outsiders, Securities Bureau officials welcomed the changes, for they recognized that they were severely understaffed and that they would need greater expertise to regulate the increasingly sophisticated securities markets.[65] In fact, the press accused the ministry of turning the outrage of the stock scandal to its own advantage. By increasing their own regulatory powers, the press critics claimed, MoF officials were shamelessly practicing *yakebutori* (getting fat after the fire, that is, profiting from misfortune).

As for the financial system reform legislation itself, it passed through committees in June 1992 with only minor revisions. In committee hearings, Diet members occasionally challenged MoF officials to liberalize a bit more here or to regulate a bit more there, but they did not challenge the basic outlines of the legislation. LDP members were primarily concerned with creating a new securities regulator and strengthening securities regulation in order to appear responsive to the problems underlying the compensation scandal and the "bubble" economy. In their discussions with LDP leaders, MoF officials stressed that they had been working on the legislation for six years, and that they had thought it out carefully and discussed the issues at length with the financial institutions themselves. At the eleventh hour, MoF officials grew a bit anxious as opposition protests to the LDP proposal to send peacekeeping forces abroad threatened to prevent passage before the Diet recessed for the summer. To their relief, the LDP pushed the bill through just in time, on June 19.[66]

Ministry officials consciously designed the reform legislation to make it easier to restructure the industry. For example, they included a provision in the legislation allowing the long-term credit banks and the Bank of Tokyo to merge with other banks, and thereby to acquire large branch networks without giving up the privilege of issuing bank debentures.[67] In a subtler move, the ministry inserted a clause whereby banks could enter the securities business without creating a subsidiary *if* they bought out ailing securities firms. This provided a special incentive for large banks to take on the costly task of saving these securities firms, but it also posed a credible threat that could push reluctant securities firms to assume this role—just to keep the banks out. In the first such case, Japan's ninth-

---

[65] Interview with MoF official (June 1992).

[66] *Nihon Keizai Shimbun* (June 20, 1992).

[67] The Bank of Tokyo, under the leadership of former MoF official Toyoo Gyohten, announced its merger with the Mitsubishi Bank in March 1995.

largest bank, Daiwa Bank, took over control of the eleventh-ranked securities firm, Cosmo Securities, in August 1993.[68]

In December 1992, the MoF issued more detailed guidelines regarding firewalls between parent institutions and their subsidiaries and the scope of businesses in which subsidiaries would be able to engage. As expected, banks would be allowed to underwrite bonds but not to sell stocks. Banks and securities firms starting trust subsidiaries could introduce nonmoney trusts such as real-estate and bond trusts, but they would not be able to manage pension funds.[69] The ministry would issue the first securities subsidiary licenses to the long-term credit banks and trust banks in July 1993, and city banks would have to wait one more year.[70] The city banks voiced a perfunctory protest over the delay, but did not go any further. "As bank executives we would like things to move more rapidly," explained one senior city bank official, "but we can appreciate what the ministry is trying to do."[71] IBJ was clearly the most prepared and the most eager to enter new lines of business, with most other financial institutions less than enthusiastic about expansion, given the depressed market. But this mood fit in nicely with the ministry's strategy of "bearing small and growing big." Despite the abrupt end to the LDP's one-party rule in July 1993, ministry officials have proceeded with the implementation of financial system reform virtually unaffected by the political turmoil around them. As of December 1995, banks had established seventeen securities subsidiaries and six trust subsidiaries, and the "Big Four" securities houses had each set up a trust subsidiary. But by this time, the authorities were beginning to consider a more radical solution to the system reform problem, revising antitrust law to allow financial institutions to form holding companies incorporating different types of financial institutions.

THE NEW REGIME

Beyond the two central cases outlined above, Japanese authorities have enacted reforms that touch almost all aspects of the financial system. They have introduced new financial products, improved foreign access, internationalized the yen, and strengthened regulation. Let us briefly review reforms in three other areas—securities commission liberalization, corpo-

---

[68] *JEI Report*, No. 31B (August 20, 1993). Then in October 1994, the MoF allowed Mitsubishi Bank to take over a troubled trust bank, Nippon Trust. *Tokyo Business Today*, March 1995, p. 8.

[69] *Asian Wall Street Journal* (December 19, 1992).

[70] The MoF approved the applications of IBJ, the Long-Term Credit Bank, and the Nōrinchūkin Bank (the central agricultural cooperative bank) for securities subsidiaries on July 5, 1993. *JEI Report*, No. 25B, July 9, 1993.

[71] Interview with Fuji Bank executive (August 1993).

rate bond market reforms, and non-bank regulation—in order to fill out our picture of financial reform Japanese-style. In stark contrast to their British counterparts, MoF officials have not made securities commission liberalization a priority. They have not been particularly concerned that high commissions would make Tokyo less attractive as a financial center, and they have been far more concerned with the potential impact of liberalization on domestic securities firms, particularly the smaller firms.[72] And unlike the British with their Big Bang approach, they have liberalized with painstaking deliberation. Under MoF guidance, the Tokyo Stock Exchange (TSE) reduced commission rates four times from 1985 through 1990.[73] The Securities and Exchange Council began deliberations on outright liberalization in 1992 and began by liberalizing trades over ¥1 billion in April 1994.[74]

As of the early 1980s, MoF officials were reluctant to reform the corporate bond market in part because they feared that corporate bonds might crowd out the market for government bonds. Furthermore, the banks were adamantly opposed to any expansion of the corporate bond market so long as they were excluded from this market. In fact some banks preferred *not* to be allowed into the market, because they would rather make easy commissions as trustees than compete more openly for underwriting commissions.[75] Thus corporate bond market reform became hostage to the larger debate over financial system reform. Ministry officials only proceeded with reform once they had established that banks would be able to underwrite bonds through subsidiaries under the terms of the system reform. Since 1991, they have taken several cautious steps toward reform. For example, they have relaxed the criteria for shelf registration and expanded the number of eligible issuers from about 300 to 600.[76]

The MoF has naturally had more difficulty controlling financial institutions in those segments of the financial system that lie beyond its jurisdiction, such as the non-bank sector supervised by MITI. In the past, MoF officials have not been too eager to usurp MITI's authority in this area because they could influence the non-banks indirectly through affiliated banks, and they could not regulate the huge number of non-banks effec-

---

[72] The Big Four securities houses have been less adamant in defending fixed commissions. In fact, one insider reports that in 1983 Nomura tried to wager the liberalization of commissions—on behalf of the rest of the industry as well as itself—in exchange for a trust banking license. Interview, July 1991.

[73] The TSE lowered rates in April 1985, November 1986, October 1987, and June 1990. Commission rates for trades of ¥50–100 million, for example, went from 0.55 percent in 1985 to 0.225 percent in June 1990. *JEI Report*, No, 20A, May 20, 1994, p. 4.

[74] *JEI Report*, No, 20A, May 20, 1994, p. 4.

[75] One Japanese bank executive reports that MoF officials resorted to virtually "kidnapping" bank executives to present a lecture on why banks *should* want a stronger corporate bond market. Interview, June 1991.

[76] Sneider (1993).

tively anyway. And non-banks do not have depositors, so they pose less of a systemic risk than banks. The MoF seized some regulatory powers over non-banks, however, in 1991 after the non-banks became the scapegoats for real estate speculation and the resulting boom-and-bust "bubble" economy.[77] The LDP took up the issue of non-bank regulation, apparently in response to public concern. But a key Diet member revealed that the actual impetus came from the MoF: "Let's just say the ministry encouraged us to deal with the situation," commented Tetsuo Kondoh, chairman of the party's Research Council for Financial and Banking Problems.[78] In 1992, MITI wrought partial revenge on the MoF, introducing its own bill to allow non-banks to securitize certain assets and thereby decrease their reliance on banks for funds. Nevertheless, MITI had to negotiate closely with MoF officials in the process, and the resulting bill leaves the MoF with a substantial role in non-bank regulation.[79]

In each of these cases, the MoF's own agenda powerfully shaped the outcome. Frances Rosenbluth offers an alternative perspective, suggesting that financial institutions have driven policy change. Although most decisions grew out of bargaining between the financial institutions and the ministry, she contends, the ministry was narrowly constrained in its actions because financial institutions could appeal to the LDP if they did not like the ministry's settlement. Even when the party was not involved, ministry officials understood that decisions that did not reflect the prevailing interests of the finance industry *could* provoke an appeal to the party. In fact, the ministry made roughly the same decisions that the party would have if there had been such an appeal, for both ministry and party respond to the same balance of political forces.[80]

In contrast, I argue that in practice the ministry's scope for discretion was wide rather than narrow. Of course, ministry officials must respond to industry preferences. But they are insulated enough from the specific demands of particular industry segments that they can insert their own preferences into policy outcomes. In the face of a divided industry, they can decide which groups to favor and which groups to compensate. And they can manipulate the deliberation process in order to gain industry accep-

---

[77] The general public was actually critical in this episode. Both the ministry and the party acted out of the fear of public outrage. Once again, this is consistent with Goodhart's theory (Chapter 5) and not with the theory of regulation. Rosenbluth (1989) and others underestimate the political power of Japanese consumers because they assume that consumers would push for deposit interest rate liberalization and other measures that would promote the consumer interest as defined in economic theory. In fact consumers are influential, but primarily in pushing for *more* regulation in the wake of financial scandals.

[78] Interview (July 11, 1991). A MoF official also confirmed this interpretation. Interview, June 1991.

[79] Sneider (1993).

[80] Rosenbluth (1989).

tance. They rarely have anything to fear from an industry appeal to the LDP, for financial institutions would only appeal to the party if they could be confident that the LDP would respond favorably *and* the potential benefits would outweigh the costs of a deterioration in relations with the ministry, or outright retaliation by the ministry. In practice, financial institutions have little incentive to appeal as long as their interests are divided, for one group's appeal would only be nullified by another group's counter-appeal.[81]

The evidence from this chapter suggests that MoF officials have followed their own priorities more than those of financial institutions or party politicians. Ministry bureaucrats have demonstrated their ability to manipulate the LDP for their own purposes, and even to defeat the party in head-to-head conflict. For example, a strong majority within the LDP favored the creation of an independent securities regulator on the model of the U.S. SEC, yet the ministry was able to fend off this threat through a massive lobbying effort combined with a persuasive rationale. Likewise, the ministry has pursued its own agenda in the face of indifference or ambivalence in the finance industry and even overcome strong industry opposition when necessary. For example, the Securities Bureau took up the laborious task of redefining securities in order to bring new financial instruments under the regulatory regime, even though neither the banks nor the securities houses ever lobbied for this change.[82] And the ministry overcame rabid industry opposition as it opened holes in the monopolies of the long-term credit banks, the trust banks, and the securities houses.

The MoF's approach to financial reform reflects its own biases: it has guided the process in a gradual and orderly manner, managed liberalization to protect domestic financial institutions, and designed the reforms to maintain its own authority over these financial institutions.[83] The ministry has been able to dictate the pace and the sequence of reform because the ministry itself has been the dominant arena for both deliberation and implementation. The ministry process has been slow, but this slowness has served a purpose. The ministry has used the lead time to persuade dissenting industry groups to accept their fate, to arrange compensation packages for these groups, and to prepare these institutions to face new

[81] In the case of the Banking Law of 1982, analyzed at length by Rosenbluth (1989), the financial institutions did appeal to the Diet. But this represents an extreme scenario, in which industry-ministry relations were unusually strained and the industry was united in opposition to a blatant ministry attempt to strengthen its authority through stricter disclosure rules.

[82] To the disappointment of some foreign observers but to the surprise of no one, the MoF retained the right to permit new financial instruments on a case-by-case basis rather than issuing a general permission for certain classes of instruments.

[83] In a similar vein, Lincoln (1988) characterizes the MoF's goals in the reform process as promoting the stability of financial institutions and the financial system as a whole, holding down the cost of government debt, and maintaining its own power.

competition. Where financial institutions have been close to failure, MoF officials have arranged private mergers or bailouts to prevent outright failure. In fact, as we have seen, they tailored the financial system reform legislation to enhance their ability to orchestrate these mergers.

Furthermore, ministry officials designed the reforms to maintain and even to enhance their own power—something the financial institutions would hardly have endorsed. They recognized that they would lose some sources of leverage over the finance industry, so they were determined to create others. In the past, the ministry's most powerful lever over banks was its ability to deny or delay applications for new branches, or to attach specific conditions to its approval. But this lever has lost much of its impact as the number of branches is no longer a bank's most critical competitive advantage. Instead, ministry officials acquired an equally powerful tool in the authority to issue licenses for financial institutions to establish subsidiaries for new lines of business, and to determine the conditions of entry. The ministry has already begun to manipulate this leverage in order to push financial institutions to bail out weaker institutions. In Britain, of course, the practice of regulation has moved in precisely the opposite direction: regulation has become less discretionary, and the authorities have experienced a substantial net loss of control.

Although ministry officials have tenaciously defended their authority over financial institutions, they have also proven themselves able to adapt to changing times. The ministry itself has transformed from a conservative and stingy regulator to more multifaceted supervisor, monitor, and adviser.[84] The ministry no longer sets prices for bank loans, but occasionally "advises" IBJ, the market leader for the long-term prime rate, instead.[85] Practitioners suggest that the ministry has become somewhat more market-oriented since the mid-1980s, when it gained a more direct interest in markets as the secondary market in government bonds developed and the ministry became majority shareholder in the country's largest corporation, NTT.[86] The ministry has reorganized in order to enhance its capabilities as a market monitor. The Banking Bureau created a new Markets Division, and the Securities Bureau merged its Capital Markets Division and its Secondary Markets Division.[87] At the same time, the ministry has gradually strengthened its requirements for disclosure from both financial institutions and corporations. This gives investors the ability to make more informed decisions in the marketplace, but it also gives the ministry access

[84] Mabuchi (1990) offers an interesting variation on this interpretation. He suggests that the ministry's transformation is part of Japan's transition from a "soft state"—with lighter control over a wider array of activities, to a "hard state" with tighter control over a narrower array of activities.

[85] Interview with IBJ executive (June 1992).

[86] Interviews with Japanese financial executives (1991–92).

[87] Nihon Keizai Shimbun (1992), pp. 205–10.

to more information for its own purposes. Ministry officials have even tolerated some formalization of regulation, although not nearly to the degree we observed in the United Kingdom. In the wake of the 1991 securities scandal, the Securities Bureau reviewed its inventory of regulations, eliminating some measures and codifying some of its "voluntary rules" as TSE regulations. Then in a January 1995 financial reform package linked to the U.S.-Japan "Framework" talks, the ministry pledged greater transparency in regulation and strict adherence to the Administrative Procedures Law.[88]

Even so, there are increasing signs that the MoF has not adapted enough. Although the ministry has managed the reform process and retained leverage over the industry, it has increasingly lost control over developments in the marketplace. With respect to regulating an increasingly complex securities market, ministry officials themselves recognize that they need more manpower and greater expertise. The stock market's prolonged slump has definitively demonstrated that the ministry cannot defy the logic of the market—at least not forever. In fact, one could argue that MoF manipulation delayed a market correction and thus made the eventual plunge much worse than it otherwise would have been. When the New York market crashed in October 1987, MoF called in top executives from the Big Four brokerage firms to ask them to stop the decline by buying shares. Not surprisingly, they asked the brokers to buy the one stock in which the ministry had the greatest stake: NTT.[89]

In the banking sector, asset deflation compounded with mismanagement to produce a full-fledged crisis, with banks holding an estimated ¥50–100 trillion in nonperforming loans. Confident that the MoF would bail them out in a pinch, bank managers had generously extended massive loans during the bubble years of the late 1980s only to find that borrowers were unable to repay the loans once the bubble burst in the 1990s. The crisis has erased the MoF's perfect record of no bank failures, forced the ministry to come up with public funds to support ailing financial institutions, strained relations between the ministry and the banks, and soiled the ministry's reputation as an effective regulator. As of December 1995, the ministry had participated in bailouts of four credit cooperatives and one commercial bank. Meanwhile, the ministry has collaborated with financial institutions to hide losses and bolster profits, and has attempted to consolidate the industry by pressing larger and stronger banks to take over their more fragile counterparts. Nonetheless, the postwar system re-

---

[88] The ministry also pledged to liberalize asset management and corporate securities markets and to ease restrictions on cross-border financial transactions. *JEI Report*, No. 2B, January 20, 1995.

[89] Schaede (October 1990) compares New York's "Black Monday" with Tokyo's "Blue Tuesday."

lied so heavily on the perceived omnipotence of the ministry itself that the crisis has seriously undermined confidence in the financial system. This has led to a new wave of MoF-bashing, and more calls for the reorganization or dismemberment of the ministry.[90]

Despite all of their troubles, MoF officials remain surprisingly unconcerned about losing power. For the Banking and Securities Bureaus, regulatory reform has become close to a full-time job. A cynic might say that the MoF has become the ministry of perpetual reform, just as MITI has become the ministry of trade conflicts. As former Banking Bureau director general Tsuchida put it, MoF officials will start worrying about losing their power once all financial markets are liberalized. But the way the MoF liberalizes, that day is a long way off.[91]

---

[90] In a rare move, the *Asahi Shimbun* (September 17, 1995) made an open plea on its editorial page: "Break Up the MoF."
[91] Interview (June 13, 1991).

Chapter Nine

Regulatory Reform Japanese Style: The Strategy Behind Slowness

As in the British cases, Japanese telecommunications and finance reveal a common pattern to regulation and its reform. Under the rubric of administrative reform in the 1980s and deregulation in the 1990s, the Japanese government has extended its program of regulatory reform to a wide array of other sectors as well. Before we attempt to generalize about an overall Japanese pattern to reform, let us survey some of these other sectors.

REGULATORY REFORM IN OTHER SECTORS

Broadcasting

In broadcasting, the Ministry of Posts and Telecommunications (MPT) used the same heavy-handed approach to controlling market entry that it demonstrated in telecommunications. In fact, the MPT has only managed competition in telecommunications so adeptly because of its prior experience with broadcasting regulation. Throughout the postwar era, the MPT has carefully balanced the promotion of the public television network, the Japan Broadcasting Corporation (*nippon hōsō kyōkai*, or NHK), with the regulation of private competitors. In the 1980s, it then took on the task of managing entry into satellite broadcasting. The government originally conceived its plans for satellite broadcasting in the late 1960s. NHK and MITI were particularly enthusiastic, NHK because it wanted to increase its research and development budget and promote broadcasting in general and MITI because it wanted to use the plan as an industrial policy for domestic satellite producers. As in telecommunications, the MPT used regulatory reform in the 1980s as an opportunity to usurp NHK's role as the leader in broadcasting-related research and development. Japan launched the broadcast satellite BS-2B in 1984, and two NHK stations began pay satellite TV service in 1989. The commercial TV stations strongly opposed even this limited market liberalization, but quickly stopped trying to buck the trend and began vying for the one available license. Thirteen companies applied, and the ministry responded in classic fashion by putting all thirteen together into an unwieldy consortium known as Japan Satellite Broadcasting, which began service in 1990.[1] The ministry then declared that it would add more channels in 1997 and again around the year 2000.[2] In the meantime, it manipulated the potential applicants to enforce administrative guidance. MPT officials enlisted "voluntary" private sector support in national telecommunications projects, regional Teletopias, and even planted government-sponsored documentary programs on private stations.[3] As Tetsurō Tomita, the former MPT official and managing director at Fuji TV, puts it: "MPT likes us to wait for our licenses, because this means that we will be more cooperative in the meantime."[4] As the prospects for the business dimmed somewhat by the mid-1990s, however, private firms became somewhat less zealous about seeking new licenses. In 1992, the ministry licensed six private satellite stations using communications satellites. Because these use a different technology, viewers must buy a separate dish, tuner, and decoder to use the service, so not surprisingly subscribers were slow to hook up. In September 1993, the ministry tried to help out the ailing commercial satellite broadcasters by easing regulations such as restrictions on advertising time.

Through the early 1990s, MPT authorities deliberately impeded the expansion of cable television. Historically, they had restricted cable television companies to small geographic zones in order to protect broadcast television, especially at the local level. Thus cable companies focused primarily on rebroadcasting television to remote areas. MPT officials then continued this policy into the 1990s because they had committed themselves to satellite broadcasting. As of 1993, only 2 percent of Japanese homes subscribed to cable, compared to 60 percent for U.S. homes.[5] But they performed a major shift in 1993, deciding to promote rather than impede the convergence of telecommunications and broadcasting. They had become accustomed to a strict separation between the two domains, one that was institutionalized in the form of distinct bureaus within their

[1] The Japanese refer to this approach as "making [them] one" (*ipponka*).

[2] Interview with MPT official (August 1992) and T. Itō (1992), pp. 217–46.

[3] Interview with Toshiyuki Shinohara, professor of media and communication at Juntendō University and former representative of the Private Broadcasting Association (Minpōren) (June 24, 1993).

[4] Interview (June 22, 1993).

[5] *New York Times* (November 18, 1993).

own organization. But eventually they recognized that they stood to benefit from the growth of multimedia services, those services that transcend
these two domains.[6] With respect to cable television, this meant switching
from restricting growth to promoting it. In December 1993, the ministry
announced that it would allow cable companies to offer service covering
two or more geographical zones and to offer telecommunications services
including telephony, and it would abolish restrictions on foreign investment in the cable business. Then in April 1994 it unveiled a plan to encourage cable operators to link up with each other to extend their area of
coverage. NYNEX was one of the first to react to the regulatory changes,
announcing a joint venture with the Tomen Corporation to provide interactive programming and telephone service. But NYNEX subsequently
withdrew from the venture, apparently because it recognized that remaining regulatory barriers would continue to stifle the growth of the cable
market. NYNEX and the other American Baby Bells would be unlikely to
match their success in the British market.[7]

Transportation

The Ministry of Transportation (MoT) has the reputation of being one
of Japan's stodgiest and most rigid regulators, and in general the reputation is well deserved. But when the administrative reform movement took
hold, ministry officials were determined not to be forced into a reactive
stance. So they zealously proposed the "deregulation" of one sector that
they could not really control anyway: trucking. New companies can enter
trucking much more easily than they can rail or air transport, for all they
need is a truck, a driver, and perhaps a garage. And given the size of the
industry—with about 40,000 companies—the ministry cannot possibly
monitor the companies' behavior in any detail. In fact, this may be one
case in which the nominal level of regulation, "licensing," overstated
rather than understated the ministry's actual level of control. Thus MoT
officials were more than willing to downgrade nominally from a license to
a permit system. In addition, they calculated that modest liberalization
would not lead to much entry into the market anyway, because there was
already a shortage of drivers and garages in major urban centers. They
could have "deregulation" without disruption, in fact virtually without impact. The ministry actually preempted the second Provisional Council on
the Promotion of Administrative Reform (Gyōkakushin)—the council
designated to oversee the implementation of the Rinchō's recommendations—by several months when it proposed this reform in 1988. This

---

[6] Interviews with MPT officials (1993–94).
[7] *Tokyo Business Today* (November 1994), pp. 6–9.

made it much easier to control the content of the reform than if it had allowed the Gyōkakushin to take the initiative. The MoT's policy council recommended that trucking companies would no longer need licenses, but only permits; the separate forwarding laws for different modes of transportation would be streamlined into a single law; and the sector would be subject to new regulations to improve safety standards. Under the new safety regulations, the ministry itself, in addition to the police, would be able to punish violators of rules concerning truck weight and the number of hours per day that a driver can work. The ministry would also be able to punish the corporate users of trucking services if they were found to have encouraged the trucking companies to violate safety standards. Most trucking companies opposed the legislation because they feared that it implied more competition and lower profits. The trucking companies lobbied Diet members, particularly enlisting the support of their industry association chairman, senior LDP Diet member Mutsuki Katō. Meanwhile, the ministry tried to convince the industry to accept the reform. Ministry officials emphasized to the truckers that there would be no massive entry into the market, and the results to date support this prediction. Those MoT bureaucrats who were involved in pushing through the bills got high marks within the ministry for guiding the reform so smoothly.[8]

MoT officials have taken the art of managed liberalization to its highest form in the airline industry. The MoT developed the market on the basis of clear segmentation, with a niche for each of three players. Japan Air Lines (JAL) monopolized international routes; All Nippon Airways (ANA) dominated the major domestic routes; and Japan Air System (JAS) specialized in local routes. In 1986, the ministry slowly began to allow second or even third carriers to operate on those routes where demand was greatest. It opened up specific routes to second carriers one by one through an extended process of tacit barter, with each carrier receiving approximately one "second-carrier" route for every one of its own routes on which it would have to tolerate a competitor. As of 1995, ANA and one other carrier had been allowed on twenty-seven of JAL's international routes, and JAL and one other had been allowed on forty of ANA's domestic routes.[9] In designating the new carriers, the ministry gave particular consideration to carriers serving the fifty-three routes with very low demand, such as those serving small outlying islands. These carriers were given priority to move into lucrative new routes and were protected from entry in their own most profitable routes. In 1989, the ministry revised its system of price regulation so that fares could fall within plus or minus 10 percent of

---

[8] Interview with MoT official (August 1991); *JEI Report* 17A (27 April 1990); Takahashi (October 1989); and Yūsō Keizai Shimbun (1989).
[9] Ministry of Transportation data.

a specified pricing curve based on distance. Since then, ministry officials have been increasingly confounded by discount travel agencies that offer lower prices by breaking up block purchases and then reselling them to individuals. They have been unable to crack down on this practice, given the public campaign for deregulation since 1993. They went further in 1994, reducing the level of regulation over price changes from permit to notification, and allowing carriers to lower prices substantially. Even so, they insist on retaining some regulatory control, noting that Japan has a shortage of facilities and airspace so that complete liberalization would lead to higher and not lower prices.[10] Economists remain unconvinced.[11]

Keidanren and the Management and Coordination Agency (MCA) have also pushed for the deregulation of taxis.[12] Not surprisingly, MoT officials were reluctant. They offered a sophisticated version of the rationale for supply and demand adjustment tailored to taxis: you need to regulate the supply of taxis because supply has a tendency to move precisely counter to demand. In good times, demand rises but supply falls, because taxi drivers look for better work. In bad times, demand decreases but supply booms because everyone suddenly wants to be a taxi driver. The ministry tries to smooth out this cycle through its licensing system. If the industry were deregulated, the number of taxis would soar, profits would plummet, and eventually the number of taxis would stabilize around its present level. Why allow such disruption? Ministry officials had studied U.S. deregulation—and did not like what they saw.[13] Then in 1993, the entrepreneurial manager of one taxi company, MK Taxi, made a breakthrough when he took advantage of the new Morihiro Hosokawa administration's pledge to deregulate the Japanese economy—and successfully applied to lower prices. This unprecedented price competition lasted from December 1993 through March 1994, when MoT officials decided to embark on broader regulatory reform.[14] In October 1994, they formally liberalized fares in Tokyo and Osaka, yet not a single company applied to reduce fares. In fact, a group of companies applied to raise prices by 12 percent, but requested that the ministry respond with permission for the entire group so they could keep their prices in line. The ministry approved the price hike in 1995, but linked this action with a program to create 10 percent discounts for those passengers racking up a fare of ¥10,000 (U.S. $100) or more.[15] But if one is to believe a survey conducted by the Tokyo taxi association and distributed to passengers,

[10] Interviews with MoT officials (July 1992 and September 1994).
[11] See, for example, T. Itō (1992), pp. 85–89. Uekusa (1991) provides an analysis of the economics of Japanese regulation more broadly.
[12] *Nihon Keizai Shimbun* (July 5, 1992).
[13] Interview with MoT official (August 1991).
[14] *Ekonomisuto* (June 7, 1994), pp. 60–63.
[15] *Nihon Keizai Shimbun* (January 6, 1995).

then consumers really do not mind. Fully 59.2 percent of those surveyed responded that "the fare adjustment is unavoidable in order to improve working conditions for taxi drivers"; 33.0 percent stated that "fares should be kept down by using foreign drivers and taking other such measures, although this may cause problems of geography, language or safety." The remaining 7.8 percent comprised the "other" category.[16]

The Public Utilities

MITI, viewed by many as the most liberal of all Japanese ministries, actually overtook the MoT as the ministry with the greatest number of regulations in 1993 (Table 13), largely because of its heavy regulation of the energy sector.[17] The ministry only began serious regulatory reform in the early 1990s, when it became increasingly concerned that high energy prices were slowing economic recovery. In April 1992, a policy council subcommittee recommended the liberalization of gas prices for large users. It proposed that gas companies be permitted to supply large users outside their normal operating area, and that non-gas companies should be able to supply gas to these users within certain restrictions.[18] Gas companies generally supported these measures: they had no real desire to break down their own regional monopolies and compete with one another but they hoped to take business from electric and oil companies by offering lower prices to large users. Electric companies did not oppose the measure too forcefully, for they did not feel terribly threatened by competition from gas companies. Oil companies protested more strongly, but their influence was muted by the fact that the reforms do not technically concern oil. Here again, jurisdictional boundaries proved to be critical. Because the reform came under the jurisdiction of MITI's gas division, this gave the gas companies more input and the gas division more control—dampening the opposition from electric and oil companies. The gas division was able to guide the policy process, winning passage in June 1994.[19]

The ministry then took on the electricity sector with a June 1994 report that proposed creating a wholesale market and marginally liberalizing prices. It would allow non-electric companies with their own generators to sell excess supply to electric companies and require electric companies to

---

[16] The author obtained the survey results from a dispenser in front of the passenger seat in a Tokyo taxi in October 1994. The one-page flyer is entitled *Takkun mini jōhō* [Takkun's Mini-Report] No. 32 (October 1994).

[17] See Muramatsu, ed. (1990), for a comparison of policy orientations across ministries.

[18] Ministry of International Trade and Industry (May 1992).

[19] Interviews with utility executives and MITI officials (July 1992 and September 1994). See Samuels (1987) on Japanese energy policy more broadly, and Suetsugu (1994) on energy reforms through 1993.

Table 13. The changing number of regulations imposed by Japanese government agencies, 1986–1995 (as designated in Japanese law)

	1986	1987	1988	1989	1990	1991	1992	1993	1994	1995
Prime Minister's Office	27	27	29	32	32	32	33	33	32	32
Fair Trade Commission	26	26	26	28	28	26	26	26	26	26
National Public Safety Commission	81	95	97	100	100	99	114	134	144	141
Management and Coordination Agency	29	29	29	34	34	34	34	37	35	35
Hokkaido Development Agency	26	26	28	31	31	31	31	32	31	31
Japan Defense Agency	26	26	28	31	31	31	31	31	31	31
Economic Planning Agency	26	26	26	31	31	31	31	31	31	31
Science and Technology Agency	218	260	263	291	291	298	298	303	301	297
Environment Agency	149	149	156	159	162	164	165	188	194	199
Okinawa Development Agency	27	27	27	32	32	32	32	32	32	32
National Land Agency	81	81	81	86	86	86	89	89	88	87
Ministry of Justice	146	146	148	149	153	154	166	172	172	168
Ministry of Foreign Affairs	37	37	39	42	46	46	50	53	50	50
Ministry of Finance	1116	1134	1143	1173	1195	1210	1236	1387	1391	1374
Ministry of Education	310	308	317	314	315	312	322	333	327	327
Ministry of Health and Welfare	936	945	985	1015	1033	1106	1170	1221	1246	1221
Ministry of Agriculture, Forestry, and Fisheries	1263	1256	1270	1270	1299	1315	1357	1427	1419	1400
Ministry of International Trade and Industry	1870	1886	1883	1900	1908	1916	1915	1986	1769	1780
Ministry of Transportation	2017	1976	1977	1962	1988	1966	1966	1893	1700	1607
Ministry of Posts and Telecommunications	265	273	279	284	306	308	313	319	291	292
Ministry of Labor	532	559	563	560	559	565	579	631	629	633
Ministry of Construction	742	770	776	804	808	842	870	910	879	841
Ministry of Home Affairs	104	107	108	113	113	113	114	134	127	125
TOTAL	10054	10169	10278	10441	10581	10717	10942	11402	10945	10760

SOURCE: MCA data.

transport this electricity over their own power lines. It would also reduce the level of regulation over seasonal or time-of-day discounts from a permit to a notification requirement.[20] In the same month, another policy council recommended reforms in the oil sector. MITI has historically been especially protective of the industry, giving oil companies a monopoly on the import of oil and allowing them to sell gasoline at comparatively high prices.[21] At the same time, it has pushed these same oil companies to maintain kerosene and light-oil prices at more reasonable levels. The report pledged to allow the special law giving the oil companies a monopoly on imports to expire in March 1996 and to consider more modest reforms in gasoline retailing.[22] In May 1994, a rice retailer by the name of Kanare Beikoku set off a national furor by purchasing surplus gasoline from wholesalers and then selling it for only ¥100 per liter. MITI eventually forced the company to purchase its supplies through more established channels.[23] Keidanren itself divided on the issue of oil industry reform, when the industry association—housed in Keidanren's own building—refused to endorse deregulation. Keidanren ended up deleting oil from its deregulation proposal of November 1994, only recommending reform in a separate report.[24] The electricity and oil industry reform bills passed in April 1995.

Deregulation Since 1993

Like the Deregulation Unit of the British Department of Trade and Industry (DTI), the Administrative Management Bureau of the MCA is responsible for coordinating the overall deregulation effort. This bureau has worked particularly closely with the various administrative reform councils and deregulation councils since 1993. To support this effort, the agency has developed a data base of regulations incorporated into Japanese laws. Their data show that the overall number of regulations has remained fairly steady. The number of regulations increased marginally from 10,054 in 1985 to 10,760 in 1995 (Table 13). They claim, however, to have made some real progress in deregulation because they have downgraded the stringency of some of these regulations.[25] They have separated regulations into three broad types: permits and licenses that rely on ministerial discre-

---

[20] Ministry of International Trade and Industry (June 1994).

[21] Gasoline prices are high for at least three reasons: controlled competition, inefficient distribution, and high taxes. Upham (Summer 1991) records the notorious case of Lion's Oil, a rebel company, which tried—and ultimately failed—to defy MITI by importing oil directly.

[22] Interview with MITI official (September 1994) and *Nihon Keizai Shimbun* (January 10, 1995).

[23] *AERA* (June 13, 1994), pp. 6–9.

[24] *Nihon Keizai Shimbun* (November 18, 1994) and interview with Keidanren official (September 1994).

[25] Interviews with MCA officials (1991–93).

tion, certifications that depend on more objective criteria, and notifications that simply require the submission of information (Table 14). The statistics do not show any downgrading overall, but MCA officials contend that these statistics do not reveal the level of real deregulation because many new regulations have been added in response to the privatization of public corporations and the appearance of new regulatory issues. In other words, holding the line on regulatory expansion is no small achievement in a world that is becoming more and more complex. Nevertheless, they readily admit that the number of regulations is at best a very crude measure of the degree of government control over private actors.[26] For precisely this reason they have begun to take up those regulations that do not even make it into the books, those that come under the heading of "administrative guidance."[27] Potentially the most significant change has come in the form of the Administrative Procedures Law, which passed in July 1994. It seeks to push ministries either to eliminate or to codify administrative rules that are not currently in law, thus directly threatening the tradition of administrative guidance. In practice, however, ministries are changing rules in the formal sense without letting this undermine their discretion in practice.

When Prime Minister Morihiro Hosokawa's coalition government took power in the summer of 1993, it lacked much of a policy platform. Hosokawa himself was vague on his intentions, but did take a clear stand on political reform, decentralization, and deregulation. As a former prefectural governor, he had experienced the frustrations of dealing with central government bureaucrats first hand. He declared that he would be able to push through meaningful deregulation, for unlike his LDP predecessors, he was not wedded to vested interests. He was particularly eager to promote deregulation because of the prolonged recession: he hoped to use deregulation to stimulate the economy and to appease Japan's trading partners by facilitating imports. Skeptics suggested that even the most successful deregulation program would not be likely to deliver these results.[28] He promptly appointed a new study group on deregulation to be headed by Keidanren chairman Gaishi Hiraiwa. He tried to outmaneuver bureaucratic resistance by keeping bureaucrats and former bureaucrats out of the group. The only flaw in his logic was that members had no choice but to rely on bureaucrats for information because they were unfamiliar with the

[26] Interviews with MCA officials (1991–93).

[27] Reports surveying Japanese deregulation efforts and future prospects include Economic Planning Agency, Comprehensive Planning Bureau (1986 and 1989); Keidanren (March 1988); Fair Trade Commission, Study Committee on Government Regulations and Competition Policy (October 1989); and Tanaka and Horie (December 1990 and May 1991). Independent studies include Haley (1989), Hayashi (1990), Matsubara (1991), Kanō, ed. (1991), T. Itō (1992), and Kakurai, ed. (1992).

[28] See, for example, Glen Fukushima, "Deregulation Is Not Enough," *Tokyo Business Today* (January 1994), p. 56.

Table 14. Japanese government regulations categorized by type, 1995

Type of regulation	Number of regulations (percent of total)	
Permit (*kyoka*)	1149	(10.7)
Authorization (*ninka*)	1624	(15.1)
License (*menkyo*)	100	(.9)
Approval (*shōnin*)	1113	(10.3)
Designation (*shitei*)	254	(2.4)
Consent (*shōdaku*) & other	25	(.2)
SUBTOTAL for Licenses and Permits	4265	(39.6)
Recognition (*nintei*)	474	(4.4)
Confirmation (*kakunin*)	125	(1.2)
Verification (*shōmei*)	126	(1.2)
Validation (*ninshō*)	17	(.2)
Examination (*shiken*)	113	(1.1)
Inspection (*kensa*)	247	(2.3)
Certification (*kentei*)	33	(.3)
Registration (*tōroku*)	181	(1.7)
Investigation (*shinsa*) & other	20	(.2)
SUBTOTAL for Certifications	1336	(12.4)
Notification (*todokede*)	3435	(31.9)
Filing (*teishutsu*)	555	(5.2)
Report (*hōkoku*)	572	(5.3)
Submission (*kōfu*)	89	(.8)
Statement (*shinkoku*) & other	79	(.7)
SUBTOTAL for Notifications	4730	(44.0)
OTHER	429	(4.0)
GRAND TOTAL	10760	(100.0)

SOURCE: MCA data.

existing regulations and were under pressure to produce immediate results. Thus when the study group reported in December 1993, it essentially reproduced the bureaucracy's own list of measures already targeted for deregulation. The more official administrative reform council (Gyōkakushin) had already issued its final report in October 1993. Meanwhile, the bureaucracy struggled behind the scenes to retain control over the eventual outcome. For example, bureaucrats insisted that the Hiraiwa group, which was less susceptible to their control than the Gyōkakushin, be referred to as a study group (*kenkyūkai*) rather than a committee (*iinkai*) or a policy council (*shingikai*), and that the cabinet resolution could only promise to "refer" (*sankō*) to its recommendations, and not to "honor" (*sonchō*) them. As one official stressed, "These nuances are important."[29]

[29] Interview (September 1994). See Johnson (1995), pp. 157–82, on the political implications of nuances in the Japanese language.

A cabinet resolution in February 1994 set up a new deregulation head-quarters in the Cabinet Office and promised to produce a five-year plan for deregulation in June. This structure differed substantially from the old administrative reform program, because the new headquarters in the Cabinet Office gave politicians a greater ability to influence the outcome. The government also took the important symbolic step of allowing foreign company executives to serve on one of the subcommittees to propose deregulation measures. Yet the deregulation effort soon stalled due to political turmoil. Hosokawa resigned in April amid a minor scandal, and LDP defector Tsutomu Hata took his place. Then in June, the coalition collapsed as Social Democratic Party of Japan (SDPJ) representatives broke off and formed a new coalition with their former arch-rivals in the LDP. In one of its final acts, the Hata government produced a long list of proposed deregulation measures. The government had failed to produce a five-year plan by the original target, but it pledged to do so by March 1995.

Bureaucrats within the MCA and the Cabinet Office then set out to turn this list into a workable five-year plan. This meant working with each of the relevant ministries to see just how many of the June proposals were feasible. If an individual ministry opposed a particular deregulation measure, it would have to defend its position and negotiate a resolution with the Cabinet Office. For MCA and Cabinet Office bureaucrats, it was only natural that they should control the process at this stage. The advisory bodies had done their job, and it was the bureaucracy's function to turn recommendations into feasible policy. In November, however, Keidanren suddenly demanded that the government set up a second private sector committee to oversee the compilation of the five-year plan. Keidanren officials did not trust the bureaucrats to cut their own powers, and they had found that the committee approach gave them a much better window into the reform process.[30] MCA bureaucrats objected, arguing that they would have the Gyōkakushin's successor organization in place by spring 1995 so there was no need for yet another committee. In addition, they argued that they would not have time to incorporate the committee's recommendations in time to put them into the five-year plan. Keidanren took its case directly to Prime Minister Murayama, who consulted with the MCA director-general before ultimately agreeing to set up the committee in accordance with Keidanren's wishes. The committee, however, disappointed the deregulation zealots. At the behest of the ruling parties, the new committee included representatives of two of the groups most wary about deregulation: small businesses and consumers. And in any case, the committee was only active for about two months in early 1995, so it was not

---

[30] Interview with Keidanren official (July 1995).

able to come up with major revisions to the earlier proposals. Most critically, however, the bureaucrats insisted on consistency between the committee's recommendations and the five-year plan. They argued that as an advisory organ to a decision-making body, the committee would have to offer proposals that were consistent with government policy. If there were a discrepancy, the bureaucrats would then coordinate a resolution between the committee and the relevant ministry. This had the effect of impeding or diluting proposals that would meet with the objection of the lead ministries.

The government produced its five-year plan in March 1995, and most academics and journalists pressing for reform were less than impressed. While the government came up with an impressive list of 1091 measures, these were not as substantive as many had hoped. The plan left timetables vague, gave the ministries considerable discretion in implementation, and in some cases merely downgraded the level of regulation (from license to permit, for example) rather than eliminating regulations outright. In December 1995, the new Gyōkakushin successor council, the Administrative Reform Committee (Gyōkakui), reported on the state of the deregulation program. Progress was still insufficient, it declared, so the government must redouble its efforts.[31]

THE JAPANESE PATTERN OF REGULATORY REFORM

The Japanese regulatory regime described in Chapter 3 has produced a distinct pattern of regulatory reform, which I call "strategic reinforcement." The pattern is "strategic" because the government has not liberalized for the sake of liberalization, but has selectively introduced competition in specific markets while simultaneously ensuring that domestic firms survive and prosper with as little disruption as possible. I use the term "reinforcement" because the government has not retreated from intervention but has reorganized its apparatus for intervention and rearranged its particular mix of interventionist policies by reinforcing critical mechanisms of control. This pattern of regulatory reform has four basic characteristics (see Table 15).

1. *The government selectively promotes competition, managing market entry and minimizing "exit."* In other words, the ministries continue their legacy of protection and promotion beyond "deregulation." The Japanese government has been strongly inclined toward strategic reregulation, sculpting reforms to advantage domestic firms or at least to minimize any negative impact on them (see Table 1 for the typology of reregulation). And unlike

---

[31] *Asahi Shimbun* (December 8, 1995).

Table 15. Comparing patterns of regulatory reform in the United Kingdom and Japan

United Kingdom	Japan
Regime orientation: Regulatory	Managerial
Regime organization: Segmented	Fused
Overall pattern of reform: Pro-competitive disengagement	Strategic reinforcement
1. The government aggressively promotes competition without managing entry or exit. (bias toward *pro-competitive* reregulation)	1. The government selectively promotes competition, controlling entry and exit. (bias toward *strategic* reregulation)
2. The government fragments regulatory authority.	2. The government retains centralized regulatory authority.
3. The government codifies and juridifies regulation. (bias toward *juridical* reregulation)	3. The government maintains ministerial discretion. (bias toward *expansionary* reregulation)
4. The government implements reform in an uneven and adversarial manner.	4. The government implements reform in a smooth and coherent manner.

their British counterparts, Japanese authorities have been relatively shy with pro-competitive reregulation. Instead, they have responded to market shifts more selectively, liberalizing only in those areas where they were convinced that competition would be beneficial. The lead ministries have typically prepared industry for greater competition while at the same time working on legislation to permit more competition. Ministry officials have combined several tactics in their "prepare and liberalize" strategy. First, they employ strategic delay, giving firms time to adjust. For example, the MPT delayed its approval of a new mobile telephone system in part as a way of giving NTT and NEC time to catch up with Motorola in mobile telephone technology. Second, they use early warnings, announcing liberalization well before it is implemented as a way of pushing firms to adapt. The MoF used this approach to encourage small banks to modernize. Third, they intervene directly to encourage or to coerce firms to adjust. For example, the MoF has actively brokered mergers and tie-ups to help financial institutions cope with financial system reform. This approach to market control contrasts markedly with that in the United Kingdom, where the whole point of liberalization is to push inefficient service providers out of the market.

Furthermore, the ministries have orchestrated the process of entry itself. Despite the liberalization of telecommunications services, the MPT insisted on a notification requirement even for VAN service providers and devised license and permit requirements for other satellite, mobile, and telephone services. Likewise, the MoF retained the right to determine the timing and scope of cross-entry between banks and securities firms by issuing licenses for the brokerage subsidiaries of the banks and the banking subsidiaries of the brokerage houses. In all the sectors we have examined, the ministries have desegmented the market only partially, meaning that they then orchestrate an ongoing process of slow and gradual cross-entry. Whereas British officials would tend to let the market determine how many players could survive in a newly liberalized sector, the Japanese government tries to determine this number ahead of time. For example, the MPT preselected the appropriate number of players for each segment of the telecommunications market: long-distance telephone service, international, mobile, and satellite. In satellites, the ministry refused to grant a license to a third consortium—because three would be a crowd—until U.S. pressure forced the ministry to give in. In contrast, the DTI explicitly decided in its duopoly review not to hold any more "beauty contests" to choose entrants, but to allow any qualified company to enter the market. Once the ministries allowed entry, they have been determined to ensure that all new entrants survive. They do this not only by limiting further entry, but also through detailed price and service regulation. The MPT has been the most aggressive in this respect, carefully weighing each regulatory decision to make sure that all of the new common carriers survive. When firms are having difficulty, the MPT follows the approach mastered by the Ministry of Finance (MoF): brokering mergers rather than letting firms fail outright.

2. *The government retains centralized regulatory authority.* Japanese regulatory reform differs strikingly from British reform in that it has not entailed any significant reorganization of the bureaucracy or decentralization of authority. The U.S. government developed a system of independent regulatory agencies, intentionally separating them from sponsoring departments. British regulatory reform has been characterized by a transition from a system closer to Japan's, with central government departments as both sponsors and regulators, to a system closer to that of the United States, with independent regulatory agencies. In the case of the MoF, part of the ministry's strategy for financial system reform was to prevent its jurisdiction from being parceled out to new agencies. As noted in the previous chapter, the ministry fought off a campaign to create an independent securities regulator in the wake of the securities loss compensation scandal of 1991. The ministry was determined to prevail because it derives its strength and its ability to orchestrate bargains precisely from the broad scope of its authority. Likewise when members of the third Gyōkakushin mentioned the creation of a foreign policy advisory office outside the Min-

istry of Foreign Affairs (MFA) on the lines of the U.S. National Security Council, the MFA protested immediately. Commentators noted with some irony that the MFA responded to this particular proposal with uncharacteristic speed.[32] Ironically enough, the only reorganization undertaken under the administrative reform program involved the very agency promoting administrative reform, the Administrative Management Agency (AMA), which became the MCA.

3. *The government maintains ministerial discretion.* The most distinctive feature of Japanese regulatory reform has been the remarkable prevalence of expansionary reregulation. Ministry officials have been so eager to expand the authority of their own ministry, and to protect their jurisdiction from encroachment by other ministries, that they have made the generation of new sources of authority a major goal of reform. They have been particularly zealous in defending and extending their own power because regulatory reform presents the very real threat that this authority could be usurped, not so much by market players as by other ministries. As we have seen, the erosion of jurisdictional boundaries between sectors has inevitably generated conflict over jurisdiction, such as that between the MPT and MITI, or between the Banking and Securities Bureaus within the MoF. Ministry bureaucrats have manipulated the reform process to create new sources of authority or to replace lost powers with new ones. Their greatest new source of power comes in the ability to control an extremely valuable resource: permits and licenses for entry into new markets. The ministries have written the reform laws in a way that maximizes their own discretion in interpreting and implementing them. This discretion generates power because it expands their freedom to interpret the laws to their own liking, and it makes companies more reliant on the ministries to implement them in a manner that suits the industry. Furthermore, it gives the ministries the ability to discriminate between market players, and this ability is critical to their power to enforce compliance with administrative guidance.

The ministries have engaged in some juridical reregulation as well, but they have tried to avoid letting the juridification and codification of rules go so far that it undermines ministerial discretion. In some cases, ministries have been forced to accept formal rules in order to make them more compatible with international regulatory standards. In other cases, they have had to codify regulations in greater detail simply to keep up with the increasing complexity of the markets they govern. In addition, the Administrative Procedures Law will gradually push them to make regulation more transparent. But the ministries still rely heavily on administrative guidance to control the behavior of private sector actors. In practice, of

---

[32] *Nihon Keizai Shimbun* (June 5, 1991).

course, the degree to which they are able to rely on informal channels depends on the structure of the industry. Ministries have been much more willing to formalize regulatory procedures in sectors with thousands of players, like trucking or the non-bank sector, than they have in the case of industries with fewer but bigger players, like banking or the airline sector.

4. *The government implements reform in a smooth and coherent manner.* The Japanese political process has made regulatory reform slow, and slow reform is qualitatively different from rapid reform. As noted above, ministry officials have often deliberately delayed reform in order to give weaker companies time to prepare for competition. This pattern has only been broken in cases where the United States has applied strong pressure for immediate results.[33] In addition, the decision-making process has typically incorporated those interest groups most likely to oppose regulatory reform, formally through the policy councils and informally through regular discussion between bureaucrats and businessmen. The ministries have tried to convince at least some of the opponents to accept their fate, and this often involved developing a compensation package for them.

The government's structure allows it to approach reform in a coherent manner. Japanese regulatory reform occurs more gradually and more smoothly, and it is implemented more effectively than reform in the United States or the United Kingdom. Japanese ministries cannot ignore societal interests any more than U.S. or British departments can, but they can package their response in order to promote more effectively their own interests and the public interest as they define it. And because the policy process is centralized in the ministries, they can implement reforms in a deliberate sequence. They are better able to conceive and implement coherent strategies because they do not have to share power with independent regulatory agencies and are rarely subject to appeals to the court system or the ruling party.[34] Furthermore, the ministries are in a better position to prepare private sector actors for the changes to come. In the finance case, for example, MoF officials were able to give the financial institutions a good idea of the timing and terms of liberalization well in advance, which allowed them to plan in a way that U.S. financial institutions could not emulate.

Although Japanese ministries have generally succeeded in crafting regulatory reforms as they pleased, this is not to say that they have not had to adapt to changing circumstances. In fact, they have only managed to re-

---

[33] Webber (April 1990) argues that the German government has been able to overcome domestic resistance to reform only in those sectors where considerable international pressure has been present. Many have made a similar argument concerning Japan. Tadokoro (1988), for example, argues that U.S. pressure was critical in breaking the domestic opposition to financial liberalization.

[34] Litt et al. (1990).

tain so much authority because they have been willing to adapt. They have faced real threats to their power, but they have largely managed to fend off these threats thus far. The MPT could have entered the 1990s as the regulator of nothing, with MITI exercising light *de facto* control over the information technology sector. MoF officials could have ended up with market players simply running circles around them, helpless without any levers to manipulate. Japan's bureaucrats have had to transform from domestic enforcers to international negotiators, from rigid regulators to more flexible market monitors, and from defenders of the status quo to innovative reformers. In the process, they have had to relinquish some of their powers and redefine some of their goals.

The particular combination of continuity and change in regulation reveals two clear trends. First, the regulators have clung more tenaciously to their authority to formulate and implement policies than to specific policies themselves. For example, MoF officials have liberalized interest rates, but have not surrendered their authority over financial institutions or their relative autonomy from politicians, independent regulators, and the courts. The MPT abruptly switched its policy on cable television, but it has not relinquished its power to manage the competition in cable television or in telephone service. Second, they have abandoned specific policies but not overarching policy goals. For example, they have largely given up trying to control the cost of capital or allocate credit to firms, but they have not given up their fundamental orientation toward the protection and promotion of domestic industry. Despite having embraced a rhetoric of consumer sovereignty and globalization, the regulatory ministries have not shifted their priorities from the industries they supervise to other segments of Japanese society or to the international community.

Rather than resist regulatory change, the ministries ironically have made the ongoing process of internationalization and regulatory reform into a new heroic task. Most commentators view internationalization as a force taking power away from national governments, because it makes these governments more vulnerable to outside economic and political pressures. But this misses a critical point: a country as important as Japan gains in influence over other countries more than it loses power over its own economy. The MoF may not be able to stabilize the yen, but it can destabilize the dollar or the deutschmark. The Securities Bureau may have less control over domestic markets, but the International Finance Bureau is more powerful than ever as a central player in the "Group of Seven" (G-7) financial talks. Japan's emerging international role gives the ministries a new source of status domestically as well as a new source of influence abroad. Likewise, the ministries have turned economic liberalization into a growth industry. MPT officials have gained in status because so many companies want to know the ministry's plans for liberalization and want licenses and permits once new lines of business are open to them. "These days we are always being harassed, asked for favors or for information," explains one MPT official, "and we could not be happier about it."[35] Even the MCA has gained a new lease on life. It is imposing its own sort of revenge on the higher prestige ministries—forcing them to demonstrate that they have truly deregulated.

[35] Interview with MPT official (July 1991).

PART IV

THE POLITICS OF REGULATORY REFORM

CHAPTER TEN

Other Countries:
The Many Roads to Reregulation

Having outlined patterns of regulatory reform in two countries, the United Kingdom and Japan, let us briefly review reforms in three other countries: the United States, France, and Germany. In doing so, we test, extend, and refine the broader applicability of the framework developed in earlier chapters. By specifying elements of the story not captured by the framework, we can begin to put together a more sophisticated and complex model to supplement the more parsimonious one. Although the U.S. experience has appeared at points in previous chapters, let us now examine it more systematically in light of the findings for the United Kingdom and Japan.

THE UNITED STATES: FROM CHALLENGE TO APPEAL

The U.S. postwar regulatory regime prior to reform most closely resembled that of the United Kingdom. In fact, its orientation was more liberal than the British and its organization was more fragmented. U.S. government officials and business leaders were even more convinced that government should guide macroeconomic policy and protect property rights, but in principle should not intervene in industrial affairs beyond these basic functions. The U.S. government only pursued an industrial policy in the defense sector, where it heavily supported both basic research and product development. Otherwise, industrial intervention followed a purely political rather than rational logic. The regime organization was fragmented in the sense that the federal government itself was decentralized with a wide range of independent regulatory agencies; the judiciary played a substantial role; and regulatory power was often shared between federal and state agencies. As in the United Kingdom and unlike Japan, government agencies were not linked into tight networks of coordination with industry, and thus they have not tried to protect such relationships from the potential ravages of liberal reform. Therefore, we would expect U.S. regulatory reform to follow the British "disengagement" pattern, only U.S. reforms should go even further. At the same time, however, the reforms may be less dramatic in the sense that the U.S. regime was already quite liberal, legalistic, and decentralized prior to the deregulation movement that began in the mid-1970s.

Telecommunications

The U.S. telecommunications regime prior to reform incorporated many of the assumptions common elsewhere: a single carrier should provide service because telecommunications is a natural monopoly; the carrier should put top priority on developing the network infrastructure; and the carrier should provide fair and equal access to the network for all. The U.S. system, however, differed from the post, telegraph, and telephone (PTT) model in two critical respects: the U.S. carrier, American Telegraph and Telephone (AT&T), was a private company rather than a government administration, and it was decentralized into local operating companies. Although it was a private company, AT&T performed critical public functions, providing universal service irrespective of cost and conducting research of benefit to the economy as a whole. It developed an in-house research and development system centered around the famous Bell Labs, which performed basic as well as applied research.[1]

The unity of the network contrasted with the fragmentation of the regulatory system. Individual states began to set up regulatory commissions in 1907. As in many other sectors, the federal government established its regulatory system in the wake of the Great Depression, creating the Federal Communications Commission (FCC) as an independent regulatory body in 1934. The FCC regulated prices, equipment standards, and service. State and federal regulatory authorities shared responsibility for the telecommunications system, leaving them with the awkward task of trying to separate out intrastate and interstate service for regulatory purposes. The FCC was the lead regulator at the federal level, but Congress oversaw the FCC and could intervene to pass legislation related to telecommunications. In addition, FCC decisions were subject to judicial review, meaning that the FCC would have to consider the possibility of review even

---

[1] On the development of the U.S. telecommunications system, see Brock (1981); Schiller (1982); Hills (1986), pp. 50–61; and Horwitz (1989), pp. 90–125.

when no appeal was actually made. The Department of Justice was also involved by virtue of its role in enforcing antitrust policy.

AT&T was unusual among U.S. companies for its sheer size and the scope of its activities. Despite its considerable achievements, it provoked popular fears of corporate power and violated the prevalent ideology of antitrust. In 1919, under the Kingsbury Commitment, AT&T responded to a Department of Justice antitrust investigation by agreeing to divest its telegraph division, Western Union, and to stop acquiring competitive independent operators. In 1938, an FCC report accused AT&T of overcharging its operating companies for telecommunications equipment and passing these costs on to consumers through higher telephone rates.[2] And in 1949, the Justice Department launched an antitrust investigation aimed at forcing AT&T to divest its manufacturing arm, Western Electric. The Pentagon lobbied against divestiture, arguing that it would impair the nation's unified military command and control system. Under a 1956 Consent Decree, AT&T kept Western Electric but agreed not to enter unregulated communications markets such as data services or cable television.

The U.S. experience contrasts with those of the United Kingdom and Japan in the degree to which private sector actors aggressively challenged the regulatory system. As noted in Chapter 1, the development of new terminal equipment, the advent of microwave and satellite technology, and the convergence of communications and computers provided opportunities for private actors to test the existing regime. Private firms could test the regime in the marketplace, or they could appeal to a wide range of political actors, including the FCC, the Justice Department, the courts, Congress, or state regulatory authorities. In the terminal equipment market, the Hush-a-Phone Company was the first to contest AT&T's monopoly by developing a device that could be attached to a telephone to make it easier to communicate in noisy places. The FCC ruled that the device could not be used with Bell telephones, but an appeals court overturned this decision in 1956. Not surprisingly, AT&T interpreted this decision narrowly and continued to try to keep out non-Bell attachments other than the Hush-a-Phone. The Carter Communications company then tried to market its "Carterphone," a telephone that could translate voice signals into radio signals for mobile communications systems. In 1968 the FCC ruled that the Hush-a-Phone decision implied that Carter should be allowed to sell its telephone as well. AT&T continued to discourage foreign attachments, primarily by requiring that they be attached through a Bell connecting device. In 1975 the FCC ordered AT&T to cease this practice.[3]

[2] Hills (1986), pp. 54–56.
[3] Bickers (1991), pp. 97–98.

In the transmission market, a coalition of corporate users applied to the FCC for permission to set up private telecommunications lines using microwave technology at frequencies above 890 megacycles. The FCC granted this permission in its 1959 *Above 890* decision, but did not allow joint usage of private facilities and did not rule on the question of interconnecting these private lines with the public network. In 1963 Microwave Communications International (MCI) proposed a microwave link between St. Louis and Chicago, which it would lease to companies for private use. The FCC launched a broad investigation in response, finally judging to allow MCI to create this link in 1969. In 1971 the FCC made a more general judgment, the *Specialized Common Carrier* decision, allowing firms to lease private lines. The legal and political battle continued as AT&T challenged MCI's right to offer Execunet service, a telephone service designed for corporate customers. AT&T charged that this service represented message toll service rather than private line service. The FCC supported AT&T in 1974 by refusing to accept MCI's proposed rate schedule, but the courts overturned this decision in 1977, thereby sanctioning network competition.[4]

In the market for value-added services, the FCC launched its own inquiry in 1966 to devise regulatory responses to the new technological possibilities. In the Computer I decision of 1971, it established four categories of service, ranging from pure communications to pure data services, with two hybrid categories in between. It would allow competition in data services and the hybrid category of data services with incidental communications service included, but not in pure communications or the hybrid category of communications with incidental data services included. As it became clear that there was no way to distinguish between the two hybrid categories, the FCC moved toward a distinction between "basic" and "enhanced" services in its Computer II report in 1980.[5]

The regulatory debate came to a head in 1974, when the Department of Justice brought an antitrust suit against AT&T. The department accused AT&T of predatory pricing and using its monopoly power to unfair advantage in the market for value-added services. The suit transformed the debate by forcing all parties who were troubled with the department's initiative, especially AT&T, to formulate concrete alternatives. As the suit dragged on, Congress intervened in 1977. AT&T executives debated at length how to respond to the suit, with some actually favoring divestiture, but eventually they decided to oppose it with their full force. Most AT&T executives still believed in the merits of monopoly, an integrated network, and uniform technical standards. AT&T proposed legislation that would

[4] Temin (1987), pp. 134–36.
[5] See Bar and Borrus (October 1989) on the Computer Inquiries.

effectively eliminate the threat of competition and enlisted the support of prominent members of Congress. Congress deliberated AT&T's proposal and other possible bills at some length in 1977 and 1978, but ultimately failed to take action. Congressional leaders saw political costs to accepting AT&T's bill, and they were never able to create a consensus on a proposal for more comprehensive reform.[6] Judge Harold Greene, who presided over the antitrust suit, never completed the case, but his interim statements clearly indicate that he planned to judge against AT&T. Recognizing the imminent threat, AT&T revised its strategy and began to lobby to improve the terms of a potential settlement. In 1982, AT&T finally reached an agreement with the Department of Justice whereby it would divest all of the Bell operating companies, but in exchange would be allowed to enter new lines of business including data communications. Judge Greene then engaged in extended deliberations over the practical details of the settlement, finally issuing his Modified Final Judgment in 1984.

The fragmented nature of the U.S. political system operated in favor of a highly pro-competitive solution to the telecommunications regulatory debate. Unlike Japan's Ministry of Posts and Telecommunications (MPT), the FCC never tried to centralize regulatory authority within its own jurisdiction and willingly ceded power to the court in the 1970s.[7] The repeated process of appeal favored reform because a decision in favor of liberalization was much harder to reverse than one against it.[8] And AT&T could not concentrate its efforts to forestall liberalization on any one agency, because no one agency was in control of the process. In any case, the arena for the most important stage in the process, Judge Greene's court, was the least vulnerable to AT&T's lobbying efforts. Derthick and Quirk suggest that Congress could never have come to such a bold decision because it would have had to be more sensitive to AT&T's interests.[9]

The U.S. approach to telecommunications reform reflects an antitrust tradition combined with a passion for liberalization that swelled in the 1970s. Academic critiques of regulation played an important role in the

---

[6] On the political battles involved, see Derthick and Quirk (1985), Temin (1987), and Horwitz (1989).

[7] Heffron (1983) argues that the FCC attempted some domain expansion in the 1960s, but then actively sought to limit its own authority in the 1970s.

[8] Thus whereas many have argued that the U.S. political system is particularly prone to gridlock (e.g., Cohen, McCubbins and Rosenbluth, 1995) because it provides so many "veto" points—opportunities to forestall change—this actually depends on the nature of the policy issue. The system also provides many "access" points whereby actors can challenge the status quo, thus facilitating change in areas where it is hard to reverse changes once they are made. When liberalizing markets, for example, it is both practically and politically difficult to revert to monopoly once new players have entered the market.

[9] Derthick and Quirk (1985).

process, as they did in the broader deregulation movement.[10] Peter Temin argues that William Baxter, the Justice Department prosecutor in the anti-trust case, was determined to break up AT&T, given his belief in economic theories of regulation, and this pushed the case toward a far more radical solution than his staff might have otherwise proposed.[11] The U.S. response to technological advances differs from that of France or Germany because American political actors overwhelmingly interpret them as developments that require more competition and less government intervention. Leaders in other countries understand technological evolution just as well, but are far less convinced that these changes necessitate a liberal or "deregulatory" response.

Even though the final settlement was reached out of court, Judge Greene has continued to preside over regulatory debates ever since by virtue of his authority to interpret the Modified Final Judgment. When the Judgment was made in 1984, Justice Department officials involved hoped that it would resolve the issue of telecommunications competition for good: AT&T would be able to diversify into new areas, whereas the Bell Operating Companies (BOCs) would be restricted to the provision of basic service. Yet Judge Greene's court and federal and state regulators soon found themselves confronted with an endless series of judgments on the detailed conditions of competition.[12] The BOCs filed a stream of applications for exemptions to the prohibition on moving into new lines of business and launched a lobbying effort for more blanket rights to provide these services. The Reagan administration supported the BOC's position.

In the 1990s, private sector innovations, state and federal regulatory decisions, and court judgments have continued to chip away at the barriers between cable television, local telephone service, and long-distance service. The BOCs have pushed for the right to move into new areas, and cable and long-distance companies have tried to intrude upon the BOCs' turf while simultaneously protecting their own. In 1992, the FCC struck a first blow at the BOC's monopoly by allowing specialized communications companies greater access to BOC networks.[13] Later that same year, AT&T stormed into the cellular telephone business by taking a 33 percent stake in McCaw Cellular Communications, the industry leader, with an option to take majority control at a later date.[14] In 1994, the Baby Bells filed a motion in federal court to throw out the Consent Decree altogether, arguing that technological advances and market liberalization had rendered it obsolete. The House of Representatives passed a comprehensive telecom-

---

[10] Ibid.
[11] Temin (1987), especially pp. 217–35.
[12] Morgan and Pitt (1991); Huntley and Pitt (1990).
[13] *New York Times* (September 18, 1992).
[14] *Economist* (November 14, 1992), pp. 75–76.

munications bill in July 1994 that would have allowed the Baby Bells into the long-distance telephone market, but the bill failed in the Senate in September after a standoff between the long-distance carriers and Commerce Committee Chairman Ernest Hollings. Hollings had insisted on provisions requiring the Baby Bells to face competition in local markets before moving into the long-distance business, and they had refused to go along. Then in June 1995 the Senate passed a bill to allow local and long-distance carriers to compete head-to-head, to permit telephone companies to offer cable television, and to liberalize cable prices, and the House followed with its own bill in August. Congress then managed to reconcile the bills just prior to an agreed deadline of year-end 1995. Congress members and industry representatives crafted a delicate compromise on the terms of the Baby Bells' entry in the long-distance market. The Justice Department would be given partial authority to determine when the Bells were facing sufficient competition in their own local markets, and only then would they be allowed to expand into long-distance service.[15] After further posturing by the two parties and wrangling over details, Congress finally passed the bill in February 1996.

Financial Services

The U.S. financial system is unusual to the extent that both financial institutions and regulators are decentralized. Financial conglomerates began to emerge in the late nineteenth century, but legislators who feared the power of large banks restricted their growth by refusing to renew national banking charters after 1910. Banks were effectively limited to doing business within a single state, with only holding companies allowed to operate across state lines. The regulatory system was characterized by a dual structure of regulation. Banks could choose whether to be chartered at the state or federal level, but only those chartered at the federal level could be members of the Federal Reserve system.[16]

The present regulatory regime began to take shape in the 1930s after a series of reforms following the market crash of 1929 and the ensuing Great Depression. The architects of these reforms blamed structural flaws in the financial system for the Depression and designed the new system to prevent similar market upheavals in the future. Under the Banking Act of 1933, commonly known as the Glass-Steagall Act, Congress divided the banking and securities sectors in order to eliminate conflicts of interest between bankers and underwriters. The government also separated commercial banks from savings and loan institutions (S&Ls), which were de-

---

[15] *New York Times* (December 21, 1995).

[16] Bloch (1981) and Kane (1987) stress the virtues of this dual regulatory system.

signed to promote home ownership. The S&Ls were required to invest in long-term housing loans rather than short-term commercial loans in exchange for certain privileges, including the right to offer slightly better deposit interest rates than commercial banks. In the banking sector, in 1933 the Federal Reserve Board established Regulation Q, whereby interest rates for bank deposits were fixed. It also strengthened the deposit insurance system, setting up separate government insurance agencies for commercial banks and for S&Ls. Under the 1934 Securities Act, Congress created an independent securities regulator, the Securities and Exchange Commission (SEC), which developed an elaborate new regulatory system. SEC officials relied on extensive disclosure requirements, which they believed were necessary to support a market-driven financial system. Without the aversion to legalism evident in the United Kingdom and Japan, the regulatory system became more juridical and complex over time.[17]

The structure of financial markets influenced regulatory debates in several ways. First, as in Japan, the division between banks and brokerage firms shaped regulatory policy debates by creating two distinct groups of institutions whose interests conflicted on many regulatory issues. Second, the barriers inherent in the system gave financial institutions greater incentives to innovate in order to take advantage of or to circumvent regulatory barriers. But unlike their Japanese counterparts, U.S. financial institutions were not constrained from testing the authorities by moral suasion or other forms of governmental "guidance." And third, as in the United Kingdom, the lack of strong ties between financial institutions and industry meant that debates over financial reform focused on the financial sector itself rather than on its role in financing industry.

The fragmented structure of regulation also influenced the process of financial reform. As in telecommunications, firms wishing to challenge the rules had multiple avenues for appeal. They could state their case before self-regulatory organizations, state or federal regulatory agencies, or the courts. This facilitated pro-competitive reform over the long run because firms challenging the status quo could always appeal a defeat, whereas those who were opposed could not easily reverse a decision to liberalize. The pluralistic nature of governance in the sector made policy coordination very difficult and subjected the rules to constant challenge and renegotiation.

The U.S. financial revolution took on full force in 1975 with the abolition of fixed commissions on stock transactions in the New York Stock Exchange (NYSE). Beginning in 1963, several investment firms outside NYSE membership challenged the system by offering a discount brokerage service on some listed stocks. The NYSE responded by ordering its

[17] Moran (1991), pp. 21–54.

members not to do business with such discounters, and the discounters then sued the Exchange in court. Although these court challenges were unsuccessful, the Department of Justice officially criticized the Exchange's anticompetitive behavior in a report in 1968. Meanwhile, institutional investors protested the fixed commission structure for subsidizing individuals at the expense of institutions and began bypassing the NYSE. The SEC finally decided to force the NYSE to liberalize commissions in 1975, in part because the Exchange's reputation had been further tarnished by a series of scandals.[18]

The macroeconomic changes of the 1970s provided a significant challenge for regulators in the major financial centers. The transition to flexible exchange rates encouraged national authorities to take greater liberties with fiscal and monetary policy. This resulted in large imbalances, increasing international capital flows, and more "leakage" from domestic financial systems. The problem was particularly acute in the United States because inflation was very high, threatening the structure of regulated interest rates.[19] The Regulation Q ceilings were not a major issue prior to 1966 when the ceilings first fell below market rates. But high inflation put severe pressure on these regulations in the 1970s as deposit interest rates sometimes did not even keep up with retail price increases. This pushed savers to look for alternative investments with better returns.

In 1961 Citibank invented the negotiable certificate of deposit (CD), a CD that could be traded on secondary markets. Although CD rates were regulated, they could move freely in secondary transactions. This gave banks a new source of funds at market rates, meaning that they could expand lending without having to gather matching deposits.[20] The CD market expanded rapidly after the authorities liberalized CD rates between 1971 and 1973. Most individual investors, however, were still not able to benefit from this market because of high minimum denominations. Investment banks overcame this problem by packaging money market instruments together into money market funds for these investors. Banks then demanded that they be allowed to offer market rates as well. Meanwhile, in 1972 Massachusetts banks began to offer negotiable order of withdrawal (NOW) accounts, checking accounts that pay interest, and these accounts were available nationally by 1980. Under the 1980 Deposit Institutions and Monetary Control Act, Congress mandated that deposit interest rate ceilings be lifted by 1986. And under the 1982 Garn-St. Germain Act, Congress allowed "super" NOW accounts and money market deposit accounts.

---

[18] Moran (1991), pp. 36–46.
[19] Meerschwam (1991), pp. 90–91.
[20] Ibid., pp. 90–91.

The advent of "hybrid" instruments such as negotiable CDs and money market accounts struck an early blow at the Glass-Steagall barrier between commercial and investment banks. Both commercial and investment banks subsequently became more aggressive in challenging these barriers, devising more and more sophisticated ways of circumventing the restrictions. Unlike the Japanese authorities, the U.S. government never consolidated the various issues involved into a single coherent debate. Instead, the process took the form of challenges to the status quo by entrepreneurial firms, followed by a series of responses by regulatory agencies and the courts. In their study of the debate over regulating commercial paper markets, David Litt et al. suggest that the U.S. reform process has been characterized by "post-clearance" decision making: the initial decision (clearance) only launches the debate, as it is then challenged repeatedly in the courts and in Congress.[21] Bankers Trust tested the accepted interpretation of the Glass-Steagall Act—that banks could not underwrite or distribute commercial paper—by placing commercial paper with investors for several corporate customers in 1978. This led to a protest to the Federal Reserve Board, which denied the petition; an appeal to the Supreme Court, which reversed this denial in 1984; subsequent clarifications by the Board; and finally a 1987 decision by the Board to permit three major commercial banks, including Bankers Trust, to set up securities subsidiaries. This established the principle that banks and brokerage firms could cross Glass-Steagall lines through subsidiaries. The Securities Industry Association then successfully lobbied Congress to suspend this decision for one year while Congress worked on comprehensive regulatory reform legislation. But Congress failed to deliver, and the Board's decision went into effect in March 1988.[22]

Before reform, the U.S. financial regulatory system was much more fragmented than that of other countries, including the United Kingdom, and reform has fragmented it even more. The government has created several new regulatory bodies, and the courts have become more involved. The liberal economic ideology and the fragmented nature of the political system have both worked in favor of strongly pro-competitive solutions. Unlike their Japanese counterparts, U.S. officials have not manipulated the liberalization process in order to protect or promote domestic financial institutions. If anything, they have felt that freer market competition should make these institutions stronger. Yet the period of liberalization has coincided with a precipitous decline in the world market share of major U.S. financial institutions. Liberalization may not have directly caused U.S. financial institutions to falter, but it has accelerated the process

---

[21] Litt et al. (1990).
[22] Ibid., pp. 383–403.

whereby they have been replaced by Japanese and European institutions in the rankings of the world's richest. Furthermore, U.S. authorities have designed financial reforms primarily to provide financial services to consumers more efficiently rather than to promote investment in industry. In Japan, France, and Germany, in contrast, we find that authorities are much more concerned with finance as a servant of industry.[23]

Since the late 1980s, U.S. financial authorities have been confronted with a crisis of daunting proportions: the collapse of the S&L industry. No one knows the true cost of the crisis, which will include interest payments extending for several decades, but some estimate that it will eventually exceed $500 billion. And this does not include indirect costs, such as lower confidence in the financial system, unemployment, and other social costs. Experts disagree fundamentally in their analysis of the crisis, with some blaming excessive liberalization, and others insufficient liberalization. Those who defend liberalization tend to stress that the deposit insurance system provided S&Ls with a perverse incentive to take risks because they could always count on the government's safety net. More fundamentally, the crisis was rooted in the structure of the S&L industry itself, which relied on short-term deposits to make long-term loans. This mismatch between liabilities and assets made S&Ls vulnerable to large swings in interest rates, a problem they did not really experience until the late 1970s. But these problems only produced a crisis because the authorities liberalized *before* they addressed these deeper problems.[24]

Financial liberalization created new investment and loan alternatives that took business away from the S&Ls. Depositors took their money out of S&Ls to seek higher returns in money-market funds, and home buyers borrowed from securities firms that could package and resell the loans as securities. The government responded by liberalizing the S&Ls' use of funds. This was supposed to help them compete, but with the deposit insurance system still in place it only invited disaster. Asset-side liberalization combined with the insurance safety net meant that S&Ls had both the freedom and the incentive to take greater risks—and this ultimately produced the crisis. The structure of the U.S. government made it difficult for the authorities to coordinate the sequence of reforms, and in this case sequence was particularly critical. In addition, U.S. authorities failed to respond quickly once the crisis emerged, since both bureaucrats and Congress members were inclined to put off paying the bill for

---

[23] Allen (September 1994) makes this contrast with respect to the United States and Germany.

[24] For three contrasting perspectives on the crisis, see Eichler (1989), Kane (1989), and White (1991). Eichler places deregulation as a major cause of the crisis, Kane disagrees, and White charts a middle course, suggesting that it was one of several factors that only in combination produced a crisis.

the S&L industry's weakness.[25] Ironically, the S&L crisis prompted the U.S. Congress to pass far-reaching reregulatory legislation in 1991. Under the Federal Deposit Insurance Corporation Improvement Act, the government introduced a system of deposit insurance premiums scaled on the basis of bank risk, set out stricter guidelines for bank lending, tightened reporting requirements, and increased bank liability for errors or fraud.[26]

In the same year, however, the Bush administration failed to pass comprehensive financial reform legislation to permit interstate banking and to free banks to underwrite securities and sell mutual funds. The reform effort stalled in October 1991 when Henry Gonzalez, chairman of the House Banking Committee, struck a deal with John Dingell, chairman of the House Energy and Commerce Committee, whereby financial institutions would have to establish formidable firewalls between their banking, securities, and insurance divisions. The banks then swiftly turned against the bill, arguing that this compromise undermined meaningful reform. Even the administration switched its position and lobbied against the bill, which was overwhelmingly defeated in the House on November 4.[27] Then in 1994, the Clinton administration pushed through a reform bill to permit interstate banking. Banks had been able to operate across state lines in most states through separate subsidiaries, but the new legislation finally gave them the freedom to link interstate networks and to merge across state lines. But the administration failed to achieve its goal of consolidating bank regulation. The Treasury Department had proposed to join the bank regulation functions of the Office of the Comptroller of the Currency, the Federal Reserve Board, and the Federal Deposit Insurance Corporations and the Office of Thrift Supervision into a single agency, but it ran into fierce opposition from the Federal Reserve. In addition, many of the banks opposed the proposal because they enjoyed the right to choose among regulators.[28] In 1995, Congress attempted once again to repeal the Glass-Steagall Act. A broad coalition of Republicans, Democrats, the Federal Reserve Board, big banks, and many securities firms strongly supported the effort. The House Banking Committee passed a repeal, but attached a rider to appease the insurance industry by keeping banks out of the insurance business indefinitely. The banks then dropped their support for the bill, and the drive for reform stalled once more.[29]

[25] See the special issue on the S & L crisis in *PS: Political Science and Politics* 24:3 (September 1991).

[26] *Economist* (February 27, 1993), p. 77.

[27] *New York Times* (November 6, 1991).

[28] *Economist* (August 6, 1994), pp. 59–60.

[29] *New York Times* (November 2, 1995).

Regulatory Reform American Style

Like the United Kingdom and Japan, the United States has extended its deregulation movement to a wide array of sectors. In fact, the U.S. movement predates those of other countries, and provided some of the inspiration for the Thatcher and Nakasone reforms. It differs in that it was not initiated by a specific administration, but by a variety of political entrepreneurs. The movement dates back to the Gerald Ford administration (1974–77), when Senator Edward Kennedy and others began to herald the cause of deregulation in congressional hearings. Kennedy began with the airlines, but the movement quickly spread to other areas, including trucking and energy. Ronald Reagan (1981–89) made deregulation a pillar of his supply-side economic program and extended reform beyond economic regulation to social regulation as well. George Bush was accused by die-hard Reaganites of permitting creeping reregulation, but his Council on Competitiveness did push for regulatory relief, and he declared a three-month moratorium on new regulations in early 1992—just in time for the reelection campaign. Bill Clinton, who defeated Bush, asked Vice President Albert Gore to run a program to "Reinvent Government" by streamlining regulatory procedures and cutting red tape. Then in February 1995, the new Republican majority in the House raised the ante, declaring a moratorium on new regulations for the rest of the year and passing a bill to make it much harder to issue new regulations. The bill subjects new regulations to strict risk assessment and cost-benefit tests and gives regulated firms the right to sue if these tests are not properly conducted.[30]

The U.S. government has gone even further than the British government with regulatory reform in that it eliminated one regulatory agency, the Civil Aeronautics Board; broke up the telecommunications carrier; and decentralized power even further—in particular by giving the courts a larger role in regulatory policy. Nevertheless, the U.S. reforms exhibit the same essential characteristics we found in the United Kingdom. U.S. authorities have not attempted to control the disruption inherent in the process of liberalization, and they have accepted and sometimes even encouraged the exit of less competitive firms. The breakup of AT&T caused massive disruption to the industry, and other countries have not followed suit precisely because they see this as too high a price to pay for theoretical gains in efficiency.[31] And financial deregulation has contributed to—if not exactly caused—the enormous upheaval of the S&L crisis. Likewise, the U.S. government has further decentralized the regulatory process and ju-

---

[30] *Los Angeles Times* (March 1, 1995).
[31] Kraus and Duerig (1988) and Stone (1989) both argue that the costs of breakup have outweighed the benefits.

ridified regulation. In telecommunications, the courts have taken on a permanent role in interpreting the Modified Final Judgment regarding the activities of AT&T and the BOCs. And in finance, reregulation in the wake of the S&L crisis has added a new layer of rules. Finally, even more than in the United Kingdom, the process of reform itself has been uneven, unpredictable, and adversarial. Because no one agency controls the process, it tends to progress in fits and starts, with any apparent resolution likely to be challenged at a later stage.

Despite the similarities between the U.S. and British patterns, the U.S. experience represents a difference in kind—and not only of degree— from the British case. That is, U.S. private sector actors challenged the rules much more aggressively than their counterparts in the United Kingdom, or in any other country for that matter. They did so through both marketplace innovation and political action. And they were only able to do so because of the highly codified and legalistic regulatory regime. Under a more discretionary system, such as that of Japan, private actors rarely try to outmaneuver the system because they understand that they must comply with the spirit and not the letter of the rules, and they risk being sanctioned if they defy the authorities' intent. In the United States, however, both private sector actors and public officials understand that challenging the interpretation of the rules is part of the adversarial system of regulation.[32] The courts play a much more central role in the process of regulatory change than they do in the United Kingdom. The British government demonstrated its intolerance for judicial policymaking when it agreed to suspend the Office of Fair Trading (OFT) case against the Stock Exchange. Likewise, the U.S. government has demonstrated a remarkable tolerance for it by allowing Judge Greene's court to take over telecommunications regulation.

FRANCE: THE STATE REFORMS ITSELF

In the postwar era, the French government, like its Japanese counterpart, actively intervened in the economy to foster long-term economic growth. Although France has a historical tradition of strong central government, the present structure of government really only took shape with reforms after the Second World War. Constitutional changes, civil service reforms, and financial restructuring, among other measures, produced a system characterized by a strong centralization of power, a powerful elite bureaucracy, and close ties between the bureaucracy and industry. As in Japan, the French government used its ability to allocate credit through

[32] Kagan (1991) describes the U.S. process as one of "adversary legalism."

the banking system as its most fundamental tool in pursuing a state-led development strategy.[33] Yet French *dirigisme* also had important features that distinguish it from the Japanese variety. The French government relied much more heavily on nationalization, routing funds to industry through nationalized banks and controlling industry directly through ownership. It also developed a more elaborate system of planning, using plans to influence corporate behavior. French authorities used their flexibility in the implementation of regulations as leverage over industry, but they did so differently from their Japanese counterparts. As we have seen, Japanese bureaucrats designed legislation as a general framework, leaving much of the detailed implementation up to their own discretion. In contrast, French authorities relied on much more extensive and formal regulations, but generated leverage over industry by selectively granting exemptions to these onerous regulations.[34] Thus while the mechanisms of control differ somewhat, France clearly fits the "managerial" approach to industry, and we should expect French regulatory reforms to incline toward the Japanese "reinforcement" pattern.

Telecommunications

The French government's propensity to liberalize sectors without liberating them is particularly evident in telecommunications. The French telecommunications system developed as a typical Continental PTT: telecommunications carrier, postal service, policymaker, and regulator all in one. The postal and telecommunications ministry (Ministère des Postes, des Télécommunications, et de l'Espace, or PTE Ministry) had a small administrative staff overseeing two enormous service monopolies, the Direction Générale des Télécommunications (DGT) and the Direction Générale de la Poste (DGP). This integration of ministry and operator facilitated the pursuit of national objectives such as investing in infrastructure, expanding service, and maintaining uniform technical standards. Even more than elsewhere, the French PTT embodied a culture of public service. The state-run Centre National d'Etudes des Télécommunications (CNET) served as a training ground for a corps of telecommunications engineers and as a research center that organized the effort to develop the infrastructure. The CNET cultivated a team of domestic suppliers, including its national champion, Alcatel.

The French infrastructure historically lagged behind most of its neighbors, but massive investment brought France to the leading edge within ten years. The turning point came in 1974, when President Valéry Giscard

---

[33] Zysman (1983), pp. 99–169.
[34] Hall (1986), p. 153.

d'Estaing designated telecommunications as a national priority and assigned Gérard Théry, director of the DGT, the task of modernizing the system. The DGT was more successful in investing in infrastructure than the British Post Office because it had a superior mode of financing this investment. It was able to borrow from international capital markets through the Caisse Nationale des Télécommunications (CNT), a government financing organization created in 1967. Théry restructured the DGT, obtaining considerable budgetary freedom from the Ministry of Finance.[35] By the late 1980s, France was leading in the global race toward digitalization.[36]

The government used the DGT as a tool of industrial policy, building up the technical expertise of the telecommunications equipment manufacturers and providing a modern infrastructure for business as a whole. The government managed the development process and directed an effort to stimulate demand. Under the "Plan Cable," the DGT envisioned using cable networks both for telecommunications and for broadcasting as the country moved more toward interactive data communications and video transmission. The Plan was not entirely successful, mostly because it was ahead of its time and so demand was lower than anticipated. In the area of videotext, the government provided "Minitel" terminals free to households. This program stimulated demand for telecommunication services in general and educated the public in the use of telematics. The DGT was far more aggressive than Britain's Post Office in moving into new services. It reorganized itself several times in order to cultivate a more entrepreneurial style, and it created semi-autonomous subsidiaries to provide new services such as value-added networks (VANs) and mobile telephone service. It even allowed limited competition in some areas, notably value-added services. The DGT's dominance had its limitations as well, however, since it overlooked some new markets (cable, facsimile) in its zeal to move into others (VANs, mobile).

Although DGT officials professed no desire to emulate the deregulatory initiatives of the United States or the United Kingdom, by the mid-1980s they had recognized the need to undertake more modest reforms. They worried about competition with British Telecom (BT) in international telephone service and access to the U.S. market in telecommunications equipment. The U.S. government had declared that an open market at home was the price to pay for access to the U.S. market, by far the world's largest. DGT officials estimated that French equipment manufacturers would need an 8 to 10 percent world market share to survive in international competition, yet the French market only accounted for 3 to 4 percent of this market.

[35] Cawson et al. (1990), pp. 122–24.
[36] Duch (1991), p. 174.

Furthermore, DGT officials realized that they would have to make changes in order to comply with European Community (EC) directives. The EC did not have a major role in British telecommunications reform because the key decisions were made in the early 1980s, when the EC was still a minor player in the sector. By the late 1980s, however, when France and Germany initiated their reforms, they did so in conjunction with EC-level developments The EC Commission issued a Green Paper in 1987 proposing that European telecommunications regulation be harmonized and that national regulatory authorities be separated from telecommunications operators.[37] The European Union (EU) has taken over an increasing role in telecommunications regulation in the 1990s, such that member government policies have begun to lose some of their distinct national flavor. At the same time, however, EU policy itself represents an interesting compromise between the contrasting regulatory ideologies of the member countries.[38]

Few in the French government or in the private sector had recommended substantial reforms prior to the mid-1980s. After all, the system was functioning well, particularly in comparison to the situation before 1974. In contrast to the British Post Office, the DGT was respected within government and popular with the larger public. Even as the United States, and then the United Kingdom and Japan embarked on major reforms, French telecommunications policymakers broadly agreed that France had no need to follow suit. Users did not actively lobby for reforms. For the most part, they were genuinely satisfied: the DGT had met most of their needs even as these needs became more complex, and they were willing to let the DGT continue to try to adapt.[39] In addition, many of the most powerful users were nationalized companies, and those that were not were still, like Japanese companies, tied into relationships of dependence on the government and the nationalized sector, the difference being that formal government ownership was more important in France, whereas informal obligational ties were more important in Japan. Household users predictably provided a constant flow of complaints about service quality and standards, but made few demands for broader reform.

Thus the DGT itself took the lead. It had a near monopoly on information and expertise, so it was the only actor in a position to assess the need for change. The DGT was not unified: in fact, major factions opposed change, and the unions protested vehemently.[40] Yet DGT managers and

[37] Commission of the European Communities (1987).
[38] Woolcock, Hodges, and Schreiber (1991); Cowhey and Zysman (April 1992); Sandholtz (January 1993).
[39] Interview with user association representative (October 1990).
[40] Several disgruntled DGT executives express their misgivings under a collective pseudonym in A. de Guers (1987).

engineers were attracted by the opportunity to break loose from the postal service and to become a more autonomous corporation. They were opposed to competition in basic telephone service, but favored reorganization.

In 1986, a coalition of the Right recaptured the French parliament, creating the country's first experience with "cohabitation": a president of the Left presiding over a government of the Right. Gérard Longuet, the liberally inclined new postal and telecommunications minister, immediately began work on telecommunications reform.[41] The prime minister, Jacques Chirac, was surprisingly reluctant to provoke the postal and telecommunications unions. Although his conservative coalition did not rely on union support, he was well aware of the unions' ability to cause trouble. He remembered only too well the telecommunications strike of 1974, which had severely disrupted the economy. The government did not give in to union pressure as much as it anticipated union pressure: that is, it designed reforms in order not to antagonize the unions too much. It began with a decree in September 1987 permitting firms to sell VANs to third parties on leased lines. As in Japan, the ministry distinguished between two types of VANs, and it retained for itself the right to authorize the larger and more sophisticated VANs.[42] The government then began to work on broader reform legislation, but decided to wait until after the elections to introduce it.

As it turns out, the coalition narrowly lost the election of 1988, but the new Socialist administration pressed ahead with the reforms. The Chirac administration had been inclined to begin with further liberalization first, but the Socialists realized that this would not be effective without a reorganization of the operator, so they decided to proceed with the reorganization right away. In preparation for the changes, they renamed the telecommunications operator France Télécom (FT) in 1988, with the Direction de la Réglementation Générale (DRG) serving as its regulatory arm. In December 1988, the new minister, Paul Quilès, asked Hubert Prévot, an adviser with a union background, to organize a public debate on the reorganization of the PTT. The government sought to use the Prévot process to create a consensus for a reform that it had essentially already designed. Prévot toured the country for a full year, holding large public meetings and engaging in more restricted encounters with interested parties. Prévot produced a report so diplomatically worded that it could not be opposed. He avoided controversial points and went to great lengths to adopt the rhetoric of those who might oppose reform. Thus he stressed the continuing importance of a commitment to "public service,"

[41] See Longuet (1988).
[42] Thimm (1992), pp. 97–98.

responsiveness to social needs, and investment in infrastructure and research and development. He also granted an important symbolic concession to the unions, promising that workers would still be considered civil servants.[43] The Prévot process neutralized the union opposition by inviting all interested parties to hearings on the proposed legislation, especially those users and potential market entrants who favored reform. This put the unions on the defensive, for they were made to look like reactionaries unwilling to accept change.[44] Even after the government announced its draft law, it avoided bilateral negotiations with the unions. On April 3, 1990, the Conseil Général de Travail (CGT), the union with the largest number of postal and telecommunications workers, called a general strike to protest the proposed reforms. But with only 15 to 20 percent of workers participating, the strike ended in complete failure. The bill passed on June 28, 1990, and the next day the non-CGT unions—Force Ouvrière (FO), Confédération Française des Travailleurs Chrétiens (CFTC), and the Confédération Française Démocratique du Travail (CFDT), signed an agreement with the minister whereby workers were reclassified and compensation levels were boosted by a total of Fr 5 billion. The government had bought off the unions, but many believed that this was a small price to pay for social peace.

The DGT submitted the telecommunications and postal bills jointly to parliament. This made it that much easier for the telecommunications bill to pass smoothly, for deputies focused on the more politically sensitive postal side. They wanted to ensure that post offices would continue to serve the needs of rural communities, and that post offices would not threaten commercial banks by moving further into the banking business. Some right-wing deputies argued that the government should set up an independent regulator like the FCC or Oftel, but the ministry insisted that the government should maintain centralized regulatory control.[45] Originally, the government had suggested that it would transfer some regulatory powers to the new Commission Nationale de la Communication et des Libertés (CNCL), but it never carried this through.[46] Instead, it established two regulatory bureaus: the DRG, which was essentially in place already, and the Direction du Service Public (DSP). The DRG regulates competition in the telecommunications market, and the DSP regulates FT.[47]

The government passed a second bill on December 29, 1990, clarifying the delineation between the monopoly and competitive sectors and ex-

---

[43] Prévot (July 1989).
[44] Interviews with DRG officials (1990–91).
[45] Interview with DRG official (April 1993).
[46] Vedel (1988), p. 296.
[47] On the politics of French telecommunications reform, see Darmon (1986), Vedel (1988), Coriat (October 1989), Cawson et al. (1990), and Duch (1991).

tending the liberalization process that had been progressing on an *ad hoc* basis throughout the 1980s. The legislation permits competition in mobile and satellite communications and value-added services, but requires service operators to obtain ministry authorization and to abide by a ministry charter that specifies conditions for operation. Likewise, the bill affirmed the liberalization of the equipment sector, while stipulating that suppliers must obtain ministry approval and satisfy all ministry technical standards.[48]

As in Japan, the ministry remained the primary locus of debate through much of the process, and thus it was able to design a reform that served its own goals. It enhanced the industry's ability to meet diverse and changing needs while maintaining its own capacity to shape the sector's evolution. It did this by retaining regulatory and supervisory powers that enable it to influence the behavior of the major marketplace players, especially FT. During the legislative process, FT executives lobbied to expand their own business freedom, and the ministry sought to maximize its discretion in implementing regulation. Neither side wound up entirely satisfied, for FT faces a rather daunting regulatory regime, and a constitutional commission ruling dictated that the ministry make its regulatory system as transparent as possible. The ministry's new regulatory wings are both staffed with former DGT officials, so the regulators and FT share a common heritage. Beyond its regulatory responsibilities, the ministry supervises FT through its participation in three advisory commissions.[49] More important, FT must develop its three-year business plans in coordination with both the PTE and the Finance Ministries. The government demonstrated its continued control over FT in April 1991—after both reform bills had passed—when it channeled a Fr 8.5 billion bailout of electronics giants Thomson and Bull through FT.[50] The PTE Ministry still enjoys close ties to the operator, the research institutes, and the manufacturers. As a result, like Japan's MPT, it possesses the authority to formulate and implement telecommunications policy and to regulate the competition within the new regime.

By the mid 1990s, the French government was busily preparing for the liberalization of telephone service across Europe, scheduled by EU directive for 1998. French authorities planned to privatize FT by 1998, but were unable to make a formal decision or to set a timetable given powerful resistance from the unions. Meanwhile, they agreed to clarify plans for domestic telephone competition in order to assure U.S. government ap-

---

[48] Thimm (1992), pp. 114–16.
[49] Commission Supérieure du Service Public des Postes et Télécommunications, Conseil National des PTT, and Commission Supérieure du Personnel et des Affaires Sociales. *Télécoms Magazine* (July–August 1990), pp. 60–61.
[50] Thimm (1992), p. 105.

proval of "Phoenix," an alliance between FT, Deutsche Telekom, and Sprint. Despite its commitment to liberalization and privatization, however, the French government remained determined to promote the sector through large-scale industrial policy projects (*grands projets*) at both the national and the European levels.[51]

Financial Services

In financial services French authorities broke with the past more radically. They faced more powerful market pressures and a more profound erosion of their traditional policy tools, but they also enjoyed more decisive leadership. Top government officials led the financial reform process even more than in the United Kingdom or Japan. Insiders describe a situation in which one brilliant official at the Finance Ministry (Ministère de l'Economie, des Finances et du Budget), Jean-Charles Naouri, single-handedly engineered the Paris "Big Bang."[52] Although this characterization overstates the case, Naouri and his colleagues at the ministry clearly orchestrated the process. In the short period from 1983 to 1987, they reduced exchange controls, removed credit controls, created new money markets, liberalized interest rates, and reformed the Bourse. In doing so, they fundamentally curtailed many of the core instruments of *dirigisme*, and yet they did so less as an exercise in disengagement than as a restructuring of regulatory powers in the face of powerful market changes.[53]

Traditionally, the French financial system, like the Japanese financial system, has relied very heavily on bank credit to finance industry. There was no absolute wall between banking and brokerage as in the United States or Japan, but the government intentionally created a financial system biased toward bank lending. The authorities felt that they had better control over the flow of funds with a credit-based financial system, and they used a deliberate policy of tight credit to direct funds to priority sectors.[54] The Paris stock exchange, the Bourse, remained underdeveloped well into the 1980s. The government influenced financial flows even more directly than in Japan: it operated a wide array of semipublic financial institutions, owned the largest commercial banks, and participated on the boards of the most prominent investment banks. And as in Japan, private sector banks were organized into compulsory industry associations that institutionalized a close working relationship between the government and the financial sector.[55]

[51] Bar (September 1995).
[52] Interviews (1990–91).
[53] Cerny (March 1989); Loriaux (1991).
[54] Zysman (1983), especially 112–33.
[55] Coleman (April 1993).

As in other countries, institutional investors and other interested parties began to call for financial reforms by the early 1980s. Yet these voices were unusually faint in France, and most of the financial community solidly favored the status quo. The banks were afraid that reform would take business away from their traditional lending business and shift it to the Bourse and off-market securities markets. They also feared that reform would lead to deposit interest rate liberalization, which would erode their strong base of cheap funds. In addition, many of the largest financial institutions were disinclined to criticize the system given their nationalized status. Industrial concerns were equally cautious, for many of them benefited from the prevailing system of subsidies and preferential credit.

The government itself took the critical early steps in financial innovation.[56] Finance Ministry officials either directly introduced new financial instruments themselves or manipulated incentives in order to induce the private sector to innovate. In 1978, for example, Finance Minister René Monory promoted a shift of funds into equity markets by offering an income tax deduction for new purchases of French shares. In 1981, Finance Minister Jacques Delors tightened the regulation of deposit rates so that savers could not index deposits to money market rates. This encouraged savers to switch their investments into open-ended unit trusts and mutual funds.

In 1983, French financial regulation and *dirigisme* more broadly encountered a watershed as the new Socialist government performed its famed U-turn. After seizing power in 1981, President François Mitterrand's administration embarked on an inflationary program of increased social spending that combined with a stubborn global recession to produce a daunting balance of payments crisis. The government devalued the franc in October 1981, but this failed to stem the crisis. As the crisis deepened, it became clear that the government faced a cruel dilemma: either pull out of the European Monetary System (EMS) or defend the franc through an austerity program. It began a reverse course with a second devaluation and an austerity program in June 1982 and completed it with a third devaluation and an even more drastic austerity program in March 1983.[57]

By this point, government authorities had reasons to consider broader financial reforms. First, they sought to bolster their strong franc policy by creating a more attractive "menu" of investment instruments. Second, they wanted to create more efficient channels for investment into French industry. They increasingly recognized that state efforts to finance industry directly had not always produced the desired results, and in any case

---

[56] See De Boissieu (1990) on public versus private financial innovation.
[57] Hall (1986), pp. 192–202.

the austerity program would greatly impede their ability to keep this up. Thus they sought reforms that would make it easier for financial institutions themselves to invest in industry. They especially hoped to design financial instruments that could serve the particular needs of two privileged sectors: nationalized industries and smaller companies.[58] Third, as in the United Kingdom and Japan, the authorities were concerned about financing the budget deficit, which was considerable at the time. They wanted to find ways to fund the deficit without monetization, in order to avoid creating additional inflationary pressures, and they recognized that deeper and more sophisticated secondary markets could make this easier. And finally, they wanted to promote Paris as a financial center, and to do this they would have to dramatically reform the Bourse.

Mitterrand's finance minister, Jacques Delors, introduced an initial set of reforms in early 1983, creating new savings instruments, organizing a "second market" in unlisted securities to give smaller firms access to financial markets, and strengthening the powers of the financial regulators.[59] Then in January 1984, the government passed a new banking law that unified regulations over different categories of banks, centralized regulatory powers in a new agency, the Comité de la Réglementation Bancaire (CRB), and created a new umbrella industry association for the sector. This both strengthened the government's control over the banking industry and enhanced the mechanisms of policy coordination between the government and the banks.[60]

The real explosion of financial reform began in November 1984 under Delors's successor, Pierre Bérégovoy, who came to be known as the socialist who brought capitalism to France. Bérégovoy's personal deputy Naouri both encouraged him to move forward and organized a core group of ten to twenty officials within the Trésor, the super-elite division within the ministry that deals with finance, to design reforms. Although many within the financial community were still hesitant, Trésor officials felt they had to take charge. As one official notes: "We decided here in the Trésor to create a futures market, to create an open money market, to suppress exchange controls, to eliminate credit controls, and to modernize monetary policy. Neither the Bank of France nor the banking community initiated these measures. We convinced the various parties, and they all played along."[61] A representative from the main banking association, the Association Française des Banques (AFB), depicts the process in strikingly similar terms: "The ministry took the initiative: we participated in a classic dialogue with the authorities, but we did not initiate. We did not accept every-

[58] De Boissieu (1990), pp. 186–87.
[59] Cerny (March 1989), pp. 179–80.
[60] Coleman (April 1993).
[61] Interview (October 1991).

thing, but in general we played along right from the start."[62] In fact, the ministry used the AFB to persuade the financial institutions of the need for reform.[63] Of course, ministry officials understood the interests of the financial institutions and took these into account when designing their reforms. They even got some of their specific ideas from interested parties. For example, they first considered the creation of a market for medium-term notes in response to a suggestion from the association of corporate treasurers.[64] Nonetheless, only the ministry was able to overcome resistance within the financial community, to resolve conflicts within this community, and thus to determine the timing, the scope, and the nature of reform.

The government was boldest in its creation of new money market instruments. The government eased this transition politically by allowing the banks themselves to deal in many of these instruments, thus softening the blow of disintermediation. The Trésor authorities announced new debt instruments, including *obligations renouvables du Trésor* (ORTs) and *obligations assimilables du Trésor* (OATs). They also introduced certificates of deposit and commercial paper. In the case of CDs, Bérégovoy anticipated bank resistance so he simply announced his decision without any consultation outside the ministry.[65] The government proceeded gradually with both CDs and commercial paper, introducing larger denominations first and then moving on to smaller denominations. The authorities also established a futures market, MATIF (Marché à Terme d'Instruments Financiers), in 1986.

Chirac's finance minister, Edouard Balladur, extended the reforms the Socialists had launched. He abolished exchange controls, ended credit ceilings, created yet more instruments to encourage savings, and liberalized interest rates on bonds and long-term deposits.[66] As to interest rates, the banks argued that liberalization would force them to charge commissions for checks and other services in order to break even, which caused a furor in the press. The government decided, rather than go further, to wait for the EC to do the job for them. The authorities also moved forward with a wholesale reform of the Bourse, although they moved gingerly when abolishing the monopoly of the *agents de changes,* brokers who have the status of public officials with statutory responsibilities. They liberalized commissions and opened the *agents* to outside ownership in three stages, giving the *agents* a full six years to adapt to a more competitive environment.[67] At the same time, they substantially strengthened the powers of the Commission des Opérations de la Bourse (COB), the official regulator

[62] Interview (July 1990).
[63] Interview with AFB official (October 1991).
[64] Interview with Trésor official (October 1991).
[65] Cerny (March 1989), p. 183.
[66] Loriaux (1991), pp. 271–72.
[67] *The Banker* (May 1987), p. 41.

of trading activity, giving the COB the ability to fine or bar from the market traders or firms who violate regulations.

The French authorities have introduced reforms in a carefully calculated manner. As in telecommunications, they appeared immune to international pressures up to a point and yet moved swiftly once they decided to act. The institutional structure of politics makes French authorities less responsive to societal pressures for reforms than their counterparts in Britain or the United States, yet more capable of implementing these reforms once they have determined they are necessary. Only French (or Japanese) authorities could produce a program with such internal coherence. As French economist Jacques Melitz notes, the French authorities sculpted their reforms according to a very deliberate plan:

> As one contemplates the panoply of measures that took effect in France from late 1984 to the end of 1986, there is no doubt that the changes were inspired by a general vision. This was no mere lifting of controls: new instruments were created; new markets were added, including markets in futures; and the importance of permitting every individual agent to hedge his risks was clearly recognized. The whole program smacks of a close acquaintance with the principles of the theory of finance.[68]

These authorities had no passion for liberalization *per se*, but they wanted to modernize the French financial system. In this effort, they willingly abandoned some of the tools they used to allocate credit. But they were still left with considerable influence over the behavior of financial institutions.[69] They have actually strengthened regulatory agencies such as the CRB and the COB. And they continue to exercise authority over the large banks, even after privatization. Jean-Yves Haberer—ironically a former directeur at the Trésor—lashed out at this lingering *dirigisme* after being dismissed as chairman of Crédit National due to his previous performance running the Crédit Lyonnais. Refusing to accept responsibility for the misfortunes of the Crédit Lyonnais, Haberer blamed a government that still instructs financial institutions to support influential sectors of the economy regardless of financial good sense.[70]

Regulatory Reform French Style

France never experienced a full-fledged deregulation movement like that of Japan, yet in real terms the French break with *dirigisme* has been

---

[68] Melitz (1990), p. 397.
[69] Cerny (March 1989) argues that they have left themselves with the capability for a "tactical" sort of *dirigisme*.
[70] *Los Angeles Times* (April 1, 1994).

more profound than Japan's attack on overregulation. The Socialists' U-turn in 1983 brought on a public renunciation of *dirigisme* and ushered in a campaign of privatization, decentralization, and financial liberalization that only intensified when the Right returned to power in 1986. The French break with statism was more radical than Japan's because France faced a more intense economic crisis, a more obvious failure of state activism, and a more powerful international constraint in the form of the maturing European Community. All industrialized countries faced a similar set of pressures for regulatory change, but these pressures were more acute in France because of its particular monetary crisis of 1982–83 and its position within the EC.

Nevertheless, the French pattern of reform still features the same basic characteristics we saw in Japan. As in Japan, seemingly bold moves toward the market were coupled with compensatory measures designed by state officials to buffer French firms from the full force of competition and to retain strategic sources of control for themselves. Telecommunications officials designed reforms that did not threaten national champions in equipment manufacturing, and finance officials managed the process in order to avoid undermining the standing of French financial institutions. The financial authorities helped banks cope with disintermediation by giving them a larger role in securities markets, and they helped the *agents de change* to survive stock exchange reform by orchestrating a reform as elegant and slow as any reform carried out in Japan. In fact, as a whole French authorities have orchestrated the reform process in an extremely smooth and deliberate fashion. Relatively insulated from interest group pressures, government officials have postponed reform longer than officials elsewhere, yet have pushed it through with relative ease once they decided to act. They have tailored reforms that resemble their own blueprints much closer than those of U.S. or British officials. They have also managed to structure liberalization in a way that limited the loss of regulatory power. As in Japan, they have retained regulatory and policy functions within the same agency. In accord with EC guidelines, they have separated the telecommunications operator (FT) from the regulator (DRG), but the PTE Ministry remains both policymaker and regulator. The Finance Ministry did create a new securities regulator, the Conseil de Bourse, but it retains effective control over the Conseil's functions.

French officials have compensated themselves for losses of regulatory power in some areas by undertaking new initiatives in others. They have not done this in the Japanese manner, using control over the liberalization process itself as a new lever over industry, but have maintained regulatory authority in a manner more consistent with their traditional mechanisms of control. Thus French authorities have manipulated privatizations to retain their influence over the privatized firms, appointing their own preferred directors and allocating controlling blocks of shares (*noyaux durs*) to reliable allies.[71] They have also sought more novel ways to achieve their policy goals in a changed environment. They have tried to create new intermediary institutions, such as stronger local authorities, to fill in the gap for diminished state power. They have encouraged banks to follow the German model and to assume more of a public role. And where the French state has lost the capacity to perform as it used to, as in industrial policy, the authorities have increasingly looked to the EU to take over their responsibilities.[72]

GERMANY: THE PRUDENCE IN PIECEMEAL CHANGE

At first, the German postwar regime appears to defy the contrast intro-duced in Chapter 3 between a "regulatory" and a "managerial" orientation, and between a "segmented" and a "fused" structure (see Table 5). The Ger-man government espoused a relatively liberal ideology, yet in practice it was more involved in the industrial adjustment process than either the British or the U.S. government. The German political system resembles that of the United States, with power relatively decentralized within the fed-eral government and substantial responsibilities devolved to the state level, and yet the German government is more capable of coordinating policies for industrial sectors. In its essence, the German regime is closer to the Japanese than to the British or U.S. model. The German government in-tervenes in the economy far more actively than one might expect from its liberal rhetoric. Leaders of both conservative and socialist inclinations sup-port the ideals of a "social market economy," a notion that simultaneously respects the market and legitimizes economic regulation and social wel-fare.[73] And the German government partially compensated for its decen-tralized structure through close cooperation between agencies and a dense network of parapublic institutions.[74] It substituted informal coordination for the centralization of governmental power characteristic of Japan or France. In addition, Germany's large universal banks played a public role, supporting the government's capacity to manage the economy.[75] Given this, we should expect German reform to follow the broad pattern of Japanese "reinforcement," but we may discover some interesting variations traceable to features unique to the German political economy.

---

[71] Bauer (October 1988).

[72] Levy (1994) argues that these efforts have largely failed, because the intermediary and EC-level institutions have not had the capacity to fulfill these responsibilities.

[73] Lehmbruch (1992), pp. 31–35.

[74] Katzenstein (1987 and 1989).

[75] See Zysman (1983), pp. 251–65.

Telecommunications

Telecommunications reform in Germany resembled that of Japan and France: a government ministry orchestrated a gradual and orderly process of liberalization. As in other European countries, the German telecommunications system evolved around a PTT administration, the Deutsche Bundespost (DBP). The federal government's leading role in telecommunications and the DBP's monopoly was written into Article 87 of the Basic Law (*Grundgesetz*), Germany's constitution. The Bundespost embodied a tradition of public service, with a strong commitment to universal service at a uniform price. The DBP was formally run by a council with representatives from the conservative and progressive parties, the states (*Länder*), the unions, and industry. Thus both the unions and telecommunications equipment makers had considerable influence over policy because they were formally incorporated into the policy process, and this formal representation provided an opportunity for informal influence as well. The unions not only represented the interests of DBP workers, but also reinforced the DBP's commitment to welfare goals. Meanwhile, the equipment manufacturers essentially formed a production cartel, with research and development activities centered around a government research institute. The DBP itself manufactured some equipment and had a monopoly on the first telephone. The equipment market was relatively open in theory, although in practice the DBP used strict standards to keep out foreign products.

As in the French case, the government ministry and the operator were integrated into a single organization. The DBP was relatively free from interference by other government agencies, but was subject to intervention on specific matters. The Economics Ministry, which was controlled by the liberal Free Democratic Party (FDP), had to approve all tariff rates. The Finance Ministry, which had to approve spending and borrowing, made sure that about 10 percent of DBP earnings went to the government's general funds. And the Interior Ministry had the right to approve salary scales.[76] Like the French DGT, the Bundespost was fairly successful in modernizing the telecommunications system, and users were generally satisfied with its service. In the 1970s, however, the DBP stumbled in its effort to develop an indigenous switching system that was supposed to bridge the gap between analog and digital technology. The system, known as "EWS" (*elektronisches Wahlsystem*), ended up being outmoded by the time it came out.[77] In 1978, the DBP officially abandoned EWS and moved to the international digital standard. Telephone rates remained high by European standards, in part because telecommunications operations were

[76] Cawson et al. (1990), pp. 152–53.
[77] Ibid., pp. 162–65.

used to subsidize the postal service and to provide funds to the government.

The underlying forces pushing the government to enact reforms were similar to those in other countries. The sweeping reforms in the United States, and later in the United Kingdom and Japan, pushed officials to consider some changes. Despite the relative strength of the infrastructure, business people and government officials alike became concerned that Germany was falling behind in advanced services. As early as 1979, the Monopoly Commission came out with a report recommending that the equipment and service markets be liberalized. Then in the 1980s, the U.S. government began to pressure the DBP to open its procurement system. This pushed the equipment manufacturers, Siemens in particular, to support domestic liberalization as the *quid pro quo* for a presence in the U.S. market. As in France, the European Community played a major role. The German government, which was pushing for liberal reforms at the EC level in other sectors, was in the awkward position of lagging in the telecommunications sector. The government felt pressure to be more consistent across sectors, for other EC members would be only too ready to point out inconsistencies in the German position. German officials actually took a more liberal stance on telecommunications reform within the EC arena than they did at home. This suggests that domestic political constraints produced a disjuncture between the actual preferences of government elites and the more moderate reforms they proposed for their home market.

In 1982, a new conservative coalition government came to power promising to bring a "New Direction" to German politics. The Christian Democrats (CDU) dominated the coalition, with support from the Bavarian Christian Social Union (CSU) and the FDP. As it turns out, the coalition was powerfully constrained in its ability to pursue liberal reforms, but it did turn its attention to the telecommunications sector early on. The notoriously liberal Economics Ministry and computer makers such as IBM and Nixdorf strongly advocated telecommunications liberalization. The new minister for posts and telecommunications, Christian Schwarz-Schilling, who had been a strident critic of the Bundespost in opposition, took up the task of reform with considerable enthusiasm. Realizing that it would be difficult to push through any reform, and unsure how to proceed anyway, the government announced an independent inquiry on telecommunications reforms in 1984. It then spent an entire year on the delicate task of appointing the members of the commission, who were meant to represent a broad array of interests. The twelve-person commission, chaired by Professor Eberhard Witte, included representatives from the unions, the CDU, the Social Democratic Party (SPD), the state governments, and the media. Yet the commission remained dominated by the established sectoral policy network, a network centered within the ministry itself.[78]

The federal structure of government provided a substantial barrier to reform. Any reform would have to pass the upper house of the legislature, the Bundesrat, which is made up of state representatives. The states were wary of reform because it would diminish their control over telecommunications policy. To make matters worse, this conflict between the federal and state governments was linked to a parallel dispute over sovereignty in broadcast policy. Furthermore, the states were afraid that reform would undermine the universal service obligation, leading to regional disparities in service. This contrasts with the situation in the United States, where the states have actively participated in the liberalization process.

The equipment manufacturers were divided on the question of reform. The smaller manufacturers were steadfastly opposed because they relied on steady orders from the DBP. Siemens executives were more ambivalent. With liberalization, they would lose the stability of fixed DBP orders, but the overall market for equipment would probably grow. They were most adamant in defending the network monopoly. If they could keep earning rents in the network infrastructure sector, this could become a major strategic advantage in competitive sectors.[79] Over time, Siemens executives became more favorably disposed toward reform, and individual executives actively lobbied for change.

The postal workers union, the Deutsche Postgewerkschaft (DPG), adamantly opposed reform. Unlike Britain's POEU, the DPG unified telecommunications and postal workers. But the postal workers dominated the union, and thus the telecommunications workers were in no position to support a reform that would help them at the expense of the postal workers. The postal workers were likely to lose more jobs, whereas the telecommunications workers might benefit from higher salaries. The union's influence was muted, however, because Schwarz-Schilling had excluded it from the traditional corporatist partnership. Whereas union leaders boasted that they had participated in all major DBP decisions under the SPD government, they found themselves excluded from the core group of policy staff under the new coalition. This then forced the union to adopt an "outsider" strategy of classic pressure politics.[80] Beginning in April 1986, the union launched a massive campaign to protest the proposed separation of the telecommunications and postal divisions of the Bundespost. They organized public demonstrations and appealed to the SPD and other progressive politicians at both the federal and state levels.

[78] Lehmbruch (1992), p. 38.
[79] Cawson et al. (1990), p. 177.
[80] Grande (April 1987).

Critically, the DBP itself gradually shifted in favor of reform. Schwarz-Schilling and a small group of advisers were committed to reform, but many still favored the status quo. The postal side of the organization was strongly opposed. As in Britain and Japan, many of the telecommunications engineers opposed competition because it would threaten the integrity of the network. They argued that so long as the DBP was a public administration with social responsibilities, competition could never be fair. Private companies would simply indulge in "cream skimming," to the benefit of no one except these companies themselves. At the same time, however, DBP officials recognized that they stood to obtain substantial salary raises with reforms, and they welcomed the idea of independence from the postal service. Most were willing to accept reform as long as the DBP could maintain its monopoly in basic services and increase its independence as a telecommunications operator. The majority within the DBP gradually shifted as younger officials less wedded to the traditional system gained influence, and Schwarz-Schilling and his core group of reformers consolidated power.[81]

The Witte Commission finally came up with its report in 1987, proposing reforms somewhat bolder than many had expected. It recommended separating the telecommunications from the postal divisions of the DBP, and the operator (the DBP) from the regulator (the ministry). The ministry would have its own staff to regulate the DBP and other competing firms in the telecommunications market. The DBP would maintain a monopoly over the "transmission path" and voice telephony. The Commission defined the scope of the monopoly as covering the transmission path rather than the network because it recognized that the term "network" would include private switching equipment. The Commission was not able to come to a unanimous decision. Two members dissented; three others added supplementary opinions arguing that the recommendations did not go far enough. Interestingly, although SPD representative Peter Glotz ultimately voted against the proposals, his written opinion supported liberalization in principle.[82] The Witte Commission report ended up coming out after the EC's "Green Paper" on telecommunications policy, but the two were prepared simultaneously, and the Witte Commission's recommendations mirrored those of the Green Paper very closely. Insiders suggest that the Witte Commission had as much impact on the Green Paper as vice versa.[83]

The DBP itself heavily influenced the content of the Witte Commission report, and some suggest that DBP officials wrote large portions of it.[84]

[81] Grande (1989).
[82] Witte (1989).
[83] Interviews (October 1991).
[84] Webber (April 1990), p. 38.

These officials began drafting a proposal for legislation in 1987 before the Witte report came out. The government draft, released in November 1987, resembled the Witte report very closely, with several important differences. Most critical, the proposed law presumed that the DBP's monopoly would endure, whereas the Commission argued that the monopoly would have to be abandoned in the medium term as technological progress continued. The law would allow the DBP to extend its monopoly to new types of basic service so long as these were still designed for voice transmission. The government indicated that it would retain the cross-subsidization of local rates and would not allow pricing according to usage for leased lines.[85]

The union's continuing resistance to the reforms pushed the government of Helmut Kohl, which was at an all-time low in popularity in 1989, to offer several concessions. The proposed law had included a plan to abolish the DBP's governing council, which would mean less representation for the states and for the union. As a compromise, the government agreed to create a new board with union representation. In addition, the government would establish an Office of Welfare within the DBP to protect workers' rights. Finally, as in France, the government consented to leave some organizational ties between the postal and telecommunications divisions. The union was particularly fearful of a complete split because this could divide the union.

Volker Schneider and Raymund Werle conclude that of all the actors involved in the reform, the one that dominated the process and most influenced the result was the Bundespost itself: "Those who wanted more liberalization as well as those who wanted less had considerable power resources, but they neutralized each other so that the PTT Ministry could maintain control and mobilize the allies it needed to get the law passed."[86] Politically, therefore, the most important transition was the one that took place *within* the DBP. As in the Japanese and French cases, ministry officials were in the position to formulate the reform law and to implement it as well. They constructed a reform whereby they could allow more competition without sacrificing social obligations, and without surrendering their own influence over the sector.

The reform law, passed in 1990, left considerable leeway for interpretation. The battle between the reformers and the conservatives would only be resolved at the implementation stage. The freshly detached ministry and the operator, Deutsche Bundespost Telekom, began their new roles while in the awkward position of still sharing the same building. In fact, DBP Telekom executives occasionally found—to their delight—that their

---

[85] Schmidt (June 1991), pp. 215–16.
[86] Schneider and Werle (November 1989), pp. 53–54.

new competitors sent license applications to the DBP Telekom fax machines by mistake.[87] Prior to reform, most officials within the DBP felt that the operator would have more power and prestige than the ministry, not to mention better salaries. Few volunteered to stay with the ministry, and the ministry ended up recruiting 50 percent of its post-reform personnel from outside.

Telekom executives who had hoped for sympathetic treatment from their former colleagues at the ministry have been bitterly disappointed. In fact, the ministry surprised many with an aggressively pro-competition stance. In the area of mobile communications, the ministry quickly issued a license to a competing consortium led by Mannesmann and ordered DBP Telekom to provide access at reduced rates.[88] Even more surprising, it allowed an exception to the transmission path monopoly for satellite links between the newly reunited eastern and western parts of Germany. Ministry officials judged that Telekom would not be able to provide new infrastructure quickly enough, so they granted licenses to private satellite operators. This required Cabinet approval, so that by the time the change had been made Telekom had made substantial progress in developing land-based links. Thus the "window of opportunity" for competitors was partially closed. Nonetheless, the ministry licensed ten operators for this service and boldly demonstrated its willingness to move ahead with competition.[89] The ministry thus produced competition with a minimum of controversy by granting substantial concessions during the public debate, and then undermining these concessions at the implementation stage.[90]

Reunification has created its own new problems. Telekom had to sacrifice some of its modernization plans in order to finance basic infrastructure for the former East Germany. Meanwhile, the Ministry of Finance demanded that Telekom continue to route funds to the government to help offset the extraordinary financial demands of reunification. Ministry officials worried that this added burden would make Telekom less competitive internationally.

In November 1993, the German government decided to partially privatize DBP Telekom, beginning with the sale of a 25 percent stake in 1996. This gives Telekom access to private capital markets and positions the firm to compete more effectively in the global marketplace. In particular, it helps Telekom play the game of global alliances and mergers that has begun to characterize the sector. The government has retained substantial

---

[87] Interview with Federal Ministry of Posts and Telecommunications official (October 1991).

[88] *Economist* (June 1, 1991), pp. 67–68.

[89] Interview with Federal Ministry of Posts and Telecommunications official (October 1991). See Federal Ministry of Posts and Telecommunications (March 1991).

[90] Schmidt (June 1991), p. 220.

control, with government officials filling five of the ten nonemployee positions on the Telekom board.[91] Private sector players were particularly critical of the decision to appoint a former ministry official, Gerhard Pfeffermann, to the board. This decision, along with several minor scandals, prompted the resignation of Telekom Chief Executive Helmut Ricke, and his replacement by Ron Sommer, a youthful outsider who spent most of his career with Sony. Meanwhile, with EU-mandated liberalization scheduled for 1998, the ministry remains torn between an interest in greater competition and a commitment to preserve Telekom's monopoly in the transmission path until 1998. Several utility firms have begun putting together their own networks and have applied for licenses to compete with Telekom. Wolfgang Bötsch, the postal and telecommunications minister, publicly ruled out full liberalization of basic network services before 1998 but suggested that he would consider smaller projects in competition with Telekom prior to that time.[92]

Finance

The distinctive features of the financial system have made financial reform less pressing an issue in Germany than in other countries. Germany has not had to deal with the problem of the eroding boundaries between the banking and brokerage businesses because the country's "universal banks" have always been allowed to do both. In addition, Germany deregulated deposit interest rates early on, in 1967 (although banks still offer closely similar rates); however, in those areas where Germany has encountered pressures for change since the 1980s, such as stock exchange reform and money market liberalization, it has lagged behind all four of the other countries in this study.

The proponents of financial reform have encountered barriers inherent in both the political system and the structure of financial regulation. The federal system has enabled state governments to delay or even block change in some cases. The decentralization of regulatory authority has also made it difficult to push through comprehensive reform. The Federal Finance Ministry has overall responsibility for financial regulation, but delegates regulatory powers over banking and insurance to subsidiary agencies. Germany's notoriously independent central bank, the Bundesbank, provides a rival power center for the ministry and is particularly vocal on matters relating to its primary function of conducting monetary policy. The state governments have authority over the regional stock exchanges, although these are largely self-regulating in practice. While this

---

[91] *Economist* (December 17, 1994), p. 68.
[92] *Economist* (February 11, 1995), p. 58, and *Los Angeles Times* (March 31, 1995).

decentralized structure has prevented sweeping reform, it has actually made it easier to push through minor changes in those areas where a single institution has autonomy.[93]

German government officials have traditionally taken a more liberal approach to financial regulation than to telecommunications regulation. They espouse a philosophy of considerable reliance on self-regulation, recognizing the banks' status within the economy. Federal Finance Ministry officials view their role as one of supervising and monitoring a financial system that normally operates and regulates itself.[94] German banks, unlike their British counterparts, are heavily oriented toward the long-term financing of industry. As in Japan and France, this means that the banks' interests are much more closely tied to the welfare of industry. But the strength of bank lending has come at the expense of growth in capital markets.

Because of Germany's unique political and financial system, there was never a purely domestic impetus to reform in the way there was in the United States, the United Kingdom, and Japan. Pressure to reform generally came from abroad, in the form of competition from other financial centers and from EC initiatives.[95] The development of futures markets in London and Paris made German officials and financiers alike worry that German stock markets might lose out to these European rivals. The stock exchanges were particularly vulnerable to international competition, since trading was dispersed among eight regional exchanges. Frankfurt is the largest exchange, with more than half of total turnover, but it does not dominate in the way that London dominates in Britain or Paris prevails in France. The division of Germany after World War II made it impossible for Berlin, the major market up to that point, to attain a dominant position. By the late 1980s, the major banks and federal financial officials agreed that the stock exchange required substantial reform, including a further centralization of activity in Frankfurt.

The state governments, afraid that any reform would benefit the Frankfurt exchange at the expense of the smaller exchanges, balked. The regional exchanges and small brokerage firms protested as well. On the other side, the major banks, the Finance Ministry, the Bundesbank, the Frankfurt exchange and the state government of Hesse (where Frankfurt is located) all advocated reform.[96] The banks argued that business had to be concentrated in Frankfurt in order to meet the competition from Paris and London, and they even recommended shutting down several of the

---

[93] Moran (October 1989).

[94] Interview with Federal Finance Ministry official (October 1991).

[95] This contrasts with France, where financial reforms began before the EC declared its plans for a single financial market in 1985.

[96] Webber (April 1990).

smaller exchanges in order to strengthen Frankfurt. In addition, they proposed creating a futures market and modernizing the trading system.

The stock exchanges had the authority to make some organizational changes on their own, but the creation of a futures market and the transformation of the regulatory system would require legislation. Thus the political battles took place in two distinct arenas: within the exchanges themselves, and in political circles in Bonn and Frankfurt. Within the exchanges, the situation was complicated by the presence of the banks. Thus the major proponents of change were represented in the deliberations within regional exchanges that would otherwise oppose reform without hesitation. The opponents thus lacked a forum where they could dominate. In 1987 the banks tried to consolidate their power over the exchanges by creating the Federation of German Stock Exchanges.[97] Voting rights within the federation were determined by turnover, meaning that Frankfurt controlled more than 50 percent of the votes. In response, the Stuttgart and Munich exchanges began to put together a federation of the non-Frankfurt exchanges because the existing federation so blatantly favored the interests of the big banks.

In 1989, the government proposed a bill to reform the stock exchanges and to create a futures market. The Bundesrat, which represents state interests, proposed a daunting array of amendments to the bill. Although this could have easily led to deadlock, the major banks intensively lobbied to break the impasse, appealing to the chancellor himself. The bill eventually passed without the amendments, owing to the persistence of the large banks backed by the threat of foreign competition.[98]

With the passage of the 1989 stock exchange reform bill the government then prepared legislation for the reorganization of the stock exchange and the creation of a new centralized regulatory agency under the Federal Finance Ministry with enhanced enforcement powers. It encountered a more difficult struggle with this bill, since state governments fiercely opposed the extension of new regulatory responsibilities to the federal government.[99] The state governments had fought a similar battle when the government set up federal regulators for the banking and insurance industries. The states proposed that the government set up a federation of state regulators, but the federal government successfully argued that this would be unconstitutional because it would create a new level of administration between the state and the federal level. The government coupled this legislation with reforms of insider trading regulation following EC directives, finally passing the omnibus reform bill in November 1993.

[97] Ibid.
[98] Ibid.
[99] Interview with Federal Finance Ministry official (October 1991).

The German government has been even more cautious about money market reforms, largely because of the Bundesbank's concern that reforms might impede monetary policy. "We have always attached a very high importance to our product, the deutschmark," explains one Bundesbank official, "even at the expense of Germany as a financial center."[100] The bank reluctantly permitted CDs in 1986, but effectively stifled the market by subjecting CDs to minimum reserve requirements.[101] Likewise the bank resisted money market funds, which could threaten its open market intervention and money supply targets. The 1993 reform bill provided the legal foundation for the introduction of money market funds, and the bank finally dropped its opposition in May 1994. Even so, the bank has slowed their development by discouraging the issuance of short-term government securities, a primary investment for such funds.[102]

Although the Federal Finance Ministry served more as a coordinator of the reform process than as primary author, it has managed to enhance its own authority at the expense of the states. At the same time, it has accepted that it will lose some of its sovereignty to Brussels over the long term. As in telecommunications, the government's response to political constraints has not been to abandon reform, but to repackage it in smaller, more individually acceptable pieces in areas where the need for reform has been most obvious.

Regulatory Reform German Style

Despite the conservative government's promise to bring a new direction to economic policy, it has lagged behind all of the other countries included in this study in the realm of regulatory reform. In December 1987, the government did appoint a commission on deregulation, but the commission itself adopted a selective and cautious approach and its efforts have not translated into major reforms.[103] The move toward German unification beginning in 1989 initially revived the government's enthusiasm for neoliberal reforms, but by 1991—when the imposing costs of unification became all too clear—it all but abandoned the cause.[104] German officials have been less convinced than their counterparts elsewhere that regulation needed to be reformed, and they have been constrained by the structure of German politics. The weakness of coalition government makes it hard for the ruling coalition to impose change on the opposition, and the federal structure of government makes it more difficult for cen-

---

[100] Interview (April 1993).
[101] Schaede (1989), p. 36.
[102] *Economist* (May 14, 1994), p. 81.
[103] Donges (1991); Dyson, ed. (1992), pp. 263–66.
[104] Lehmbruch (1992), pp. 29–30.

tral government agencies to impose change on the states. Despite these institutional barriers, however, the government has adeptly enacted a series of pragmatic piecemeal revisions in existing practices.

Where the government has taken action, its approach resembles that of the Japanese government. As in Japan, German ministries have considerable autonomy within their specific domains.[105] This produces a pattern of relatively independent policy networks in the various industrial sectors, typically centered around the responsible government agency. This structure slows regulatory change, because ministerial and private sector actors with a stake in the status quo have greater control over the process. It also produces the strong bias toward orderly and consensual change that we saw in the Japanese cases. And as in both Japan and France, government officials rather than outside academics or think tanks initiated the shift in regulatory paradigms, giving them a greater ability to define the terms of debate.[106]

Although the unique features of the German approach to regulatory reform should not be ignored, it still falls within the basic parameters of the "reinforcement" pattern. Rather than simply opening new markets and seeing what happens, the German government reviewed the potential impact of proposed measures on incumbent firms first. In telecommunications, the government deliberately protected equipment manufacturers from a hasty and disruptive deregulation, and in finance, it buffered regional stock exchanges and their industrial clients from the full force of competition. Likewise, the government structured reforms to minimize the loss of its own ability to formulate coherent policies for individual sectors. As noted above, it achieved the "fusion" of governmental functions not by centralizing activities in a few powerful central ministries as in Japan or France, but through a more complex system of coordinating multiple authorities. The German state has retained this capacity for strategic coordination. Overall, the government has moved very deliberately, trying not to cause undue disruption through change. By incorporating interest groups into the decision-making process, it has also prepared them for changes. The large banks have played an important role in implementation, which they have only been able to do because they were incorporated into the policy process.

Nonetheless, several distinct features of the German experience stand out. As noted above, the German government has a much more fragmented political structure than the Japanese or French government. This has forced it to rely more on informal networks to coordinate policy change, and this in turn implies greater reliance on private sector actors.

---

[105] Ibid.
[106] Ibid., pp. 35–36.

Whereas governments in Japan, France, and Germany all rely heavily on private sector cooperation, the delegation of public responsibilities to private actors is more complete in Germany. The German government does not enjoy as powerful an arsenal of rewards and punishments, and it does not have the same institutional capacity to structure and enforce political bargains. In particular, the government relies on private banks to assume public functions. In the case of financial reform, this has meant that the banks themselves played a more powerful and autonomous role in producing regulatory solutions than Japanese or French banks. This then suggests that a full understanding of German reforms must include an analysis of private organization (the role of the banks), an element outside the central framework developed in Chapter 1. This is an important lesson for our model, and we shall return to it in the concluding chapter.

CHAPTER ELEVEN

The Irony of State-Led Deregulation

In this final chapter we consolidate the evidence from the cases, identify national and sectoral patterns, and reconsider our three original propositions regarding the nature of regulatory reform.

NATIONAL AND SECTORAL PATTERNS

With the benefit of the mini-cases in the previous chapter, we can now refine the explanatory framework and specify more clearly what it can and cannot explain. We can accomplish this by distinguishing three different levels of analysis: overall patterns, specific national cases, and specific sector cases. Each new level adds more focus to the analysis, but does so at the expense of simplicity. At the level of overall patterns, evidence from the United States, France, and Germany confirms that preexisting ideas and institutions powerfully shape the basic direction of regulatory change. That is, those countries with more of an "arms-length" approach toward industry and looser sectoral networks turned regulatory reform into an exercise in disengagement. And those countries with a tradition of government intervention in industrial affairs and tighter sectoral networks structured regulatory reform to maintain critical government capacities and protect valued institutional arrangements. As shown in Table 16, the pattern of regulatory reform in the United States was largely consistent with disengagement, and in France and Germany with reinforcement. At this level, however, the model cannot account for much of the detail of regulatory reform outcomes. That is, it explains deep-seated biases in how countries responded to new challenges, but does not account for variation within the two broad pat-

Table 16. Patterns of regulatory reform in five advanced industrial countries

	United States	United Kingdom	Japan	France	Germany
Eagerness to liberalize markets fully	High	High	Low	Low	Low
Willingness to reduce control over industry	High	High	Low	Relatively low	Relatively low
Reform process	Uneven	Uneven	Coordinated	Coordinated	Coordinated
Pattern	Disengagement	Disengagement	Reinforcement	Reinforcement	Reinforcement

terns of response (disengagement and reinforcement). In the cases of the United Kingdom and the United States, this is not so problematic. The U.S. process differed from the British because private actors challenged the status quo more aggressively. And British reform was far more radical in its impact because the U.S. regulatory regime was already rather legalistic and fragmented prior to reform. Beyond this, however, British and U.S. outcomes are broadly similar, not only because British reform was modeled after economic and legal notions already popular in the United States, but also because disengagement is primarily a negative action whereas reinforcement is a creative process. Thus in the case of Japan, France, and Germany, the variation within the broad pattern is more troublesome.

We can account for the variation between Japan, France, and Germany much better if we move to the next level of analysis. Here we find that the particular mode of reinforcement is linked to the specific mechanisms of intervention under the old regime. Thus in Japan, where government officials have traditionally relied on administrative guidance as a critical tool of policy, and administrative guidance has in turn relied on discretionary authority over industry, officials have been particularly keen to create new sources of this authority. This explains the most distinctive feature of Japanese reform: the ministries' effort to turn liberalization into a protracted process in which their ability to determine the timing and conditions of new market entry generates a powerful new source of leverage over industry. Likewise in France, where officials have used nationalized industries as a critical tool of policy, we find that these officials have structured privatization in a way that leaves them with some influence over the privatized industries. And in Germany, where the government has never enjoyed as much direct authority over industry as in Japan or France, government officials have been less determined to protect specific mechanisms of control than to maintain informal channels of influence, with considerable variation across sectors. In telecommunications the government retained influence by appointing its own agents to the DBP Telekom board, whereas in finance the government has been more willing to cede responsibilities to the banks.

Thus at a third level of analysis, national patterns give way to significant sectoral variations. Some may prefer to abandon the national level of analysis altogether, but the evidence demonstrates that national patterns are alive and well. The British and Japanese patterns hold up remarkably well across a wide range of sectors. We found no sector cases in the United Kingdom fitting the reinforcement pattern, and no sector cases in Japan fitting the disengagement pattern. Nonetheless, the analysis remains incomplete without looking at sectoral variations. Sectors may vary from national patterns in one of three basic ways. First, sectors have *generic market features*: intrinsic market characteristics that distinguish them from one another across all countries. For example, the financial services sector is characterized by rapid innovation and intense international competition, and these basic characteristics hold true across all the countries we have examined. Second, sectors have *country-specific market features*: characteristics specific to that sector within a particular country. For example, the Japanese financial sector is highly segmented, whereas the German financial sector is not. Third, sectors have *country-specific political, or "regime," features*. For example, the federal ministry is the dominant player in the German telecommunications regime, whereas the large banks are the dominant players within the finance regime. As noted in the preceding chapter, the German story cannot be told without looking at the banks. And yet they can only be incorporated into the model meaningfully at the sectoral level, for they play a much greater role in some sectors, such as finance, than in others.

These features help to explain some of the variation in regulatory reforms across sectors. For example, the dynamism of the telecommunications, finance, and broadcasting sectors helps to explain why reforms in these sectors have been more extensive within each country and more pervasive across countries than reforms in less dynamic sectors, such as trucking or water supply. Likewise, sectoral features help to explain more specific variations across sectors within particular countries. In Germany, for example, the government was historically more protective of the telecommunications sector than the finance industry, and the structure of government control was more centralized. As a result, the government was more reluctant to relinquish control over telecommunications than over finance. Thus in the finance case, the government has allowed regulatory authority to devolve to a wide range of authorities and permitted the banks to play a leading role in stock exchange reform.

Combining sector studies with an analysis of national patterns adds to the picture by showing how sectoral regimes relate to the national norm.

We understand the British and Japanese telecommunications stories better by recognizing that the reforms reflected adjustments in sectoral regimes that in some ways did not fit the national norm. Telecommunications was unusual among British sectors in that government control was relatively high and power was relatively centralized. Thus we should not be surprised that reform brought the sector more in line with the national norm. Likewise, telecommunications was unusual among Japanese sectors in that the lead ministry did not really control the sector. Thus reform represented a reassertion of the ministry's "rightful" authority.

Figure 3 helps sort out how national and sectoral variables interact. Naturally, any judgment about the degree and the orientation of regulatory change within such broad sectors is bound to be subjective and imprecise. Nonetheless, I have crudely categorized the sixteen cases from this study along with nine not specifically addressed in this study to clarify how the degree and direction of regulatory change varies across countries and sectors. The five countries divide neatly into two camps, with the United States and the United Kingdom in the "disengagement" camp, and Japan, France, and Germany in the "reinforcement" camp. As noted above, however, the degree of regulatory change has been greatest in those sectors with the greatest degree of market change—and this has been true across

Figure 3. Patterns of reform by country and sector

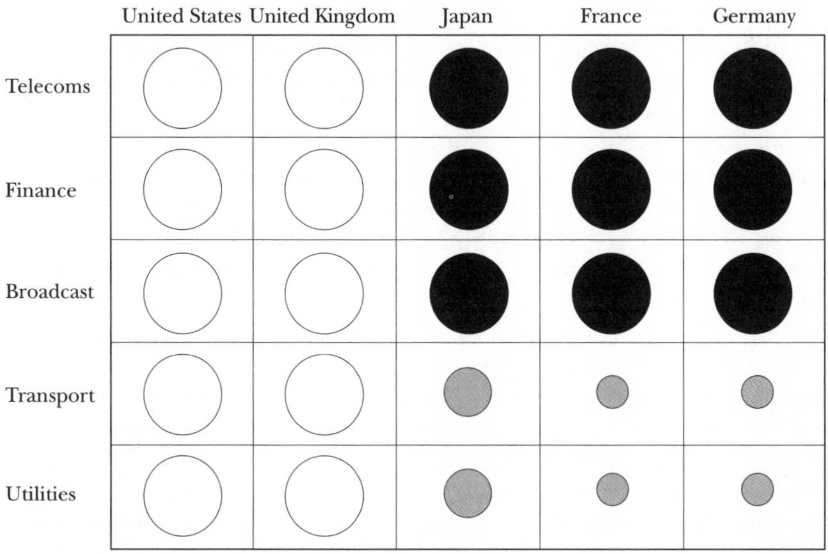

NOTE: Shade of circle represents the orientation of reform (white = procompetitive disengagement, black = strategic reinforcement, screened = mixed) and size of circle represents the extent of regulatory change.

all five countries. And those governments inclined toward the reinforcement pattern have been less inclined toward strategic or expansionary reregulation in those sectors less subject to international competition, such as transportation and utilities, so I have classified these cases as mixed.

NATIONAL PATTERNS OR INTERNATIONAL CONVERGENCE?

Let us now return to the three propositions regarding regulatory reform originally advanced in the Introduction. The first proposition suggested that the regulatory reforms common to many advanced industrial countries since the early 1980s were not primarily "deregulatory" in their substance. Rather, these reforms combined liberalization with reregulation, with the emphasis often on reregulation. The case studies overwhelmingly support this proposition, demonstrating both the prevalence and the wide variety of reregulation policies. The British government established a new regulatory agency, the Office of Telecommunications (Oftel), just to handle all the new regulation that liberalization would require. And Oftel used its own brand of pro-competitive reregulation to "create" competition (see Table 1 for the typology of reregulation). In the financial services sector, the Financial Services Act embodied the very notion of juridical reregulation—the juridification and codification of regulation— eventually producing five new regulatory bodies, three distinct grades of regulations, and vastly more complicated compliance requirements. Japan's Ministry of Posts and Telecommunications (MPT) took the notion of expansionary reregulation to its most absurd extreme. Rather than relinquishing existing regulatory powers, it cultivated a whole range of regulatory powers that it had not previously enjoyed. And the Ministry of Finance (MoF) practiced its own peculiar form of strategic reregulation, trying to manipulate the sequence, timing, and extent of liberalization measures in order to protect financial institutions from the full force of more open competition.

Whereas the evidence with respect to the first proposition speaks for itself, the second and third propositions are more complex and thus require more extended treatment here. At one level, the case studies unquestionably support the second proposition, that governments have responded to similar pressures in strikingly different ways. After all, the distinct national patterns summarized above demonstrate just that: differential responses to common challenges.[1] Still, these clear national varia-

---

[1] Among others, Wilensky (1991), Berger (December 1992), and Zysman (1994) have articulated this basic point: national patterns remain remarkably resilient despite the globalization of markets.

tions have combined with elements of convergence. The governments in this study have converged the most in that they have all liberalized: they have opened markets to more competition. And they have varied to the extent that they have reregulated in different ways. They have converged to the extent that they have been compelled in a specific direction by common market forces, and they have varied to the extent that different ideas and institutions have pushed them to respond in different ways. The question then becomes: is the variation profound or trivial? For those most enamored with the ineluctable power of markets, the national variations may be minor in comparison to a larger global trend toward convergence.

My answer is that the variation is substantial, and that it challenges the very notion of any convergence in regulatory practice. We can clarify this point by distinguishing between *market outcomes*, or changes in the nature of competition, and *regulatory outcomes*, or changes in the form of regulation. We observed a convergence in market outcomes in Tables 2 and 3: all governments have lifted exchange rate controls, and all governments have allowed microwave operators to compete with the dominant telecommunications carrier. And we have seen a distinct variance in regulatory outcomes in Tables 15 and 16: some governments have formalized regulation more than others, and some governments have relaxed their supervision over industry whereas others have intensified this supervision. I would argue, however, that regulatory outcomes ultimately structure market outcomes. That is, by favoring particular modes of reregulation, governments set the terms of market competition. The mode of reregulation affects which companies enter the market, what services they offer, what investments they make, and what strategies they pursue. Although regulatory reforms have unleashed both British Telecom and NTT on international markets, the behavior of these firms in overseas markets still reflects the distinct context of regulation within their respective home markets. And although regulatory reforms have allowed AT&T to invade both the British and Japanese markets, AT&T's strategy and its prospects remain powerfully shaped by the context of regulation within these two distinct host markets. Thus corporate strategy responds not simply to signals from an abstract market, but from a particular market structured by home-country regulations, host-country regulations, and the interaction of the two. In other words, the subtle interaction between government and industry continues to influence the nature of competition within a given market even after it has been formally liberalized. For precisely this reason, I have focused on regulation as it is practiced and not as it is preached. And we have found that regulatory practice remains remarkably different across countries, regardless of the power of international market pressures.

Thus the evidence does in fact contradict the popular wisdom that the overwhelming power of international markets has forced national regulators in a common direction. The market shifts described in Chapter 2 have provided a major stimulus for regulatory change, but governments have had considerable leeway in how they respond. The market-centered perspective misleads us by portraying markets as determinants of outcomes rather than as stimuli to which national governments respond in distinct ways. We can see this point more clearly by reformulating the market-centered perspective outlined in Chapter 1 as three specific propositions.

1. *The telecommunications revolution compels a liberal response.* Rapid advances in telecommunications technology require that governments deregulate because government control only stifles the exploitation of this new technology.
2. *The financial revolution compels a liberal response.* The globalization of financial markets requires governments to deregulate to prevent the flight of capital and financial activity abroad.
3. *The competitive dynamic between regulators compels a liberal response.* In global markets with competing national regulators, authorities must reduce the regulatory burden as much as possible in order to attract business activity to their own country and to prevent its flight to other countries.[2]

I contend that these are not universal laws of the marketplace but subjective interpretations of it. They are not descriptions of how governments have actually responded so much as prescriptions of how some people think they should have responded. U.S. and British authorities have embraced the logic of these propositions, but French, German, and Japanese authorities have not—and these ideological differences have powerfully influenced their respective reform policies.[3] Thus Bank of England officials designed the Big Bang precisely with this logic in mind: the United Kingdom had to deregulate commission rates to prevent financial activity from shifting away from London. MoF officials have been far less convinced that regulatory advantages determine business location. They have focused much more on protecting domestic securities firms, so they have naturally been much slower to deregulate commissions. In essence, market pressures are most constraining when leaders believe them to be all-powerful, and least constraining when leaders do not. This supports my assertion from Chapter 2 that one cannot understand national differences in regulatory reforms without looking at ideas—for ideas provide the filter through which decision makers interpret market forces.[4]

---

[2] Wriston's (1992) work articulates the first proposition, McKenzie and Lee's (1991) the second and third.

[3] See Maital (Summer 1992), for example, on the case of telecommunications.

[4] More broadly, one could suggest that economic "laws" rely on subjective interpretations, and their predictive power depends heavily on the pervasiveness of particular cultural norms. Thus to the extent that different countries have different market cultures, economic "laws" that apply in one cultural context may not apply in another. See Eckstein (1994).

EVALUATING PATTERNS OF REFORM

Before we tackle the third proposition, let us briefly consider the ramifications of the national patterns described above. If there are distinct national patterns, then how do these matter? This study's primary purpose has been to explain policies and not to evaluate them, and thus to this point I have tried not to judge the various outcomes. Yet, it is important to note that regulatory outcomes are not neutral: they have implications for everything from economic performance to political legitimacy. If we accept for a moment that there are two broad patterns of regulatory reform—"disengagement" and "reinforcement"—then which is better? Ultimately this judgment depends on how one ranks certain values such as efficiency, stability, fairness, and flexibility. In one sense, each pattern is naturally likely to surpass the other in terms of those values that its proponents cherish most. The disengagement pattern should produce greater efficiency, because U.S. and British officials disengaged precisely to improve efficiency. And the reinforcement pattern should allow more government control, for Japanese, French, and German officials reinforced some of their powers precisely in order to retain this control. Each pattern thus represents a bias in how government officials evaluate the costs and benefits of specific reform measures. Thus the British government has pursued bold liberalization in sectors where more caution may be warranted, such as financial services, and Japan has clung to control in sectors where it may not be necessary, such as buses. So if we assume that the proper regulatory balance lies somewhere between disengagement and reinforcement, then the United Kingdom has gone too far in some areas, whereas Japan has not gone far enough in others.

If we define efficiency as most economists do, however, then disengagement clearly wins out.[5] In this view, Japanese officials' continuing unwillingness to surrender control could undermine the country's industrial strength in the long run. But the reinforcers have also reserved a greater ability to formulate and implement industrial policy as a means to promote economic growth, and to use regulation as a source of competitive advantage. Whether this is good or bad ultimately depends on whether one believes that industrial policy tends to promote economic growth or to hinder it.[6] On the one hand, one could say that the reinforcers have an advantage over the disengagers because they maintain the capacity for effective intervention—intervention which at least has the potential to be beneficial. On the other hand, however, governments that possess this ca-

---

[5] In fact, many economists think that even Britain should disengage further. See, for example, Kay, Mayer, and Thompson, eds. (1986).

[6] For contrasting views, see Johnson, Tyson, and Zysman, eds. (1989), and Trezise (1983), Komiya (Summer 1986), or Beason and Weinstein (1993).

pacity may be prone to intervene even when such intervention is not warranted.

The difference between the two patterns also implies a difference between fast and slow, and early and late liberalization. In the United Kingdom, government officials stressed that more competition would strengthen domestic industry in the long run, and therefore they tried to accelerate the liberalization process. In Japan, in contrast, government officials stressed that more competition could make domestic industry vulnerable to foreign competition in the short run, and so they tried to slow down the process. British authorities hoped to use liberalization to strengthen industry, whereas Japanese authorities sought to strengthen industry *before* liberalization. If we can take trends in market share as any indication, then the early "deregulators" have lost decisively in the strategic game of regulatory reform. By liberalizing first, they opened domestic industry to foreign competition before ensuring access to not-yet-liberalized foreign markets. This is most evident in the telecommunications equipment industry where U.S. and British producers faced an onslaught of imports while they still lacked reciprocal access abroad. Table 17 shows how the U.S. and British trade balances deteriorated sharply in those years when the U.S. and British governments had liberalized these markets and their trade partners had not. Still, although slowness may be strategic in some cases, in others it may just be slow. Both the Japanese and the Germans have shown signs of political immobility that could be a real liability in the long run.

The choice between disengagement and reinforcement also implies a tradeoff in the style of regulation after reform, with each approach enjoying several distinct advantages. The disengagement pattern favors a fairer and more judicial system of regulation because the separation of regula-

Table 17. Trade balances in telecommunications equipment in five countries, 1978–1985 (millions of dollars)

Year	United States	United Kingdom	Japan	France	Germany
1978	155	97	336	121	392
1979	129	105	364	117	406
1980	136	52	374	162	492
1981	159	66	545	212	595
1982	203	35	764	286	647
1983	−419	−79	906	434	579
1984	−1040	−92	1076	495	—
1985	−1196	−132	1321	492	—

SOURCE: OECD (1988).

NOTE: British, French, and German figures converted at average exchange rates for the year. 1985 figures for France estimated; 1984–85 figures for Germany not available.

tory and promotional functions makes the regulator more impartial. Otherwise, a ministry that is simultaneously regulator and sponsor might be biased in favor of the industry it sponsors. This approach also makes it easier for government officials to tailor regulation to those areas where regulation is truly necessary, without imposing excessive constraints. Japanese regulators still emphasize broad structural regulations such as licensing systems, whereas British authorities have developed more ways to target specific behavior. In terms of regulatory "technology," the United States leads the world, with fine-tuned mechanisms to mimic market forces in markets where competition is insufficient or nonexistent. At the same time, however, governments that adopt the reinforcement approach maintain the ability to formulate policies in a more coherent manner and to implement them more smoothly. Sometimes governments have to resolve difficult questions that involve conflicting values, and a "fused" regime (see Table 5) allows them to weigh the aggregate costs and benefits more effectively. In addition, by maintaining coordinated networks joining the public and private sectors, authorities keep private sector actors better informed of policy developments, and this helps them to plan for the future.

Overall, regulatory reform has had a positive net effect in both the disengagement and reinforcement variants. The clearest benefits have come from market liberalization: household consumers and businesses now enjoy a much greater variety of telecommunications equipment and services at lower prices than they would have without liberalization. Likewise, investors can tap a wider menu of financial instruments to maximize returns, and borrowers have more avenues to raise funds in a manner tailored to their needs. Even reregulation has probably done more good than harm. The disengagers have found fairer and more effective ways to maintain telecommunications quality standards and to protect investors from fraud, and the reinforcers have generally replaced unreasonable regulations with more beneficial ones.

The State and Regulatory Reform

Finally, the case studies support the third proposition, that state actors have powerfully shaped reform. At a superficial level, the cases overwhelmingly support this proposition. We have seen how state actors actively pursued reforms in order to generate revenue, to facilitate the servicing of the debt, or to make regulation itself more effective. Bank of England officials designed the Big Bang well before the famed Goodison-Parkinson agreement, and Japanese ministry officials outlined telecommunications reform a full decade before the broader debate over reform began. But at a deeper level, even if state actors were central to the process, how can we tell whether they acted autonomously or simply on behalf of private interest groups?

Two distinct bodies of literature suggest that state actors may serve private interests even in the absence of direct interest group pressures. First, some scholars suggest that the interests of state actors and big business are so tightly bound that the state bureaucracy almost naturally acts as a servant of private interests.[7] In recent case studies of government-industry relations, this argument has most frequently been applied to France and Japan. Although these countries do not fit the model of pluralist pressure politics, some scholars contend that state actors and big business enjoy a broad consensus on goals such that the state spontaneously acts in the interest of the country's largest corporations.[8] Second, the literature on agency and delegation, particularly with reference to the United States, suggests that state bureaucrats are constrained by political oversight even when politicians delegate decisions to these bureaucrats. And the politicians, in turn, serve as agents of interest groups. Thus bureaucrats are constrained even when politicians and interest groups do not directly pressure them because they understand that politicians could intervene if they did not produce an acceptable decision.[9]

I contend, however, that state actors can and do act autonomously of interest group pressures—and that this matters for policy outcomes. Concerning regulatory reform, moreover, I suggest that one cannot explain policy outcomes *without* looking at the autonomous preferences of state actors. We can demonstrate this by reviewing the four central cases, focusing on the *process* and the *outcome* of reform. To trace the process, one must ask: Who initiated and controlled the process? And to analyze the outcome, one must ask: Who most powerfully influenced the outcome?

In the case of British telecommunications, private sector actors—producers or users—did not push for either of the two most critical elements in reform: privatization or network competition. In fact, no one outside of the government had seriously considered either option before the Thatcher government came to office. Privatization and liberalization served the interests of corporate users, but also threatened the interests of powerful corporations such as BT's favored equipment suppliers. The Thatcher government chose which of these interests to favor. The outcome of the reform process reflects the ideological leanings of the

---

[7] Broad theoretical statements of this basic argument range from Karl Marx to Lindblom (1977).

[8] See, for example, Ridley and Blondel (1969) or Bauer and Cohen (1985) on France.

[9] See Noll (1989), pp. 1277–81, for the theoretical argument; Weingast (Winter 1981) and Weingast and Moran (1983) on the United States; and Rosenbluth (1989) and McCubbins and Noble (1995) on Japan.

Thatcher government combined with the government's more narrow interest in raising funds without increasing taxes. It also incorporates the particular agendas of the Treasury, the Department of Trade and Industry (DTI), and Oftel—none of which can be equated with specific private sector interests. These agencies were biased primarily by their own functional responsibilities: the Treasury sought to generate revenue, Oftel heralded the cause of pro-competitive regulation, and the DTI tried to use competition to promote the information technology sector.

It is also somewhat easier to argue that in financial services in the United Kingdom the Big Bang reflected the interests of major City practitioners. After all, institutional investors wanted negotiable commissions and major banks wanted to be able to participate in the Stock Exchange, and the Big Bang delivered both of these changes. And unlike the beneficiaries from telecommunications reform, some financial institutions openly advocated reforms before they happened. Still, this does not account for how other powerful City interests—the jobbers and the brokers, for example—adamantly opposed reform. Only government actors had the ability to break the deadlock between the various City actors, and this gave them the leeway to set the terms of a resolution. The Bank of England took the lead, building the Big Bang upon its own "Blue Skies" plan for reform. The Financial Services Act , meanwhile, cannot be described as serving the interest of any private interest group—with the possible exception of the lawyers' association. City institutions certainly did not demand it. Rather, DTI officials initiated the reform process because they recognized that the existing legislation had ceased to function. The supposedly omnipotent City was caught off guard, and only seriously responded to the DTI's initiative after the bill had already passed.

The state's influence on the reform process is even more pronounced in Japan. In the telecommunications case, no major private group recommended privatization or network competition until the administrative reform council, the Rinchō, proposed these measures. The Rinchō's recommendations may have served the interests of Keidanren, the big business federation, but the eventual outcome of the process begun by the Rinchō more closely reflects the priorities of MoF and MPT bureaucrats. Once the Rinchō report was out, the MPT took control of the reform process and reoriented the reforms in a manner that blatantly defied the council's deregulatory intent. The MPT made token concessions to various interest groups, such as the telecommunications manufacturers, but sculpted the legislation to increase its authority, to constrain NTT, and to create an elaborate new MPT-run regulatory regime. And as in the British case, the MoF's concern with revenue generation also colored the privatization debate, effectively precluding the breakup of the privatized carrier.

Finally, in Japanese finance, the MoF orchestrated the process according to its own sense of priorities. As with the Big Bang, this case is more vulnerable to a "capture" argument because many of the reforms did serve the interests of powerful industry groups. Although these institutions did not lobby very strenuously for reform prior to the yen-dollar talks, some groups did express support for limited reforms. In fact, Frances Rosenbluth (1989) argues that this case is largely consistent with the theory of regulation. Still, Japan's financial institutions were divided over many reform questions, and Rosenbluth's approach cannot explain why one group won one battle only to lose another, or why many reform measures reflected the MoF's independent agenda. Although ministry officials made some compromises, they also dealt major setbacks to some of Japan's most powerful financial institutions, including the Industrial Bank of Japan (IBJ) and Nomura Securities. Furthermore, they structured the reforms to maximize their own power, something the finance industry would hardly have endorsed.[10]

Thus we have established that state actors held autonomous preferences, acted upon these preferences, and influenced outcomes in ways that we cannot understand by focusing on private interests alone. As noted in Chapter 1, however, private sector interests clearly shaped these outcomes as well. So given that both state and societal actors matter, then how can we best characterize the relationship between them? At an abstract level, we can suggest that state actors are *relatively* autonomous from society.[11] But then what does this really mean? In concrete terms, it means that ambivalence within society and divisions between societal groups leave state actors as the interpreters and arbiters of these interests. And state actors do not interpret or arbitrate in a neutral fashion. They bring to this role specific ideological biases and institutional capabilities. Thus they pursue their own agenda while trying to satisfy important societal groups at the same time. Alternatively, we can understand the relative autonomy of the state in terms of state actors pursuing a particular conception of the public interest—but one that only partially transcends those of societal groups. In the case of the regulation and promotion of industry, state actors strive for better economic performance. Their conception of performance transcends the interests of specific firms or sectors, yet it is not unrelated to these interests either. That is, their view of the public interest necessarily incorporates a notion of what is good for the leading sectors of the economy, and perhaps even what is good for Toyota or Rolls-Royce. I simply suggest that the ideological and institutional context

---

[10] See Vogel (July 1994), especially pp. 237–40.
[11] A wide range of authors have characterized this relationship in terms of relative autonomy, from neo-Marxists (Poulantzas, 1978) to new institutionalists (Skocpol, 1985).

in which state actors operate powerfully shapes how they interpret this public interest, and how they pursue it.

In the end, the paradoxes all but disappear. Once we recognize that regulatory reform has been more about reregulation than deregulation, then it starts to make sense that different governments have reregulated in different ways. A common movement toward deregulation implies convergence, for deregulation is a negative action and thus one would not expect to see much difference from one deregulation to the next, but reregulation is a creative process, and thus we should not be surprised to find distinct national variants. Likewise, we should not be surprised that state actors have played a central part in the process. Deregulation would imply a retreat of the state, and we would hardly expect state actors to rally to the cause of retreat. But reregulation merely implies a reorganization of control, and state actors are deeply interested in the terms of this reorganization. In fact, regulatory reform has involved a fundamental restructuring of the core functions of the state: finding new ways to raise revenue and to service the debt, and developing more effective mechanisms of policy implementation. So should we really be surprised that government officials try to influence reforms that concern their ability to perform core functions? Or that their ideas about these functions and the institutional context in which they perform these functions shape the outcome of these reforms? If what seemed so paradoxical at the outset now appears almost commonsensical—well then so be it.

References

Allen, Christopher. (September 1994). "New Institutionalism and the Politics of Financial Reform: Ideas vs. Institutions." Unpublished.

Allinson, Gary D., and Yasunori Sone, eds. (1993). *Political Dynamics in Contemporary Japan.* Ithaca, Cornell University Press.

Anchordoguy, Marie. (1989). *Computers Inc.: Japan's Challenge to IBM.* Cambridge, Mass., Council on East Asian Studies.

Anderson, Stephen J. (1990). "The Political Economy of Japanese Saving: How Postal Savings and Public Pensions Support High Rates of Household Saving in Japan." *Journal of Japanese Studies* 16:61–92.

Aoki Masahiko. (1988). "The Japanese Bureaucracy in Economic Administration: A Rational Regulator or Pluralist Agent?" In John B. Shoven, ed., *Government Policy towards Industry in the United States and Japan,* pp. 265–300. Cambridge, Cambridge University Press.

Arora, Dayanand. (1991). *Investment Banking in Japan: Retrospect and Prospects.* Frankfurt, Peter Lang.

Atkinson, Michael M., and William D. Coleman. (April 1992). "Policy Networks, Policy Communities, and the Problems of Governance." *Governance* 5:154–80.

Bar, François. (September 1995). "Linked Destinies? Telecommunications Reform in France and Germany." Unpublished.

Bar, François, and Michael Borrus. (October 1989). "From Public Access to Private Connections II: Network Strategy and National Advantage in U.S. Telecommunications." In OECD-BRIE.

Bauer, Michel. (October 1988). "The Politics of State-Directed Privatization: The Case of France, 1986–88." *West European Politics* 11:49–60.

Bauer, Michel, and E. Cohen. (1985). *Les Grandes Manoeuvres Industrielles.* Paris, Belfond.

Beason, Richard, and David Weinstein. (1993). "Growth, Economies of Scale, and Targeting in Japan, 1955–90." Harvard Institute of Economic Research Discussion Paper 1644.

Becker, Gary S. (August 1983). "A Theory of Competition among Pressure Groups for Political Influence." *Quarterly Journal of Economics*, pp. 371–400.

Beesley, Michael E. (1981). *Liberalisation of the Use of British Telecom's Network*. London, HMSO.

Beesley, Michael E., and Bruce Laidlaw. (1989). *The Future of Telecommunications: An Assessment of the Role of Competition in U.K. Policy*. Institute of Economic Affairs Research Monograph No. 2. London, IEA.

Beller, Alan L., Tsunemasa Terai, and Richard M. Levine. (1992). "Looks Can Be Deceiving—a Comparison of Initial Public Offering Procedures under Japanese and U.S. Securities Laws." *Law and Contemporary Problems* 55:77–118.

Berger, Suzanne. (December 1992). "The New Politics of Convergence." Unpublished.

Berrill, Kenneth. (Summer 1986). "Regulation in a Changing City—Bureaucrats and Practitioners." *Midland Bank Review*.

Bickers, Kenneth N. (1991). "Transformations in the Governance of the American Telecommunications Industry." In Campbell, Hollingsworth, and Lindberg, eds., pp. 77–107.

Bishop, Matthew, and John Kay. (1988). *Does Privatization Work? Lessons from the U.K.* London, Centre for Business Strategy.

Bloch, Ernest. (1981). "Regulation and Deregulation of Financial Institutions." In Jules Backman, ed., *Regulation and Deregulation*, pp. 149–74. Indianapolis, Bobbs-Merrill.

Boaz, David, and Edward H. Crane, eds. (1993). *Market Liberalism: A Paradigm for the 21st Century*. Washington, D.C., Cato Institute.

Boleat, Mark. (August 1987). "Building Societies: The New Supervisory Framework." *National Westminster Quarterly Review*, pp. 26–34.

Borrie, Gordon. (1991). "Office of Fair Trading: Reflections on Regulation." In Veljanovski, ed., pp. 85–93.

Borrus, Michael, François Bar, Patrick Cogez, Anne Brit Thoresen, Ibrahim Warde, and Aki Yoshikawa. (May 1985). *Telecommunications Development in Comparative Perspective: The New Telecommunications in Europe, Japan, and the U.S.* Berkeley Roundtable on the International Economy (BRIE) Working Paper No. 14.

Bosanquet, N. (July–September 1981). "Sir Keith's Reading List." *Political Quarterly* 52:324–41.

British Telecommunications Act 1981. (1981). London, HMSO.

Brock, Gerald. (1981). *The Telecommunications Industry: The Dynamics of Market Structure*. Cambridge, Harvard University Press.

Calder, Kent E. (1988). *Crisis and Compensation: Public Policy and Political Stability in Japan*. Princeton, Princeton University Press.

——. (1993). *Strategic Capitalism: Private Business and Public Purpose in Japanese Industrial Finance*. Princeton, Princeton University Press.

Campbell, John C. (1984). "Policy Conflict and Its Resolution within the Governmental System." In Ellis S. Krauss, Thomas P. Rohlen, and Patricia G. Steinhoff, eds., *Conflict in Japan*, pp. 294–334. Honolulu, University of Hawaii Press.

Campbell, John L., J. Rogers Hollingsworth, and Leon N. Lindberg, eds. (1991). *Governance of the American Economy*. Cambridge, Cambridge University Press.

Cave, Martin. (August 1995). "Telecommunications." In Economic Planning Agency, *International Comparison of Privatization and Deregulation—the Case in the*

United Kingdom. Discussion Papers No. 60, pp. 1–52. Tokyo, Economic Planning Agency.

Caves, Richard E., Jeffrey A. Frankel, and Ronald W. Jones. (1990). *World Trade and Payments.* 5th ed. Glenview, Ill., Scott, Foresman / Little, Brown.

Cawson, Alan, Kevin Morgan, Douglas Webber, Peter Holmes, and Anne Stevens. (1990). *Hostile Brothers: Competition and Closure in the European Electronics Industry.* Oxford, Clarendon Press.

Cerny, Philip G. (March 1989). "The 'Little Big Bang' in Paris: Financial Market Deregulation in a *Dirigiste* System." *European Journal of Political Research* 17:169–92.

——. (1991). "The Limits of Deregulation: Transnational Interprenetration and Policy Change." *European Journal of Political Research* 19:173–96.

Civil Aviation Authority. (1984). *Airline Competition Policy.* Paper 500. London, CAA.

Cohen, Linda, Matthew McCubbins, and Frances Rosenbluth. (1995). "The Politics of Nuclear Power in Japan and the United States." In Cowhey and McCubbins, eds., pp. 177–202.

Coleman, William D. (April 1993). "Reforming Corporatism: The French Banking Policy Community, 1941–1990." *West European Politics* 1:122–43.

Commission of the European Communities. (1987). *Towards a Dynamic Economy: Green Paper on the Development of the Common Market for Telecommunications Services and Equipment.* Brussels, CEC.

Committee to Review the Functioning of Financial Institutions [Wilson Committee]. (1978). *Evidence on the Financing of Industry and Trade.* London, HMSO.

——. (1980). *Report.* Cmnd. 7937. London, HMSO.

Conservative Party. (1979). *The Conservative Manifesto 1979.* London.

Coriat, Benjamin. (October 1989). "Régime Règlementaire, Structure de Marché, et Compétitivité d'Entreprise." In OECD-BRIE.

Cowhey, Peter F., and John Zysman. (April 1992). "Telecom Policy at a Crossroads: Stalemate or Starting Point?" Unpublished.

Cowhey, Peter F., and Matthew D. McCubbins, eds. (1995). *Structure and Policy in Japan and the United States.* Cambridge, Cambridge University Press.

Crozier, Michel J., Samuel P. Huntington, and Joji Watanuki. (1975). *The Crisis of Democracy.* New York, New York University Press.

Curran, Timothy J. (1982). "Politics and High Technology: The NTT Case." In I. M. Destler and Hideo Sato, eds., *Coping with U.S.-Japanese Economic Conflicts,* pp. 185–241. Lexington, Mass., Lexington Books.

Curtis, Gerald L. (1988). *The Japanese Way of Politics.* New York, Columbia University Press.

Dahrendorf, Ralf. (October–December 1980). "Effectiveness and Legitimacy: On the 'Governability' of Democracies." *Political Quarterly,* pp. 393–410.

Darmon, Jacques. (1986). *Le Grand Derangement: La Guerre du Téléphone.* Paris, J. C. Lattes.

Davidson, Andrew. (1992). *Under the Hammer: Greed and Glory inside the Television Business.* London, Mandarin.

De Boissieu, Christian. (1990). "The French Banking Sector in the Light of European Financial Integration." In Jean Dermine, ed., *European Banking in the 1990s,* pp. 182–226. Oxford, Blackwell.

De Guers, A. (1987). *Casse Avenue de Segur: La France dans la guerre des Communications.* Paris, Alain Moreau.

Department of Industry. (July 1977). *Report of the Post Office Review Committee* (Carter Report). London, HMSO.

——. (July 1978). *The Post Office.* London, HMSO.

Department of Trade and Industry. (1988). *DTI—the Department of Enterprise.* Cmnd. 278. London, HMSO.

——. (November 1990). *Competition and Choice: Telecommunications Policy for the 1990s.* Cmnd. 1303. London, HMSO.

——. (March 1991). *Competition and Choice: Telecommunications Policy for the 1990s.* London, HMSO.

Department of Transport. (1984). *Airline Competition Policy.* Cmnd. 9366. London, HMSO.

——. (July 1984). *Buses.* Cmnd. 9300. London, HMSO.

Derthick, Martha, and Paul J. Quirk. (1985). *The Politics of Deregulation.* Washington, D.C., Brookings Institution.

Donges, Juergen. (1991). *Deregulating the German Economy.* San Francisco, ICS Press.

Dosi, Giovanni, Laura D'Andrea Tyson, and John Zysman. (1989). "Trade, Technologies, and Development: A Framework for Discussing Japan." In Johnson, Tyson, and Zysman, eds., pp. 3–38.

Duch, Raymond M. (1991). *Privatizing the Economy: Telecommunications Policy in Comparative Perspective.* Ann Arbor, University of Michigan Press.

Dyson, Kenneth. (October 1986). "West European States and the Communications Revolution." *West European Politics* 9:10–55.

——, ed. (1992). *The Politics of German Regulation.* Aldershot, U.K., Dartmouth.

Eads, George, and Kozo Yamamura. (1989). "The Future of Industrial Policy." In Yamamura and Yasuba, eds., pp. 423–68.

Ebato Tetsuo. (1987). *Kasumigaseki no kōbō* [The ups and downs of Kasumigaseki]. Tokyo, Chikuma Shobo.

Eckstein, Harry. (1975). "Case Study and Theory in Political Science." In F. I. Greenstein and Nelson W. Polsby, eds., *Handbook of Political Science,* pp. 79–138. Reading, Mass., Addison-Wesley.

——. (1994). "Social Science as Cultural Science: An Essay in Honor of Aaron Wildavsky." Unpublished.

Economic Planning Agency, Comprehensive Planning Bureau. (1986). *Kisei kanwa no keizai-teki kōka* [The economic benefits of deregulation]. Tokyo, Ōkurashō Insatsukyoku.

——. (1989). *Kisei kanwa no keizai riron* [The economic theory of deregulation]. Tokyo, Ōkurashō Insatsukyoku.

Eichler, Ned. (1989). *The Thrift Debacle.* Berkeley and Los Angeles, University of California Press.

Eisner, Marc Allen. (1993). *Regulatory Politics in Transition.* Baltimore, Johns Hopkins.

Ellison, I. K. C. (1990). *The Telecommunications Duopoly Policy Review: Proposals for Policy Changes.* London, Robert Fleming.

Ely, Bert. (1993). "Government Regulation: The Real Crisis in Financial Services." In Boaz and Crane, eds., pp. 115–28.

Evans, Peter, Dietrich Reuschemeyer, and Theda Skocpol, eds. (1985). *Bringing the State Back In.* New York, Cambridge University Press.

Fair Trade Commission, Study Committee on Government Regulations and Competition Policy. (October 1989). "Kyōsō seisaku no kanten kara no seifu kisei no minaoshi" [A review of government regulation from the perspective of competition policy]. Tokyo.

Federal Ministry of Posts and Telecommunications. (March 1991). "Principles for Granting Licenses for the Telephone Service via Satellite in and with the New Federal States." Bonn.

Foster, C. D. (1992). *Privatization, Public Ownership, and the Regulation of Natural Monopoly.* Oxford, Blackwell.

Foundation for Advanced Information and Research, Japan. (1991). *Japan's Financial Markets* (FAIR Fact Series II). Tokyo, FAIR.

Fowler, Norman. (1977). *The Right Track: A Paper on Conservative Transport Policy.* London, Conservative Political Centre.

Francis, John. (1993). *The Politics of Regulation: A Comparative Perspective.* Cambridge, Mass., Blackwell.

Frankel, Jeffrey A. (1984). *The Yen/Dollar Agreement: Liberalizing Japanese Capital Markets.* Institute for International Economics, Policy Analyses in International Economics 9. Washington D.C., IIE.

———. (April 1990). "Japanese Finance: a Survey." Unpublished.

Fuji Bank Research Department. (September 1987). "Kinyū seido minaoshi no hitsuyōsei to hōkō" [On the necessity for a review of the financial system]. *Fuji Times,* pp. 2–8.

Fuji Research Institute. (September 1990). "Beikoku no faiyauōru" [American firewalls]. *Fuji Times,* pp. 2–8.

Funabashi, Yōichi. (1988). *Managing the Dollar: From the Plaza to the Louvre.* Washington, D.C., Institute for International Economics.

Gamble, Andrew. (1988). *The Free Economy and the Strong State: The Politics of Thatcherism.* Durham, Duke University Press.

George, Alexander L. (1979). "Case Studies and Theory Development: The Method of Structured, Focused Comparison." In Paul G. Lauren, ed., *Diplomacy: New Approaches in History, Theory, and Policy,* pp. 43–68. New York, Free Press.

Gerschenkron, Alexander. (1962). *Economic Backwardness in Historical Perspective.* Cambridge, Harvard University Press.

Glaister, Stephen. (1991). "U.K. Bus Deregulation: The Reasons and the Experience." *Investigaciones Economicas* 15:285–308.

Glaister, Stephen, and Tony Travers. (April 1993). "The Politics and Economics of British Rail Privatisation." Unpublished.

Glencross, David. (1991). "ITC: The Reform of Broadcasting Regulation." In Veljanovski, ed., pp. 141–51.

Goldstein, Judith. (1993). *Ideas, Interests, and American Trade Policy.* Ithaca, Cornell University Press.

Goldstein, Judith, and Robert Keohane, eds. (1993). *Ideas and Foreign Policy: Beliefs, Institutions, and Political Change.* Ithaca, Cornell University Press.

Goodhart, Charles. (1987). "What Is the Purpose of Regulating Financial Services?" Unpublished.

———. (Summer 1987). "The Economics of 'Big Bang.'" *Midland Bank Review.* 6–15.

Gourevitch, Peter. (1986). *Politics in Hard Times: Comparative Responses to International Economic Crises.* Ithaca, Cornell University Press.

Gower, L. C. B. (January 1982). *Review of Investor Protection: A Discussion Document.* London, HMSO.

——. (January 1984). *Review of Investor Protection, Report: Part 1*. Cmnd. 9125. London, HMSO.

Grande, Edgar. (April 1987). "Telecommunications Policy in West Germany and Great Britain—a Comparative Analysis of Political Configurations." Unpublished.

——. (1989). *Vom Monopol zum Wettbewerb?* Wiesbaden, Deutscher Universitätsverlag.

Grant, Wyn. (1989). *Government and Industry: A Comparative Analysis of the U.S., Canada, and the U.K.* Hants, U.K., Edward Elgar.

Haas, Richard, and Oliver Knox, eds. (1991). *Policies of Thatcherism: Thoughts from a London Thinktank.* Lanham, Md., University Press of America.

Haley, John O. (1986). "Administrative Guidance versus Formal Regulation: Resolving the Paradox of Industrial Policy." In Gary R. Saxonhouse and Kozo Yamamura, eds., *Law and Trade Issues of the Japanese Economy: American and Japanese Perspectives*, pp. 107–28. Seattle, University of Washington Press.

——. (1989). "The Context and Content of Regulatory Change in Japan." In Kenneth Button and Dennis Swann, eds., *The Age of Regulatory Reform*, pp. 124–38. Oxford, Clarendon Press.

Hall, Peter A. (1986). *Governing the Economy: The Politics of State Intervention in Britain and France.* New York, Oxford University Press.

——. (April 1993). "Policy Paradigms, Social Learning, and the State: The Case of Economic Policymaking in Britain." *Comparative Politics*, pp. 275–96.

——. (September 1994). "The Comparative Political Economy of Europe in an Era of Interdependence." Unpublished.

——, ed. (1989). *The Political Power of Economic Ideas: Keynesianism across Nations.* Princeton, Princeton University Press.

Hall, Peter A., and Rosemary Taylor. (September 1994). "Political Science and the Four New Institutionalisms." Unpublished.

Hamada, Kōichi, and Akiyoshi Horiuchi. (1987). "The Political Economy of the Financial Market." In Yamamura and Yasuba, eds., pp. 223–60.

Hansard Society. (1979). *Politics and Industry—the Great Mismatch.* London, Hansard Society.

Hayashi, Toshihiko. (1990). *Kōeki jigyō to kisei kanwa* [Public utilities and deregulation]. Tokyo, Tōyō Keizai.

Heffron, Florence. (1983). "The Federal Communications Commission and Broadcast Deregulation." In John J. Havick, ed., *Communications Policy and the Political Process*, pp. 39–70. Westport, Conn., Greenwood.

Her Majesty's Treasury. (1978). *The Nationalized Industries.* Cmnd. 7131. London, HMSO.

Hibbs, John. (1989). "Privatisation and Competition in Road Passenger Transport." In Cento Veljanovski, ed., *Privatisation and Competition: A Market Prospectus*, pp. 161–77. London, Institute of Economic Affairs.

Hills, Jill. (1986). *Deregulating Telecoms: Competition and Control in the United States, Japan, and Britain.* Westport, Conn., Quorum.

——. (1989). "Neo-Conservative Regimes and Convergence in Telecommunications Policy." *European Journal of Political Research* 17:95–113.

Hiwatari, Nobuhiro. (1991). *Sengo nihon no shijō to seiji* [Markets and politics in postwar Japan]. Tokyo, Tokyo Daigaku Shuppankai.

Hobsbawm, E. J. (1969). *Industry and Empire.* Harmondsworth, U.K., Penguin.

Hollingsworth, J. Rogers, Philippe Schmitter, and Wolfgang Streeck, eds. (1994). *Governing Capitalist Economies: Performance and Control of Economic Sectors.* New York, Oxford University Press.

Horwitz, Robert Britt. (1989). *The Irony of Regulatory Reform: The Deregulation of American Telecommunications.* New York, Oxford University Press.

Huntley, John A. K., and Douglas C. Pitt. (1990). "Judicial Policymaking: The Greeneing of U.S. Telecommunications." *International Review of Law and Economics* 10:77–100.

Hutton, Will. (September 1991). "Why Britain Can't Afford the City." *Management Today,* pp. 46–51.

Iio Jun. (1993). *Mineika no seiji katei* [The political process of privatization]. Tokyo, Tokyo Daigaku Shuppankai.

Ikenberry, G. John. (1990). "The International Spread of Privatization Policies: Inducements, Learning, and 'Policy Bandwagoning.' " In Ezra N. Suleiman and John Waterbury, eds., *The Political Economy of Public Sector Reform and Privatization,* pp. 88–110. Boulder, Colo., Westview.

Imai, Kenichi. (August 1989). "Japan's Financial System and Industrial Innovation." Unpublished.

InfoCom Research, Inc. (1991). *Jōhō tsūshin handobukku '92-nemban* [Information and communications handbook 1992]. Tokyo, InfoCom.

Information Technology Advisory Panel, Cabinet Office. (1982). *Cable Systems.* London, HMSO.

Inoguchi, Takashi, and Tomoaki Iwai. (1987). *"Zoku giin" no kenkyū* [A study of "Zoku" Diet members]. Tokyo, Nihon Keizai.

———. (1990). "The Political Economy of Conservative Resurgence under Recession: Public Policies and Political Support in Japan, 1977–1983." In T. J. Pempel, ed., *Uncommon Democracies: The One-Party Regimes,* pp. 189–225. Ithaca, Cornell University Press.

Inter-Bank Research Organization. (1973). *The Future of London as an International Financial Center.* London, HMSO.

Itō, Daiichi. (1988). "Policy Implications of Administrative Reform." In J.A.A. Stockwin, ed., *Dynamic and Immobilist Politics in Japan,* pp. 77–105. London, Macmillan.

Itō, Takatoshi. (1992). *Shōhisha jūshi no keizaigaku: kisei kanwa wa naze hitsuyō ka* [An economics with the emphasis on consumers: Why deregulation is necessary]. Tokyo, Nihon Keizai.

Itō, Yōichi. (1986). "Telecommunications and Industrial Policies in Japan: Recent Developments." In Marcellus S. Snow, ed., *Marketplace for Telecommunications: Regulation and Deregulation in Industrialized Democracies,* pp. 201–30. New York, Longman.

Jaffer, S. M., and D. J. Thompson. (November 1986). "Deregulating Express Coaches: A Reassessment." *Fiscal Studies,* pp. 45–68.

Johnson, Chalmers. (1982). *MITI and the Japanese Miracle.* Stanford, Stanford University Press.

———. (1989). "MITI, MPT, and the Telecom Wars: How Japan Makes Policy for High Technology." In Johnson, Tyson, and Zysman, eds., pp. 177–240.

———. (1995). *Japan: Who Governs? The Rise of the Developmental State.* New York, Norton.

Johnson, Chalmers, Laura D'Andrea Tyson, and John Zysman, eds. (1989). *Politics and Productivity: The Real Story of Why Japan Works.* Cambridge, Mass., Ballinger.

Kagan, Robert. (1991). "Adversarial Legalism and American Government." *Journal of Policy Analysis and Management* 10:369–406.

Kakurai, Yasuo, ed.(1992). *Kisei kanwa mondai to keizai minshu-shugi* [The deregulation problem and economic democracy]. Tokyo, Shin Nippon Shuppansha.

Kambara, Masaru. (1986). *Tenkanki no seiji katei* [The political process in a period of transition]. Tokyo, Sōgō Rōdō Kenkyūjo.

Kane, Edward J. (May 1981). "Accelerating Inflation, Technological Innovation and the Decreasing Effectiveness of Banking Regulation." *Journal of Finance* 36:355–67.

——. (1987). "Competitive Financial Reregulation: An International Perspective." In R. Portes and A. Swobosa, eds., *Threats to International Stability*, pp. 111–47. Cambridge, Cambridge University Press.

——. (1989). *The S&L Insurance Mess: How Did It Happen?* Washington, D.C., Urban Institute Press.

Kanō, Yoshikazu. (1991). *"Mineika" ga nihon o kaeru* [Privatization will change Japan]. Tokyo, PHP Kenkyukai.

Kasuya, Shinji. (1989). "Nihon ni okeru shin-hoshushugi no isō" [The neo-conservative phase in Japan]. In Kawakami and Masuda, eds., pp. 382–456.

Katō, Hiroshi. (1984). *Kangyō Kaikakuron* [A theory of governmental reform]. Tokyo, Chūō Keizai.

——, and Yōichi Sandō. (1983a). *Dokō-san to tomo ni 730-nichi* [730 days with Mr. Doko]. Tokyo, Keizai Ōraisha.

——. (1983b). *Kokutetsu denden sembai: saisei no kōzu* [A plan for revitalization: JNR, NTT, and Japan Tobacco & Salt]. Tokyo, Tōyō Keizai.

Katzenstein, Peter J., ed. (1978). *Between Power and Plenty: Foreign Economic Policies of Advanced Industrial States.* Madison, University of Wisconsin Press.

——. (1987). *Politics and Policy in West Germany: The Growth of the Semi-Sovereign State.* Philadelphia: Temple University Press.

——. (1989). "Stability and Change in the Emerging Third Republic." In Katzenstein, ed., *Industry and Politics in West Germany: Toward the Third Republic*, pp. 307–53. Ithaca, Cornell University Press.

Kavanagh, Dennis. (1990). *Thatcherism and British Politics: The End of Consensus?* 2d ed. Oxford, Oxford University Press.

Kawakami, Tadao, and Toshio Masuda, eds. (1989). *Shin-hoshushugi no keizai shakai seisaku* [The economic and social policies of the new conservativism]. Tokyo, Hōsei University Press.

Kawakita, Takao. (1985). *Tsūsan yūsei sensō* [The MITI-MPT wars]. Tokyo, Kyōikusha.

Kay, John, Colin Mayer, and David Thompson, eds. (1986). *Privatisation and Regulation: The U.K. Experience.* Oxford, Clarendon Press.

Keeler, Theodore E. (1984). "Theories of Regulation and the Deregulation Movement." *Public Choice* 44:103–45.

Keidanren. (January 1987). "Keidanren jōhō tsūshin kankei ikenshū" [Keidanren opinions on information technology]. Tokyo.

——. (March 1988). "Kisei kanwa ni kansuru yōbō" [Recommendations regarding deregulation]. Tokyo.

Kerr, Ian M. (1986). *Big Bang.* London, Euromoney.

Komiya, Ryūtarō. (Summer 1986). "Industrial Policy in Japan." *Japanese Economic Studies* 14:51–81.

Komori, Masao. (1988). *Denden mineika no butaiura* [Behind the scenes of NTT's privatization]. Tokyo, Gōdō Tsūshinsha.

Krasner, Stephen. (January 1984). "Approaches to the State: Alternative Conceptions and Historical Dynamics." *Comparative Politics* 16:223–46.

Kraus, C. R., and A. W. Deurig. (1988). *The Rape of Ma Bell: The Criminal Wrecking of the Best Telephone System in the World.* Secaucus, N.J., Lyle Stewart.

Kumon Shumpei. (Spring 1984). "Japan Faces Its Future: The Political-Economics of Administrative Reform." *Journal of Japanese Studies* 10:143–63.

Kusano, Atsushi. (1989). *Kokutestu kaikaku* [JNR reform]. Tokyo, Chūō Kōronsha.

Lehmbruch, Gerhard. (1992). "The Institutional Framework of German Regulation." In Dyson, ed., pp. 29–52.

Levy, Jonah D. (1994). "The Crisis of Identity in Post-*Dirigiste* France." Unpublished.

Leys, Colin. (1983). *Politics in Britain.* London, Heinemann.

Liberal Democratic Party. (April 1992). *Seimu chōsakai meibō* [Policy Research Council directory]. Tokyo, LDP.

Lijphart, Arend. (September 1971). "Comparative Politics and the Comparative Method." *American Political Science Review* 65:682–93.

———. (July 1975). "The Comparable-Case Strategy in Comparative Research." *Comparative Political Studies* 8:158–77.

Lincoln, Edward J. (1988). *Japan: Facing Economic Maturity.* Washington, D.C., Brookings Institution.

Lindblom, Charles E. (1977). *Politics and Markets: The World's Political-Economic Systems.* New York, Basic Books.

Litt, David G., Jonathan R. Macey, Geoffrey P. Miller, and Edward L. Rubin. (1990). "Politics, Bureaucracies, and Financial Markets: Bank Entry into Commercial Paper Underwriting in the United States and Japan." *University of Pennsylvania Law Review* 139:369–453.

Littlechild, Stephen. (February 1983). *Regulation of British Telecommunications Profitability.* London, Department of Industry.

———. (1991). "Office of Electricity Regulation: The New Regulatory Framework for Electricity." In Veljanovski, ed., pp. 107–18.

Llewellyn, David T. (August 1987). "Competition and the Regulatory Mix." *National Westminster Quarterly Review,* pp. 4–13.

Longuet, Gérard. (1988). *Télécoms: La conquête de nouveaux espaces.* Paris: Dunod.

Loriaux, Michael. (1991). *France after Hegemony: International Change and Financial Reform.* Ithaca, Cornell University Press.

Lynn, Jonathan, and Antony Jay. (1989). *The Complete Yes Minister.* Omnibus edition. London, BBC Books.

Mabuchi, Masaru. (1990). "Ōkurashō ni okeru gyōsei sutairu no henka" [The Ministry of Finance's changing policy style]. In Muramatsu, ed., pp. 41–80.

Magaziner, Ira C., and Thomas M. Hout. (1980). *Japanese Industrial Policy.* Berkeley, Institute of International Studies.

Maital, Shlomo. (Summer 1992). "The Global Telecommunications Picture: Is America Being Outstripped by France?" *Brookings Review,* pp. 40–43.

March, James G., and Johan P. Olsen. (1989). *Rediscovering Institutions: The Organizational Basis of Politics.* New York, Free Press.

Matsubara, Satoru. (1991). *Mineika to kiseikanwa* [Privatization and deregulation]. Tokyo, Nippon Hyōronsha.

McCubbins, Matthew, and Gregory Noble. (1995). "The Appearance of Power: Legislators, Bureaucrats, and the Budget Process in the United States and Japan." In Cowhey and McCubbins, eds., pp. 56–80.

McKean, Margaret. (1993). "State Strength and the Public Interest." In Allinson and Sone, eds., pp. 72–104.

McKenzie, Richard B., and Dwight R. Lee. (1991). *Quicksilver Capital: How the Rapid Movement of Wealth Has Changed the World.* New York, Free Press.

Meerschwam, David M. (December 1989). "The Japanese Financial System and the Cost of Capital." Unpublished.

——. (1991). *Breaking Financial Boundaries: Global Capital, National Deregulation, and Financial Services Firms.* Boston, Harvard Business School Press.

Melitz, Jacques. (1990). "Financial Deregulation in France," *European Economic Review* 34:394–402.

Ministry of Finance, Banking Bureau. (1983). *Ginkō kyoku kinyū nenpō* [Banking Bureau finance annual], no. 32. Tokyo, Ōkurashō Insatsukyoku.

——. (1991). *Ginkō kyoku kinyū nenpō* [Banking Bureau finance annual], no. 40. Tokyo, Ōkurashō Insatsukyoku.

Ministry of Finance, Banking Bureau, Financial System Research Council. (May 1989). "Atarashii kinyū seido ni tsuite" [On the new financial system]. Subcommittee report. Tokyo.

——. (July 1990). "Atarashii kinyū seido ni tsuite" [On the new financial system]. Second subcommittee report. Tokyo.

——. (May 1991). "Atarashii kinyū seido ni tsuite" [On the new financial system]. Final subcommittee report. Tokyo.

Ministry of Finance, Banking Bureau, Study Group on Financial Issues. (May 1990). "The Liberalization of Interest Rates on Time Deposits of Less than 10 Million Yen." Tokyo.

Ministry of Finance, Securities Bureau, Securities and Exchange Council. (June 1990a). "Shōken torihiki shingikai kihon mondai kenkyūkai daiichi bukai hōkoku" [First subcommittee report, Fundamental Research Committee of the Securities and Exchange Council]. Tokyo.

——. (June 1990b). "Shōken torihiki shingikai kihon mondai kenkyūkai daini bukai hōkoku" [Second subcommittee report, Fundamental Research Committee of the Securities and Exchange Council]. Tokyo.

——. (May 1991). "Shōken torihiki shingikai kihon mondai kenkyūkai hōkoku" [Report of the Fundamental Research Committee, Securities and Exchange Council]. Tokyo.

Ministry of International Trade and Industry. (May 1992). "*Sōgō enerugii chōsakai toshi netsu enerugii bukai gasu kihon mondai kentō shōiinkai chūkan torimatome*" [Comprehensive Energy Research Council, Thermal Energy Committee, Gas Basic Problems Subcommittee interim report]. Tokyo.

——. (June 1994) "*Denki jigyō shingikai jukyūbukai denryoku kihon mondai kentō shōiinkai chūkan hōkoku*" [Electric Industry Council, Supply and Demand Committee, Electricity Basic Problems Subcommittee interim report]. Tokyo.

Ministry of Posts and Telecommunications. (May 1991). "Yochokin kinri no jiyūka to yūbin chokin" [Postal savings and the deregulation of interest rates for savings and deposits]. Report of the Study Group on Postal Savings, Committee on Interest Rate Deregulation. Tokyo.

Ministry of Posts and Telecommunications, Telecommunications Policy Council. (March 1990). "Nihon denshin denwa kabushiki kaisha-hō fuzoku daini-jō ni motozuki kōzuru beki sochi, hōsaku-tō no arikata" [Measures and policies for consideration regarding article 2 of the NTT law]. Tokyo.

Ministry of Posts and Telecommunications, Telecommunications Policy Issues Study Group. (June 1971). *Tsūshin gyōsei no tembō (yosetsu)* [The future of telecommunications policy (summary)]. Tokyo.

Miwa, Toshirō. (1993). *Kinyū gyōsei kaikaku* [Financial administrative reform]. Tokyo, Nihon Keizai.

Mochizuki, Michael. (1993). "Public Sector Labor and the Privatization Challenge: The Railway and Telecommunications Unions." In Allinson and Sone, eds., pp. 181–99.

Moon, Jeremy, J. J. Richardson, and Paul Smart. (1986). "The Privatisation of British Telecom: A Case Study of the Extended Process of Legislation." *European Journal of Political Research* 14:339–55.

Moran, Michael. (October 1981). "Finance Capital and Pressure-Group Politics in Britain." *British Journal of Political Science* 11:381–404.

———. (1986). *The Politics of Banking.* 2d ed. London, Macmillan.

———. (January–March 1988). "Thatcherism and Financial Regulation." *Political Quarterly* 59:20–27.

———. (October 1989). "Regulatory Change in West German Financial Markets." Unpublished.

———. (1991). *The Politics of the Financial Services Revolution: The U.S.A., U.K., and Japan.* New York, St. Martin's.

Morgan, Kevin, and Andrew Davies. (October 1989). "Seeking Advantage from Telecommunications: Regulatory Innovation and Corporate Information Networks in the UK." In OECD-BRIE.

Morgan, Kevin, and Douglas Pitt. (1991). "Communities, Communications, and Change: The Dialectic of Development in U.S. Telecommunications." In Wilks and Wright, eds., pp. 233–55.

Muramatsu, Michio. (Spring 1988). "Mineika, kisei kanwa to saikisei no kōzō: denki tsūshin seisaku no henka" [The structure of privatization, deregulation, and reregulation: The change in telecommunications policy]. *Leviathan* 2:118–35.

———, ed. (1990). *Shakai keizai no henka to gyōsei sutairu no henyō ni kansuru chōsa kenkyū hōkokusho* [A report of research on socioeconomic change and the transformation of policy style]. Tokyo, Management and Cordination Agency.

Muramatsu Michio, and Ellis S. Krauss. (1987). "The Conservative Policy Line and the Development of Patterned Pluralism." In Yamamura and Yasuba, eds., pp. 516–54.

Naisbitt, John, and Patricia Aburdene. (1990). *Megatrends 2000: Ten New Directions for the 1990s.* New York, Avon Books.

National Economic Development Office. (1976). *A Study of UK Nationalised Industries.* London, HMSO.

Nihon Keizai Shimbun. (1983). *Jimintō Seichōkai* [The Liberal Democratic Party's policy research council]. Tokyo, Nihon Keizai.

———. (1992). *Ōkurashō no yūutsu* [The MoF's lament]. Tokyo, Nihon Keizai.

Nippon Telegraph and Telephone Public Corporation. (1977). *Nihon denshin denwa kōsha nijūgonenshi* [A twenty-five year history of NTT]. Vol. 1. Tokyo, Denki Tsūshin Kyōkai.

Nippon Telegraph and Telephone Public Corporation Management Structure Study Group. (November 1982). "Kokunai kōshū denki tsūshin jigyō no keiei keitai-tō ni kansuru chōsa kenkyū" [A study regarding the management structure of the domestic telecommunications business]. Tokyo.

Nippon Telegraph and Telephone Public Corporation, Management Survey Bureau. (May 1971). *Dēta tsushin o meguru kakushu iken seron hihan shiryō* [Materials on various views, opinions, and criticisms concerning data communications]. Vol. 3. Tokyo, NTT.

Niskanen, W. A. (1971). *Bureaucracy and Representative Government.* Chicago, Aldine-Atherton.

———. (1993). "Reduce Federal Regulation." In Boaz and Crane, eds., pp. 103–14.

Noble, Gregory W. (1989). "The Japanese Industrial Policy Debate." In Stephan Haggard and Chung-in Moon, *Pacific Dynamics: The International Politics of Industrial Change*, pp. 53–95. Boulder, Colo., Westview.

Noguchi, Yukio, and Eisuke Sakakibara. (August 1977). "Ōkurasho-nichigin ōchō no bunseki" [An analysis of the Ministry of Finance—Bank of Japan dynasty]. *Chūō Kōron* 1085:96–150.

Noll, Roger G. (1989). "Economic Perspectives on the Politics of Regulation." In R. Schmalensee and R. D. Willig, eds., *Handbook of Industrial Organization*, pp. 1253–87. New York, Elsevier Science Publishers.

Noll, Roger G., and Bruce M. Owen, eds. (1983). *The Political Economy of Deregulation: Interest Groups in the Regulatory Process.* Washington, D.C., American Enterprise Institute.

Noll, Roger G., and Frances M. Rosenbluth. (1995). "Telecommunications Policy: Structure, Process, Outcomes." In McCubbins and Cowhey, eds., pp. 119–76.

Nordlinger, Eric. (1981). *On the Autonomy of the Democratic State.* Cambridge, Harvard University Press.

NTT Corporation. (1986). *Nippon denshin denwa kōsha shashi* [The history of NTT public corporation]. Tokyo, Jōhō Tsūshin Sōgō Kenkyūjo.

O'Connor, James. (1973). *The Fiscal Crisis of the State.* New York, St. Martin's.

OECD-BRIE. *See* Organization for Economic Cooperation and Development and the Berkeley Roundtable on the International Economy.

Ohmae, Kenichi. (1990). *The Borderless World: Power and Strategy in the Interlinked Economy.* New York, Harper Business.

Okimoto, Daniel. (1989). *Between MITI and the Market: Japanese Industrial Policy for High Technology.* Stanford, Stanford University Press.

Organization for Economic Cooperation and Development. (1988). *The Telecommunications Industry: The Challenges of Structural Change.* Information, Computer, and Communications Policy Paper No. 14. Paris, OECD.

Organization for Economic Cooperation and Development and the Berkeley Roundtable on the International Economy. (October 1989). *Information Networks and Business Strategies.* OECD-BRIE Project on Competitiveness and Telecommunications Policy. Paris, OECD.

Ōtake, Hideo. (1994). *Jiyūshugi-teki kaikaku no jidai* [The era of liberal reform]. Tokyo, Chūō Kōronsha.

Ozawa, Ichirō. (1993). *Nihon kaizō keikaku* [Blueprint for a new Japan]. Tokyo, Kōdansha.

Peltzman, Sam. (August 1976). "Toward a More General Theory of Regulation." *Journal of Law and Economics* 19:211–40.

——. (1989). "The Economic Theory of Regulation after a Decade of Deregulation." In *Brookings Papers: Microeconomics 1989*, pp. 1–59. Washington, D.C., Brookings Institution.

Pitt, Douglas C. (1980). *The Telecommunications Function in the British Post Office: A Case Study of Bureaucratic Adaptation*. Westmead, U.K., Saxon House.

Polanyi, Karl. (1944). *The Great Transformation: The Political and Economic Origins of Our Time*. Boston, Beacon Press.

Poulantzas, Nicos. (1978). *State, Power, and Socialism*. London, New Left Books.

Prestowitz, Clyde V., Jr. (1989). *Trading Places: How We Are Giving Our Future to Japan and How to Reclaim It*. New York, Basic Books.

Prévot, Hubert. (July 1989). *Rapport de Synthèse*. Paris, Ministère des Postes, des Télécommunications et de l'Espace.

Ramseyer, J. Mark, and Frances McCall Rosenbluth. (1993). *Japan's Political Marketplace*. Cambridge, Harvard University Press.

Reid, Margaret. (1988). *All-Change in the City*. London, Macmillan.

——. (1989). "Mrs Thatcher and the City." In Dennis Kavanagh and Anthony Seldon, eds., *The Thatcher Effect*, pp. 49–63. Oxford, Oxford University Press.

Ridley, F., and J. Blondel. (1969). *Public Administration in France*. London, Routledge.

Rosenbluth, Frances McCall. (1989). *Financial Politics in Contemporary Japan*. Ithaca, Cornell University Press.

Rōyama, Shōichi. (1989). *Kinyū jiyūka no keizaigaku* [The economics of financial liberalization]. Tokyo, Nihon Keizai.

Sakakibara, Eisuke. (1990). *Shihon-shugi o koeta nihon* [Japan—beyond capitalism]. Tokyo, Tōyō Keizai.

Samuels, Richard J. (1987). *The Business of the Japanese State: Energy Markets in Comparative and Historical Perspective*. Ithaca, Cornell University Press.

Sandholtz, Wayne. (January 1993). "Institutions and Collective Action: The New Telecommunications in Western Europe." *World Politics* 45:242–70.

Satō, Seizaburō, and Tetsuhisa Matsuzaki. (1986). *Jimintō seiken* [The LDP government]. Tokyo, Chūō Kōronsha.

Schaede, Ulrike. (1989). "Liberalization of Money Markets: A Comparison of Japan and West Germany." *Journal of International Economic Studies* 3:25–43.

——. (1990). *Der neue japanische Kapitalmarkt—Finanzfutures in Japan*. Wiesbaden, Gabler.

——. (October 1990). "Black Monday in New York, Blue Tuesday in Tokyo: The October 1987 Crash in Japan." Unpublished.

Schiller, Dan. (1982). *Telematics and Government*. New York, Ablex.

Schmidt, Susanne K. (June 1991). "Taking the Long Road to Liberalization: Telecommunications Reform in the Federal Republic of Germany." *Telecommunications Policy*.

Schneider, Volker, and Raymund Werle. (November 1989). "Governance by Policy Networks: The German Telecommunications Sector." Unpublished.

Schreiner, J., and K. Smith. (Summer 1980). "The Impact of Mayday on Diversification Cost." *Journal of Portfolio Management*.

Schwartz, Frank. (1993). "Of Fairy Cloaks and Familiar Talks: The Politics of Consultation." In Allinson and Sone, eds., pp. 217–41.

Seisaku Kōsō Fōramu. (December 1980). *Katsuryoku aru bunkenteki jōhō shakai e* [Toward an active and decentralized information society]. Tokyo, Seisaku Kōsō Fōramu.

Seldon, Arthur, ed. (1988). *Financial Regulation—or Over-Regulation?* London, Institute of Economic Affairs.

——. (1989). "Economic Scholarship and Political Interest," In Andrew Gamble et al., *Ideas, Interests & Consequences*, pp. 75–98. London, Institute of Economic Affairs.

Shafer, D. Michael. (1994). *Winners and Losers: How Sectors Shape the Developmental Prospects of States.* Ithaca, Cornell University Press.

Shintō, Hisashi. (1982). *Denden zakkubaran* [NTT straight-talk]. Tokyo, Tōyō Keizai.

——. (1985). *NTT o tsukuru* [Creating NTT]. Tokyo, Tōyō Keizai.

Shiota, Ushio. (1988). *Issennichi no jōho* [A thousand days of concessions]. Tokyo, Shinchōsha.

Shonfield, Andrew. (1965). *Modern Capitalism: The Changing Balance of Public and Private Power.* New York, Oxford University Press.

Skocpol, Theda. (1985). "Bringing the State Back In: Strategies of Analysis in Current Research." In Evans, Reuschemeyer, and Skocpol, eds., pp. 3–37.

Sneider, David A. (1993). "Recent Developments in Japan's Securities Market." In *International Securities Markets 1993*, Practicing Law Institute, Corporate Law and Practice Handbook Series B-798. New York, Practicing Law Institute.

Society of Telecom Executives. (July 1983). "Liberalisation, Privatisation, and Regulation: What Future for British Telecom?" London.

Solomon, J. H. (September 1986). "Telecommunications Evolution in the UK." *Telecommunications Policy*, pp. 186–92.

Steinmo, Sven, Kathleen Thelen, and Frank Longstreth, eds. (1992). *Structuring Politics: Historical Institutionalism in Comparative Analysis.* Cambridge, Cambridge University Press.

Stelzer, Irwin. (Summer 1988). "Britain's Newest Import: America's Regulatory Experience." *Oxford Review of Economic Policy* 4:69–79.

Stigler, George. (Spring 1971). "The Theory of Economic Regulation." *Bell Journal of Economics and Management Science* 2:3–21.

Stone, Alan. (1989). *Wrong Number: The Breaking Up of AT&T.* New York: Basic Books.

——. (1991). *Public Service Liberalism: Telecommunications and Transitions in Public Policy.* Princeton, Princeton University Press.

Suetsugu, Katsuhiko. (1994). *Enerugii kaikaku* [Energy reform]. Tokyo, Denryoku Shimpōsha.

Swann, Dennis. (1988). *The Retreat of the State: Deregulation and Privatisation in the U.K. and the U.S.* Hertfordshire, U.K., Harvester Wheatsheaf.

Tachibanaki, Toshiaki. (June 1991). "The Economics of the Regulation and Deregulation of the Financial Industry in Japan." Unpublished.

Tadokoro, Masayuki. (1988). "Aru gaiatsu no jirei kenkyū—nichibei en-doru kōshō no seijigaku-teki kōsatsu" [A political analysis of the U.S.-Japan yen-dollar negotiations—a case study of foreign pressure]. *Himeji Hōgaku* 1:209–55.

Takahashi, Shima. (October 1989). "Torakku unsō jigyō no kisei kanwa to sono eikyō" [The deregulation of the trucking business and its impact]. *Ryūtsū Mondai Kenkyū* 14.

Tanaka, Kakuei. (1972). *Nihon Rettō Kaizōron* [A plan for remodeling the Japanese archipelago]. Tokyo, Nikkan Kōgyō Shimbunsha.

Tanaka, Kazuaki, and Masahiro Horie. (December 1990). "Mineika to kisei kanwa" [Privatization and deregulation], part 1. *Kōkyō Sentaku no Kenkyū* 16:72–84.

——. (May 1991). "Mineika to kisei kanwa" [Privatization and deregulation], part 2. *Kōkyō Sentaku no Kenkyū* 17:65–86.

Temin, Peter. (1987). *The Fall of the Bell System: A Study in Prices and Politics*. Cambridge, Cambridge University Press.

Thatcher, Margaret. (1993). *The Downing Street Years*. New York: HarperCollins.

Thimm, Alfred. (1992). *America's Stake in European Telecommunication Policies*. Westport, Conn., Quorum.

Thomas, David. (1986). "The Union Response to Denationalisation." In Kay, Mayer, and Thompson, eds., pp. 299–321.

Toffler, Alvin. (1990). *Power Shift: Knowledge, Wealth, and Violence at the Edge of the 21st Century*. New York, Bantam.

Tomita, Tetsurō. (1984). "Dendenkaikaku hōan no rippō katei" [The legislative process of the NTT reform laws]. In Moriya Koyama et al., *Nihon no jōhō/tsūshin benchā* [Japan's information/communications venture], pp. 30–55. Tokyo, Diamond.

Toshikawa, Takao. (1995). *Ōkurashō "kenryoku no himitsu"* [The secret of MoF power]. Tokyo, Shōgakkan.

Trezise, Philip H. (1983). "Industrial Policy Is Not the Major Reason for Japan's Success." *Brookings Review* 1:13–18.

Tsuru Shigeto. (1993). *Japan's Capitalism: Creative Defeat and Beyond*. Cambridge, Cambridge University Press.

Tyson, Laura D'Andrea, and John Zysman. (1989), "Developmental Strategy and Production Innovation in Japan." In Johnson, Tyson, and Zysman, eds., pp. 59–140.

Uekusa, Masu. (1991). *Kōteki kisei no keizaigaku* [The economics of public regulation]. Tokyo, Chikuma Shobō.

Upham, Frank. (1991). "The Man Who Would Import: A Cautionary Tale about Bucking the System in Japan" (Review). *Journal of Japanese Studies* 17:323–43.

Vedel, Thierry. (1988). "La Déréglementation des Télécommunications: Politique et Jeu Politique." In Institut Français des Sciences Administratives, *Les Déréglementations: Etude Comparative*, pp. 281–312. Paris, Economica.

Veljanovski, Cento, ed. (1991). *Regulators and the Market: An Assessment of the Growth of Regulation in the U.K.* London, Institute of Economic Affairs.

Vickers, John, and George Yarrow. (1988). *Privatization: An Economic Analysis*. Cambridge, MIT Press.

Vogel, David. (1986). *National Styles of Regulation: Environmental Policy in Great Britain and the United States*. Ithaca, Cornell University Press.

——. (Winter 1992). "Consumer Protection and Protectionism in Japan." *Journal of Japanese Studies* 18:119–54.

Vogel, Steven K. (July 1994). "The Bureaucratic Approach to the Financial Revolution: Japan's Ministry of Finance and Financial System Reform." *Governance* 7:219–43.

Webber, Douglas. (April 1990). "Institutions, Structures, and the Intermediation of Interests under the Christian-Liberal Coalition in West Germany." Unpublished.

Weingast, Barry R. (Winter 1981). "Regulation, Reregulation, and Deregulation: The Political Foundations of Agency Clientele Relationships." *Law and Contemporary Problems* 44:147–77.

Weingast, Barry R., and M. Moran. (1983). "Bureaucratic Discretion or Congressional Control: Regulatory Policymaking by the Federal Trade Commission." *Journal of Political Economy* 91:765–800.

West, Joel. (February 1995). *Building Japan's Information Superhighway.* Japan Policy Research Institute (JPRI) Working Paper No. 7.

White, Lawrence J. (1991). *The S&L Debacle: Public Policy Lessons for Bank and Thrift Regulation.* New York, Oxford University Press.

Wilensky, Harold L. (March 1991). *The Nation-State, Social Policy and Economic Performance.* Institute of Industrial Relations, University of California, Berkeley, Working Paper No. 25.

Wilensky, Harold L., and Lowell Turner. (1987). *Democratic Corporatism and Policy Linkages: The Interdependence of Industrial, Labor-Market, Incomes, and Social Policies in Eight Countries.* Institute of International Studies, University of California, Berkeley, Research Series No. 69.

Wilks, Stephen. (Autumn 1989). "The Department of Trade and Industry under Lord Young." *Public Policy and Management,* pp. 43–46.

Wilks, Stephen, and Maurice Wright, eds. (1991). *The Promotion and Regulation of Industry in Japan.* New York, St. Martin's.

Wilson, James Q. (1979). "The Politics of Regulation." In Wilson, ed., *The Politics of Regulation.* New York, Basic Books.

Witte, Eberhard, and the Government Commission for Telecommunications. (1989). *Restructuring of the Telecommunications System.* Heidelberg, R. v. Deckers Verlag, G. Schenck.

Wolf, Charles, Jr. (1988). *Markets or Governments: Choosing Between Imperfect Alternatives.* Cambridge, MIT Press.

Woolcock, Stephen, Michael Hodges, and Kristin Schreiber. (1991). *Britain, Germany, and 1992: The Limits of Deregulation.* London, Royal Institute of International Affairs.

Wriston, Walter B. (1992). *The Twilight of Sovereignty: How the Information Revolution Is Transforming Our World.* New York, Scribner's.

Yamada, Takahiro, with Michael Borrus. (February 1992). *Change and Continuity in Japan's Telecommunications Policy.* Berkeley Roundtable on the International Economy (BRIE) Working Paper No. 57.

Yamagishi, Akira. (1985). *Ze wa ze, hi wa hi* [Right is right, and wrong is wrong]. Tokyo, Nippon Hyōronsha.

———. (1989). *NTT ni asu wa aru ka* [Is there a tomorrow for NTT?]. Tokyo, Nippon Hyōronsha.

Yamamura, Kōzō, and Yasukichi Yasuba, eds. (1987). *The Political Economy of Japan: Volume 1—the Domestic Transformation.* Stanford, Stanford University Press.

Young, Hugo. (1989). *One of Us: A Biography of Margaret Thatcher.* London, Macmillan.

Yūsō Keizai Shimbun. (1989). *Butsuryū shin-jidai no shōhizei to kisei kanwa* [The consumption tax and deregulation in a new era for cargo]. Yasuda Kasai Booklet Series. Tokyo.

Zysman, John. (1983). *Governments, Markets, and Growth: Financial Systems and the Politics of Industrial Change.* Ithaca, Cornell University Press.

——. (1994). "How Institutions Create Historically Rooted Trajectories of Growth," *Industrial and Corporate Change* 3:243–83.

Index

Cornell Studies in Political Economy
A Series Edited by Peter J. Katzenstein